M000290279

RACISM, MISO
OTHELLO ᴍɪ ɪ ʜ

Through readings of texts spanning four centuries, and bridging the Atlantic – from genres as diverse as English Renaissance drama, abolitionist literature, Gothic horror, and contemporary romance – Daileader questions why Anglo-American culture's most widely read and canonical narratives of inter-racial sex feature a black male and a white female and *not* a black female and a white male. This study considers the cultural obsession with stories patterned on Shakespeare's *Othello* alongside the more historically pertinent, if troubling, question of white male sexual predation upon black females. Daileader terms this phenomenon "Othellophilia" – the fixation on Shakespeare's tragedy of inter-racial marriage to the exclusion of other definitions and more optimistic visions of inter-racial eroticism. This original book argues that masculinist-racist hegemony used myths about black male sexual rapacity and the danger of racial "pollution" in order to police white female sexuality and exorcise collective guilt over the sexual slavery of women of color.

CELIA R. DAILEADER is Associate Professor of English at Florida State University. She is the author of *Eroticism on the Renaissance Stage: Transcendence, Desire, and the Limits of the Visible* (Cambridge, 1998), and has published numerous articles on feminist theory and criticism, critical race studies, and Renaissance literature. She is co-editor with Gary Taylor of John Fletcher's *The Tamer Tamed*, and co-editor with Rhoda Johnson and Amilcar Shabazz of *Women and Others: Re-thinking Gender, Race, and Empire*.

RACISM, MISOGYNY, AND THE *OTHELLO* MYTH

Inter-racial Couples from Shakespeare to Spike Lee

CELIA R. DAILEADER

Florida State University

CAMBRIDGE
UNIVERSITY PRESS

CAMBRIDGE UNIVERSITY PRESS
Cambridge, New York, Melbourne, Madrid, Cape Town, Singapore, São Paulo

Cambridge University Press
The Edinburgh Building, Cambridge, CB2 2RU, UK

Published in the United States of America by Cambridge University Press, New York

www.cambridge.org
Information on this title: www.cambridge.org/9780521613149

© C. Daileader 2005

This publication is in copyright. Subject to statutory exception
and to the provisions of relevant collective licensing agreements,
no reproduction of any part may take place without
the written permission of Cambridge University Press.

First published 2005

Printed in the United Kingdom at the University Press, Cambridge

A catalogue record for this book is available from the British Library

ISBN-13 978-0-521-84878-7 hardback
ISBN-10 0-521-84878-4 hardback
ISBN-13 978-0-521-61314-9 paperback
ISBN-10 0-521-61314-0 paperback

Cambridge University Press has no responsibility for the persistence or accuracy of URLs for external
or third-party internet websites referred to in this publication, and does not guarantee that any
content on such websites is, or will remain, accurate or appropriate.

To Gary Taylor
for taking me there

Contents

List of illustrations   *page* viii
Acknowledgments   ix

Introduction. Othellophilia   I

1   White devils, black lust: inter-racialism in early modern drama   14

2   The Heathen with the Heart of Gold: Othellophilia comes
    to America   50

3   Holes at the poles: Gothic horror and the racial abject   75

4   Sisters in bondage: abolition, amalgamation, and the crisis
    of female authorship   III

5   Handsome devils: romance, rape, racism, and the
    Rhet(t)oric of darkness   143

6   Invisible men, unspeakable acts: the spectacle of black male
    violence in modern American fiction   170

Conclusion. "White women are snaky": Jungle Fever and its
discontents   208

Notes   223
Index   254

Illustrations

3.1 "'To be shady,' – whence all the inflections of shadow or darkness." *page* 82

3.2 "With a very slight exertion of the imagination, the left . . . of these indentures might have been taken for the intentional, though rude, representation of a human figure standing erect, with outstretched arm." 82

3.3 E. W. Clay, *The Fruits of Amalgamation* (1839). Courtesy of the American Antiquarian Society. 88

3.4 Frontispiece to Mary Shelley's *Frankenstein* (1831). Courtesy of the New York Public Library. 91

3.5 "Othello! Othello! Everywhere. There is no getting away from Othello." Courtesy of the Shakespeare Birthplace Trust. 103

4.1 Johann Moritz Rugendas, *Voyage pittoresque dans le Brésil*: "Nègres à fond de calle." Courtesy of the National Library of Jamaica. 140

Acknowledgments

I wish to thank the Research Advisory Council at the University of Alabama for supporting work on an early version of this project. I am also indebted to my colleagues Utz McKnight, Robert Young, and Philip Beidler for their feedback on individual chapters and for overall support, and I am especially grateful to Emma Smith and an anonymous reader at Cambridge University Press for extensive comments on the entire manuscript. The Hudson Strode Program in Renaissance Studies provided crucial funding toward illustrations permissions and research, and my research assistants – Ed Geiswiedt, Oliver Hennessey, and Alissa Nutting – were indispensable resources. I owe to Hunt Hawkins the late discovery of a newly published but vital source for Chapter 4. I also wish heartily to thank all the students – both graduate and undergraduate – upon whom I tested this book's central arguments, particularly (but not exclusively) those enrolled in "Origins of racial discourse," "Inter-racialism," and "Women in literature." My gratitude to these young, adventurous minds is as profound as their talent. Finally, I owe immeasurable thanks to Gary Taylor for inspiration, for encouragement, for feedback, for sharing of books, and for putting up with my brain-picking – around the clock and seven days a week. Without his support and his faith in my work, this project would never have come to fruition.

Introduction. Othellophilia

> *Othello*: She's like a liar gone to burning hell:
> 'Twas I that killed her.
> *Emilia*: O, the more angel she,
> And you the blacker devil!
> William Shakespeare, *The Tragedy of Othello, the Moor of Venice*

Before black men were lynched for alleged sex with white women, white women were burned alive for alleged sex with a devil described as black. For this we cannot blame racism: though the rhetoric of demonism would be incorporated into racial discourse as it developed, the black devil figure pre-existed the large-scale contact with and enslavement of African peoples that generated racism as a hegemonic, pseudo-scientific discourse. The color of the medieval and early modern devil was allegorical. Indeed, the devil himself – from a secular point of view – is allegorical. I do not believe he exists, and neither do, I daresay, many of my readers. If the historical phenomenon in question is not racism, then, what is it? The devil is an ideological fabrication, yet droves of real women died owing to alleged relations with him. To call it misogyny is only the beginning. Here is some anecdotal evidence:

The Devil's penis was the obsession of every Inquisitor and the "star" of nearly every witch's confession. The women invariably said it was cold but there was disagreement on other details . . . Most reported it was black and covered with scales . . . One likened the Devil's penis to that of a mule, which the Evil One constantly exposed, so proud was he of its massive size and shape.[1]

Uncannily familiar? Indeed, the women's testimony oddly prefigures the modern myth of the hyper-sexual black male. Sometimes, in fact, the discourses of witch-craft treat the Devil's blackness as *literally* African, as in the 1324 trial of Lady Alice Kyteler, wherein a witness claimed to have seen her with "three large Negroes bearing iron rods in their hands."[2] These racialized demons seem perplexingly "modern," and the narratives

I

in which they appear suggest certain constants in the development of racial stereotype. Yet there is one other historical constant here that deserves pointing out: these narratives justify a woman's death on the basis of her sexuality – even, very often, on the basis of one single (if singular) sexual act.

For as long as women have existed they have died as a result of sex. When it didn't happen "naturally" – as a result of childbirth – male power found ways to make it happen, either literally or symbolically. This, for me, is the story of Shakespeare's *Othello* (1603): it is the story of a woman killed – smothered in her bed – for having sex.[3] Which *particular* man she is killed for having sex *with* matters less to me than the sexual nature of the transgression she dies for: that is, her "innocence" of the charge of adultery with Cassio strikes me as immaterial, as from the standpoint of masculinist–racist hegemony it is her defiance of paternal authority and the miscegenation taboo that results (and rightly so) in her death.

In the apt phrasing of Michael Neill, *Othello* "has rightly come to be identified as a foundational text in the emergence of modern European racial consciousness – a play that trades in constructions of human difference at once misleadingly like and confusingly unlike those twentieth-century notions to which they are nevertheless recognizably ancestral."[4] I don't set out to resolve this "like/unlike" problem, although it will underlie many of the book's discussions: the problem has generated abundant excellent and fascinating scholarship, and is as yet to be resolved. Perhaps it never can be. And indeed the question "Is *Othello* a racist play?" may be, at least at this juncture in the play's critical history, somewhat beside the point. Othello himself, the character, does not exist; he is as much a construct as the devil in the witch-craft trials mentioned above, the devil to whom Shakespeare's text frequently compares him. Rather, my own problem with the play, and the reason why – almost despite myself – I have returned to it again and again in my research, like that nagging insect bite or eternally crooked painting, can be summed up in a single comment by one of my undergraduate students: "If *my* wife cheated on me, *I'd* kill her."

That relatively few objections to Shakespeare's politics in this play have focused on its treatment of domestic violence – as opposed to its treatment of race – seems to me worthy of comment. Indeed, even those critics who categorize the play as "domestic tragedy" overwhelmingly resist applying the language of domestic violence,[5] a subject confined, seemingly, to the domain of journalists, psychologists, law enforcement officers, consciousness-raising groups, and other traffickers in the mundane world of the real. Yet this attitude – implicitly elevating literary violence to a level above social or cultural critique – leaves uninterrogated the ways in which the text naturalizes Othello's extreme reaction to a set of otherwise unremarkable circumstances. To argue that this reaction – "jealousy," in the universalizing language of liberal humanist interpretation – is "natural" not just to black men, but to people (to men?) "in love" is *not* to rescue the play's message for progressive post-modern politics. As Linda Charnes argues, "The love story has been one of the most pervasive and effective – yet least deconstructed – of all ideological apparatuses: one of the most effective smokescreens available in the politics of cultural production." Charnes points to "the historical popularity of crime stories purveyed as love stories" in arguing that "love" is not a universal human truth, but rather a culturally constructed "genre" – "one whose coercive influence is camouflaged by its very obviousness."[6] I would like to treat *Othello* as one of those "crime stories": wife-murder, after all, is a *crime*. Wife-murder is a crime – in Shakespeare's culture as in our own – *even when the wife is "guilty" of adultery.*[7]

The language of criminality, indeed, seems appropriate to a reading of *Othello,* yet in a way that only underscores the feminist point here. As critics such as Katherine Maus have demonstrated, the play is deeply fascinated by legalist questions of guilt and innocence, with the notion of "ocular proof."[8] Yet this language, throughout the better part of the play, is most often applied to Desdemona, not Othello; indeed, discussions of "domestic tragedy" repeatedly misapply the language of crime and punishment, criminalizing the wife's adultery rather than the husband's murder.[9] That this reversal of culpability is culturally over-determined does not excuse *our own* failure of attention to it as critics who allegedly "know better" than to say that wives who commit adultery deserve violence. And in fact, attention to the (often inconsistent) details of the play brings to light the fact that sexual infidelity of one type or another is rampant amongst Shakespeare's *dramatis personae.* Cassio, for instance, is "almost damned in a fair wife" (1.i.12), yet flagrantly courts (and scornfully boasts of) Bianca, all the while worshiping Desdemona.[10] More strikingly, Iago suspects that Othello has cuckolded him, and he mentions this as one of his many motives for revenge – against Othello, not against Emilia. Critics tend to ignore this point of plot, but in my reading it sheds significant light on the play's treatment of female sexuality. No one wonders why Iago – the character whose villainy my students often cite as evidence that the text is not racist ("But Iago is *white,* and look how evil *he* is . . .")[11] – does *not* consider his own wife's alleged adultery as grounds for violence against *her*. This is not, of course, to praise Iago at Othello's expense: eventually, Iago too kills his wife. But Iago's violence is practical, not symbolic – he kills Emilia to prevent her from incriminating him, not because she has "contaminated" his marriage bed (IV.i.205), as Othello believes Desdemona has done. Is this why readers so seldom notice, let alone believe in, the suggestion that Othello and Emilia have committed adultery? Is this why Iago has been so famously held up as an example of "motiveless malignity"[12] – why he does not seem, to us, to believe in his own motives? Because a sexually jealous Iago would act precisely the way he urges Othello to act – he would lash out in misogynistic violence. Perhaps the homoerotic reading of Iago's interactions with Othello might explain his apparent indifference toward his wife – it is Othello, as Iago's primary love-object, who bears the brunt of his jealousy. But this does not explain the critical silence surrounding the *other* adultery plot – a silence that underscores our complicity in the notions that perpetuate domestic violence.[13]

Let us return briefly to the subject of witch-trials and consider the status of the women who confessed to knowledge of the devil's penis. What happened to their bodies as a result of the confession? What happens to bodies that burn? They char, they blacken. The witches thus join with their devil-lover in the sooty blackness associated with hell-fire. The transformation, of course, is irreversible; innumerable proverbs of the period insist on the indelibility of blackness as a moral signifier. The notion of "washing the Ethiope," indicating an exercise in futility, is only one. Another such expression is "Pitch defiles."[14] Pitch defiles; it does not just dirty; and it does so by physical contact. Moreover, it does not merely rub off on someone; rather, it sticks. Like the cultural inscription of the hymen as, not a minuscule and biologically useless membrane, but rather an irreplaceable (and tenuous) state of moral purity, the reification of blackness has little to do with the physical properties of, say, pitch (which is hard to wash off) or soot (which isn't) and has everything to do with the addressee of the proverb, the potential handler of the pitch. Along the same lines, the discourse of racial blackness and its proscriptions against inter-racial sex have little to do with real people of color. As Toni Morrison says, "The subject of the dream is the dreamer."[15]

One aspect of Shakespeare's controversial play that has *not* been the subject of debate is whether we should credit Othello's statement in the epigraph to this Introduction, his characterization of the dead Desdemona as "gone to burning hell" (V.ii.127). The question may seem naïve or overly literal from the stand-point of a secular, post-modern community of scholars, readers, and play-goers, but early modern audiences would have been acutely aware that Othello, as a murderer-suicide (never mind a Moor and born heathen) would be going to hell. Yet Desdemona also compromises her spiritual status in this scene, for she has taken on the blame for her death: "*Emilia*: 'O, who hath done this deed?' *Desdemona*: 'Nobody. I myself. Farewell'" (121–2). Othello immediately underscores this as a lie, and one that re-casts her death as a suicide and hence symbolically damns her. Othello, not wishing to "kill [her] soul" (33), has given her a chance to pray, and she makes only a feeble effort: asked to "Think on [her] sins," she oddly confesses, "They are loves I bear to you," and he, even more oddly, replies, "Ay, and for that thou diest" (39–41). The audience may well have agreed with them both: her love for the Moor could not be anything less than a sinful perversion, and one that ensured her ultimate destruction, physically and spiritually.[16] Though Emilia's speech emphatically attempts to redeem her dead mistress and re-assert moral binaries, she, as a female and a servant, is the least authoritative voice in the scene, and she promptly dies anyway. Of all the men onstage in the final 119 lines of the play (there are six, plus an unspecified number of "officers"), only the murderer himself says anything good about the victim, calling her a "pearl . . . / Richer than all [my] tribe" (345–6). The final speech refers to Desdemona only obliquely and grimly in the "tragic loading of this bed." Notably, the dead lovers are indistinguishable – and indistinguishably hideous – in death: "This object poisons sight, / Let it be hid" (361–3).

The early modern Prince of Darkness was indisputably black, but some lesser devils were known to wear white. Thomas Adams' popular sermon *The White Devil; or, the Hypocrite Uncased* (1613) developed Martin Luther's notion of "the white devil" as "black within . . . but white without";[17] just one year before, John Webster's *The White Devil* (1612) had dramatized, in the words of the title page, "The life and death of Vittoria Corombona the famous Venetian curtizan." Desdemona is from Venice too. Even if she has not committed adultery with Cassio (and we know she hasn't), the "foul disproportion" and "unnatural" desires (III. iii.237) that led her to elope with the Moor risk placing the "fair devil" (481) in the same moral category.

Pitch defiles. Or, in the more positive terms of the contemporary African-American sexual boast, "Once you go black, you never go back."

The devil, iconographically speaking, is no longer black. In the popular imagination, he is generally a cartoon figure in red tights with a goatee, horns, and a pointy tail. Hardly an intimidating figure. And so it should be:

does anyone miss witch-hunts? This is not to say our culture lacks demons: from the Cold War to the "War on Drugs" to the "War on Terrorism" our demons are increasingly ideological – or, at least, more overtly so.

One could even say that in the official discourse of post-modern, white democracy, the devil is racism itself. That is why so many scholars, theatre-goers, and readers have been struggling, for so many years, to prove that *Othello* either is or is not racist, either is or is not "about race." I have a different set of questions to ask of the play and of the discussions surrounding it: namely, *Why this play? Why Othello?* Of all seventeenth-century treatments of blackamoors, why was *Othello* singled out for all this attention? Mary Floyd-Wilson situates the play "at a crossroads in the history of ethnological ideas when an emergent racial discourse clashed with the still-dominant classical and medieval" paradigms. At the same time that the play reflected these changing views, however, it also, in Floyd-Wilson's analysis, helped to solidify them: she explains, ". . . it is the legacy of Shakespeare's play that this portrait of 'Moorish behavior' [as irrational, jealous, and lascivious] established many of the strains of modern racial discourse."[18] Floyd-Wilson's arguments are persuasive; they do, however, raise the question of whether this "legacy" or impact owes itself to the intrinsic literary merit of the play, to some preternatural ability of the play to anticipate more modern (albeit offensive) attitudes toward racial difference, or to the mere fact that Shakespeare wrote it. This book aims to explore this set of questions.

Let me introduce a term that will be central to this analysis: *Othello-philia,* the critical and cultural fixation on Shakespeare's tragedy of inter-racial marriage to the exclusion of broader definitions, and more positive visions, of inter-racial eroticism. I originally coined the term to address a very specific problem in contemporary classical theatre: the habit of casting black actors in "color-blind" roles that uncannily recalled the role of Othello. Thus, Hugh Quarshie, the actor who broke the color-line in the Royal Shakespeare Company, managed to make a name for himself *without* playing Othello, a play that he views as reinforcing racial stereotypes.[19] But, as I argue in my essay on black actors, the role continued in many ways to haunt his career, cropping up in the language of reviews, alluded to in the semiotics of costuming and blocking. Likewise with Quarshie's successor, Ray Fearon, whose 1996 roles as Bracchiano in *The White Devil* and Paris in *Troilus and Cressida* subtly evidenced his status (as one critic put it parenthetically) as "a future Othello." Indeed, even Fearon's acclaimed performance as Romeo (1997) – despite, seemingly, the director's best intentions – inspired Othellophile musings, at least in the critics.[20] When he went on finally to play Othello – opposite the same actress who'd played Juliet to his Romeo (a fact I will return to later) – I could not help but wonder whether the critical enthusiasm didn't owe something to collective relief at seeing Fearon's professional destiny fulfilled.

My work on Othellophilia in casting opened my eyes to the way Anglo-American culture *generally* "casts" black men as Othellos. The fixation on the coupling of a black male and a white female, with the attendant cultural anxieties played out in the story's tragic result, is not unique to the RSC or even to English "classical" drama. The discourse I call Othellophilia is not solely theatrical – or even, necessarily, consciously Shakespearean.

An exemplary phenomenon is the popular approach to modernizing *Romeo and Juliet* – namely, the device of translating the medieval blood-feud into the language of modern, particularly American, racial conflict. In my fact-gathering about so-called "non-traditional" casting, I discovered that these inter-racial productions almost inevitably cast Romeo, not Juliet, as black – an observation that says as much about contemporary racial discourse as its early modern progenitor in the portrayal of black-amoors like Othello.[21] Thus, something that appeared as a mere, awkward note in my essay on racial casting – that is, the practical invisibility of black *female* performers in Anglocentric, classic theatre – becomes the aporia this book aims to explain, if not to fill. Why, for instance, have white performers monopolized the role of "tawny" or "black" Cleopatra – as the text calls her (*Antony and Cleopatra*, 1.i.6; 1.v.28) – throughout the play's 400-year performance history? This puzzling stage legacy occupies the flip-side of Othellophilia, and points toward its own suppressed counter-discourse: the more historically pertinent if more ideologically troubling story of white male sexual use of black females, the slave-holder's secret.

This book proceeds from the simple observation that in Anglo-American culture from the Renaissance onward, the most widely read, canonical narratives of inter-racial sex have involved black men and white women, and not black women and white men. Why? True, Anglocentric beauty standards might discourage authors from setting up women of color as objects of lyric praise, but conventions can always be played with – as indeed Shakespeare does with Cleopatra, as well as the "Dark Lady" of the Sonnets. Moreover, historical fact simply does not bear out the myth that women of color are sexually repugnant to white men. If anything, the opposite.

For the first miscegenists were European males. The very first documented case of inter-racial sex in English history involved an African
woman impregnated and abandoned during the famous expedition of Sir
Francis Drake.[22] And the pattern continued: there were no women on
board the first ships to arrive on the shores of Africa or the New World,
and European women were in short supply in the colonies into the
eighteenth century. Furthermore, until 1800 the vast majority of women
sailing to America were non-European.[23] This means that unless the
European colonists remained doggedly chaste (or insisted only on homosexual relations) any sexual interest would have been directed at either
native or enslaved females – that is, Indians or blacks. Correspondingly,
the first miscegenation statute in Virginia in 1662 specifically addressed
the offspring of white masters and their slaves: "Children got by an
Englishman upon a Negro woman shall be bond or free according to
the condition of the mother, and if any Christian shall commit fornica-
tion with a Negro man or woman, he shall pay double the fines of a
former act." The wording of this infamous statute barely acknowledges
the possibility that an English*woman* might fornicate with a Negro man,
though that is clearly covered in the second clause. In any case, Virginia
law did not address the children of such a union until 1691.[24] Indeed,
the widespread prostitution – literal and de facto – of women of color in
the West Indies has been well documented, and historians have noted the
disproportionate number of female versus male manumitted slaves,
manumission being a frequent reward for sexual service.[25] The practice
of West Indian concubinage was so deeply entrenched that by the early
1800s white males openly commented on the comeliness of "the ladies of
color." One historian notes that "white males possessed a sexual typology
in which white women were valued for domestic formality and respectability, coloured women for exciting socio-sexual companionship, and
black women for less-structured covert sexual adventurism."[26] If there is a
class hierarchy affording relations with "coloured" (i.e., part European)
women a prestige denied those covert relations with blacks, this doesn't
discount the latter group as erotic objects. In fact, the very presence of
those "coloured" women evidences the sexual desirability of their black
mothers.

This book claims that masculinist racist hegemony used myths about
black male sexual rapacity and the danger of racial "pollution" at least
partly to exorcise its own collective psychological demons: the slave-
master's sexual guilt, and his fear of the products – filial and social – of
the inter-racial trysts so powerfully portrayed in slave autobiographies.

Another motive, of course, was the control of white women. According to Kim F. Hall's ground-breaking *Things of Darkness: Economies of Race and Gender in Early Modern England*, women's bodies in the discourses of English colonialism become "the symbolic repository of the boundaries of the nation."[27] Yet this description also applies to American racism, as is made obvious by the title of the white supremacist propaganda film *Birth of a Nation* (1915). As stated in the first sentence of the first novel written by an African-American, William Wells Brown's *Clotel; or, The President's Daughter* (1853), "With the growing population of slaves in the Southern States of America, there is a fearful increase of half whites, most of whose fathers are slave-owners, and their mothers slaves."[28] Thus, the historical popularity of *Othello* on American stages – even despite squeamishness about inter-racial marriage – makes perfect sense. Whatever might have been Shakespeare's point in telling the story, it has served well as a cautionary tale for white women who might besmirch either their own (sexual) "purity" or that of their race. In lynching, white female sexuality justifies racist violence: in Othellophilia the woman is lynched too.

I had originally conceived of this as a study of inter-racial eroticism, and that is how a draft title phrased it. But the further my work proceeded, the less erotic the "eroticism" of the material appeared. Many of the texts are, indeed, obsessed with (generally female) sexuality; many contain scenes bordering on pornographic; but the ideology these images serve is, at basis, profoundly sex-phobic. The paradox is only an apparent one: as I have argued elsewhere, many sexually explicit representations are colored by loathing of the flesh, designed to chastise, purge, annihilate, or contain the erotic body.[29] When one body is female and white and the other black and male the ideological stakes are especially high.

This project is ambitious in its chronological scope: in tracing the impact of a cultural trope across four centuries and across the Atlantic, I am consciously flouting the central dictate of New Historicism: that of avoiding comparisons across what Foucault calls "epistemes."[30] In doing so, I align myself with an increasing number of scholars critical of that by-now orthodox critical practice.[31] I feel I need not apologize for the project's trans-historical reach, having garnered ample evidence of a trajectory of racialized sexual discourse that originated in Shakespeare, that achieved dominance in and through his reputation, and that continues to shape Anglo-American cultural fantasies. In this respect, the book is a kind of critical history of Shakespeare's *Othello*, but one with broader political and theoretical implications. New Historicism's caution in discussing race in the early modern period, its insistence on scare-quoting, qualifying, and piling syllable upon syllable to the term (from racism to racialism to proto-racism to proto-racialism) is all well and good if these habits do not function to silence or de-legitimize scholars looking for continuity as well as change across historically defined discourses. Foucault himself, after all, attempted to write a complete *History of Sexuality*. Arthur J. Little, Jr., in one of the books that inspired my project here, points out that New Historicism's "narratives about how early modern culture is discrete, about how it is not us" in effect posit "a virginal Renaissance culture (a Renaissance or Shakespeare of transcendent signification), outside the fictions through which we engage in it."[32] Little here is concurring with Neil L. Whitehead, who states, "If historicism achieved the aim of understanding a past culture 'in its own terms,' the result would be totally unintelligible, except to that culture and at that moment."[33] Finally, I believe that a feminist or black feminist – or, in my shorthand, black/feminist[34] – theoretical framework to some degree requires a kind of "retroactive" reading. Bell hooks, for instance, traces color rivalry among African-American women back to those first generations of lighter-skinned ("coloured") daughters born of the slaves the masters abused.[35] In an academy obsessed with classification, stratification, and specialization, with the accumulation of detail, of intellectual minutiae, it is sometimes necessary to state and re-state what so many of us in our personal lives know (insofar as we can know anything) to be an obvious truth: that certain forms of oppression and discrimination have endured, and that moreover they will continue to endure without the very kind of analysis and discussion scholars like Little and Hall propose. As Ania Loomba observes, "It is as necessary to confront the long histories of race as it is to show that racial thinking has a history and is not fixed and universal."[36]

My approach to Shakespeare is first and foremost political, and my approach to the literary canon first and foremost revisionist. I argue in this book that Othellophile narratives are less concerned with the praise or blame of their black male protagonists than with the sexual surveillance and punishment of the white women who love them. In other words, Othellophilia as a cultural construct is first and foremost *about women* – white women explicitly, as the "subjects" of representation; black women implicitly, as the abjected and/or marginalized subjects of the suppressed counter-narrative. The topic of female authorship arises naturally out of the book's concern with canonicity, as well as its feminism. We will find that the intervention of female authors – as early as Aphra Behn in 1676 – alters the discourse in interesting and often surprising ways.

Anti-essentialist caution, however, must temper our approach to the authorship question, as female authors do not by any means agree, and female-authored texts as often participate in hegemonic discourse as counter it – on grounds of either race or gender. Aphra Behn may have been the first author to valorize an enslaved African prince in *Oroonoko; or, The Royal Slave* (1688), but this is by no means to say that her gender "naturally" inclines her toward anti-racist sympathies (indeed, it does not even guarantee her feminist sympathies). Jyotsna Singh rightly points out that "Contemporary, Western feminist engagements with race . . . in trying to chart the complexities of the relation between race and gender oppressions, implicitly *collapse* the categories of difference by assuming a common history of marginalization."[37] In part, this project aims to problematize the notion of that "common history" by highlighting complicity on both sides of the race–gender divide. I argue, for instance, that female authors (and readers) have been responsible for the largest-scale outgrowth of Othellophilia in mass-marketed prose: the romance novel. *White* female authors, that is. It should perhaps come as no surprise that women of color authored two of the most subversive texts to be discussed in this book, Harriet Jacobs' *Incidents in the Life of a Slave Girl* (1861) and Alice Randall's parody of an American racist classic, *The Wind Done Gone* (2000). By the same token, black male authors fairly consistently critique the master discourse, but more often on the grounds of race rather than gender. That is, the plight of the Othellophile hero seems the focus of black male authors who intervene in the discourse: sympathy for his white victim is rare (and, when present, condescending), and sympathy for her black female counterpart almost non-existent. Indeed, as I argue in Chapter 6, Ralph Ellison's *Invisible Man* almost completely excludes black women: it is they who, at the textual level, are truly (ironically) invisible.

This book's organization is roughly chronological, with some overlap and some backward glances: the first two chapters, on the Renaissance and Restoration/eighteenth century, are the most linear, with the final four chapters dividing nineteenth- and twentieth-century texts by genre. Each chapter comprises a central black/feminist argument and a secondary (though usually related) discussion about the relative canonicity of individual texts, and how each text's politics may account for its status in (or out of) the canon. Throughout, evidence will be garnered for a canon-building process favoring texts that neither too overtly critique *nor* endorse hegemonic notions of white supremacy and female subordination. In this respect the book's chronological structure belies its central argument, which emphasizes the consistency rather than the mutability of Othellophilia as a cultural trope. These are variations on a (Shakespearean) theme.

In addition to bridging historically defined "fields" of literary studies, this project also bridges the Atlantic, a move made possible by Joseph Roach's paradigm of an "oceanic interculture"[38] epitomized by figures such as Olaudah Equiano, an important voice in the discourse as it sailed to America. From Chapter 2 on, the book will increasingly concern itself with American literature, not because English authors ceased participating in Othellophilia in the eighteenth century, but because American slavery and its aftermath rendered Shakespeare's play a political touchstone in the hands of authors, critics, and commentators on both sides of these heated American debates. In fact, it may prove the case that Othellophilia "belongs" as much to American as to Anglo-American culture, in the same way that American slavery and racism bear a particular thumb-print, and the Salem witch-trials – though certainly part of a centuries-old, Anglo-European history of persecution – symbolize the problematic principles on which my "Nation, under God" was founded. My point here is that English bardophiles along with American Anglophiles may rest assured I will not "blame" early modern England or Shakespeare for the uses to which American racism has put *Othello*. Nonetheless, America and England have always been joined at the hip politically. As is evident in the partnership (I will resist calling them partners in crime) of these two nations in the recent, calamitous, and internationally deplored invasion of Iraq, neither side can claim the devil made us do it.

In fact, if America "owns" the most heinously racist revisions of *Othello* – say, the *Othello* burlesques, or, later, the hysterically miscegenation-phobic *Birth of a Nation* – it can also claim ownership of the most compelling and bold correctives to the discourse. Two cases in point are the female African-American authors mentioned above, Jacobs and Randall. Harriet Beecher Stowe's famous *Uncle Tom's Cabin* (1852) was decried by critics for its "unwomanly" willingness to allude (however obliquely) to the sexual abuse of female slaves by their masters, even while offering its own softened Othellofication in the central martyrdom of the resplendently white little Eva. But Jacobs' more forthright autobiography makes a point of exposing the sexual secrets of slavery along with – perhaps even more daringly – the brutal, inter-racial, woman-to-woman rivalries that resulted, a legacy that arguably continues to thwart the realization of a truly inter-racial feminism. Similarly, Randall's artistic parody of Margaret Mitchell's *Gone with the Wind* (1936) exposes the evasions of the master discourse, this time in overt opposition to a canonical, white female author. Critics and biographers of Margaret Mitchell have, I believe, settled the question of "How black was Rhett Butler?"[39] and the occluded inter-racialism of the American classic becomes perfectly legible in Randall's creative critique. But the debate extends beyond these two texts to the cultural meta-text of the lawsuit that postponed publication of Randall's book. Othellophilia's status as a hegemonic discourse is perhaps nowhere more evident than in this attempted suppression of the story told by Scarlett's mulatto half-sister. Like the question of whether Mitchell's central "love-scene" is a rape – or an even grimmer question: whether historical lynchings punished (or prevented) actual rapes, as the lynchers alleged – the issue here is not who is telling the "truth." The question is, rather, which lies hurt the most.

Gary Taylor, commenting on the American news media's Othellophile treatment of the O. J. Simpson murder trial, calls *Othello* "The greatest lie ever told."[40] In determining whether the play can be saved for post-modern anti-racist sensibilities, the conclusion of this book takes up the most recent filmic retelling of Shakespeare's story, Tim Nelson's *O.* (2001). Particularly pertinent to my argument is the fact that the film's white co-star, Julia Stiles, not only starred in two other pseudo-Shakespeare films for the American teen screen (*Ten Things I Hate about You* [1999] and *Hamlet* [2000]); she also starred in another inter-racial, pop-culture love-story, *Save the Last Dance* (2001). Noting this "type-casting" of a white female in inter-racial romances will bring the book full-circle back to the problems raised in relation to the RSC. In an entertainment industry that routinely discriminates against women of color, can we afford to keep telling the same old story?

We know the old expression: "All cows are black at night." This ugly reduction of all women to one featureless mass of tamed and branded sexuality demonstrates, on the one hand, the longevity of the masculinist logic by which Desdemona – for merely marrying a Moor – becomes a "strumpet," "that cunning whore of Venice" (iv.ii.84, 93), and "fair devil" (iii.iii.481). But the expression can also be turned outside-in, and appropriated in the name of feminist solidarity. This project is driven in part by my discomfort with the grand omission of Othellophilia: that is, the black woman in Desdemona's shadow. Virginia Woolf once searched for Shakespeare's sister: I would like to ask, where is Othello's sister? I never had a *sistah*, white, black, or even gold. This book is my attempt to find her.

CHAPTER I

White devils, black lust: inter-racialism in early modern drama

Paulina: . . . I will turne Turke.
Gazet: Most of your tribe doe so
When they begin in whore.
Philip Massinger, The Renegado

In 1609 English authorities were shocked by the circulation of a pseud-onymous pamphlet attacking the King and his predecessor, and specific-ally accusing "Queen Elizabeth, who styled herself head of the Anglican Church and virgin . . . of immodesty, of having given birth to sons and daughters, of having prostituted herself to many different nationalities, of having slept with blackamoors."[1] Sex with (an unspecified number of) "blackamoors" (or, in the original Latin, *populus aethiopum* – Ethiopians) seems to have been the most perverse act imaginable. On the other hand, it is notable that the above-quoted summary, spoken by the English Ambassador to Italy, where the author (a Jesuit) was believed to have sought asylum, places miscegenation on a continuum with transgression of the xenophobic taboo, only one step beyond in severity. Either way, the anecdote is significant as evidence of inter-racialism's historical utility – first and foremost – in the sexual slander of English women. Who might the Queen's international lovers have been? They might have been – like Portia's scorned suitor Morocco in *The Merchant of Venice* (1598) – princes. The identities of these blackamoors – anonymous in both the original pamphlet and the synopsis of it we find in state documents on the scandal – does not matter: what matters is their pollution of the (now dead) female sovereign.

As Kim Hall points out, "black" in the early modern period very often stands in opposition not to a necessarily racial sense of "white" but rather to "fair," meaning beautiful, and the word held particular, moral reson-ances for women. Correspondingly, to be "foul" was to be of dark complexion and hence unlovely and therefore lascivious (presumably out of desperation, though the logic is often unclear). "In practice this means that the polarity of dark and light is most often worked out in representations of black men and white women."[2] My thesis here and throughout this book picks up from Hall's point, tracing a Shakespearean racialist rhetoric that pairs a black man and a white woman in such a way as to render the former a vehicle for misogynist figurations of a woman's sexual sullying, with all the racist–voyeuristic titillation that such a spectacle provides. There is also a secondary, more theoretical thesis that addresses, in deconstructive fashion, the flip-side of Othellophilia: that is, the suppressed counter-narrative of the black woman seduced or raped by a white man or men. The comparative obscurity of these stories works against my coining a term with which to discuss them (though I will suggest one below). But behind this shadow-discourse lurks a very real, if painful history: as noted in the Introduction, the black woman impregnated on the Drake voyage was left, when her time to give birth approached, "to take her adventure" on a desert island.[3] This anecdote is mentioned in passing in the accounts of the voyage – indeed, some versions do not mention the unfortunate woman at all. What prevented someone like Shakespeare from dramatizing this sad and enigmatic tale – from telling, as it were, Sycorax's side of the story? It is not enough to say that the black population in pre-emancipation London, for reasons to be discussed later, was predominantly male: there were also more Protestants than Catholics, precious few Jews, and (probably) no fairies, witches, or ghosts.

The relative paucity of black female characters in early modern literature has been well noted by critics.[4] When visible at all in the period, black womanhood tends simply to further misogynistic humor, as in *The Merchant of Venice*, when the clown character is blamed for "getting up of the Negroes' belly" (III.v.32). As in the Drake narrative, the black woman appears only when pregnant – indeed, in Shakespeare she does not literally appear at all: she is not a character but an offstage belly, to be brought up and dismissed in the space of five lines. Onstage black females fare little better: when George Peele – Shakespeare's collaborator on *Titus Andronicus*[5] – marries a black woman to a blind man in *The Old Wives Tale* (1594?), the joke is on both of them. Likewise, in Richard Brome's *The English Moore; or, the Mock Marriage* (1630?) and Philip Massinger's *The Parliament of Love* (1624), the heroine puts on black-face in order to preserve her chastity. When it so happens that an Englishman finds the disguise no impediment to lust, the point is not her desirability but his depravity – indeed, to prepare us for this astonishing lapse in taste, Brome's *dramatis personae* list labels the horny bastard "Nathaniel

(A Wencher)." This Wencher might seem exceptional, in bearing the kind of sexual stigma generally reserved for women in the period (the other "w" word being far more common in these plays). Yet one could also say that the black-face disguise has the same metonymic function *vis-à-vis* the heroine's own (perhaps latent) sexuality, manifesting what Jack D'Amico calls "The Moor within."[6] As Hall points out in what I consider her book's most powerfully insightful statement, often "women are only 'black' or fair in competition with, or in relation to, each other."[7] Taken to its logical conclusion, this means a woman can also be fair or black in relation to herself, in relation to her soul.

Indeed, I suspect that black characters – male and female – in early modern English drama tell us more about the "fair" women with whom they associate than they tell us about the real or imagined qualities of "Moors," "blackamoors," "Negroes" or "Ethiopes."[8] To that end, this chapter reads early modern inter-racialism for tropic patterns, particularly the demonic and the bestial, that link two characters across racial binaries. These biracial dyads may be gendered in either direction – either Othello-wise or otherwise (though the latter is, as we'll see, rarer) – and they may or may not involve consummated sexual desire, but they all work according to the same curious alchemy: white + black = black. We end up, almost inevitably, with a moral that is anti-black, anti-feminist, and even anti-sex.

In placing *Othello* in context with early modern plays like John Webster's *White Devil* (1612), Thomas Dekker's *Lust's Dominion; or, the Lascivious Queen* (1600), the collaborative *The Knight of Malta* (1618), or Thomas Rowley's *All's Lost by Lust* (1619–20) – all of which involve inter-racial couples – I wish to highlight what I perceive as a conversation about the topic amongst English authors, a conversation in which there was agreement as well as dissent, mimicry as well as innovation. I relay this discussion because, in the centuries following the death of Shakespeare and his "reinvention" as cultural icon, other early modern voices have been silenced, often undeservedly.[9] Indeed, even Shakespeare's own voice has been edited out of the transcript, as not all of his statements on the topic are afforded the centrality of his play *Othello*. Why, when invoking what still remains the ultimate in "star-crossed love" – that is, love that defies the miscegeny taboo – do we think of Othello and Desdemona before (for instance) Antony and Cleopatra? This chapter aims to answer that question.

In my amassing of incidents of inter-racialism in early modern English drama, I have posited three rules. Rule number one: inter-racial sex is a prospect to be avoided by all means, in the minds of all characters – even, generally, the perpetrators. Shakespeare's Morocco may boast of his red blood and his (black) amorous conquests, but his sole purpose in the play – prince or no prince – is to be rejected as a suitor to the fair Portia. Rule number two: inter-racial sex is rarely raised as a possibility – and if so, it is emphatically thwarted – when one party is English, as opposed to Italian or Spanish. Perhaps the most amusing example of such an aborted seduction is Thomas Heywood's *The Fair Maid of the West, Part 2* (1631) wherein an African King and Queen lust, respectively, for the English heroine and hero; the problem is resolved by one of those ubiquitous, racialized bed-tricks: they sleep with each other without knowing it. Finally, here is rule number three, which will largely constitute my argument in this chapter: inter-racial sex never involves a consenting and a sympathetic white woman.

Desdemona would seem, to some, to be an exception to the last. But Desdemona was not Shakespeare's first Moor-loving woman, and much insight can be gained by reading her against her predecessor, Tamora in *Titus Andronicus* (1592), who commits adultery with perhaps the most villainous Moor – if he is not the most villainous character of any genus, species, or kind – on the English stage. In this most sensationally violent of Shakespeare's plays, the inter-racialist sub-plot is strongly associated with the numerous acts of butchery and the cannibalistic climax, and that sub-plot indeed proved so memorable to audiences that Edward Ravenscroft's popular Restoration adaptation brought it to the foreground.[10] Also powerfully linked in Shakespeare's play are the adulterers themselves. Aaron's first speech in the play is about Tamora:

> Now climbeth Tamora Olympus' top,
> Safe out of fortune's shot, and sits aloft,
> Secure of thunder's crack or lightening flash,
> Advanced above pale envy's threat'ning reach.
> As when the golden sun salutes the morn
> And, having gilt the ocean with his beams,
> Gallops the zodiac in his glistering coach
> And overlooks the highest peering hills,
> So Tamora. (11.i.1–9)

The imagery of height, flight, light and divinity works to set Tamora upon a pedestal from which she will quickly topple. Aaron goes on to imagine, with an obvious innuendo, mounting with (or simply mounting) the queen, whom he "Has prisoner held fettered in amorous chains, / And . . . bound to Aaron's charming eyes" (13–16). "I will be bright," he boasts, "and shine in pearl and gold" (19), adorned like those "decorative" Moors of portraiture, pageantry, and coats of arms in early modern Europe.[11]

The companion speech of Tamora's, as she woos Aaron in the woods, takes up the imagery of light and flight, and then plunges into the shadows:

> My lovely Aaron, wherefore look'st thou sad
> When everything doth make a gleeful boast?
> The birds chant melody on every bush,
> The snakes lies rolled in the cheerful sun,
> The green leaves quiver with the cooling wind
> And make a chequered shadow on the ground.
> Under their sweet shade, Aaron, let us sit,
> And whilst the babbling echo mocks the hounds,
> Replying shrilly to the well-tuned horns
> As if a double hunt were heard at once,
> Let us sit down and mark their yellowing noise;
> And after conflict such as was supposed
> The wandering prince and Dido once enjoyed,
> When with happy storm they were surprised
> And curtained with a counsel-keeping cave,
> We may, each wreathed in the other's arms,
> Our pastimes done, possess a golden slumber,
> Whiles hounds and horns and sweet melodious birds
> Be unto us as is a nurse's song
> Of lullaby to bring her babe asleep. (11.ii.10–29)

The passage comments on and completes Aaron's earlier soliloquy in the descending movement of its tropes: there are birds, but they are perched (on bushes, not even trees) and lazily singing, and are no sooner mentioned than linked to snakes, with all their demonic and sexualized connotations. The repetition of "let us sit" and "let us sit down," the alliteratively marked movement from "cheerful sun" to "chequered shadow" to "sweet shade" to "counsel-keeping cave" anticipate all the imagery of valleys and pits (with their obsessively vaginal and uterine troping) surrounding the murder of Bassanius and the rape and dismemberment of Lavinia. Notably, the references to gold echo both Aaron's earlier description of Tamora's glory and his burial of a bag of gold, immediately preceding the above-quoted speech. Tamora here makes her preference for darkness clear not only by wooing a blackamoor, but by wooing him in these particular terms, praising shadows, "a happy storm," and a curtaining cave. The brightness Aaron had attributed to her is only dimly recalled in Tamora's synesthetic "yellowing noise" (Shakespeare's somewhat forced pun on "bellow" and "yell") and in the post-coital "golden slumber" she predicts, sound and slumber being concepts alien from, if not antithetical to, light and sunshine. The tropes of earthliness, descent, darkness, and enclosures will culminate in Tamora's accidental cannibalizing of her sons – that is, her literalizing of this scene's metaphorical "swallowing womb" (239) – and in the final punishment of the miscegenous lovers: her body will be cast out as prey to the same scavenging birds she invokes in this scene, and he will be buried up to his neck and starved.

Aaron's reply to her seduction speech continues, as it were, the metaphorical duet, while also setting up an important distinction between them:

> Madam, though Venus govern your desires,
> Saturn is dominator over mine.
> What signifies my deadly-standing eye,
> My silence and my cloudy melancholy,
> My fleece of woolly hair that now uncurls
> Even as an adder when she doth unroll
> To do some fatal execution? (30–6)

The complex gendering of these images itself is worthy of pages: the "deadly-standing eye" combined with the serpentine hair suggests Medusa or the gorgons (the adder is also a "she"), while the fact that "eye" is singular, and that it *stands* – particularly in the context of the scene's overdone sexual symbolism – suggests a phallic symbol.[12] The action of the hair is more remarkable still: Tamora's rolled snakes become unrolling adders' tails, and her (also serpentine) wreathing of arms becomes his preternaturally uncurling hair. All in all, although his verbs here suggest an undoing or reversal of Tamora's, the shared tropes serve to confuse their bodies in a way that anticipates Bassianus' statement that Aaron makes her "honour of his body's hue" (73); the ambiguously coiled, perhaps copulating, snakes become the lovers' four, indistinguishable arms, then are multiplied in the strands of Aaron's strangely phallic hair. Despite the sexualized imagery, however, Aaron's point seems to be that Tamora is the hornier of the two – and my crass use of contemporary slang will be forgiven, I hope, in light of the close reading that follows. This distinction is not, I believe, strong enough to counter the reader's sense of these two as kindred spirits, but it is a distinction at least as important as that of complexion, and important in grasping the hyper-sexualization of subsequent inter-racialist heroines.

Though Aaron claims to be ruled by Saturn and not Venus, the
sexualized nature of the revenge plot (thoughts that provoke, it seems,
the displaced erection of his adder-tail hair) allows Tamora to take his
rebuff in her stride and redirect her energies toward the impending sexual
violence. When Bassanius and Lavinia stumble on the couple and he
sarcastically likens Tamora to Diana, she seizes hold of the irony, replying, "Had I the power that some say Dian had / Thy temples should be
planted presently / With horns, as was Actaeon's, and the hounds /
Should drive upon thy new-transformed limbs / Unmannerly intruder
as thou art" (61–5). A punning twist on the "hounds" / "horns" refrain of
her earlier wooing speech, this rhetorical move is significant in casting
Tamora herself – not the three men involved in the rape – as the one who
cuckolds Bassanius. Lavinia takes the "horning" joke and redirects it
toward Tamora and her absent, apparently cuckolded, husband, and these
racialized images follow:

> BASSIANUS: Believe me, queen, your swart Cimmerian
> Doth make your honour of his body's hue,
> Spotted, detested and abominable.
> Why are you sequestered from all your train,
> Dismounted from your snow-white goodly steed,
> Accompanied but with a barbarous Moor,
> If foul desire had not conducted you?
> LAVINIA: . . . . . . Let her joy her raven-coloured love.
> This valley fits the purpose passing well. (72–84)

In response to this goading, Tamora turns "pale and wan." Cued by the
arrival of her sons, she launches into a strange revision of her speech to
Aaron, this time describing the place as a "barren detested vale" where the
trees "though summer" bear no leaves but only "moss and baleful mistle-
toe" (93–5). She goes on to contradict herself, claiming "Here never
shines the sun, here nothing breeds / Unless the nightly owl, or fatal
raven" (96–7); the snakes reappear in her anticipation of a maddening
midnight chorus of "A thousand fiends, a thousand hissing snakes, / Ten
thousand swelling toads" and so on (100–1). The reptilian imagery need
not be belabored here (the child of Aaron and Tamora will be called
"toad" and "tadpole" later in the play [IV.ii.77, 84], and toads and
other slimy creatures also feature in *Othello*'s racialist menagerie); what
becomes interesting in retrospect is the shift to the conventional use of
these images. What accounts for the sudden change in perspective? The
speech is, in part, a plea for vengeance from her sons, and a prelude
and incitement to the rape. But these rhetorical goals might have been

served without the contradictory images: rather, the two speeches, side by side, manifest the split nature of Tamora herself, who, in Lavinia's memorable formulation, "*bearest* a woman's face" (136; emphasis mine) that is nonetheless belied by her monstrous actions.

There is also something curious about the speech-act that concludes the passage: it seems gratuitous. The rape and cutting out of the tongue had already been planned: Tamora's charge, "Away with her, and use her as you will– / The worse for her the better loved of me" (ii.iii.166–7), only serves to render herself culpable as well. Indeed, her participation in the rape is even more direct than that of Aaron, who exits the moment the victim enters; it is Tamora who hears and rejects Lavinia's pleas for mercy. The First Folio even sexualizes Tamora's part in the rape: she describes it as "the honey *we* desire" (131; emphasis mine). Tamora's and Aaron's mutual complicity in sexual violence seals their identification: it is no wonder the state ordains similar means of their bodily destruction, Aaron devoured by earth and Tamora by animals.

In Aaron, Shakespeare gives us the first in a series of black rapists who, in the drama of the period, are never permitted to commit the crime. Arthur Little has theorized this curious phenomenon:

Throughout early modern drama, the black man maintains a peculiar relationship to the rape narrative: although often enjoying the role of most nefarious and flagrant villain in a play in which a rape is the most catastrophic and constitutive act, his black body and the woman's white one become the twain that never do meet. His blackness serves to mark rape with racial pollution without insisting on a literalization of that contamination.[13]

Perhaps the most graphic example of this is the frustrated rape-plot in John Marston's *Sophonisba* (1606); here the would-be rapist is not explicitly black (although, as King of Libya, he certainly could be), but he does enlist two "blacke knaves" who, as he obscenely threatens the victim, her "limbes all wide shall straine."[14] Like the black bodies required for so many bed-tricks in drama (there's one in this play, when the King almost takes his Negro man-servant for the heroine), the blackness of these "blacke knaves" functions emblematically. The blackness itself stands in for the rape that cannot be staged, even if it can (and it usually cannot) take place in the action of the play. Indeed, Shakespeare's *The Rape of Lucrece* (1594) – a text Little reads as a source for *Titus* – presents rape itself as "so black a deed" it literally blackens the victim's blood (1742–3). Because, as Little explains, masculinist classical ideology views rape as a property crime, not a violation of a woman's right to bodily integrity,

"Being raped by one's own" – by one's owners? – "isn't really rape." Little
goes on to observe, "Within the misogynistic frame of the nation-empire,
rape really comes to mean something when its perpetrator comes from
outside; and rape comes into its most visual, catastrophic sign when it is
committed by a black outsider."[15] Rape and race – these nearly identical
four-letter words – thus become mutually constitutive categories: "rape"
is what the other "race" wants to do to your women. This circular logic
allows a masculinist-racist culture safely to stage its own rape fantasies,
projected upon a dark-skinned alter ego. There should be a term for this:
rapism. It is as a rape, for instance, that Peter Greenaway's *Prospero's Books*
visualizes the offstage inter-racial marriage that begins *The Tempest* – and
Greenaway did not misread the text. Shakespeare only mentions the
Claribel–Tunis match in passing, but he establishes the bride's unwilling-
ness in the very same breath: this makes it effectually, if not explicitly,
rape. Let's not forget that rape is also a sub-text in *Othello*: Brabantio does
not believe that his daughter would consent to the Moor and claims

> She is abused, stol'n from me, and corrupted
> By spells and medicines bought of mountebanks.
> For nature so preposterously to err,
> Being not deficient, blind, or lame of sense,
> Sans witchcraft could not. (1.iii.60–4)

[margin handwritten: between a black man & white woman]

In sum, miscegeny, from a racist point of view, is always at some level rape.
   And if it isn't rape, if she "wanted it," it is not miscegenation, but
rather proof that a woman is not truly white, but whitewashed. Francesca
Royster argues that Tamora, racially marked as a Goth, is not just white in
relation to Aaron, but "hyper-white," representing the opposite pole of a
graduated complexional–climatological model according to which Romans were the "golden mean." Hence all the attention to her "hue."[16]
When Aaron calls Tamora's sons "white-limed walls" and "alehouse
painted signs" (iv.ii.100), he indicts their mother by association: it is,
after all, women whose "painting" or cosmetic use drew most criticism in
the period. If Aaron has "his soul black like his face" (iii.i.204) then
Tamora's soul is black like *his* face. Indeed, as I hope to prove in this
chapter, masculinist-racist discourse views the inter-racial couple as a unit,
as, to quote Iago, a "beast with two backs" (*Othello*, 1.i.117).

[margin handwritten: or vice versa?]

   And here perhaps we may return to Desdemona. In one editorially
vexed passage, Othello muses, "Her name that was as fresh as Dian's
visage / Is now begrimed and black as mine own face" – or, alternatively,
"My name that was as fresh as Dian's visage / Is now begrimed and black

[bottom handwritten note: Is skin color/race not an actual physical aspect of one's person? Here it appears to be contingent on external matters... (p. 16, 21, and above)]

as mine own face" (III.iii.391–2), and here the crux itself underscores the identification. The former reading recalls the ironized comparison of Tamora to Diana and anticipates Othello's "Was this fair paper, this most goodly book, / Made to write whore upon?" (IV.ii.73); the latter recalls, in reverse, Desdemona's own reading of Othello's inner nature: "I saw Othello's visage in his mind" (I.iii.251). Critics have made much of the color binaries in the play, without noting the way many of these binaries work to set up the two lovers not so much as opposites, but as photo negatives: for instance, in looking at Iago's potent formulation, "old black ram /. . . tupping your white ewe" (I.i.88–9), it is easy to forget that both parties are likened to animals, and thus are placed on the same side of another dichotomy, that of human–animal. Similarly, most of the animal tropes in the play are plural and thus gesture toward both members of the inter-racial couple. In *Merchant of Venice* the despised Jew is frequently called "dog," but there is no suggestion that Venice is over-run by animals: contrastingly, *Othello's* most pornographic moments are peppered with expressions such as "goats and monkeys" (IV.i.260) or the even more memorable "cistern for foul toads / To knot and gender in" (IV.ii.63–4). The knotting of the toads has a similar feel to the rolling, reptilian nuances of Tamora's and Aaron's exchange in the woods; underlying these textual subtleties one senses a horrified fascination with the mechanics of sexual congress, the twisting of limbs and constriction of orifices (particularly, the vagina).

These copulative images highlight the idea that inter-racial sex creates a new creature – and not only in the future progeny ("you'll have your nephews neigh to you, you'll have coursers for cousins and jennets for germans" [I.i.113–15]), but at the very moment of sexual union. Sometimes that creature is recognizable in the natural order – like the "tadpole" produced by Aaron and Tamora – but sometimes it is not – like the "anthropaphagi" that populate Othello's homeland (I.iii.43), or the centaur alluded to in the name of the inn to which he escapes with his bride. Iago's "It is engendered. Hell and night / Must bring this monstrous birth to the world's light" (II.i.385–6) references not only his evil scheme, but also, more allusively, the fruits of the inter-racial sex so obsessively, so pornographically imagined through the first two acts of the play.[17] Most importantly, however, the "monstrous birth" is the inter-racial couple itself. When Othello worries that "a horned man's a monster and a beast" (IV.i.59) he imagines Desdemona's cuckolding him with Cassio as something that will transform him bodily, as something that will make him monstrous; yet the rhetoric of the play suggests that his deflowering of

Desdemona the very night before has already rendered *her* a monster and a beast.

Or, to use the play's most recurrent epithet, a devil. The devil, proverbially black in the period, was, as noted in my Introduction, the world's first miscegenist. Indeed, *Othello*'s pervasive tropes of magic and the demonic incorporate references to both characters: this includes their names, Ot-HELL-o and Des-DEMON-a.[18] Othello himself calls Desdemona "fair devil" and, in the end, imagines her in hell (v.ii.138).

The central point of my reading of *Othello*'s and *Titus*' inter-racialism is quite simple: that Desdemona is not so much the antithesis of the monstrous Tamora, but a more psychologically sophisticated version of her – one with, in fact, a few touches of Lavinia thrown in for pathos and aesthetic effect. It is as though, not satisfied with his depiction of a barbaric villainess who conspires in the rape and mutilation of an immaculate Roman virgin, Shakespeare decided to try something even more challenging: having the racially and sexually immaculate victim conspire in her own degradation and murder. Hence her final, baffling, self-erasure and self-blame for her death: "Who has done this deed?" – "Nobody, I myself. Farewell" (v.ii.132–3).

Indeed, Desdemona's complicity in her own murder is embedded in the role, in a way that performance history would more clearly underscore if critics were as attentive to the gender politics of performance as to the racial issues surrounding the casting of Othello. For instance, one commentator on Ira Aldridge's performance noted that the actress playing Desdemona "was seized with such fright on seeing the terrible expression" on the (black) actor's face "that she jumped out of bed and ran away screaming with real terror."[19] This comment is typical of the racist responses to the play so well documented by critics and theatre historians, but underlying its demonstration of the actress's (and the critic's) racism is a more subtle point about the portrayal of Desdemona. The "real terror" exhibited by the actress clearly undermined her performance – that is to say, the role itself requires an unrealistic response from a woman in danger. Desdemona knows that Othello intends violence:

> DESDEMONA: Talk you of killing?
> OTHELLO: Ay, I do.
> . . .
> DESDEMONA: . . . I hope you will not kill me.
> OTHELLO: Hum!
> DESDEMONA: And yet I fear you, for you're fatal then
> When your eyes roll so . . . (v.ii.33–40)

He goes on to make the threat explicit with "Thou art on thy deathbed" (55) and "Thou art to die" (61). She, in response, pathetically pleads, "O, banish me lord, but kill me not" (85), "Kill me tomorrow; let me live tonight" (87), and finally begs "But half an hour" (89). Her failure to resist has always struck me as psychologically implausible, and the handling of the scene by directors has more often exacerbated than forestalled my own resistance to the scene's message about women and violence. Thus Charlotte Vandenhoff's 1851 Desdemona "meekly" accepted her death "while kissing the hand which [gave] it"[20] – an approach in vogue at least as late as 1995, when Oliver Parker's film adaptation required the victim to stroke her killer's shaved head in the final stages of her suffocation.

Early (male) critics used to argue about the degree to which Desdemona is or is not – potentially or at heart – "that cunning whore of Venice that married with Othello" (IV.ii.93–4).[21] To me it hardly matters. After all, the grammar of the jibe brooks no debate: the marriage – even in her husband's eyes – defines her as a whore, defines the marriage, in other words, as its ideological opposite, not merely a "frail vow between an erring barbarian and a super-subtle Venetian" (I.iii.356) but a precondition and guarantee of eventual whoredom. But we need not take Othello's or Iago's word for it: Desdemona herself has a knack for damning herself in the very terms with which she attempts to assert her innocence – as when on her death-bed she names her "loves . . . to" Othello as "sins" (V. ii.43). The addition to the source of the courtesan Bianca as Desdemona's foil (named for the white skin which is Desdemona's most emphasized physical feature) clearly also pertains here.[22] Let us not forget that her ill-fated voyage from Venice to Cyprus is expressly sexually motivated: "The rites for why I love him are bereft me" (I.iii.257). As Dympna Callaghan notes, "Such a display of apparently insatiable female sexual appetite severely problematizes Desdemona's characterization as a virtuous woman."[23] Why did Shakespeare alter the source to make it virtually physically impossible for her to commit adultery between her wedding and her death? To exaggerate Othello's gullibility, surely – but perhaps also to invite these very speculations about her sexual appetite. In the eyes of misogyny, all women are whores: chastity is merely a sign of failed opportunity or lack of wit ("fairness and wit / The one's for use, the other useth it" [II.i.132–3]). Desdemona is not chaste because she is good, but because she doesn't have the smarts to capitalize on her beauty: hence the infuriating naïveté – not to say flat absurdity – of statements like "Am I that name?" (IV.ii.121) and "I cannot say whore" (165). Her virtue is passive, not active; accidental, not essential.

My reading of Desdemona is self-consciously eccentric; there is, however, a broader and less debatable point. If Desdemona is taken as sympathetic, or as sexually innocent, she must be acknowledged as one of a kind, *vis-à-vis* other lovers of black men in early modern drama, and the rhetorical overlap between and amongst these texts invites a verdict of guilt by association. Thomas Dekker's *Lust's Dominion; or, The Lascivious Queen* (1600) impugns the miscegenous Queen in its very sub-title; indeed, her lover himself, the wicked Moor Eleazar, berates her in the post-coital first scene, calling her "strumpet" (three times) and "harlot" (twice).[24] Their exchange begins with a moment straight out of *Titus Andronicus* – the first of several seeming borrowings from Shakespeare (Shakespeare will return the favor in *Othello*). The Queen asks him, "Why is my love's aspect so grim and horrid?" and begs him to sing to her and kiss her (1.i.7–14). He shunts her away and she, strangely playing the rapist herself, replies "No, no saies I; and twice away saies stay; / Come, come, I'le have a kiss, but if you strive, / For one denial you shall forfeit five" (15). In a typical early modern portrait of the deleterious effects of sexual congress, he complains that he is "now sick, heavie and dull as lead" (20), that she is now "ugly as hell" to him (65), and that she has "melted all [his] spirits, / Ravish'd [his] youth, deflour'd [his] lovely cheeks, / And dried this, this to an anatomy / Only to feed [her] lust." Again, we note that the language of sexual violation ("ravish'd," "deflour'd") is applied to him (78–81). When the Queen, angered, has her sons "cry murder" against the Moor, he repents and offers to tear his tongue (Lavinia-like?) "From this black temple for blaspheming" her (14–15). The scene goes on to echo *The Merchant of Venice* where the Prince of Morocco offers to "make incision for [Portia's] love" in order to "prove whose blood is reddest" (11.i.6–7). Eleazar offers to kiss the Queen and stab his flesh "And quaffe carowses to [her] of [his] blood" (*Lust's Dominion*, 1.i.121–2). Another *Merchant* borrowing – this one conflating Shakespeare's Moor and his Jew – follows the Queen's departure to her dying husband's bedside: when asked whether the Queen was with him, Eleazar replies: "The Queen with me, with me, a Moore, a Devill, / A slave of Barbary, a dog; for so / Your silken countries christen me, but father / Although my flesh be tawny, in my veins, / Runs blood as red, and royal as the best / And proud'st in Spain" (151–6). The scene ends with a soliloquy wherein Eleazar – bragging, like Aaron, that he has "bewitch'd" the Queen – lays out his vengeful plans, including her murder; the concluding line declares "To shed a harlots blood can be no sin" (198).

The language of demonism pervades the play in a way that anticipates *Othello*, while also highlighting Shakespeare's lighter touch. Eleazar is called "devil" no fewer than twenty times (sometimes in the emphatic form of "black devil") and is called "fiend" five times (variously "black fiend," "damned fiend," "hell-begotten fiend"); there is also "black Prince of Devils," "son of hell," "Prince of Hell," "hell-hound," and "damned hell-hound." Some of these epithets appear in compounds with the term Moor, suggesting an equivalence between the racial marker and the epithet, as in "That damned Moor, that Devil, that Lucifer" (ii.i.51–2). More pertinent to this analysis, however, is the observation that, towards the end of the play particularly, Eleazar's lover begins to share in this linguistic demonization through formulations such as the irresistibly alliterative "The Devill, and his dam, the Moor, and my Mother" (iv.iv.96). Indeed, the lovers themselves partake in the devil-and-dam rhetoric: she calls him "Devill of hell" and he spits right back "And Devill's dam" (v.iii.113, 115). Dekker also conflates the characters by way of that familiar reptilian imagery: in the same scene in which Eleazar calls the Queen a serpent, the couple is introduced as "This woman, and this Serpent" (v.i.142). Our favorite amphibian also appears in a line spoken by all onstage : "Moor, Devill, toad, Serpent" (v.ii.45).

Also reminiscent of *Titus* and prefiguring of *Othello* are the racialized moral binaries: "this disgrace / Shall dye thy soule, as Inky as my face" (i.ii.190–1); "Your cheeks are black, let not your souls look white" (ii.ii.81); "Black faces may have hearts as white as snow . . . The whitest faces have the blackest souls" (v.iii.9/11). In fact, the latter maxim (speciously spoken by Eleazar) is not borne out by the events of the play: the Moor himself has a "fair" Spanish wife, Maria, who commits suicide in order to evade seduction by the King of Spain (a plot in which her husband is complicit). She vows, ". . . Before foul lust / Shall soil the fair complexion of mine honor / This hand shall rob Maria of her life" (ii.iii.179–81). Lest it seem that we have stumbled upon an exception to my third rule of inter-racialism in the period, however, I should point out that Maria does not quite escape the language of sexual denigration; she is called "strumpet" by (ironically) the Lascivious Queen herself (iii.ii.90).

Dekker's play ends with an explicitly racist moral: "And for this Barbarous Moor and his black train / Let all the Moors be banished from Spain" (v.iii.182–3). The play was successful enough that Aphra Behn revised it in the Restoration as *Abdelazar; or, The Moor's Revenge* (1676),

which was also fairly popular (we will discuss Behn in the next chapter).²⁵
Like other plays of the period featuring Moors, the popularity of *Lust's
Dominion* may have had as much to do with its anti-Spanish sentiment as
its racialist excesses; indeed, its title insults not the Moors, but the domain
of the Spanish Queen. Xenophobia and nationalism are always hard to
distinguish from racialism. As I've argued elsewhere, the sexualized, racial
imaginary of *Othello* is colored by anti-Italian stereotype – an observation
that prevents Iago's villainy from exonerating Shakespeare from general
bigotry.²⁶

While we are on the subject of lascivious queens, we should consider
Shakespeare's *Antony and Cleopatra* (1606–7) and its most consistently
whitewashed of dark heroines. For the longest time, I was not sure
whether Cleopatra belonged in this study, but my uncertainty might well
owe more to the stage-history of the play, in its insistence on her
theoretical whiteness, than to the text itself. Indeed, even twentieth-
century theorists of racial discourse, with very few recent exceptions, have
either ignored or been puzzled by her racial status.²⁷ Shakespeare invites
us to imagine Cleopatra, in the very first lines of the play, as a "gipsy"
with a "tawny front" (1.i.6); she goes on to blazon herself as "with
Phoebus' amorous pinches black / And wrinkled deep in time" (1.v.28–
9) but then confuses matters by referring to her "bluest veins" (11.v.28).
That she is racially distinct from the Romans is indisputable; what
remains open to speculation is whether she would have been played
by an actor in black or brown make-up. She is never described as "fair,"
and that seems a remarkable divergence on the part of a Shakespearean
tragic (or even comic) heroine; moreover, blue veins are visible in olive-
skinned hands. One need not, I suppose, be so technical: both the tawny
front and the blue veins are rhetorical creations – in regard to the former,
Cleopatra is not onstage, and, in regard to the latter, the audience is
not close enough to observe the perhaps metaphorical color of her
veins. The same might be said of her self-description as "black"; the
modifier "wrinkled" follows it, and whereas this rings true to other
references to her age ("waned lip" [11.i.21] for instance), it clearly does
so in the mode of poetic hyperbole: the wrinkle on her face becomes a
wrinkle in the face of time in which she, larger than life in her cavortings
with Phoebus, imagines herself lovingly enfolded. The Cleopatras of
Shakespeare's contemporaries present a similarly inconclusive picture:
she can be snow-white, brown, or black, depending upon the whim of
the author.²⁸

Regardless of how Cleopatra was embodied in early modern performances, the text leaves no doubt that her affair with Antony is inter-racial,
and destructive for that very reason. Moreover, her excessive sexual
appetite, considered alongside Antony's frequent ambivalence toward
her, fits the pattern perfectly, as do the references to magic or witch-craft
and the rhetoric of whoredom to which the Romans subject her. The
difference lies in the relative sympathy Shakespeare affords her, a sympathy which no doubt goes a long way in explaining the heroine's
historical perception as not black. Indeed, John Dryden's consciously
Shakespearean adaptation, *All for Love* (1678), would go on to imagine a
Cleopatra with alabaster skin. I will have more to say about this bit of
literary whitewashing – as well as *Antony and Cleopatra*'s ambiguous
status with regard to the canon of Shakespearean "race" plays – later in
the chapter. Here suffice it to say that the relationship between Antony
and Cleopatra meets our three definitions of early modern inter-racialism
in being dangerous, exoticized, and far removed from a recognizably
English femininity.

Cleopatra is not demonized; although her love for Antony is adulterous
and politically detrimental, it is not portrayed as damnable or unnatural,
as it would be if their races were reversed. Rather, it is he whose behavior
is aberrant. Just as Othello must answer to accusations of witch-craft,
Antony must attribute his desire for Cleopatra to her enchantments,
vowing to "shake off these Egyptian fetters" – those fetters or chains a
recurring inter-racialist image – and "from this enchanting queen break
off" (i.ii.105, 117). Likewise, the Romans tend to blame wine, drugs,
witch-craft or the intoxicating effects of Egyptian cookery for Antony's
moral lapses (ii.i.19–38). Even Enobarbus' powerful and lengthy blazon –
in my opinion the most exquisite passage in Shakespeare – praises her by
way of negatives and oxymorons: her person "beggared all description" –
she "made a gap in nature" – "she did make defect perfection" – "For
vilest things / Become themselves in her" (ii.ii.204, 223, 237, 243–4). The
negativity of the blazon rings true to the understanding of black as
the absence of light, and the gaping omission at the heart of it – its
refusal to describe Cleopatra's body – may, for all its ingenuity and
theoretical richness, simply manifest Shakespeare's unease with praising
the appearance of a dark-skinned woman.

Perhaps the most conclusive evidence for Cleopatra's darkness lies in a
scene that most critics neglect: her interrogation of the messenger on the
subject of her rival Octavia.

CLEOPATRA: Is she as tall as me?
MESSENGER: She is not, madam.
CLEOPATRA: Didst hear her speak? Is she shrill-tongued or low?
MESSENGER: Madam, I heard her speak. She is low-voiced.
CLEOPATRA: That's not so good. He cannot like her long.
   . . .
What majesty is in her gait? . . .
MESSENGER: She creeps. (III.iii.11–18)

The jealous Queen goes on to ask about Octavia's age, the shape of her face, and finally the color of her hair: to all of these, she receives flattering responses, and pays the messenger accordingly. Like Enobarbus' description of Cleopatra on her barge, this passage is less remarkable for what it includes than what it excludes. Why does she not ask whether Octavia is *fair*, or whether she herself is fairer than Octavia? Clearly, Cleopatra knows she cannot compete on grounds of complexion, so she asks about particulars of stature, gait, physiognomy, voice, and age. Only when assured of her superiority on these points does she venture onto the more sensitive subject of hair-color, receiving again a comforting answer: Octavia does not have the gold hair that would give her the beauty advantage (the Queen's own presumably black hair having a Sidneyan precedent). These are simple points of plot, but they have gone unnoticed by a legion of critics – even those who have scoured the text for racial references.

That a black Cleopatra has been unimaginable to most critics should not surprise us, considering the historical tendency of Shakespeareans to gloss over his racialist language, a smoke screen we can thank Kim Hall for piercing in *Things of Darkness*. The same has been the case for the so-called Dark Lady of Shakespeare's Sonnets, who – as Marvin Hunt demonstrates in a pointed and convincing essay – may well have been inspired by a woman closer to black than brunette. Without definitively claiming a historical or racial identity for the heroine of the Sonnets, Hunt details the critical discomfort with her darkness and proffers evidence of her racial alterity by way of close-reading. In addition to the racial inflection of her "dun" breasts (130.3), black eyes (127.9), and wiry black hair (130.4), there is the idea that loving the Dark Lady renders one a "slave to slavery" (133.4). Beyond this, Hunt offers an original and pregnant gloss of 127.7 – "Sweet beauty hath no name, no holy bower" – in limning out the associations of African darkness with the anonymity attributed to the unbaptized.[29] If such a case can be made for the Dark Lady – who has consistently eluded efforts on both sides of the debate to align her with a historical personage – the same case can certainly be made for Cleopatra, historical queen of an African nation.

As noted above, Cleopatra is not overtly demonized and therefore stands apart from other, more emphatically "black" characters in early modern drama; as should be clear, however, the ambivalences embedded in her portrayal ring true to racialist constructions of difference. As tragic heroine rather than villainess she more closely resembles Juliet than Tamora: however, as "Serpent of old Nile" (1.v.25), associated with its fecundating slime and hyper-reproductive reptiles, she more closely resembles the lecherous queen (and, indeed, her adder-haired, Moorish lover) than the thirteen-year-old romantic. The word "queen," female monarch, was a homonym for "quean," whore. Shakespeare no doubt expected audiences to supply the pun.

I have been suggesting in this chapter that *Antony and Cleopatra* deserves consideration as an alternative to *Othello* as a model of inter-racial eroticism, and that the former's historically deracialized interpret-ation evidences Othellophilia's status as a critical, not just an artistic practice. By the same token, in my search for a coinage for the counter discourse, I ruled out "Cleophilia" because the name of the legendary figure has been so frequently severed from its African roots and aligned with a vaguely exoticized but fair-skinned, regal femininity. Another consideration was the aristocratic ring of the name: heroines of the counter-narrative tend to hail from the servant classes, like Webster's Zanche or Rowley's Fydella. Indeed, so clearly wedded are the racial associations with servants (versus queens), that the same black actresses who are routinely barred from playing Cleopatra almost inevitably wind up in her entourage.[30]

The blackamoor servant of Webster's *White Devil*[31] seems a compelling lower-class counterpoint to Cleopatra, to the degree that we might even speak of Zanchophilia (or Zanthophilia, to take up her more mellifluously named counterfeit in *The Knight of Malta*), if such a cultural phenomenon existed. Somewhat ironically, the racialist language of *The White Devil* first came to my attention in a seemingly "non-traditional" 1996 RSC production, which cast black actor Ray Fearon as Duke Bracchiano, the adulterous lover of the stigmatized heroine, Vittoria.[32] As Ania Loomba notes, "In *The White Devil,* 'blackness' is a signifier of various forms of socially unacceptable behavior," foremost amongst which is female sexual transgression, metaphorized in Zanche, the "black fury" to her mistress Vittoria's "devil in crystal."[33] What strikes me as unique about Webster's approach to this language is a certain critical sensibility:

many of the references to "black deeds" are self-evidently hypocritical, and the one black character in the play is – despite her scapegoating by the misogynist, anti-black, Florentine power structure – among the most sympathetic. The play is also unusual in placing the unquestionably black Zanche in an active relationship with the Machiavellian Flamineo, the brother who panders Vittoria – even if his mistreatment of Zanche bears out the patterns analyzed above.

Let me pause just a moment on the one inter-racial couple imagined by Webster (as opposed to the one literally cast into the RSC production) before going on to my reading of the racialist tropes that permeate the text. Flamineo characterizes his affair with "that Moor, that witch" as unwilling on his part, born of sexual blackmail; he loves her "as a man holds a wolf by the ears" because she knows "some of [his] villainy." He goes on, "But for fear of turning on me, and pulling out my throat, I would let her go to the devil" (v.i.153–6). Once again, inter-racial sex is non-consensual; here, as in *Lust's Dominion*, the sexual aggressor is female.

With regard to the language of demonism Webster outdoes even Dekker in *Lust's Dominion*: I counted thirty-three uses of "devil" in the singular or plural. The difference is that the term is applied more generally; none amongst the two central male and two central female characters escapes the appellation, although Vittoria is most often singled out. Most references to the devil by far are free-floating, however: twenty-one times the term appears in some form of maxim or idiomatic phrasing. Indeed, it can be argued that the title itself is ambiguous or ironic, and that Webster would resist an uncritical endorsement of the corrupt Duke's grossly hypocritical sneers against the woman he seduced, embroiled in scandal, and abandoned to a one-sided justice. Martin Luther's sense of "white devil" as arch-hypocrite applies more to him, as he sits on the side-lines at her trial.

Where tropes of demonism are prevalent, one looks for the early modern sister discourse in the language of whoredom, and here again Webster does not disappoint: I counted twenty-six occurrences of "whore" or "strumpet" in the singular or plural, and here the scales are more clearly tipped against Vittoria (twenty occurrences), even if she strives admirably, in the trial scene, to resist this linguistic imprisonment. Interestingly, the only other woman in the play who is called "strumpet" is Zanche, who also shares the stigma of "devil," along with yet a third vein of metaphor likening women to dogs or wolves. The latter two tropes come together most notably in the scene wherein mistress and servant band together against Flamineo, who linguistically pairs them as "a couple of braches" and "cunning devils" (v.vi.135, 148).[34]

Dympna Callaghan observes that "blackness and femininity are conjoined not just in Zanche, but in the way she mirrors Vittoria."[35] I would go so far as to call the two characters alter-egos. Both women are victims of the double-standard: Zanche – whose role in her mistress's seduction seems limited to laying down cushions – shares Vittoria's sentence in the "house of converted whores" because the court deems her, rather than the pandering Flamineo, the "bawd" (indeed, Flamineo himself first takes the sentence as applying to him). Moreover, the two women die together in a way that more closely resembles an erotic joint-suicide than any of the other deaths in the play. Vittoria insists on dying first, baring her breast before the sword and vowing to meet it halfway. The two women's final speeches beautifully complement one another:

> VITTORIA: I will not in my death shed one base tear,
> Or if I look pale, for want of blood, not fear.
> CARLO: Thou art my task, black Fury.
> ZANCHE: I have blood
> As red as either of theirs; wilt drink some?
> 'Tis good for the falling sickness. I am proud
> Death cannot alter my complexion,
> For I shall ne'er look pale.
> LODOVICO: Strike, strike,
> With a joint motion. [*They strike*]
> VITTORIA: 'Twas a manly blow.
> The next thou giv'st, murder some sucking infant,
> And then thou wilt be famous. (v.vi.225–34)

It is not just their bravery that unites the two women here; also dissolving of color binaries are their references to blood. Blood, the humor associated with passion and carnality, was always a problematic fluid for early modern women. However "fair" her complexion, the blood visible in a woman's blush functioned in masculinist discourse as the site for speculation about her sexual appetite, from the red of Lucrece's cheek which arouses Tarquin's desire, to the blackened blood after her rape, to Hero's blush in *Much Ado about Nothing* (1600), representing either "guilt" or "modesty" depending on the male glossator. Just as the Prince of Morocco and Eleazar boast of their red blood in challenging racial hierarchies, the blood invoked in this scene in *White Devil* symbolically solders black servant and white mistress.

This use of blood as social equalizer might be seen to work against Vittoria, figuratively lowering her rather than elevating her servant. But the passage is more complex than that. Zanche's defiant boast and invitation to blood-sucking – like Eleazar's offering "carouses" of his blood – ironically racializes the addressee; Zanche subverts stereotypes of African cannibals, attributing a cannibalistic blood-thirst to her pale-skinned executioners. Vittoria's reference to lactation interestingly elaborates on and genders the drinking trope in a way that follows from her earlier baring of her breast; it is also symbolically consistent, as early modern physiology viewed milk as refined menstrual blood. The imagistic pattern culminates in Vittoria's final confession, "O my greatest sin lay in my blood. / Now my blood pays for it" (240–1). The women's symbolic sisterhood in blood – representing passion or appetite – is literalized in their deaths. Racially and socially distinct, they become blood-sisters in sacrifice to the sexual hypocrisies of a racialist-masculinist state. Significantly, Vittoria's demand that she be killed first ("I shall be waited on in death; my servant / Shall never go before me" [217–18]) is disregarded; their deaths are dealt in one blow.

The identification of the two characters, and the tropes of blackness applied to each, make the play ripe for experimentation in racial casting. In 1991 the RSC cast Vittoria herself as black. And indeed, there is even a question as to how "white" she might or might not be. The rhetoric of fairness is remarkably absent from descriptions of Vittoria: Flamineo's introduction of her suggests black hair and even perhaps a less than lily white complexion: "What an ignorant ass or flattering knave might he be counted, that should write sonnets to her eyes, or call her brow the snow of Ida, or ivory of Corinth, or compare her hair to the blackbird's bill, when 'tis liker the blackbird's feather?" (i.ii.115–19). In the trial scene there is a suggestion that she uses cosmetics – something Zanche openly admits. As Hall explains, early modern denigrations of "painting" carried strongly racialist implications, sometimes going so far as to praise blackness (as in Aaron's attack on the "white-limed walls" of Tamora's sons) in order to suggest that the prized white complexion of the female ruling class – and the sexual purity it metonymized – might be falsified.[36] Vittoria denies the painting accusation somewhat equivocally, and in a way that anticipates Zanche's dying speech, "O, you mistake. You raise a blood as noble in this cheek / As ever was your mother's" (iii.ii.53–4). Yet, as noted above, her blushing – legible as sign of racial/moral purity as well as its opposite – can too easily be subsumed in the rhetoric of whoredom and darkness: Flamineo says, "Come sister, darkness hides your blush. Women are like curst dogs: civility keeps them tied all daytime, but they are let loose at midnight . . ." (1.ii.199–201).

In fact, the entire trial scene constitutes an attempt to penetrate Vittoria's seeming moral whiteness, and in this respect the issue of skin-color is irrelevant. One judge muses, "I do not think she hath a soul so black / To act a deed so bloody" (iii.ii.183–4). In the 1996 production, the heroine's moral "blackness" is explicit in the program illustration, wherein a darkly lipsticked and very pale Vittoria, photographed only from nose to hip level, suggestively grips her own low-cut, white bodice with hands gloved in black. Because her arms, in the image, are largely cropped out of the picture, it looks as though the black hands belong to someone else, someone – perhaps the actress's black co-star – embracing her from behind. The moral allegory written into the casting of this particular production could not be any clearer: Bracchiano is a part of her, the personification of her "black deeds" (v.vi.300), the object of her "black lust" (ii.ii.7).

The subtlety of Webster's use of racialist tropes stands out more sharply in contrast to a later play, *The Knight of Malta* (1618), by John Fletcher, Philip Massinger, and Nathan Field. The play is a hodge-podge of allusions and borrowings from contemporaries – the plot combines Shakespeare's *Othello* and *The Winter's Tale* in depicting a virtuous woman slandered, seemingly killed, and later revived; the visit to her tomb and disappearance of her body is stolen from Thomas Middleton's *The Lady's Tragedy* (otherwise known as the anonymous *Second Maiden's Tragedy*), and there is even a whiff of Romeo in her husband's soliloquy in the tomb. But to me the most interesting bit of artistic theft is what the authors did to Webster's Zanche – here Zanthia or, alternatively, Abdella (I will call her Zanthia in order to foreground the parallels with Zanche).[37]

Once again, we have an inter-racial couple demonized in relation to one another; once again, the lighter-skinned partner in crime – the villainous Frenchman Montferrat – is in the relationship reluctantly. Montferrat, a "Bloodsucker of innocence" (1.iii.190), desires the morally and racially "spotless" Oriana, but feels compelled to offer sexual promises to her Moorish maidservant, Zanthia, in order to retain the latter's aid in his seduction of the former (or revenge against her, if he fails to seduce her). Zanthia is ruthlessly sexualized and, although her introduction contains some elements of the praise-of-blackness tradition analyzed by Hall, Montferrat wastes no time in enforcing the usual racial binaries. He greets her,

> . . . Oh my Zanthia,
> My Pearle, that scornes a staine! I much repent
> All my neglects: Let me *Ixion* like,
> Embrace my black cloud, since my *Juno* is
> So wrathfull and averse; thou art more soft
> And full of dalliance then the fairest flesh,
> And farre more loving. (1.i.161–7; italics in original)

She accuses him of using her "as a property" to be discarded, which he denies, vowing damnation. She goes on to boast of the conventional virtues of blackness: her "black Cheeke" cannot "put on a feigned blush" or "cozen love" with an "adulterate red, / Nor artificial white"; her "dark locks" and (white) teeth "are not purchas'd" (172–7). Moreover, she boasts, "I am as full of pleasure in the touch / As ere a white fac'd puppet of 'em all, / Juicy, and firme . . . I can as blithely work in my loves bed, / And deck thy faire neck, with these jetty chains . . ." (181–7) – and we note here the echo of Aaron's "amorous chains." He responds by calling her his "black swan," cataloguing her charms in terms of exotic plants and spices, and promising to marry her, at which cue she outlines her progress in their latest scheme against Oriana. As soon as she exits, he informs us

> It is not love, but strong libidinous will
> That triumphs o're me, and to satiate that,
> What difference twixt this Moore, and her faire Dame?
> Night makes their hews alike, their use is so,
> Whose hand so subtile, he can colours name,
> If he do winck, and touch 'em? lust being blind,
> Never in women did distinction find. (219–25)

Nonetheless, he continues, for reasons unknown, to put off Zanthia sexually. She later presses him: "Am I not here / As lovely in my blacke to entertaine thee / As high, and full of heat, to meet thy pleasures?" He answers, Eleazar-like, "I wil be alone" (II.iii.11–14).

This deferred inter-racial seduction should by now be familiar: this particular play, however, doubles the tension, and complicates the racial topography, by introducing a second ultimately thwarted seduction, that of an enslaved "Turkish captive of incomparable beauty" by the name of Lucinda. In a surprising twist to the usual inter-racialist narrative, Lucinda is both a "fair virgin" and a Turk. A sexual "prize" who is fought over by four soldiers and who manages, like Sheherazade, to sit at bedside with a ravisher and talk him out of his lust, this proto-Orientalist heroine occupies an eroticized middle-ground between the black, hyper-sexual

Zanthia and the icy, white Oriana in a way that prefigures the white-washed but exotic Cleopatra of later stage history.

Still, there is no question as to the racial/moral hierarchy in the play. Oriana, clearly modeled on Desdemona ("My last breath cannot / Be better spent, then to say I forgive you" [iii.ii.197–96]), is called not just "fair" but "fairest," and that by a man who desires them both. Moreover, the text surpasses *Othello* in connecting the heroine's virtue to her white-ness: the terms "fair," "white," or "spotless" appear in association with Oriana's hands, person, or honor at least thirteen times in the play (as opposed to the small handful of times Lucinda is called "fair"). And whereas one might argue that the slander plot requires this insistence, one might as easily reverse the terms of the equation and say that a slander plot is required in constituting her as the "fairest" possible heroine.

And yet. And yet. By now we should be prepared to see the Desdemo-nian heroine rhetorically sullied at some crucial point. Having no Othello at hand, Oriana does it to herself. Here she responds to her disappointed suitor, when asked whether she would marry him if her husband died:

> How much you undervalue your own price,
> To give your unbought selfe, for a poore woman,
> That has been once sold, us'd, and lost her show?
> I am a garment worne, a vessel crack'd,
> A zoane untide, a Lilly trod upon,
> A fragrant flowre cropt by another hand
> My colour sullyde, and my odour chang'd;
> . . . I am rather
> Fit to adorn his Chimney, then his bed. (v.i.140–50)

The reference to chimneys (and, by association, soot and blackness) links her to Zanthia, who in the very next scene is called "chimney sweeper." The identification is momentary, of course, but it underscores the way in which black servant figures in the period were almost literally *props* for their fair mistresses. Zanthia, like Webster's Zanche, is the literary equivalent of the subordinated black sitter in portraiture: her function is to provide complexional contrast. And when there is physical contrast – metonymically linked to a binary class construct – there is always the potential irony of spiritual affinity. Just as a racial marker like "Ethiope" or "sun-burnt Blackamoor" could be used on any woman as a generic insult, mere proximity to a black female can easily impugn a play's white heroine.

Oriana's rhetorical self-sullying hardly compares to the abjection of Zanthia, but the corresponding "chimney" passage bears scrutiny as well.

She is described as "the only truth that ever issud out of hell, which her black jawes resemble" and cursed in the following terms: "a plague o' your bacon-face, you must be giving drinks with a vengeance; ah thou branded bitch: do'ye stare, gogles? I hope to make winter bootes o' thy hide yet; she feares not damning: hell fire cannot parch her blacker than she is: do'ye grin, chimney sweeper?" (v.ii.149–54).

The speaker has left no stone unturned here: the demonic, the canine (Zanthia is elsewhere "my Brache black beauty" [iv.iv.39]), and the low-class all come together in this barrage of insults. There is even an allusion to the painted face of the actor playing her (bacon grease was proverbially used in black-face performance) and an anticipation of the goggly eyes and exaggerated grins of racist caricatures. It might be worth noting that "property" – a term Zanthia twice applies to herself, as Montferrat's handmaid or instrument – was also a theatrical term which we have since shortened to "prop"; this nuance draws our attention to a subtler, theoretical connection between her and her white-skinned foil, Oriana, in light of the early modern use of boy actors for women's roles. When Oriana likens herself to "a garment worn" she tropes herself as property in both the usual and the theatrical sense, for the garments of the boy actor playing her would have been important props in constituting her gender, like (presumably) the wig and false breasts.[38] Yet the blackness of Zanthia is also prosthetic, as the above references to soot and grease underscore. Indeed, the dialogue seems to cue the actor for the sort of parodic facial gestures (grinning and eye-rolling) we associate with minstrel shows; such a performance would even further foreground her status as a racialist fiction. If, given early modern theatrical convention, we posit neither woman as materially "really there" onstage, Zanthia occupies the even more theoretically fraught position: she, as an (artificially) black (artificial) woman is even more "not there." The black female, in the ontology of transvestite theatre, is hyper-female in a way that doesn't correlate to the gendering of the black male.[39] This theoretical sisterhood-in-absence suggests that the rhetorical correspondence opened up by the chimney references might have had more impact in performance. All cows are black at night, indeed.

The vehemence and creativity of the above-quoted verbal attack is not unique to the speaker: Montferrat himself subjects Zanthia to similar linguistic abuse. Quick to turn on his partner in villainy when there is a snag in their plans (at which cue, she merely threatens to remove his hopes for Oriana, and he relents), the lustful Frenchman proves himself a veritable artist in the language of racial insult. Here he completes a sentence of hers beginning "Either the Devill"

> Or thou, thou damn'd one, worse;
> Thou black swoln pitchie cloud, of all my afflictions,
> Thou night hag, gotten when the bright Moone suffer'd
> Thou hell it self confin'd in flesh . . .
> . . . This sword shall cut thee into a thousand peeces,
> A thousand thousand, strow thee ore the Temple
> A sacrifice to thy black sire, the Devill. (IV.ii.35–44)

As is typical of their repartee, she snaps an instant come-back: "If I be devill, you created me" (160). The verbal volleyball of this exchange epitomizes the inter-racial rhetorical partnership we first saw in Aaron and Tamora. This partnership at the level of language – their own as well as other characters' – functions effectively to counteract or ironize racial difference. As in *Lust's Dominion*, the linguistic companionship develops progressively, so that by the end of the play the two are metaphorically indistinguishable.

There is, in fact, a clearly marked turning-point in this development. Zanthia's above-quoted come-back echoes almost verbatim a line Montferrat speaks in soliloquy earlier, "Thou hast made me / More devil than thyself, I am" (II.iii.17–18). The syntactic redundancy of "Thou hast made me . . . I am" enables a more/Moor pun that also appears in *Lust's Dominion*: "Moor, more than a Devill" (*Lust's Dominion*, V.ii.28). It is an unusual moment of conscience for a racialist villain, but there are others, as when he imagines himself (with a verbal echo of *Titus*) "in-viron'd with thick mists / Black as Cymerian darkness, or my crimes" (IV.i.4–5). Naturally, Zanthia talks him back into mischief, and by the end of the act she can speak of a "contract that is made. And cemented with blood" (IV.iv.30–1) between them.

The couple's joint demonization of course calls for the popular devil-and-dam trope. The *OED* defines "dam" as an animal's mother or a mother generally in the language of insult, but the word is also related to "dame" as in lady or wife. The devil-and-dam unit, hence, draws its derogatory force from the linkage of bestiality, the demonic, and a strangely sexualized, even slightly incestuous, sense of the maternal – not to mention the pun on "damn." Zanthia is first called "dam" when she and Montferrat descend to Oriana's tomb, hoping to reclaim, Romeo-like, her body as she revives. Oriana's husband, disturbed in his clichéd soliloquizing about the darkness, light, and Oriana's "bed of death," apprehends that he is not alone:

> . . . Who are ye?
> What sacrilegious villaines? false *Mountferrat,*
> That wolfe to honour, has thy hellish hunger,
> Brought thee to tear the body out oth' tomb too?
> Has thy foule mind so far wrought on thee? ha,
> Are you there too? . . .
> . . . thou bawd to mischiefe,
> Doe you blush through all your blacknesse? will not that hide it?
> . . . You are well met, with your dam, sir . . . (IV.ii.205–14).

In another grab-bag of racialist tropes, we have here again the wolf, the "black bawd," and the play on blackness versus blushing. More interesting to me, however, is the slippage from Montferrat to his co-conspirator in the unmarked pronoun "you": the speaker's confusion about who is there in the darkness mirrors the reader's confusion about the subject of the address. It is a kind of semiotic bed-trick, its point that Frenchmen too are black at night.

The dual demonization of the inter-racialist couple comes to a head in the final scene, which presents them as "a damn'd hell-hound, and his agent dam" and as "*Cacodemon,* with his black gib there, his *Succuba,* his devil's seed, his spawn of *Phlegeton* . . . bred o' the spume of Cocitus" (V.ii.184–7). The "Evill Angell" (183) Montferrat is expelled from the order of the Knights of Malta "as a rotten, / Corrupted and contagious member" (214–15) or, in another amputation trope, "an infectious putrified limb" (266). But his real punishment for his villainy is his forced marriage to Zanthia. The couple is ushered off with an insult pillaged from Shakespeare: "Away French stallion, now you have a Barbary mare of your own, go leap her, and engender young devillings" (279–80). (If you're curious, here is the precursor in *Othello*: "The devil will make a grandsire of you"; "You'll have your daughter covered with a Barbary horse" [1.i.91, 112–13].)

With such richly overlapping material it's tempting to make broad comparisons – but we are not done with our survey of the terrain. Before coming to any conclusions about inter-racialism in the period, I wish to look at an inter-racialist play that incorporates many of the above-outlined themes and tropes in a plot containing some startling twists.

William Rowley's *All's Lost by Lust* (1619–20) might be called a rape-play with a difference.[40] Among its ideological surprises are the feisty

Dionysia (she wishes to go to war with the men); the murderously jealous wife, Margaretta; their conscience-ridden, bigamous husband, Antonio; and the post-mortem *ménage à trois* that unites all three. And that is only the sub-plot: the main plot breaks from tradition in featuring a woman who takes action after her rape – escaping the King who has raped her and, even more radically, provoking a rebellion against him. Clearly this is no Lucrece, even if she frequently invokes Tarquin in her denunciations of the Spanish King. The inter-racialism comes in when the King of the Moors – initially at war with Spain – joins forces with the Spanish general, Jacinta's father Julianus, in ousting the rapist King. The catch is that the Moor, Mulymumen, wants to possess the raped Jacinta sexually in return for his military service. When she rejects him, he takes revenge by blinding Julianus, cutting out Jacinta's tongue, and tricking Julianus into killing her (thinking he stabs the Moor himself).

Once again, the Moor is not the actual rapist, although it is surely an index of his depravity that he desires a raped woman. Not surprisingly, the rape metaphorically blackens her: she describes "her white lawne of chastity" as defiled "with blacks of lust" (G3v), and her father speaks of her "fowle-faire shape" and "sullied eyes" (G3r) and of the stain that not all the clouds in the sky, "could they drowne the sea / With a perpetuall inundation / Can ever wash . . . out" (A1v). He speaks of her in the past tense (as does Titus of his raped daughter): "I had a daughter b[ut] she is ravish't now" (A1r). Moreover, Jacinta does not hesitate to link the Moor to her rapist: "Love thee? As I would my ravisher." Her distaste for him harks to the traditional notion that blackamoors are "frightfull" to look upon (here, on the other hand, she is contrasted with Dionysia, who brags, "Do you thinke a Sarazin's head, / Or a Black-amoor's face can affright me; let me then / Be afraid of any chimney sweeper" [D1r]). Jacinta rails, "Base African / Thine inside's blacker than thy sooty skin." She calls him "dragon," "hell-hound," and "monster"; true to the discourse of Othellophilia, he replies with the epithet "lustfull whore" (G3v).

Despite the insults above, neither the play's racialist language nor its surprisingly sparse vocabulary of whoredom is univocal: most of the demonizing language directed at Moors comes out of the mouth of the besieged rapist King, himself demonized by his outspoken victim (though largely indirectly, through her jail-keeper). Mulymumen is also given a defense of blackness reminiscent of Aaron and Morocco; he wears the

> stamp of the sun
> which all the ocean cannot wash away:
> Shall those cold ague cheeks that nature moulds
> Within her winter shop, those smoothe white skins,
> That with a palsey hand she paints the limbs,
> Make us recoil[?] (D2r)

We have seen the devaluing of whiteness as painted before; in addition, the references to cold and illness invoke the classical understanding of whiteness as a defect produced by intemperate northern climes, a schema shown by Mary Floyd-Wilson to persist in early modern memory.[41] As in most other cases, however, the defense is vastly undermined in context, and surely the trick by which Mulymumen kills Jacinta ends the play with the standard racialist collapsing of dark skin, darkness, blindness, and evil. At the same time, as Jack D'Amico points out, there is a certain poetic justice to the Moor's sentence against Jacinta and Julianus, which targets "the organs of sight and speech" and thus, figuratively, "how he [the Moor] is seen and what he is called."[42] It also may be a re-working of *Titus*. As the blinded Julianus prepares his literal stab in the dark, he (absurdly) claims he can still see the Moor's "Cymerian face" (I3v); the Moor laughs demoniacally, and thrusts Jacinta before the sword. The conclusion is somewhat less brutal than that of *Titus*; it is even in some ways subversive. Here, the father kills the raped and mutilated daughter by accident; she has had a chance, between her rape and Philomela-like silencing, to decry her ravisher and see justice done, and the Moor, while certainly demonized by his actions, ultimately is not punished. Quite the contrary: he ascends the throne and concludes the play on a stunningly non-Shakespearean, darkly ironic, triumph-of-evil note.

On the other hand, all this might simply mean that the anti-black language of the play is subsumed in its anti-Spanish moral. Anthony Gerard Barthelemy views the Moorish maidservant in the sub-plot, Fydella, as an allegorical figure: "The general state of faithlessness that pervades *All's Lost* augments the irony of Fydella's name. Infidelity exists on all levels of this society: Margaretta's husband commits bigamy, the Spanish king rape, Julianus treason, and Mulymumen all manner of crimes." It is as if, Barthelemy posits, "fidelity itself . . . is blackened."[43] Spain and Mulymumen deserve one another. Indeed, the point could be made of any other play discussed here: as noted above, inter-racialism in the early modern English psyche only seems to be imaginable in Spain and Italy. I am less interested in the question of which came first, the racist or the xenophobe, than I am in teasing out the way both forms of chauvinism participate in and perpetuate misogyny.[44]

These issues also come together in the sub-plot. I have not had much to say about Fydella because her role seems limited to being just what her name means: a faithful servant to her mistress. However, in contrast to other black maidservants in the drama, her mistress is not a sexually sullied "white devil" but rather the direct opposite: a faithful wife whose husband commits adultery. Or, put another way, Margaretta is a female Othello. More astonishing still is the way Rowley subverts the usual Moor-assisted bed-trick. The bigamous husband, fooled by a letter from his wife wherein she pretends to accept the second marriage on the condition that he still sleep with her occasionally, sends his friend as a sexual surrogate, whose identity would be proclaimed afterward; thus framed for adultery, Margaretta would have no choice but to concede the marriage as null and void. Margaretta, however, has planned to murder her husband in bed, and in this act she enlists Fydella. Here we have the same partnership in crime dramatized by Webster, but hinging on willful murder rather than adultery and suspicion of collusion in murder. Moreover, just as Webster unites mistress and servant in death, Rowley renders the two indistinguishable in the act of murder: no stage directions indicate who has the more hands-on role in the strangling. Oddly, Margaretta encourages Fydella to flee the country, while she goes on to publicize her own guilt in the crime and, eventually, to commit suicide. Both Moors, male and female, get off scot-free in this play. Perhaps it should be no surprise that *All's Lost by Lust* never made it into the canon.

Indeed, of the six plays discussed so far, this is by far the hardest text to come by, there being no modern edition. I resorted to squinting over a photostat facsimile in negative. Its illegibility encapsulates a final irony: the black text brooks no marginalia, and the white letters disorient the untrained eye. Jacques Derrida was right: most binaries must be reversed in order to be seen at all.

The cumulative effect of these close readings might lead one to wonder why, of all the inter-racialist stories in circulation in early modern England, it was Shakespeare's *Othello* that survived. It is too pat to say that Shakespeare's play was "the best," because Shakespeare went on to write another, and in my opinion better, inter-racialist tragedy: *Antony and Cleopatra*.[45] Indeed, perhaps we are ready to take up the question of why the latter was not canonized as Shakespeare's great "race" play, why it was never as popular as *Othello,* and why, to the degree that it has survived, it has only done so with a white actress in the starring role. I have a simple answer, and I hope I will be forgiven a measure of bluntness. Shakespeare's audiences are not interested in women of color. Not in the leading role, certainly. Not in the role of Queen.

And what of *Titus Andronicus?* Original audiences loved it; indeed, it was named in the Induction of Ben Jonson's *Bartholmew Fair* (1614) as one of the two most popular plays of the age (the other being Thomas Kyd's *The Spanish Tragedy* [1594?]). But eighteenth-century critics abhorred its sensationalism and virtually ejected it from the canon of Shakespeare's works (not without some justification on the grounds of authorship, as it seems he did not write the first act). Only in recent years have critics rescued the play from relative obscurity amongst Shakespeare's works: when Peter Brook revived it in 1957, he called it a "dreadful play," but its very dreadfulness has since proven appealing to post-modern audiences with their penchant for black humor and imperviousness to violence. Still, though, critics and audiences do not talk of *Titus* as being "about race" in the way that they do *Othello* – perhaps precisely because its racialism is overt. In this regard, audiences may have come full circle since the eighteenth century, when the play's inclusion of a miscegenated bastard would perhaps have offended as deeply as its dismemberments, cannibalism, and sexual violence.

This in no way settles the issue of canonicity. Indeed, the process Gary Taylor calls "cultural selection" will be a central concern in this book, and we will come back to it again and again, whether in terms of *Othello* versus *White Devil,* Thomas Southerne's *Oroonoko* versus the novel it adapted, or *Uncle Tom's Cabin* versus *Clotel.* But of course we cannot interrogate *Othello*'s canonicity without interrogating Shakespeare's, as a culture's privileging of one work by an author over other works by that same author corresponds to the process whereby one artist comes to represent the achievements of an era generally. It is one of the ironies of British literary history that the most obvious way in which England had a Renaissance – the artistic flowering visible in its drama – has been obscured by the monolithic status of a single dramatist among many. Taylor writes:

Shakespeare has stimulated and influenced many artists, but the most successful beneficiaries of his influence have worked in a different medium (the painters Hogarth and Fuseli, the composers Mendelssohn and Verdi) or in a different language (Goethe, Stendahl, Hugo, Pasternak). Shakespeare provided these artists with imaginative ammunition that they used conquering their own niches without challenging his incumbency in his own.[46]

At this point in our examination of the critical history, it is important to bear in mind Shakespeare's pre-canonical status. It would not be until the late 1700s – thanks to the upsurge of British nationalism, the imperialist project, and the conservative backlash in the face of the French Revolution – that Shakespeare was proclaimed "the greatest dramatic poet in the world."[47] Indeed, the political interests served by canonizing *him* (above, for instance, Thomas Middleton, whose only "blackamoor" characters are an African King and Queen, favorably portrayed)[48] are visible in the particular plays by Shakespeare singled out for praise in this era. The same may be said of the terms in which these plays were praised: Taylor argues that the reading of Prince Hamlet as a hesitant king-killer reflected intellectual flirtation with the idea of revolution, while the canonization of *King Lear* (along with the resistance to staging it while a deranged, elderly king was on the English throne) reflected the English cultural elite's ultimate rejection of that radical possibility.[49]

It might help to look outside the cultural "niche" of theatre to see what other forces were at play in the forging of modern racial discourse centered on Shakespeare's *Othello*. Nabil Matar suggests that the stereotype of the "barbarous moor" was primarily "undertaken within theological and literary contexts" in early modern England, and bears little resemblance to the attitudes toward the Muslim Other bodied forth in "[g]overnment documents, prisoners' depositions, and commercial exchanges."[50] And, indeed, we must ever remain alert to the fact that we are looking at cultural fantasy – particularly in the playhouses, where it is often a culture's demons who come out to "play." On the other hand, drawing a hard line between literature and historical record is difficult: one sees, even in the work of historians like Matar, places where literary paradigms bleed through. Take for example one of Matar's more optimistic suggestions, namely, that attitudes toward miscegenation in England during the seventeenth century were not so severe as *Othello* would indicate. Two of his five examples are proposals that did not pan out. "In 1614 . . . negotiations were conducted for the marriage of the sultan of Sumatra and the daughter of an English 'gentleman of honorable parentage' because it was felt that such a marriage would be 'beneficial to the [East India] Company.' The marriage never took place." A bizarre anecdote follows, the wording of which I find both amusing and theoretically pregnant:

[I]n 1636, as the number of British captives rose in Algiers and funds dried up to ransom them, an anonymous suggestion was made to King Charles I that he send

English prostitutes to ransom the captured seamen – six prostitutes for every one seaman. Although the king did not act upon this advice, the idea that the English . . . women would practice the oldest profession with "Turks" suggests an environment that did not view miscegenation as totally objectionable.[51]

The insult to both the Moors and the English prostitutes is lost on this historian, whose use of the quaint euphemism, "the world's oldest profession," signals the kind of squeamishness a feminist can find both endearing and baffling. The idea is to give the Moors whores, and even then this ransom in female flesh – each valued at only one-sixth of an English sailor – is withheld. Similarly obtuse in feminist terms is Matar's quotation of Thomas Rymer, commenting – in his racist reading of *Othello* – on the 1682 marriage of the Moroccan ambassador Mohammad bin Hadou to an English servant: "With us [in England] a Moor might marry some little drab or small-coal wench."[52] The condescension of Rymer's language goes unremarked, as does the sexualized class insult of "drab" and the connotations of soiling and blackening in "coal-wench."

Once again we are looking at the equation WHITE WOMAN + MOOR = "WHORE" – or, as posited earlier, white + black = black (all whores being black at night) – that is central to the plot of *Othello*, and perhaps key to its fascination for the culture. Joyce Green MacDonald argues "that *Othello* has retained its power to reach audiences precisely because it uncannily seems to play out what they think they already know, what they have been taught, about race and sex: about black men's fundamental irreconcilability to the values of civilized society and about what happens to nice young (white) girls who defy their fathers' wishes."[53] In Othellophilia, fear of female sexual autonomy regularly shades into fear of miscegenation and vice versa; calling the one originary of the other becomes a chicken-and-egg dispute. Nor is it the case, unfortunately, that white women were innocent in this dual marginalization: the first monarch to expel the blackamoors by decree was Elizabeth I, who styled herself, significantly, "the Virgin Queen," and whose iconic self-blanching greatly encouraged what Kim Hall calls "the cult of fairness" in English women.

Perhaps one last Derridean reversal is necessary in fully grasping the discursive binary in which Othellophilia takes part. Let us start with Shakespeare's Caliban in *The Tempest* (1611), perhaps nowhere "blacker" than when he boasts of his attempted rape of Miranda: "O ho, O ho! Would't had been done! / . . . I had peopled else / This isle with Calibans" (1.iii.351–2). As in the sexual braggadocio of a Prince of Morocco or a Zanthia, early modern audiences could be counted upon to react in disgust. The prospect of an island-full of calibans could not have been much less repellent (and fascinating) than an island-full of cannibals, and surely the implied speed of the reproductive feat is part of the point. Caliban's chosen verb, "peopled," seems odd here: generally *people* don't reproduce at that rate – bugs and animals do. However, a now obscure 1668 novella describes an English shipwreck off the African coast that leads to just such a reproductive scenario: one man stranded on a desert island with four women succeeds, within the space of fifty-nine years, in fathering a nation of 1,789 people. The begetter of this colony is, of course, no "savage and deformed slave" (Caliban's description in the *dramatis personae* list), but an Englishman by the rather too-clever name of George English. Most pertinent to this discussion, however, is the fact that this fabled experiment in nation-making is partially miscegenous: the publication announces in its *précis* that of the four original mothers "one was a Negro."

It is a bizarre story – more bizarre, to me, than Shakespeare's. I end this chapter by pitting this account against Caliban's sexual boast in order to de-familiarize the notion of primitive male sexual rapacity embodied in him and hinted at in the African prince to whom Claribel (another anagram for Cannibal?) has been "loosed." (Note here the sense of that verb as "to make loose"; even Claribel, explicitly "loath" to wed a black man, is made a "loose woman" in association with him.) As argued above, the popularity of Othellofied inter-racial pairings obscures a very real counter-narrative in the history of white-on-black sexual predation. The counter-narrative has left traces: the "Negroe's belly" reference in *Merchant*, and the resemblance, in *The Tempest*, between the fate of Caliban's African mother and the anonymous "Negro wench" impregnated and abandoned by Drake and his men. So it is with this once popular narrative, Henry Neville's *The Isle of Pines*.[54]

The Negro on the isle has it somewhat better than Drake's concubine, according to the pamphlet. The sex is described as consensual, the communal life as happy, and the island as a paradise. Still the narration places the Negro at the bottom of the island hierarchy. The narrator seduces the three white women first – his favorite is, significantly, the daughter of his late "master" on-board ship, that is, the most high class – and, true to the stereotypes about people of color, it is the Negro who approaches him sexually:

None remaining but my Negro, who feeling what we did, longed also for her share; one night, I being asleep, my Negro (with the consent of the others) got close to me, thinking, it being dark to beguile me, but I awaking and feeling her and perceiving who it was, yet willing to try the difference, satisfied myself with her, as well as one of the rest: that night, although the first time, she proved also with child. (p. 6)

Here is yet another racialized bed-trick, with a touch of realism in the fact that he isn't fooled. The tryst is then passed off as curiosity rather than passion on the narrator's part; his subsequent encounters with the black lover (always termed "My Negro," in contra-distinction to the others, who become "wives") always transpired at night, for his "stomach would not serve" him during the daylight, "although she was one of the handsomest Blacks [he] had seen, and her children as comely as any of the rest . . ." (p. 6). She is, notably, the first to conceive (though one wonders how he imagines he knew so quickly), and the ablest at giving birth – again, reinforcing the stereotypes. But there is one surprise: she gives birth to "a fine white girl" (p. 6). This is noted without irony or any sense of the unusual.

The term "white" here seems to be descriptive, not taxonomic; the point is that the daughter's skin is lighter than the mother's. Still, the lack of irony is in keeping with the tone of the narrative: racial mixture is clearly not a concern of the narrator. The offspring of the miscegenous union are not differentiated from the other three clans on the island, but rather subsumed under the obviously allegorical name the narrator gives to all his descendants: English Pines, from his surname plus that of his master's daughter, Sarah Pines. The patriarch, on reaching his eightieth year, makes his eldest son "King and Governor" and teaches his people "of the manners of Europe," charging them "to remember the Christian religion, after the manner of them that spake the same Language, and to admit no other, if hereafter any should come and find them out" (p. 8). The island is – even by name – a miniature England. In the introduction of the narrative, the modifier "speaking good English" proceeds the remarkable number of the narrator's "Posterity" (p. 1).

What does this narrative teach us about miscegenation? It teaches us that one man's Caliban is another (wo)man's Prospero. There is nothing in the language of the pamphlet that suggests or anticipates the kind of horror Caliban's fantasy of peopling an island aims to arouse in Shakespeare's audience. It is no doubt attributable to my own idiosyncrasies as a modern professional woman with a certain distaste for the labor of procreation that the prospect of one white man's self-multiplication into 1,700 seems equally if not more monstrous than Caliban's attempt on Miranda. The flat, matter-of-fact tone of the Pines narrative – juxtaposed with the vituperation heaped on Caliban ("abhorred slave" – "filth" – "freckled whelp" etc.) speaks powerfully of the master discourse and its evasions. Indeed, the narrative only mentions in passing the incest committed by the first generation of English Pines: "I took the Males of one Family, and married them to the Females of another, not letting any to marry their sisters, as we did formerly out of necessity" (p. 8). No man is an island, but one man left alone on an island with four fertile women can make or break his own rules. He, like Prospero (like Shakespeare), can write the books or drown them: he can choose to wield, or to break his magic staff.

Which books get drowned and which books get saved – and what we do with the books we do save – is a question that has followed us in this chapter, sometimes obscurely, sometimes not, as the shadow cast by a ship may be thrown into view by a sand-bar. The above overview of inter-racialism in the works of Shakespeare and his contemporaries has demonstrated, I hope, both the influence of *Othello*'s representational strategies and the variations on the same theme that later generations deemed less worthy. As such esthetic judgments are always also ideological, we can look to the texts ejected from the canon in terms of the political interests these erasures served. For readers whose passion for Shakespeare's art compels them to seek liberal-minded gestures in his plays, the news is not all bad: compared to Dekker's *Lust's Dominion*, for example, *Othello* is a paragon of Anglo cross-cultural sympathy, and we can pat ourselves on the back for having canonized Shakespeare rather than Dekker. But not so fast. Restoration audiences did not have to choose between Shakespeare's "Noble Moor" and Dekker's "black fiend": both plays were revived after the theatres re-opened, the Dekker adapted by England's first professional female author. In the next chapter, we will look at Othellophilia with a woman's touch.

CHAPTER 2

The Heathen with the Heart of Gold: Othellophilia comes to America

> The English did not colonize so much of the globe *because* they had Shakespeare. Shakespeare was like a local parasite – attached to a species that eventually dominated its own niche and migrated out into others, taking the parasite along and introducing it into ecosystems that had, often, no defenses against it.
> Gary Taylor, *Cultural Selection* (New York: Basic Books, 1996), pp. 87–8

I sometimes look back with nostalgia on the days of my critical innocence – the days I believed that women authors were somehow inherently more subversive, or at least inherently more feminist. With regard to Aphra Behn and her re-admission to the canon, Joyce Green MacDonald is surely correct in observing an ideological conundrum for feminists, resulting in the critical silence surrounding Behn's play *Abdelazer*, a revision of Dekker's *Lust's Dominion*. MacDonald finds the play "particularly troubling to the feminist impulses which mark so much recent scholarship on Behn" as the play demonstrates "rigidly patriarchal views of gender and . . . reflexively white supremacist formulations of racial and political identity."[1] I myself came to the play with high hopes, not because I was impressed by the author's racial sensitivity in her later novella, *Oroonoko; or, the Royal Slave* – indeed, as we'll see in a moment, this work too has its embarrassing moments – but rather because it seemed impossible to do worse than the Renaissance source, in promulgating an oppressive racialist-misogynist, xenophobic ideology.

In fact, the first scene of Behn's play continues to nurture such hopes – not to mention simply promising better dramatic craftsmanship. The Moorish antihero does not pummel his mistress with the language of whoredom, nor does he quote the demonizing racialist insults to which the Spanish (accurately, according to the play) subject him. The hair-raising final line of the scene in the source ("To shed a harlot's blood can be no sin") is blessedly absent, and this omission plus the removal of the "Lascivious Queen" from the sub-title signals a somewhat less hatefully obvious misogyny. But one shortly realizes that this verbal restraint is just that – restraint. Behn writes according to the rule that any teacher of freshman composition must embrace and promulgate with religious fervor: it is better to "show" than to "tell," and the actions of the Queen and the Moor must first "show" the truth of their villainy.

Behn does indulge in the rhetoric of demonization, but less frequently and with more sense of dramatic timing; she also does so more even-handedly (if that is the right word) than does the source, applying the term "devil" more often to the Queen and less often to the Moor. This does not, however, make the text more palatable to modern liberal sensibilities in that these choices are part of a larger pattern whereby the villainy of the Queen is heightened, while that of her counterpart is diminished: in other words, what Behn removes of the racialism she replaces with misogyny. Behn's Queen, unlike Dekker's, complies in the "black offence" of her husband's murder. Moreover, while Abdelazer agonizes over the plot against his wife, Florella, the Queen gloats, Tamora-like, in the thought of her rival's rape and death: "My son, be like thy mother, hot and bold; / And like the Noble Ravisher of Rome, / Court her with Daggers" (III.ii.42–4). Notably, he doesn't, and so the Queen stabs Florella herself, in a scene that departs from the source in casting their rivalry in stereotypically gendered – and color-phobic – terms.

> KING: What hast thou done, most barbarous of thy Sex!
> QUEEN: Destroy'd thy Murdress, – and my too fair Rival. *Aside.*
> KING: My murdress! – what Devil did inspire thee
> With thoughts so black and sinful? Could this fair Saint
> Be guilty of a Murder! (III.iii.95–9)

The scene recalls *Othello* in its harping on the murdered Florella as a "fair saint" in contrast to which the Queen's soul is "black." The King continues to pile abuse on his mother: "Thou vilest of thy sex . . . a thing I have miscall'd a Mother" (137–8); "Peace Fury! Not ill-boding Raven shrieks / Nor Midnight cries of murder'd Ghosts, are more / Ungratefull, than thy faint and dull excuses" (152–4). Elsewhere, the Queen is "too foul" and "the worst of women" (IV.ii.62), and, finally, "the Devil['s] . . . Dam" (IV.vi.436). Correspondingly, Behn alters the source in punishing her with an on-stage death, rather than mere confinement in a nunnery.

All in all, Behn's revision of *Lust's Dominion* seems less concerned with tempering its anti-black or misogynist rhetoric than, rather, subordinating the racialist-misogynist invective to artistic design. Not surprisingly, the racialist language crescendos in the final scene, when Abdelazer lists all his villainies: here he is called "dreadfull Monster," "true born Son of Hell," "monstrous Instrument of Hell," and "Dog" (v.iii.650, 720, 730, 755). The scene also contains the most concentrated denigrations of the (now dead) Queen's sexuality: Abdelazer twice refers to her "fierce and hot . . . Lust" and profanely boasts about how he "whor'd thy Mother, the Queen." In contrast to the source, which uses this language more or less indiscriminately, Behn applies these stigmatizing terms after the characters have been shown to deserve them.

Behn's restraint in *Abdelazer* seems modeled on *Othello*, which employs racialist insults more sparingly than other Moor plays of the Renaissance, even if modern readers may find its treatment of race objectionable. Indeed, if Behn didn't have *Othello* in mind, she should have, as the latter was one of the first plays revived in 1660, and it remained immensely popular throughout the Restoration (*Abdelazer*, by contrast, seems to have been performed only three times). But as Behn scholars are well aware, the author returned to the subject of blackness in a later work that enjoyed much more success, both in its original prose form and in Thomas Southerne's adaptation for the stage. Fortunately for the critical idealist in each of us, Behn did a better job the second time around – at least insofar as *Oroonoko* valorizes rather than demonizes its African hero.

I have begun this chapter with *Abdelazer* rather than *Oroonoko* not so as to embarrass those feminist reformers of the canon whose laudable efforts have bought Behn's works into anthologies and the curriculum. As a woman author who succumbed to the siren-song of Othellophilia, Behn is not alone in Anglo-American literary history: as we shall see in ensuing chapters, Behn set the precedent followed by (white) women authors from Emily Brontë, to Harriet Beecher Stowe, to Margaret Mitchell, to authors of contemporary romance novels. Rather, I have begun with *Abdelazer* because Behn's very turn away from its organizing racialist trope epitomizes (if it did not, in fact, help create) a development that would go on to characterize eighteenth-century inter-racialism. In the transition from the "Barbarous Moor" to the "Noble Savage," one sees telescoped a broader cultural shift from the anxious insularism of Elizabethan England to the more globally conscious, if still brutally ethnocentric, discourses of colonialism. Joseph Roach's useful formulation of an "Oceanic interculture" allows our analysis to cross the Atlantic, examining texts as diverse and problematizing of genre as Behn's novella, the biography of Olaudah Equiano, Susanna Haswell Rowson's play *Slaves in Algiers* (1794), and Washington Irving's *Salmagundi* (1807). This chapter will argue that the colonialist encounter, the debates over slavery, and the negotiations over an American cultural identity, gave rise to a new moral allegory starring a figure I like to call the Heathen with the Heart of Gold – a figure ripe for cultivation by the largely female authors of the developing genre of romance. I choose the appellation Heathen with a Heart of Gold over the time-honored "Noble Savage" in a sardonic allusion to the alliterative, female equivalent: that is, the "Whore with a Heart of Gold" – or, in the original Renaissance formulation, the "Honest Whore." Most critical treatments of the so-called Noble Savage fail fully to address an important aspect of his (and it is generally his) characterization: his interactions with the (generally white) women he encounters in his adventures, and his commentary – express or implied in his actions – on western versus "African" sexual mores, the latter most conveniently figured in the seraglio. Indeed, I contend that despite his appearance as the corrective obverse of the earlier "barbarous Moor," the exotic hero of New World mythology more often than not served racist-masculinist hegemony in at least one respect: his role as castigator of women.

Set partially in Africa, partially the New World, Aphra Behn's *Oroonoko* is the only text in the current canon of English classics that celebrates an African couple – that is, a black man and a black woman. One is thus grateful for the efforts of late twentieth-century scholars who rescued the play from obscurity.[2] Despite Behn's radical choice for a subject, however, the work's politics of gender and race represent a muddy mix of the reactionary and progressive. Certainly its claim to fame as a proto-abolitionist text is shaky: critics such as Laura Brown have noted the "incoherence of the novella's treatment of slavery."[3] Though the hero decries the white traders in flesh, their cruelties and hypocrisies, he later turns on his fellow slaves for their cowardice in the aborted rebellion, regretting his efforts "to make those free, who were by nature slaves" (p. 56).[4] The point is not that slavery is wrong, but that enslaving a prince is wrong. Similarly, my undergraduates are never fooled by the blazoning of the black hero, with his "nose . . . rising and Roman instead of African and flat" and "His mouth the finest shaped . . . far from those great turned lips, which are so natural to the rest of the Negroes" (p. 13). Indeed, the whole passage is introduced by a "not" that sets even his skin-color ("perfect ebony, or polished jett") in opposition to his "brown rusty black" countrymen (p. 8): a back-handed racial compliment if there ever was one. Brown is surely right to call the hero "a European aristocrat in blackface"; indeed, I would go further, and call him a Ken-doll in ebony. Imoinda too is a mixed bag, in ideological terms: it's impressive that she can shoot a bow, but her extreme modesty and willingness to take death at her husband's hands "smiling with joy . . . for [African] Wives have a respect for their Husbands equal to what any other People pay a Diety" (p. 60), prevent the kind of feminist applause we might award the feisty heroines of Behn's other works.

Yet despite my misgivings about Behn's novella, there is one important respect in which it deserves to be hailed as subversive: this is a text that valorizes black femininity, offering in the princess Imoinda a "beautiful black Venus" worth the adoration of men both black and white. Indeed, the passage in which the narrator describes "a hundred white men sighing after her, and making a thousand vows at her feet, all in vain" (p. 14) may imply that only white men can confer value on a black woman – however, it also asks the reader to visualize white men (a hundred of them, no less!) at the feet of a black woman. The radicalism of Behn's artistic choice here is nowhere more evident than in Southerne's 1695 adaptation for the stage: Southerne made Imoinda white, and in doing so, set the standard for every subsequent adaptation (there were several) until the 1990s.[5]

Whitewashing Imoinda was a clever move on Southerne's part, allowing him both to capitalize on the popularity of *Othello* and to make use of the latter's theatrical clichés. Yet the larger ideological implications of this earliest case of Othellophilia in casting are blatantly clear in the Epilogue by Wiliam Congreve, which draws its moral from Shakespeare's play, if not directly citing it. The Epilogue begins by addressing the oddly incongruous, comic sub-plot Southerne added, wherein two English-women come to America in order to find husbands; it concludes with a comment on Imoinda's death.

> To follow fame, Knights-Errant make profession:
> We damsels fly to save our reputation:
> So they their valor shew, we our Discretion.
> To lands of Monsters, and fierce Beasts they go:
> We, to those Islands, where rich husbands grow:
> Tho' they're no Monsters, we may make 'em so.
> If they're of English growth, they'll bear't with Patience:
> But save us from a Spouse of Oroonoko's Nations!
> Then bless your stars, you happy London Wives
> Who love at large, each Day, yet keep your Lives:
> Nor envy poor Imoinda's doating blindness,
> We thought her husband kill'd her out of kindness,
> Death with a husband ne'er had shewn such charms,
> Had she once dy'd within a Lover's Arms.
> Her error was from Ignorance proceeding:

Poor Soul! She wanted some of our Town-Breeding.
Forgive this Indian's Fondness for her Spouse;
Their law no Christian liberty allows:
Alas! they make a Conscience of their Vows!
If Virtue in a Heathen be a Fault;
Then damn the Heathen school, where she was taught.
She might have learned to Cuckold, Jilt, and Sham,
Had Covent-Garden been in Surinam. (Epilogue, 13–35)

The doubly hegemonic nature of the discourse I call Othellophilia is perhaps nowhere more naked than here: English husbands are invited to flatter themselves over their greater humanity relative to the violently jealous men of African, all the while relishing the vicarious pleasure of their wives' fatal punishment at the hands of a black male alter-ego. Genre, in this case, makes the violence of the message less tolerable: one can walk away from the spectacle of a wife-murder with a sense of solemnity that forestalls feminist critique, but when the moral "You cheat, you die" is chirped with such satiric nonchalance, the author is as guilty of bad taste as bad ideas. Yet the Epilogue seems confused as to the reasons for Imoinda's sacrifice: in Behn's text Oroonoko kills her in order to prevent her rape and murder by their enemies, a justification to which Southerne adds an explicit desire to save their unborn child from slavery. Adultery as such has little to do with it. The references to cuckolding (that "horned . . . monster" again) are oddly beside the point, and only serve to underscore the cultural obsessions that drive Othellophilia – namely, the masculinist-racist obsession with the sexuality of white women.

Also telling is the confused reference to Imoinda as an "Indian," which she is not, either in Southerne's play-text or in the source. I am reminded of the editorial crux in Othello's self-eulogy before his suicide; he likens himself to "the base Judian / Indian" – either a Jew, a Judas, or an Indian – "who threw away a pearl / Richer than all his tribe" (v.ii.356–7). The intersection between Shakespeare's text and Congreve's allows a momentary identification of Imoinda with Othello, and hence a subversive counter-reading whereby the self-martyring wife is the ignorant one, casting away the pearl of her life. That is, on the other hand, precisely the reaction the Epilogue anticipates – and attempts to squelch through satire – in its urbane female auditors.

Whatever one makes of Congreve's addition to Southerne's adaptation of Behn's novella, the Epilogue makes it hard to ignore the fact that the play – like the novella before it – romanticizes a wife's death at her husband's hand.[6] However, Southerne's dialogue actually mitigates

Oroonoko's guilt by having him balk at the task of dispatching his wife: she finally forces his hand. Congreve's Epilogue, in its allusion to *Othello*, counters this effect.

There are other ways in which Southerne's version is – perhaps despite itself – more subversive than its source. The sub-plot, however troubling to formalist notions of stylistic and tonal unity, counters the essentializing, sentimentalist aspects of the central love story by highlighting marriage as a commercial enterprise, much like slavery. In one significant exchange, the cross-dressed Charlot Welldone – posing as a brother concerned to negotiate a financially desirable match for "his" sister – interrupts the suitor, "This is your Market for Slaves; my Sister is a free Woman, and must not be dispos'd of in publick" (p. 13). The sub-plot also foregrounds slavery's appropriation of black female reproductive labor: "I am a Woman my self and can't get my own Slaves as some of my Neighbors do" (p. 13). Moreover, some of the Petrarchan moments in the main plot invite feminist deconstruction for their high-flown slave-of-love poetic diction. How convincing – in a play about real slavery – are we to find statements like the thwarted rapist's "I come to offer you your Liberty / And be myself the Slave . . . You shall be gently forced to please yourself" (p. 26)? Or, from a more sympathetic speaker: "Oh! You are born always to conquer me" (Oroonoko to Imoinda). Or, even worse, Oroonoko's "To Honor bound! And yet a slave to love! . . . No man condemn me, who has never felt / A woman's power . . ." (p. 71). More compelling by far is Imoinda's own inadvertent self-portrayal as enslaved to her husband: "Indians or English: / Whoever has me, I am still a slave, / No matter whose I am, since I'm no more / *My royal master's*" (p. 31; emphasis mine).

Deconstructive maneuvers aside, the text's whitewashing of the African princess – pointed up by a slew of white/brightness/star/sun images too clichéd to merit listing – together with the Shakespearean allusions throughout, indicate Southerne's selling-out to the sensationalistic and socially suspect myth of the jealous black man. Here are some telling textual parallels:

> There is a Justice in it pleases me. (*Oroonoko*, p. 45)
>
> . . . [T]he justice of it pleases. (*Othello*, iv.i.199)

> Find yet a way to lay her beauties down
> gently in death, and save me from her blood. (*Oroonoko*, p. 78)
>
> Yet I'll not shed her blood (*Othello*, v.ii.3)

Put up your swords, and let not civil broils
Engage you . . . (*Oroonoko*, p. 79)

Keep up your bright swords, or the dew will rust 'em. (*Othello*, 1.i.60)

This object will convince you . . . (*Oroonoko*, p. 79)

This object poisons sight . . . (*Othello*, v.ii.374)

All the above are spoken by Oroonoko. There is also "Who did the bloody Deed?" – "The deed was mine" (*Oroonoko*, p. 79) followed by a reference to the sword of Justice that echos Othello's "O balmy breath, that doth almost persuade / Justice to break her sword" (*Othello*, v.ii.16–17). One hears an echo of Aaron in "No, let the guilty blush, / The white Man that betrayed me: Honest Black / Disdains to change its colour" (*Oroonoko*, p. 17). There's a bit of King Lear in ". . . a Prince every inch of him" (p. 14) and of *The Tempest* in "I did design to carry him to England, to have shew'd him there . . ." (p. 15) and of *Merchant* in "The command of a dying Father, you know, ought to be obeyed" (p. 19). And, lest we miss a single Shakespearean treatment of the exotic, there's also a borrowing from *Antony and Cleopatra*:

> This little spot of Earth you stand upon
> Is more to me, than the extended plains
> Of my great Father's kingdom. Here I reign
> In full delights in joys to power unknown;
> Your Love my Empire, and your heart my throne. (p. 34)

One can always play these games with Restoration plays, but in any case it seems clear that Southerne's adaptation owes more to Shakespeare than does Behn's original. The above quote is closer to "Here is my space / Kingdoms are clay. Our dungy earth alike / feeds beast as man" (*Antony and Cleopatra*, 1.i.36–8) than the corresponding passage in Behn's novella: "He swore he disdained the Empire of the World, while he could behold his Imoinda" (*Oroonoko*, p. 39). Yet it might also be argued that Southerne's over-the-top Shakespeareanisms reveal the subtler "Shakespeareanism" of the source. Behn's text does start out as – and end as – a kind of black *Romeo and Juliet*, its romantic hero defined as such in opposition to the sexual mores associated with Africa. As the harem setting of the story's first part emphasizes, Oroonoko's worthiness for the role of black Romeo is almost entirely premised upon his rejection of polygamy. And what theme could be more Shakespearean than that of constancy-unto-death?

Yet it is perhaps too simplistic to say that Behn selected one Shakespearean tragic hero, and Southerne swapped him with another;

Shakespeare too had sources. What interests me in reading Shakespeare through Behn through Southerne (through Congreve) is not so much the question of who "owns" the original, but rather the very difficulty in positing that point of origin. One faces the seemingly infinite capacity of these texts to escape authorial mastery – or, put another way, the capacity of the master discourse to co-opt whichever new texts come into its purview. Imoinda may not be a feminist icon, but she is, in Behn's text, a black woman whose dignity and allure walk hand-in-hand with her blackness: her emphatically raced and gendered body – not just female, but pregnant, and not just black, but tattooed – finds a pale substitute in Southerne's blushing English bride. Would it be too much to suggest that this lovingly etched black Venus is Behn's own alter-ego, her Other-ego? Jane Spencer argues that "in the story of Oroonoko and his wife [Behn's] position, as a woman, might be expected to be more analogous with Imoinda's, and that is an identification she does not want to make."[7] I see it the other way round: by resisting an identification with Oroonoko's wife, Behn resists eroticizing her own relationship to her black hero, thus preserving the integrity of the black love story. Behn closes her work with a gesture at once self-effacing and proud:

> Thus died this great man, worthy of a better fate, and a more sublime wit than mine to write his praise. Yet I hope the reputation of my pen is considerable enough to make his glorious name to survive all ages, with that of the brave, the beautiful, and the constant Imoinda. (p. 65)

For this woman author who "value[d] fame as much as . . . [a] born hero," closing the text by lauding the heroine seems, to me at least, a kind of feminist gesture. If we owe one thing to Behn other than the act for which Virginia Woolfe urged women to cast flowers on her grave – that is, earning women the right to be professional writers – it is this bit of imaginative inter-racial sisterhood.

Also significant – albeit more ideologically problematic in hindsight – is Behn's role in the transformation of Shakespeare's ageing "Barbary horse" to a genuine black beauty, worthy of white female erotic attention. Laura Brown notes the way the narrative presents an abundance of women, including the narrator and other white ladies, "as observers, beneficiaries, and consumers of Oroonoko's romantic action"[8] – her own replacement, in narrative terms, of the audience of women who enjoy *Othello* in performance. There was even a rumor circulating in Behn's own lifetime – itself another eruption of Othellophilia – that the author herself, while in Surinam, had had relations with her titular Royal

Slave. Considering the total lack of historical evidence for this charge, the number of editorial introductions that cite it is telling.

The shift in attitudes from Shakespeare's "I saw Othello's visage in my mind" (that is, in the pungent paraphrasing of Hugh Quarshie, "I know he's ugly as sin, but he has a beautiful mind"[9]) to Behn's statement that Oroonoko has "everything called beauty bating the color" represents an important turning-point in the development of the discourse, the point at which the intervention of female authors leads to the romanticization of the inter-racial hero. This is not to essentialize based on the author's gender, since Behn's earlier inter-racialist text, as we have already seen, treats the theme quite differently: it is merely to note the way that Othellophilia at this point begins to dovetail with romance as a developing and predominantly female-authored genre, while authors working in different genres – for example, satire – continue to denigrate black males. Indeed, we will see in a later chapter how Behn's African prince strangely prefigures the de-racialized but emphatically "dark" romance hero epitomized by Margaret Mitchell's "pagan prince" Rhett Butler.[10] Aside from the exigencies of genre, however, another factor in the eroticization of an African blackness would have been the increasing visibility of, in particular, men of color in Restoration and eighteenth-century England. The tradition of the "decorative" African in court life and portraiture had always competed with the demonized and proverbially ugly Renaissance stage Moor; England's increasing involvement in the slave trade meant that the fascination with the racial Other at some point was bound to compete with the phobia, and a market would spring up for softer, more patronizing, proto-racist works of art.

The real-life Oroonokos in England were, of course, seldom princes: most were servants, sailors, students, musicians, and (later in the century) refugees from the American Revolution.[11] But proportionally they were men, and thus potential lovers of white women. Indeed, the sexuality of the fashionable black page presented a problem when he reached puberty: English ladies then had to dispose of their human accessories, for the sake of social propriety. In some cases, the unfortunate young man was shipped off to the West Indies and slavery.[12] Like a boy actor, but one with no future in adult roles, the black page was not allowed to grow up. He was a social castrato – like, arguably, many black males today.

To some, the young pages in and of themselves functioned as indices to the moral failings of their white mistresses. Epitomizing the non-romantic, satiric approach to the discourse, a 1675 pamphlet sneers "The fashionable high-class whore of the period hath always two necessary

Implements about her, a Blackamoor and a little Dog; for without these she would be neither Fair nor Sweet."[13] Constitutive of her oxymoronic status as "high-class" as opposed to low-class "whore," the Blackamoor simultaneously invokes social privilege and the sexual excess permitted (according to the speaker's anti-feminist satire) by that privilege. As a symbol of her wealth, he is her ticket to respectability; as a symbol of her vanity – a weakness often viewed as leading women to whoredom – he sets her up for the speaker's scorn (and hence the reader's). The comment is of a piece with Rymer's disparaging remark about the Blackamoor and the "small-coal wench," cited in the previous chapter. One might not be able to "wash the Ethiope" clean, but blackness – as a class marker – always rubs off on a body.

The inter-racial love-story is a drama of upward mobility; this constitutes, in part, its fascination. In racist-masculinist cultures, that means the hero will be black, as males are perceived as social agents and women as their prizes. Behn's *Oroonoko* lacked this element: Southerne supplied it. This may account for the play's popularity throughout the eighteenth century.[14]

Whether or not there was a "real" Oroonoko, the popularity of Behn's novella and Southerne's play – in conjunction with the growing black population in England – meant that people were sure to find one. In 1759 art and life collided when two African men – one indeed a prince newly rescued from slavery – attended a performance of the play and received a standing ovation. Prince William Ansah Sessarakoo was a celebrated figure, nicknamed Cupid for his social graces, and the subject of sentimental poems.[15] Nor was this the only royal slave to grace the London social scene; James Albert Gronniosaw's case was similar, and he enjoyed the "happy ending" denied his literary predecessors: marriage with a white woman. Unfortunately, the two lived in poverty.[16] But that is a different tragedy.

In using terms like "real-life" to distinguish literary characters from historical personages, I may perhaps be faulted by post-structuralist critics for essentializing the difference between literary texts and historical "facts." But my aim is to trouble that very distinction. *Othello* was a popular name for slave ships, on board which real Africans suffered and died.[17] Indeed, the more fortunate of these human cargo might have been awarded the same nick-name: Julius Soubise, a freed slave taken in by the Duchess of Queensbury, was called "the young Othello" by his mistress's admiring maidservants. In a similar vein, Samuel Johnson's beloved black servant, Francis Barber, married a white woman and treated her (in the eyes of his patrons) with excessive jealousy: one account calls the wife "his Desdemona."[18] And indeed, we may now have to re-classify Olaudah Equiano – perceived for more than two centuries as a born African and the author of a factual slave narrative – as (partially) a self-invented literary character, in light of recent historical findings suggesting he was born in South Carolina.[19]

The observation about Equiano should not be taken as remotely derogatory toward this deservedly valorized early abolitionist. All autobiographies are artistic creations, and most, I daresay, contain conscious lies, if only lies of omission; it hardly matters whether the African chapters in *The Interesting Narrative of the Life of Olaudah Equiano* (1789) are drawn from the author's travel knowledge rather than the African childhood now in question by historians. I expect to make this a maxim in this book: the question is not who is telling the "truth," but rather, which lies hurt the most people. And in at least one important aspect Equiano's *Interesting Narrative* speaks a truth to which, culturally speaking, we are still often deaf: ". . . [I]t was almost a constant practice with our clerks, and other whites, to commit violent depredations on the chastity of the female slaves; and these I was, though with reluctance, obliged to submit to at all times, being unable to help them" (p. 93).[20] The rape of his country-women is clearly a central concern of Equiano's, as he returns to the subject more than once, and lists "the offensive sight of the violated chastity of the sable females" as second only to "the sound of the cruel whip" in his adieu to the horrors of slavery (p. 139). This repeated exposure to scenes of rape effectively emasculates the speaker – he is *"obliged to submit"* – and cannot help the victims, some of whom, as he tells us, are "not ten years old" (p. 93; emphasis mine).[21] This train of thought naturally leads him, in the earlier passage, to describe a literal un-manning next: "And yet in Montserrat I have seen a Negro man staked to the ground, and cut [i.e., castrated] most shockingly, and then his ears cut off bit by bit, because he had been connected with a white woman who was a common prostitute" (p. 94). The contrasting anecdote deserves note for casting the black man– white "whore" duo in a different light. Contrasting the rape of "an innocent African girl" with consensual sex with "the most abandoned woman of her species," Equiano's point is not (as the whites would have it) the lasciviousness of the black man (who is only "gratify[ing] a passion of nature" [p. 94]) nor of the white prostitute (note he avoids the usual stigmatizing terms), but rather the hypocrisy of white (sexual) justice.

Equiano's delicacy in the above-quoted passages is typical of the book. And here one notes a certain disjunction between the discourse represented by *Oroonoko* and the narrator's self-presentation: although in a letter to London's *Public Advertiser* the author advocated inter-marriage,[22] in the narrative Equiano goes out of his way to de-eroticize his persona. His relations with white women are entirely platonic, his comments on their physical appearance limited to a single mention of their slenderness (which he "did not at first like"), and any musings on their sexual behavior only implied in the subsequent comment that "they were not so much modest and shame-faced as the African women" (p. 64). Kim Hall observes the way in which the first book on Africa by an African author measures the civility of its many nations in terms of their ability to control female sexuality; Leo Africanus' *History and Description of Africa* (1600) hence adopts European masculinist notions of female propriety, while also countering stereotypes (or supporting them, depending upon the nation described) of African concupiscence.[23] Equiano here seems to prize a particularly gendered modesty; elsewhere in the book, however, he evaluates African or Indian cultures in terms of a non-gender-specific sexual continence. In these moral concerns, he recalls Africanus, yet the narrative is remarkable for its attention to male sexuality, particularly that of white males. His shock is apparent in relating an anecdote about a planter showing off the "many mulattoes working in the field like beasts of burden . . . [who] were all the produce of his own loins!" (p. 98).

More importantly, however, Equiano presents a subtle statement about his own sexuality, albeit negatively, in what he omits from his story. In one episode in Smyrna, he is offered two wives, and Equiano laconically tells how he "refused the temptation, thinking one was as much as some could manage, and more than others would venture on" (143). These and other moments are easy to miss, but given English culture's increasing obsession with the mythology of the seraglio – an obsession blatant in Behn's treatment of it in *Oroonoko* – Equiano's sexual modesty seems calculated for effect. At this point in the narrative, one may retrospectively appreciate his phrasing of the earlier description of African marriage customs: "Adultery . . . was sometimes punished with slavery or death . . . so jealous are they of the fidelity of their wives . . . The men, however, do not preserve the same constancy to their wives which they expect from them; for they indulge in plurality, though seldom in more than two" (p. 35). Again, the delicacy of phrasing manifests the narrator's conscious-ness of, and aim to negotiate around, stereotype. Like Othello, all African men are violently jealous (interestingly, though, he follows this up by telling of an adulteress who was spared the death penalty owing to pregnancy); like Oroonoko's grandfather, they "indulge in plurality" (note the moral judgment implied in the verb) – but Equiano immediately limits that plurality to two, the same number of wives he is later offered and turns down. Like his romantic literary precedent, Equiano appeals to the tastes of his white (female?) readers, in separating himself from a troubling "African" sexual excess. And here one senses a paradox: to the degree that he down-plays his sexuality, the autobiographical persona in effect makes himself a romantic hero in the eyes of the female consumer of sentimentalist fiction. The apparent contrasts with *Oroonoko* become a matter of perspective. He is monogamous (in fact, he is celibate throughout the narrative); he becomes a Christian; he feels for women whose virtue comes under attack – he even seems to feel for the adulteress mentioned above. Throughout the narrative women are prominent objects of the speaker's loyalty, from the beloved sister with whom he is captured (and whom he tragically loses), to his early, white "playmate" Mary (who once inspires him to try to wash his face white!), to various "friendly ladies" of London. Moreover, the speaker feminizes himself throughout the narrative, in ways that (like many perceived forms of effeminacy) are bound to tug at female heart-strings: he weeps frequently and effusively, he faints, prays, and writes poetry. Equiano fashions himself as the perfect sentimental hero.

Two years after the publication of his *Interesting Narrative*, Equiano married a white woman. The text's only foreshadowing of this, other than the above, is his quotation of Thomas Day's 1733 poem "The dying negro," based on an incident wherein (as Equiano tells us in a footnote), a black man committed suicide after attempting and failing to escape slavery and marry a white woman. Typically, Equiano quotes the poem in a de-eroticized context, as though it were any other anti-slavery tract. Yet, as I am trying to show here, Equiano's narrative strategies render a romantic context unnecessary. The love-story is between the hero and the reader. Does this implicate Equiano in Othellophilia? Yes and no. Like any hegemonic discourse, Othellophilia is ripe for subversion at the hands of its subjects. Equiano's story inspired countless people – many of them white women – to speak out against slavery. Malcolm X called for black power "by any means necessary";[24] certainly Equiano's romantic self-fashioning qualifies. In Greek, *pharmakon* means both medicine and poison.

A certain theme has hovered at the borders of this discussion, and that theme deserves to be brought into focus: the fascination of the seraglio.[25] In speaking of the Heathen with the Heart of Gold, I wish to keep in mind another "h" word that defines him as such: the harem. This can cut either way in terms of defining the hero's status as moral mouthpiece for the author: he is "better" than the westerners around him despite having a harem, or he is "better" than them because he could have a harem, and doesn't. The honest heathen, like the honest whore, thus points up white sexual hypocrisy, as when Behn makes the point that "the only Crime and Sin with Woman" in Oroonoko's native country is that of "abandon[ing] her to want, shame, and misery: such ill Morals are only practiced in *Christian* countries" (Behn, *Oroonoko*, p. 15; italics in original).

There is another conflicting rhetorical use of the seraglio that we have not, so far, encountered: the formula whereby the seraglio functions to foreground, by way of contrast, the so-called freedom of western women. This rhetoric can work either to further misogynist attacks on white women's (particularly sexualized) freedom, or, conversely, it can serve seemingly feminist (albeit racist) celebrations of that freedom. According to Ania Loomba, "English stories of patriarchal violence in Muslim cultures served both to define the incivility of those cultures and to offer models for domestic control of unruly women."[26] With both these formulations in mind, we turn to two ideologically counter-poised, though equally Orientalist, works of early American literature, Susanna Haswell Rowson's then-popular play *Slaves in Algiers* (1794) and John Irving's serial satire, *Salmagundi* (1807).[27] It might be useful to note here, before we embark on this chapter's final readings, that we will be leaving behind the notion of a specifically sub-Saharan blackness. As Anglo-American culture increasingly reified the heretofore fluid categories of racial difference, putting the black–white binary to the service of a historically specific form of slavery, and as imperialism gave rise to a more sophisticated grid upon which to chart racial alterity (East Indian, American Indian, Middle Eastern, etc.), the discourses of inter-racialism quite naturally began to consider the possibility of sexual contact with other Others. More pertinently, the construction of a "third category" – neither black nor white – allowed a certain imaginative safe space wherein white authors could play with issues of cultural identity without taking on the uncomfortable topic of slavery. As modern racism developed, Othellophilia whitened up: hence, the explosion of "Oriental" stage Othellos later in the 1800s. Indeed, I have been arguing all along that Othellophilia never really had much to do with black people.

Slaves in Algiers, a dramatization of white captivity in Africa, is the first work in this study that manifests something approaching what we might call a feminist sensibility. The play announces an interest in gender issues

How can she say that when she really has been talking about black people, i.e. the African slaves, the Ethiope, etc.

early on: the Prologue presents an author who "tho' a woman, pled the Rights of Man" (p. 58)[28] and in the first scene, Fetnah – a female exotic hero – speaks of the influence of a female American captive who "taught [her] woman was never formed to be the abject slave of man" (p. 60).

But let's not get too excited: if this is early feminism, it is feminism at the service of a pernicious, self-congratulatory patriotism that conceives of an America free of "persecution . . . / Where safe asylums every virtue guard, / And every talent meets its just reward" (p. 38) despite the spectacle of thousands of enslaved Africans on the streets of every American city.[29] This may be why Rowson excludes black characters from this play set in Africa: the *dramatis personae* list is divided into Americans and "Moriscans," and the latter are never described as black or even explicitly dark-skinned; both the "Moriscan" and the American women can be described as "fair." There is one reference to (apparently offstage) black characters, constituting the sole instance of out-and-out racism: the palace guards are "great, black, goggle-eyed creatures . . . [who] when one speaks to them . . . shake their frightful heads and make such a horrid noise" (pp. 72–3). But what the play lacks in racist rhetoric it makes up for in anti-Semitism: Fetnah's father is a Jew who converted to Islam – that is, he is doubly Othered – and is stereotypically greedy, not to mention speaking in a stagey "Jewish" accent. Of course there is also the lecherous Sultan figure, mocked for his whiskers, his "great beetle brows," and his habit of fondling his "huge scimitar." Discussions of the harem do carry traces of the racialist tropes analyzed in Chapter 1; the characteristic wencher amongst the Americans complains that he has "been a slave two years, six months, a fortnight, and three days; and have all that time worked in the garden of the Alcaide, who has twelve wives, thirty concubines, and two pretty daughters. And yet not one of the insensible *hussies* ever took a fancy to" him (p. 79; emphasis mine). Commenting on Fetnah, who falls for his companion, he says,

Why, 'tis a little body, but, ecod, she's a *devil* of a spirit. It's a fine thing to meet with a woman who has a little fire in her composition. I never much liked your milk-and-water ladies. To be sure, they are easily managed, but your spirited lasses require taming; they make a man look about him. Dear, sweet, angry creatures: here's their health . . . If they are saucy, why then, here – here, in this we'll drown the remembrance of the bewitching, forward little *devils*.

(p. 80; emphasis mine)

This is the closest the text comes to acknowledging complexional differences among the women in the play, the fire–milk opposition suggesting a color binary. The more frequent suggestions of physical difference are the modifiers that stress Fetnah's smallness ("my lovely little Moor";"poor little Fetnah"; "my sweet little infidel") – although these could be patronizing Orientalist pet-names rather than indications of the actual stature of the actress. More ideologically central to the play is the mention of taming, itself constituting a latent Shakespeareanism, alluding to *The Taming of the Shrew*. In this work that frames its patriotism in terms of the freedom of American women, what is the final word on gender roles? The Epilogue, spoken by the author and directly addressing the women in the audience, returns to the issue:

> Well, ladies, tell me: how d'ye like my play?
> "The creature has some sense," methinks you say;
> "She says we should have supreme dominion,
> "And in good truth, we're all of her opinion.
> "Women were born for universal sway;
> "Men to adore, be silent, and obey." (p. 94)

The following stanzas quickly retract this "flippancy," reinforcing domestic ideology by emphasizing the woman's duty of comforting her husband and "mak[ing] a paradise at home"; "By these, pursuing nature's gentle plan, / We hold in silken chains the lordly tyrant man" (p. 94). Any threat to the order of things embodied in the on-stage female author and her ability to appeal to the women in the audience is quickly dispelled; Rowson's persona here might as well be Katherine, Shakespeare's eponymous shrew, delivering her final lecture on wifely obedience. The Epilogue ends with a plea on behalf of Christian captives in the Muslim world – an appeal to sentiment more than a call to arms, but the closest Rowson comes to stating her agenda. The text's pseudo-feminist gestures turn out to have been strategic in a way that highlights the already problematic relationship between white women authors' gender and racial alliances.[30]

The echoes of *The Taming of the Shrew* deserve a bit more attention. So far this other ideologically troubled work of Shakespeare has not seemed relevant to this study, containing as it does no "blackamoor" characters. But at this point in Shakespeare's critical and theatrical history, his most popular domestic tragedy and his most dubiously "comic" treatment of marriage and male prerogative begin to inter-relate theoretically. At about mid-century David Garrick popularized what was to be the enduring convention that actors playing Petruccio, Shakespeare's swaggering poster-boy for marital hierarchy, would carry whips, thus literalizing notions of wifely subservience in a way that invites association with the painful spectacle of slavery. And whereas stage Petruccios have been, almost always, insistently, racially "white," they can tend toward the swarthy side, as the Italian setting would seem to encourage. Elizabeth Schafer's survey of the play's performance history includes an entire sub-category of "maverick" or "swashbuckling" Petruccios – a list that concludes in Morgan Freeman's performance of the role as a black cowboy in 1990.[31] Petrucciophilia shades into Othellophilia, and vice versa.

I have been trying to suggest throughout this book that Othellophilia always aims to influence women, in particular white women. In the case of the eighteenth-century exotic hero, that illocutionary force may be put to the service of divergent political ends – both misogynst-racist (Congreve) and abolitionist (Equiano) – or to no political end at all, as in Behn's failure to make a case against slavery. In the case of Behn, the gender of the author need not account for the text's relatively non-coercive or apolitical message: Rowson's capitulation to domestic ideology and anti-Muslim moral are easily as coercive as Congreve's attack on cheating English wives, in another Epilogue. Moreover, a passive political act is no less political for being passive. Rowson's focus on a (dying) form of slavery in which whites were victims, not perpetrators, constitutes, by its very evasions, a negative argument for the enslavement of blacks. Indeed, the Orientalist fixation upon a sexualized white slavery arguably contributed to, rather than merely distracting from, the catastrophic growth of the trade in black slaves.[32]

The new Orientalist variety of the discourse of Othellophilia can be, on the other hand, far more blatantly misogynistic and racist. Washington Irving's *Salmagundi* wrests the eighteenth-century exotic hero from the sentimentalist-romantic tradition of *Oroonoko*, and renders him a vehicle for (primarily misogynist) social satire. The text presents itself as a serial publication, largely consisting of letters and faux newspaper clippings. Prominent among the letter-writing personae is one "Mustapha Rub-a-Dub Keli Khan Captain of a Ketch, to Asem Hacchem, principle slave-driver to his highness the Bashaw of Tripoli"; the Mustapha character is based on one of seven captives of American military action in north Africa, whose arrival in New York caused a media stir just before *Salmagundi*'s publication. Mustapha makes his first appearance in a letter from New York lamenting the twenty-three wives he has left at home, and the wives are repeatedly invoked in order to showcase – sometimes simultaneously – both white women's superiority as sexual objects and their greater moral defects. In a master stroke of masculinist-racist having-it-both-ways, Irving sets up Mustapha as simultaneously the butt of ethnocentric sexual satire and the spokesman for misogyny. On first beholding American women, he rhapsodizes,

Yet beautiful, oh most puissant slave-driver, as are my wives, they are far exceeded by the women of this country. Even those who run about the streets with bare arms and necks . . . are lovely as the Houris that people the Elysium of true believers. If then, such as run wild in the highways, and whom nobody cares to appropriate, are thus beauteous, what must be the charms of those who are shut up in the seraglios, and never permitted to go abroad![33]

Later on, the truth dawns on him. First praising American women for their "prattle . . . as diverting as the chattering of the red-tailed parrot" and their "whim and playfulness" surpassing "the green-headed monkey of Timandi," he then bemoans the fact that "they are not treated with half the attention bestowed on the before-mentioned animals. These infidels put their parrots in cages and chain their monkeys; but their women . . . are abandoned to the direction of their own reason, and suffered to run about in perfect freedom like other domestic animals." He then sighs, "This comes . . . of treating their women as rational beings and allowing them souls" (p. 320).

Mustapha's reminiscences about his harem allow Irving simultaneously to entertain and distance himself from the notion of women as chattel. Here is Mustapha at his worst; entering what he takes to be an actual seraglio (in fact a dance-hall) and exclaiming on the "charms of these bewitching savages," he asks his companion: "To whom do these beautiful creatures belong? Certainly this must be the seraglio of the grand bashaw of the city . . ." His companion cautions him not to speak this way for fear of offending the ladies, for they "have no lord and master, but come here to catch one – they're in the market, as we term it." Mustapha then exults over having finally discovered "a fair, or slave-market, such as we have in the east" and then asks how much he might pay for "some ten or a dozen wives" (p. 329). The satire works here in a fashion similar to that of Congreve's Epilogue to *Oroonoko*; the sophisticated (male) white reader feels complacency over his own culture's relative humanity toward women, while yet enjoying the suggestion of wholesale sexual slavery of white women.[34] Mustapha goes on, Petruccio-like, to decry the "untameable disposition" of all womankind.

The "taming" reference is one of the more obscure Shakespeareanisms in a text sprinkled with allusions to the, by now, "classic" author. Tellingly, the play the text treats most fully is *Othello*. The passage presents itself as a review of a production – the only section of its kind in the work – but then concludes with the following disclaimer; "P. S. Just as this was going to press, I was informed . . . that Othello [no italics in original] had not been performed here the lord knows when; no matter, I am not the first critic that has criticised a play without seeing it . . ." (p. 142). In fact, the play was performed frequently in New York in the first decade of the 1800s. The persona, the inept and pompous critic William Wizard, Esq., attends the fictitious production with another inept critic, who complains that the actor playing Othello had not "made himself as black as a negro . . . 'for,' said he, 'that Othello was an arrant black, appears from several expressions of the play'" (p. 137). The sentence is striking in light of Anglo-American theatre history in that it precedes by seven years the accepted date of the first "tawny" or "Oriental" Othello, that of Edmund Kean on the London stage in 1814; the assumption has been that the tawny Othello was a British import via Kean's American debut in 1820.[35] Yet the view "that Othello was an arrant black" seems to be satirized here – at the very least, the text evidences awareness of a debate surrounding the issue. Would the actor playing Othello in 1807 in New York have blacked up? Early American theatre history is notoriously sketchy: George C. D. Odell's *Annals of the New York Stage* is no help here. One small clue comes from the south: according to Woodrow L. Holbein, in Charleston, South Carolina, the play was barred from performance until 1809, and one might speculate from records of the debate that a light-skinned Othello was offered as compromise. Indeed, that is the upshot of a comment by contemporary travel-writer John Lambert, who complained that actors on the Charleston stage would not "condescend to blacken their faces."[36] Lambert is an Englishman, so we cannot assume that his point of reference is theatre in the northern versus southern United States; it is not impossible that a New York performance in 1807 might have anticipated this development in Charleston, as the *Salmagundi* reference imagines. But we will return to the subject of the New York stage Moor below.

The review has a curious take on Desdemona as well. Glossing "If heaven had made her such a man," as Desdemona's wish to be a man, rather than a wish to have a man like Othello, the critic persona opines that "*she wanted to wear the breeches*" and that, thus, "Othello was . . . most ignominiously *hen-pecked*" (p. 141; italics in original). Here the William Wizard persona echoes Mustapha, who also criticizes American women for wishing to "usurp the breeches" (p. 80).

To me, however, the most significant moment in the mock-review is an allusion to Thomas Jefferson's black mistress, who we now know was foremother to an entire lineage of Jeffersonian "mulattoes," a lineage routinely and brutally effaced from American historical record.[37] The critic persona calls Desdemona "a young lady, who might possibly have had a predilection for flat noses, like a certain philosophical great man of our day." It is a stunning move, conflating Shakespeare's heroine with the American statesman, and it perfectly demonstrates the grand erasure of Othellophilia: the masking of an entire history of white male sexual predation behind the myth of its racial photo-negative. Nor is this the first allusion to Thomas Jefferson's mistress, although it is the first instance glossed as such in this edition. Earlier, Jefferson makes an appearance in a description of the New York assembly: "The *philosopher* who maintained that black was white, and that *of course* there was no such color as white, might have given some color to his theory on this occasion, by the absence of poor forsaken white muslin." The speaker then pontificates on red, the color that has apparently replaced white in New York fashions: "red is the color of Mr. Jefferson's *****, Tom Paine's nose, and my slipper" (p. 59; italics in original). The footnote in my Library of America edition cites an 1811 gloss insisting on the referent "the late President's breeches." To my knowledge no editor hazards the obvious guess – that the five asterisks stand in for the five-letter "prick" – or comments on the veiled allusion to the statesman's inter-racial affair. Chapter 1 has already discussed the symbolic use of red as a mediator between black and white in the masculinist-racialist blazon tradition: usually, this red is associated with women's sexual appetite or culpability (red cosmetics, the ambiguous red blush, etc.) but here it might well be said that the late president has been caught red-pricked if not red-handed. Even so, the redness that represents sexual guilt can be seen to refer to the un-named mistress as well, blood being both an agent in male sexual arousal and the visible marker of a woman's defloration; it also metonymizes the "black blood" of Jefferson's illicit progeny.

In a text in which race is so suppressed as a topic, these color-coded statements must be plumbed for their latent signification. Elsewhere the white–red–black triad has a more blatantly misogynistic function: interspersed amongst these parodic notes and letters are several poems addressed to the elite (white) females of the audience, cajoling them to be chaste in language ripe for deconstruction à la Kim Hall. To quote just one:

Still do I love the gentle sex
And still with care my brain perplex,
To keep the fair ones of the age
Unsullied as the spotless page . . .

The poem goes on to berate women for their efforts "To drive the rose
bloom from the face / And fix the lily in its place; / To doff the white and
in its stead / To bound about in brazen red" (pp. 125–6). The same poem
contains a beautifully ambiguous use of the term "race." Urging women
not to read (or at least to hide) the "polluted pages" of indecent poetry,
the speaker goes on to deliver a lecture on sexual morality in language that
is itself rife with salacious innuendo:

And while that purity you blight
Which stamps you messengers of light;
And sap those mounds the gods bestow,
To keep you spotless here below;
Still in compassion to our race,
Who joy, not only in the face
But in that more exalted part,
The sacred temple of the heart;
Oh! hide forever from our view,
The fatal mischief you pursue –
Let MEN your praises still exalt,
And none but ANGELS mourn your fault. (p. 127)

The primary referent of "those mounds the gods bestow" would have to
be the breasts, associated with maternity, the heart, and compassion, but
there is more than a fleeting gesture toward the *mons veneris* as well, and it
is that referent which takes over in the ensuing lines. The sequence
"mounds . . . below . . . joy, not only in the face, / But in that . . .part"
takes the reader on a head-to-crotch tour of the woman's body reminiscent of any number of erotic blazons, such as John Donne's "To his
mistress going to bed", or the more darkly misogynistic "The comparison." More intriguing still is the double-valence of the term "race." In
context, the referent appears to be "men" – the phrases "male race" and
"female race" were common enough at the time. But . . . loyalty to the
(white) "race" frequently justifies and underpins such anxieties about
female concupiscence.

The more apparent inter-racialist sub-text is, of course, that of
Mustapha's letters. American women are, apparently, sexually available
to him: he boasts that he is "honoured by the smiles and attentions of the

beautiful ladies of this city, who have fallen in love with [his] whiskers and [his] turban" (p. 178). Facial hair being a sexualized racial marker that we have seen before, it is not too much of a stretch to see a phallic symbol in the curiously disembodied turban and accompanying (pubic) whiskers. Indeed, Mustapha's ideological purpose in the text necessitates the contradiction that, despite being "tempted by these beautiful barbarians" and despite their superior desirability (proclaimed in the second paragraph of his first letter) – and even despite the possibility that he may never see his twenty-three eastern wives again – yet he will not "break the faith" he owes the latter (p. 322). Mustapha wins the reader's sympathy, and qualifies as a Heathen with a Heart of Gold, because he – unlike Jefferson – can tell black from white.

He can also tell good women from bad. The corollary to the lascivious sultan figure (a figure of which Mustapha is the positive inverse) is the retiring, veiled, "inscrutable" eastern female. Mustapha's praise of "our eastern females, who shrink in blushing timidity from the glances of a lover" echoes much of Behn's praise of Imoinda, who scarcely lifts her eyes for fear of "a rape even by the God of Day" (Behn, *Oroonoko*, p. 38). Of course, in Mustapha's case the point is to dispraise American women by contrast, in reference to the latter's forwardness and indelicacy. Often, too, he uses Orientalist tropes to indict western womanhood. For example: "A woman of this country, dressed out for an exhibition, is loaded with as many ornaments as a circassian slave when brought out for sale" (p. 322). These propensities are also, ironically, explained in reference to the American Indians, whom Mustapha mistakes for their forbears. He muses,

We heard much of their painting themselves most hideously, and making use of bear's grease in great profusion; but this, I solemnly assure thee, is a misrepresentation, civilization, no doubt, having gradually extirpated these nauseous practices. It is true, I have seen two or three of these females, who had disguised their features with paint; but then it was merely to give a tinge of red to their cheeks, and did not look very frightful. (p. 232)

Mustapha does, like Equiano, complain of the thinness of western women: he finds their figures "preposterously unseemly" and is at a loss to find "a single fat fair" like the wife he "bought by the hundred weight, and had trundled home in a wheel-barrow!" (323–4). American women's dieting is also, interestingly, described as "contaminat[ing] their pure blood with noxious recipes." The racialization of that purity immediately becomes apparent: "Ere long I shall not be surprised to see them scarring their faces like the negroes of Congo, flattening their noses in imitation of the Hottentots, or like the barbarians of Ab-al Timar, distorting their lips and ears out of all natural dimensions" (p. 324). The linkage of female self-adornment and artifice to non-white, "primitive" cultures – an association inherited from the anti-cosmetic tropes of Renaissance lyric poetry – proves long-lived indeed.

The final evidence of *Salmagundi*'s Othellophilia is the epigram to the last chapter (Letter xx): "Soft you, a word or two before we part" (p. 345). If it sounds familiar, it should: the author (perhaps quoting from memory) clearly has in mind Othello's preface to his suicidal self-eulogy – "Soft you, a word or two before you go" (v.ii.347) – an oration that concludes, notably, in Othello's self-identification as a "Turk" like Mustapha. Just as Othello here justifies his murder of Desdemona, the *Salmagundi* text goes on to deliver – in a section entitled "To the ladies" – an apology for its misogynist satire, here cast as harmless attempts "to reclaim [women] from many of those delusive follies and unseemly peccadilloes in which they are unhappily too prone to indulge" (p. 352). The text goes on to list the dangers it has warned women against – including "midnight damps," "the wildering mazes of the waltz" and "the arms of strangers" – and exhorts them to return "to the sacred asylum of home, the soil most congenial to the opening blossom of female loveliness" (p. 353). The passage is narrated by the persona "Anthony Evergreen, Gent.," but it concludes by citing an allegory of "the sage Mustapha" which describes an Arabian's search for the perfect stream to set up camp by: not surprisingly, the moral is that the "purest" stream is one that shuns "the noonday glare" (pp. 356–7). By now we should not be surprised to find an Orientalist text culminating with an endorsement of the ideology of separate spheres. The pattern established by Congreve and Rowson seems to have taken root in the discourse: where *Othello* is invoked, one is bound to find a conservative message to women attached.

This final, anti-feminist diatribe does not comprise the last few pages of the text; in fact, it is interrupted by a strange tangent of William Wizard's: typically pedantic and nonsensical, the persona ends with an incoherent set of blustering statements about his scholarship, not the least of which is his theory "that America, so far from being . . . the new world . . . is at least as old as any country in existence, not excepting Egypt, China, or even the land of the Assiniboils . . ." (p. 358). The proximity of these pontifications to the lecture "To the ladies" manifests the inseparability, in the collective subconscious, of questions of female (sexual) propriety and those of cultural identity. Wizard's claims here are set up as self-evidently ludicrous (indeed, they include his ruminations on fallen "fragments of the moon" carved with hieroglyphics): America is, indeed, a new and hence very vulnerable country in the view-point of the author. And what could be more important, in such a raw, new world, than containment of the female population?

Mustapha is not black. Nowhere, in fact, is he even described as dark-skinned. He is, however, based on a "real" African – like Othello, a soldier and a traveler, like Othello (or Oroonoko, or Olaudah Equiano), an Outsider, an Other. Incidentally, the seven original Tripolitan captives (one of whom was indeed named Mustapha) were fêted in New York by charitable patrons at the theatre. The plays were chosen to appeal to the exotic visitors: the confusedly Orientalist *Blue Beard* (featuring on-stage camels and processions of "black slaves"), followed by the popular adaptation of *The Taming of the Shrew* entitled *Catharine and Petruchio* (appealing, presumably, to Mustapha's perceived views on women), a play called *Chains of Love* (featuring "a mixed cast of Moors and Englishmen"), and *Columbus* (in which "the queer people were Indians, not Moors or Turks").[38] So, if the "real" Mustapha was not black, nor, for that matter, were the actors playing any of the Moors or black Africans or other "queer people" in these plays; indeed, had *Othello* been chosen, Mustapha might have seen an "Oriental" hero take the stage, fitted out with turban and scimitar like (perhaps) his own. Such an Othello, indeed, might have been performed by the same actor who played Petruccio, the scimitar this time replacing his whip.

Mustapha is not black (what, by the way, is the point of the nick-name "Rub-a-Dub"?). For the purposes of this chapter, however, what matters less than his skin-color is his role *vis-à-vis* the insistently white, tediously blazoned, and ruthlessly infantalized American female population, which is his (and the text's) satirical target. Like his blacker predecessors, his outsider status enables and justifies his role as moral compass in a setting removed from Old World values and traditions, a setting wherein women are perceived to be in particular jeopardy – or rather, a setting wherein women are scapegoated for a culture that perceives itself in jeopardy. The dark, sexualized, foreign male as the scourge of loose white women: this is the form in which Othellophilia arrived in America. The myth that white women *enjoy* this type of scourging will be the subject of later chapters.

CHAPTER 3

Holes at the poles: Gothic horror and
the racial abject

Talking about race in the nineteenth-century Anglo-American canon often feels like navigating around a black hole. With the obvious exception of abolitionist literature (the subject of the next chapter), black characters are either simply not there at all, or so brutally abjected, demonized, or stereotyped as to seem unworthy of intelligent critical comment. Yet, even in those works that strive to suppress a specifically African or racialized blackness, a careful reader may discern traces of what Toni Morrison would call an Africanist presence. Morrison notes in regard to American literature specifically, "in a wholly racialized society, there is no escape from racially inflected language";[1] likewise when black or otherwise Othered characters do appear, even the most marginal can be shown to perform ideological work, functioning as allegorical meditations on the self or on cultural identity. Once we pick up the critical habit of this kind of reading-through-erasure, "It requires hard work not to see this," as Morrison puts it. She goes on to present an analogy:

It is as if I had been looking at a fishbowl – the glide and flick of golden scales . . . the castles at the bottom, surrounded by pebbles and tiny, intricate fronds of green . . . and suddenly I saw the bowl, the structure that transparently (and invisibly) permits the ordered life it contains to exist in the larger world.[2]

The analogy works for both the literary artifacts and larger social and material structures that enabled their production: however much a white, educated, ruling class likes the metaphor, we never build our castles in air, but always, however indirectly, upon the backs of an exploited (largely non-white) under-class. The fish-bowl, whether it stands for slavery in particular or white privilege in general, works by containment and exclusion, but its esthetic requires a transparent structure – that is, the material that makes the fish-bowl a fish-bowl must, by definition, seem not to exist. Artifice always works best when it is concealed. Hence the invisibility of race as an explicit subject in so many texts of the period.

Indeed, it should be no surprise that Anglo-American literature in the nineteenth century should be so thoroughly whitewashed: the same can be said of Othello himself, in the hands of the new, self-elected cultural elite consisting of author-critics like Samuel Taylor Coleridge, the one who declared that "Othello must not be conceived as a negro."[3] Coleridge's own poetry – despite his oft-trumpeted interest in the poor and downtrodden – is markedly devoid of black characters (unless we count "The forsaken Indian woman"). Yet this does not foreclose the reading of racial signification in some of the poet's imagery. Consider two stanzas of *The Rime of the Ancient Mariner* (1798):

> *His* bones were black with many a crack,
>   All black and bare, I ween;
> Jet-black and bare, save where with rust
> Of mouldy damps and charnel crust
>   They're patch'd with purple and green.
> *Her* lips are red, *her* looks are free,
>   *Her* locks are yellow as gold:
> Her skin is as white as leprosy,
> And she is far liker Death than he;
>   Her flesh makes the still air cold.[4] (181–90; italics in original).

This spectral coupling hints at a necrophilic "heart of darkness" in the "white devil" myth analyzed in previous chapters. Desdemona, in marrying a Moor, effectively marries herself to her death; Coleridge's bride-of-death image suggests a reading of Shakespeare in which Othello's race works allegorically. Bizarrely, despite the bridegroom's grisly appearance, the narrator describes the woman here as "far liker Death than he" – a moment true to the discourse of Othellophilia in exposing, even at the expense of the text's logic, the misogyny underlying such images. On the one hand, it is easy to see how masculinist figurations of gender require a feminized personification of death to "wear" her flesh: woman, after all, is flesh, and is hard to imagine without it (even those *memento mori* figures of the Renaissance need their "fashion accessories" if one is to read them as female). On the other hand, Coleridge goes out of his way to endow the female figure with the conventional markers of the Petrarchan mistress – red lips and golden hair – and only denotes her deathliness halfway through the blazon. Moreover, the curious italicizing of the gendered pronouns hints at the text's own consciousness of the way gender works in this image: the particular deathliness of the female figure is bound up with the fact that she is female. Also, how are we to gloss "her looks are free"? This suggests a sexually suspect liberality in her glances that becomes particularly morbid in context. Like her demonized white predecessors in Renaissance racial discourse, this bride-of-death signifies far in excess of her physical attributes, so that her animated and otherwise comely form becomes the focus of the horrifying spectacle that her skeletal partner only frames. Once again, blackness functions emblematically, gesturing away from itself; once again, the primary referent of the blackness is female, even while the bearer of the mark himself is male. These "black bones" literalize the inward or spiritual blackness that defines the woman as white devil; beneath her "skin . . . white as leprosy," the stanzas suggest, one may find something equally black.

We might wrest an alternative signification from that oddly chosen modifier for the ghostly female, "free." This poem about a ship filled with dead men, about a catastrophic ocean voyage in which a great number of people suffer and perish, was written during the heyday of the traffic in slaves, while thousands suffered and perished in the Middle Passage. Deirdre Coleman makes the connection explicit in her analysis of Coleridge's 1795 lecture on the slave trade:

> It is easy enough to show that Coleridge's imagination was haunted by the horrors of slavery. The diseased bodies that rot on the ship's planks during the middle passage – a detail mentioned twice in this lecture – pass into *The Rime of the Ancient Mariner*: "I looked upon the rotting sea, / And drew my eyes away; / I looked upon the rotting deck, / And there the dead men lay."[5]

Indeed, as Coleman convincingly argues, much anti-slavery rhetoric – including Coleridge's own, in his lecture – explicitly appealed to or scapegoated white English women, whose appetite for sugar at the tea-table was troped as a cannibalistic consumption of African blood that rendered white women, ironically, more savage than any African. Coleman states, "In drinking the African's blood, the white English woman not only becomes black in a moral sense; the mingling of black and white is clearly a metaphor for sexual intercourse. Here the violence of slavery as a labor system merges with the gothic horror of slavery as a sexual system."[6] At the bottom of this rhetoric is an anxiety that paradoxically links abolitionism with its opposite, an anxiety that was quickly perceived and exploited by pro-slavery polemic: the fear of miscegeny. White women, themselves typed as cruelly sexually jealous mistresses of their own female slaves, were suspected of an appetite for black men as great as their appetite for sugar. Hence racist caricaturist Edward Long complains that "The lower class of women in England are remarkably fond of the blacks; for reasons too brutal to mention," and worries that their inter-racial intrigues will cause a general contamination of English blood "till the whole nation resembles the . . . Moriscos."[7]

In the context of the discourse on slavery analyzed by Coleman, Coleridge's deathly couple takes on additional racial coloring. As the spectral ship drifts away, the woman gloatingly beats her skeletal partner at dice and the wind supplies him with a responding groan "Thro' the holes of his eyes and . . . mouth" (197). In the context of this flesh–bone juxtaposition, the dead man's hollow orifices metonymically foreground the white woman's appetite: her apparent capriciousness and her guilt-by-association with his death and unnatural re-animation simply complete the effect. In this reading, describing the woman as "free" makes perfect sense: she is free in contrast to her victim, an allegorized, emaciated African dying on the planks of a slave-ship. Tellingly, the famished sailor narrator experiences this vision after having sucked his own blood in extremity of thirst. The cannibalistic resonances enforce the implication that the stakes of the spectral dice-game are high indeed: the white woman is playing for (with?) the lives of men. According to the anti-feminist vein of British abolitionism, thousands of women did so at their tea-tables daily.

This chapter will approach nineteenth-century narratives of Gothic horror with an eye to the racial interpretation of its black-on-white imagery, and with particular focus on the way tropes of cannibalism, immolation, and suffocation index otherwise suppressed fears of miscegenation. In some cases, the racial allegory is apparent – as in Edgar Allen Poe's *The Narrative of Arthur Gordon Pym of Nantucket* (1838) – in that the text contains literally black characters; in other cases, the racial subtext must be pried open, like the coffin of Bram Stoker's *Dracula* (1897). What we might call these texts' racial unconscious cannot be theorized, however, without recourse to gender, as Gothic horror thrives on – indeed, may even be constituted by – what Julia Kristeva terms abjection: broadly put, a kind of haunting by a devouring feminine principle, as fascinating as it is repellent.[8] Women have always played a constitutive role in the genre of horror: the quintessential film-scream is always a woman's. Drawing upon feminist theory and criticism of both classic and contemporary horror, this chapter will argue that a white woman is not only horror's necessary victim: the woman is both the victim and the monster.

It was Edgar Allen Poe who infamously declared that "the death . . . of a beautiful woman is, unquestionably, the most poetical topic in the world."[9] Perhaps it is stating the obvious that the woman must always be white – the whiter, the better – as beauty, particularly to a pro-slavery southerner like Poe, is so thoroughly, racially, and complexionally white as to blanche itself almost invisible.[10] What exoticism Poe affords his heroines is limited to black hair and dark eyes, always startlingly offset by their alabaster skin. Poe has it both ways in surrounding figures like Ligeia with "Oriental" artifacts and a mysterious past, all the while preserving her racial whiteness, or even implying her derivation in a mythic race of supermen. Not that Poe was intellectually inconsistent: the Egyptian sarcophagi that feature in *Ligeia* signal Poe's belief in ancient Egypt as the civilization of a superior, vanished, white race – an increasingly popular nineteenth-century mode of thought (and well suited to solidifying the notion of the white Cleopatra).[11] These touches of exoticism aside, the most prominent quality of Poe's Gothic heroine is always her ivory skin and ethereal, even spectral, radiance. This whiteness is, moreover, always symbolically linked to her necessary death – as a harbinger and sign of a fatal illness, and/or the signifier of her other-worldly nature, her status as one, like the "divine" Ligeia, "above or apart from the earth."[12] Whether glossed positively as angel, or negatively as corpse, the Poe heroine is anti-life in her bloodless whiteness. She is, to borrow Susan Gilbert and Sandra Gubar's classic feminist terminology, "killed into art" – even before she is killed in the story.[13] That she might pop back out of her grave in the end is therefore a cold comfort in feminist terms.

Yet the violence of Poe's misogyny is almost out-done by the violence of his racism, and the two attitudes are, as John Carlos Rowe points out in his reading of Poe's *Arthur Gordon Pym*, "inextricably entangled."[14] The latter work of Poe's, interpretable as a prose re-telling of Coleridge's *Mariner* as well as a racist allegory,[15] contains no trace of the quintessential Poe heroine: nor could it, as such a heroine can only be conceived by Poe in total isolation from black people. Indeed, *Pym* contains almost no women at all: rather, the primary companion of the hero is a male "half-breed" – that is, half Indian, half white – whose status as such gives the lie to Poe's suppression of miscegeny as an explicit topic. For miscegeny – or, to use the historically appropriate term, "amalgamation" – was clearly a concern of Poe's, as is evident in his notorious sneer about "those negrophilic old ladies of the North."[16] Elise Lamire argues, for instance, that Poe's "Murders in the Rue Morgue" capitalizes on public hysteria over the allegedly "amalgamationist" agenda of abolitionist lecturers in Poe's Philadelphia. Lamire places Poe's "detective story" alongside anti-abolitionist propaganda comparing black men to apes, and sex with them (by female abolitionists) to bestiality; in this light, the revelation of an orang-utan's guilt in the sexualized murder of two (white) women seems less a product of pure whimsy.[17] I would like to propose a similar reading of the subconscious of *Pym*, a text troubled, despite the dearth of female characters, by what we might call, building on Kristeva, a racial abject: that is, a feminized, racial darkness that threatens to poison or devour the white, male ego.[18]

Like *Mariner*, *Pym* involves a journey toward the South pole, into strange seas where lurk slimy creatures and where the rules of the natural order don't hold. By the time Poe was writing, a theory known as "holes at the poles" had caught the popular imagination: the theory, perhaps most thoroughly treated by the French novelist Jules Verne (1828–1905), was that one could access the inner region of the hollow globe through openings at the North and South poles. Within, one would find "a civilization of people as old as and even more advanced than the cultures of mankind on the outer surface" (Poe, *Pym*, p. xxi). Toward the end of Poe's imaginary journey, Pym and his companion, Dirk Peters, come across Tsalal, an island populated by black "savages" wherein no white or light-colored objects or animals are to be found. Indeed, even the teeth of the natives are black, although this strange fact is not disclosed until the very end, as the natives have lips so large that their teeth do not show – one of many details that manifests (in addition to Poe's fondness for racist caricature) the text's obsession with orifices. In Poe's fever-dream of racial topsy-turvy, the natives harbor a superstitious dread of the color white: they dress (when they dress at all; most of them go naked) in the black fur of an unidentified large mammal, and live in twig-covered holes in the earth or in hollow tree-boles draped with the same black pelts. The text is littered with vaginal/uterine images, from the descriptions of the hole-homes with their suggestively hairy or twiggy coverings to the narrow gorges and ravines that dominate the black, rocky terrain. The text is, moreover, preoccupied with ingestion, with the danger of poisoning and the threat of being devoured, both metaphorically and literally. The adventures that brought Pym and Peters to this island – precipitated by a mutiny led by a demonic black man – included a long, desperate period adrift without provisions, where the men were driven to an act of cannibalism; the culminating South pole sequence develops this theme of problematic consumption in a nightmare world of unspeakable bar-barism. Upon the arrival of the whites, the Tsalalans offer them a repast of "the palpitating entrails of a species of unknown animal" of which the natives "devour yard after yard": all the food is repellant to the white visitors, the water is feared "polluted" because it lacks "the customary appearance of limpidity," and the only ingestible native vegetable (a nut) seems to be toxic in large doses.

Just as pressing, however, as the danger of ingesting the wrong substance is the danger of literal immolation, that of being suffocated or consumed by another (black) body, or by the black holes and ravines in which the islanders dwell. This threat is present from the first encounter between the white men and the Tsalalans:

> We were on the ground, twelve in number, with the savages, as many as forty, sitting on their hams so closely around us that, if any disturbance had arisen, we should have found it impossible to make use of our arms, or indeed to have risen to our feet. The pressure was not only inside the tent, but outside, where probably was every individual on the whole island, the crowd being prevented from trampling us to death only by the incessant exertions of [the chief]. (p. 373)

The alarming "pressure" of the crowd manifests the anxiety that critics like Rowe see as driving the text's racial imagery – namely Poe's "repressed fears regarding slave rebellions in the South."[19] The pressure, however, is not merely metaphorical here, but also literal on the part of these naked, black bodies: the passage bespeaks a distinct – if terrifying – eroticism. The visitors pass through this particular crisis only to face the prospect of a literal burial alive: the Tsalalans, whom the narrator and his men initially trust, in fact harbor a dastardly scheme against them. In yet more sexually suggestive language, the visitors are led into a series of deep ravines, the last of which is so deep "that but little of the light of day could penetrate." It is, Pym notes, the perfect spot "for the *consummation* of an ambuscade" (p. 379; emphasis mine) – and there, indeed, they are literally consumed, when the natives cause an avalanche to entrap them. The narrator describes his horror at being "entombed alive," dwelling on "the blackness of darkness which envelops the victim, the terrific oppression of the lungs, the stifling fumes from the damp earth . . ." (p. 381). He and Peters alone manage to escape by digging furiously at the collapsed walls of the gorge with their bowie knives. The descriptions of their efforts, once again, are ripe for close-reading: "The sides of the cleft we were now attempting to ascend were . . . so excessively slippery, being wet, that we could get but little foothold upon them even in their least precipitous parts" (p. 382). After toiling up the soft, wet walls of the biologized fissure, the two are able to look back at the evidence of the "murderous work" of their island hosts in immolating the remainder of the company: the chapter concludes, grimly, "We were the only living white men on the island" (p. 384).

I find it interesting, here, that Pym calls Peters "white," as earlier in the
narrative he was repeatedly referred to as "the hybrid," after being introduced as "deformed" and "ferocious." Oddly enough, it is Peters alone
who survives these adventures, a fact that might be glossed either as Poe's
complicating his own binaries, or else as his final message of racist
despair.[20] But we will discuss the ending below.

As it turns out, the ravines in which the men were entrapped form a
pattern: Pym's sketches of their windings are legible – though not to him
– as three Coptic letters. There is a riddle written inside the chasms as
well: after scrambling the length of the gargantuan incision, the survivors
wind up in a dead-end, facing a wall carved with a humanoid pictogram
accompanied by seeming "alphabetical characters" (p. 394). Although
Pym sees this pattern as accidental and insists that the carvings are a
natural formation, a bogus editorial "note" at the end of the narrative
deciphers the characters, in both the large and small carvings, as comprising three words in Ethiopian, Arabic, and Egyptian, respectively "to be
shady," "to be white," and "the southern regions." This gloss has not
prevented one clever critic from seeing the letters EAP or EOP (Poe's
initials or surname spelled backward) in the first hieroglyph – something
which of course does not rule out the former (correct) translation of the
Coptic letters.[21] Interestingly, neither the "editor" persona in *Pym* nor the
editor of my edition of Poe comments on certain details of the pictogram.

Figure 3.1. "'To be shady,' – whence all the inflections of shadow or darkness." Diagram
from Edgar Allan Poe, *The Narrative of Arthur Gordon Pym of Nantucket* (1838).

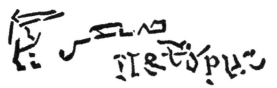

Figure 3.2. "With a very slight exertion of the imagination, the left . . . of these indentures
might have been taken for the intentional, though rude, representation of a human
figure standing erect, with outstretched arm." From Poe, *The Narrative of Arthur
Gordon Pym of Nantucket.*

Here is Poe's description: "With a very slight exertion of the imagination, the left, or most northern of these indentures might have been taken for the intentional, though rude, representation of a human figure standing erect, with outstretched arm" (p. 394). In fact, the figure is "erect" in more ways than one: neither Pym nor his "editor" (who confirms the figure as representing a human form) notes the very clear phallic protrusion, pointing in the same direction as the outstretched arms, toward the word denoting whiteness. In sum, the inscriptions all together denote a black-on-white erotic embrace – the very terms in which the white narrator's entrapment in these caves was troped.

In Poe's allegory of immolation by the Other, there is no sexuality. The natives are generally nude, except for those few in black animal hides, the symbolic redundancy of which Poe makes evident in the ambiguous – and thrice repeated – formulation "black-skin warriors." But despite all the nude bodies, there is no sex. The natives are fond of crannies, crevices, digging, disemboweling, and ingesting slimy things, but we don't read of them copulating. Their island of black rock is inscribed as if by divine force with a swallowing, treacherous hieroglyph for blackness (itself containing a microcosmic hieroglyph for whiteness) – but there is no inter-racial sex threatened on the part of the bestialized savages. My contention is that sex needn't enter the picture at all, just as it needn't in "The murders in the Rue Morgue." Arguably, most of the stories we have looked at in this book are not about sex so much as the avoidance of sex, the maintaining of the "boundaries of the self's clean and proper body."[22]

I have been speaking of *Pym* in terms of the absence of women, but there are, technically, women present in the story: the decision to turn toward the South Pacific in the first place was made (by Peters, significantly) on the basis of "the voluptuous beauty of the women" (p. 287), and the women of the island are noted, in the deceptively friendly initial encounter, as being especially "obliging in every respect" (p. 378). But this sentence is the last reference to the female Tsalalans, who immediately melt back into the undifferentiated mass of "savages." Perhaps, thus, the reason gender seems insignificant on the island is that, in a sense, the entire population is "female." Their behavior certainly fits the stereotypes: the Tsalalans are duplicitous, earthy, greedy, ignorant, fickle, and cunning. They are in awe of mirrors.[23] They are cruel in the extreme, but lack any skill or knowledge in the arts of organized warfare; their primary weapons against the white men are clubs, guile, and treachery, and in the end the disorganization and stupidity of their violence results in their destruction along with their victims (they set the visitors' ship on fire and wind up blowing themselves quite literally to pieces). And the trap into which they drive their white enemies is precisely what the masculinist imaginary presents as the female equivalent of rape: devouring by the *vagina dentata*.[24] In this case, the violation is worse than rape: a murder-in-rape, a *raptus* of life.

There is, however, a horror that underlies even this physical threat and one that allows the straightforwardly racist allegory to dissolve, in the text's final pages, into a dreamlike series of images that have supplied deconstructionist critics with an abundance of material.[25] The two survivors escape in a canoe with one native hostage and find themselves adrift in a fantastic white sea-scape, approaching the pole. The milky water, contrary to received knowledge, grows warmer as they move south, and there are strange eruptions and ashy showers all around. The captive native dies, presumably of terror at all the whiteness, but the environment's effect on the narrator is powerfully negative too: Pym's narrative ends with an enigmatic vision of a "shrouded human figure" of gigantic proportions whose skin is "of the perfect whiteness of the snow," and we find out in the "note" afterward that the narrator perished – along with the final pages of the account – in the ensuing "accident" (p. 405).

Toni Morrison places *Pym*'s final sequence in the context of similar images of "impenetrable whiteness" in American literature, frequently placed at the end of stories in which "an Africanist presence is engaged." She proposes:

Because they appear almost always in conjunction with representations of black or Africanist people who are dead, impotent, or under complete control, these images of blinding whiteness seem to function as both antidote for and meditation on the shadow that is companion to this whiteness . . . This haunting . . . suggests the complex and contradictory situation in which American writers found themselves during the formative years of the nation's literature.[26]

I find Morrison's reading compelling, and agree that these moments bespeak a specifically American "fear of boundarylessness, of Nature unbridled and crouched for attack" and the contradictory "terror of human freedom – the thing [Americans] coveted most of all." Moreover, it seems indisputable that the presence of a slave population that "offered itself up as surrogate selves for meditation on the problems of human freedom" in part enabled this peculiarly American discourse.[27] As a scholar of the English Renaissance, however, I find it hard to isolate this discourse from the racialist literary tradition that the colonists brought with them, evident in Alexis de Tocqueville's remark in 1831 that "there is hardly a

pioneer's hut that does not contain a few odd volumes of Shakespeare."[28]
To me Poe's departure from English treatments of blackness is a question
of degree and not kind: ironically enough, the racist hysteria evident in
Pym finds voice in a storyline and thematics influenced by an abolitionist-
leaning Coleridge (indeed, we have not even exhausted the parallels to
Mariner – including, for instance, an earlier ship-of-death encounter, not
to mention all of Poe's albatrosses). Moreover, we will see later in this
chapter the way Poe, in turn, influenced English authors after him, in the
creation of Gothic horror and its racial unconscious.

What is Poe's point in the bizarre ending of *Pym*? Whilst on the island
of the caves, the sailors had been removed not just from all known
geographical points of reference, but from all known referential systems;
lost in black caves in an island of black granite, surrounded by a black
population in whose semiotic system it is white that bodes evil, they find
their surroundings to be just as illegible as the inscriptions in the rock that
the gorges turn out to comprise and contain. However, when the men
emerge from these hollows and from Tsalal, Poe suddenly inverts the
paradigm, as white ash closes in on them and the white ocean threatens to
engulf their canoe. As post-structuralist theory points out, all hermeneutic
exercises require differentiation: without distinctions – subject/object,
figure/ground, self/other, black/white – signification is thwarted and
meaning collapses.[29] Neither pole (the word is doubly significant here)
of the foundational hermeneutic binary is thinkable on its own. Pure
carnality, pure earthliness, immolation by the literal and material, is no
more bearable than pure transcendence, the blank text, the void. Light
blinds as well as darkness.

This does not, of course, exonerate Poe for his portrayal of black people
as sub-human "savages" – it merely demonstrates the usefulness of racial
discourse in addressing metaphysical questions of the self, of life and
death, and of meaning. Deconstructionists, for instance, have made much
of the problem of the inscriptions on the island's face, paradigmatic of the
text's preoccupation with writing and reading.[30] One obvious riddle is
simply who wrote them. We are not invited to assume that the animalistic
and presumably illiterate Tsalalans did: they only know how to efface the
writing by filling in the gorges, which is in keeping with their more
general, perverse skill at destruction as opposed to creation (even canoe-
building seems beyond their capacities; the canoes were acquired from
some half-civilized visiting tribe). Also, the fact of their lurking in these
fissures, uncomprehending of their purpose, no less their meaning, is too
perfectly allegorical to resist a reading in light of the western exegetical

and philosophical tradition that pits the "letter" of the text against its meaning or "spirit." Yet the question of who made the carvings is perhaps less important than the fact of their inscrutability: even the "civilized" visitors fail to read them, and thus can be accused of wallowing in the letter. The macrocosmic inscription is, in fact, essentially illegible owing to the size of the characters: in this era before airplanes, such a mammoth pattern could only be discerned by its mapping from the ground. There is no doubt a subtle point about Pym himself in the fact that he cannot "read" these markings – indeed, won't recognize them as writing – even when they are right in front of him. This material is ripe for post-structuralist theoretical analysis: the travelers are literally trapped in a sentence that they cannot read. *Il n'y a pas de hors-texte* indeed!

Yet, as Rowe persuasively argues, to divorce the deconstructionist reading of *Pym* from the seemingly "crude" biographical approach to the text's treatment of race would be to "repress the subtle complicity of literary Modernism with racist ideology"; Poe's "Gnostic idealism" is indelibly linked with his class pretensions and racist politics, and his valorization of a linguistic sublime presupposes the kind of hyper-literacy inaccessible to the lower social orders. Rowe states, "Poe's contempt for the material world" (a contempt only possible, I would argue, for those whom the material world doesn't smash in the face daily) "enables his glorification of the imagination, visionary experience, and the ultimate transcendence of the alienated body."[31] And here, with the body, we come back to Poe's problem with women.

Poe's obsession with dead women has, ironically enough, proven fertile ground for feminist critique, yet the topic is far from exhausted. *Pym's* racial imagery might be said to give the lie to the absence of literal sex in the plot. Plainly speaking, sex is impossible in Poe's work, as artistic creation in his understanding always presupposes that its object – the object of male poetic adoration – is dead. In Poe's reworking of the *Mariner* myth, it is black–white contact – not the killing of a white bird (on Tsalal the albatrosses are black) – that leads to the haunting. I note in passing that *Mariner* is told to a wedding-guest, unwillingly detained from the feast; its *memento mori* function is obvious. Coleridge's female Death-in-Life, like the early modern "white devil," is an archetypal death-bearing woman.[32] Desdemona is her own *memento mori*: Othello is her partner in the Dance of Death.

I do not believe in "art for art's sake." Even if a painter could keep his politics off his palate, the viewer will find a point to the pattern: we are relentless makers and seekers of meaning. Likewise, where there is a death in literature, there is bound to be a moral. Shortly after *Pym's* publication, Poe's contemporary Philadelphian Edward W. Clay produced a series of prints satirizing the perceived inter-racial erotic desire of white female abolitionists. One of the images, entitled *The Fruits of Amalgamation* (1839), depicts an inter-racial couple in their parlor, the white woman suckling a dark infant and pillowing her black husband's feet in her lap (Figure 3.3). Directly above them hangs a large, clearly captioned and elaborately framed illustration of "Othello and Desdemona." This detail, I would argue, constitutes a threat, albeit a more subtle one than the burning of a lecture-hall wherein abolitionists have met. The message to those "negrophilic old ladies of the North" is that what happened to Desdemona will happen to them. Is it any accident that the 1830s witnessed *Othello's* unprecedented popularity in American theatres?[33]

Upon reflection, it is easy to see why the *Othello* reference was needed: otherwise the picture is too attractive. The scene of cozy domesticity is precisely what nineteenth-century audiences were expected to approve of and enjoy: the contrasting skin-tones of the inter-racial couple alone could not be trusted to convey the anti-amalgamationist point. In the semiotic system of pictorial representation, skin-color can easily register as neutral: hence the necessity that racist caricature exaggerate or make monstrous other features associated with racial difference (the shape of the mouth, etc.). And indeed, the domesticity of Shakespeare's play is precisely the site of its horror: like the murderous ape in "Murders in the Rue Morgue," Othello kills Desdemona in bed. In his discussion of another early modern domestic horror-tragedy, Gary Taylor glosses Freud's *unheimlich* – generally translated as "uncanny," but literally "un-homely" or "un-homelike" – in a way that unlocks a crucial component of horror: "What is at home is safe, secure, familiar; but the home is also a private space, walled off and hidden from the outside world, and therefore potentially secret, concealed, mysterious, threatening. The word *heimlich* (safe, familiar) thus becomes synonymous with its antonym, *unheimlich* (mysterious, threatening)."[34]

This is the genre of horror to a tee: a severed human leg thrust into the innocent wood-chipper (*Fargo*); a severed hand plopped in a plastic sandwich bag (Julie Taymor's *Titus*); or, in Taylor's analysis, a "larder scene" in a Renaissance play wherein a quartered human corpse is the "meat" hung up to drain. Along these theoretical lines, Poe's racist-horror in "Murders in the Rue Morgue" merges with the Othellophilic inter-text of *Fruits of Amalgamation*. The victims of the murder were in their

Figure 3.3. E. W. Clay, *The Fruits of Amalgamation* (1839). Courtesy of the American Antiquarian Society.

bedroom, "habited in their nightclothes" (p. 169) and one of the women was combing her hair, which the orang-utan seized and pulled out by the roots in a vicious mockery of the ministrations of a barber; the whole scene recalls Desdemona's bed-time grooming with Emilia, the homely hair-brush, nightclothes, and bedding transmogrified by the murder to *unheimlich* objects.

Freud's theory, in fact, might also help us to grasp the essence of the "white devil" figure that haunts this book: the white woman with the unwholesome secret, her appetite for black men. As a white man's sister/ mother/cousin/wife, she is famil(y)ar in the most literal sense; as sexual partner to the abject racial Other, she is monstrous. Linda Williams points out the "surprising (and at times subversive) affinity between monster and woman" in classic horror films: I believe the same applies to the literary precedent in nineteenth-century Gothic horror.[35] As Gilbert and Gubar point out, behind the angel in the house lurks a madwoman in the attic.[36]

The Gothic imagination is obsessed with enclosures in general and the home in particular, and every (un)homely interior space has its presiding angel/devil woman. Whether angel or devil, victim or monster (and I will argue that she is almost always both), she must always be white, and, as I've said of Poe's heroines, the whiter the better: to every King Kong, his Faye Wray. Moreoever, the whiteness is not accidental – but rather, the whiteness constitutes the monster as a monster (since there is nothing wrong, in the eyes of a racist culture, with preying upon black women as opposed to white) and also constitutes her as the monster's victim. I mean that possessive in its strongest possible sense, for she is not just "his" in being the victim of his violence; she is, in fact, a thing of his, and hence herself essentially monstrous. As it turns out, the woman is the monster's creature.

There has been much fascinating feminist criticism generated by the genre of horror but to my mind no one has satisfactorily answered the question of why women must be its primary victims (and I leave it ambiguous whether those victims are on screen or in the audience).[37] When men die it is "action"; when women die it is "horror." Why must the woman die? I believe the answer is this: she must die because she loves the monster. This is the pornographic secret of horror.

The climactic murder scene in Mary Shelley's *Frankenstein* (1818, 1831) takes place on the protagonist's wedding-night: his bride – "the purest creature of earth" – is murdered in her bed, strangled, before the couple has consummated the marriage (p. 150).[38] The parallel with

Desdemona – murdered on her "wedding sheets" (*Othello*, IV.ii.108) just one day after her nuptials – is obvious. This sexualized murder, moreover, is enacted by someone the text insistently describes as a member of another race. As Anne K. Mellor persuasively argues, the text of Mary Shelley's novel clearly manifests her familiarity with nineteenth-century racial science and, in particular, the notion of "'the slothful Asiatics'" – one of four categories, the others being Caucasians, Negroes, and American Indians – "as a yellow skinned, black haired, and beardless race."[39] Whether we see the monster with his large frame, yellow skin, and sleek black hair, as specifically Asian or Mongoloid, or (as other scholars have argued) Burmese, African, or just vaguely racially "Other," it seems indisputable that he is not white.[40] Indeed, in the frontispiece to the 1831 edition – which, as Mellor points out, the author herself would have seen – the monster is distinctly exoticized (Figure 3.4).[41] I would argue, moreover, that in this image the monster is also feminized, in his languid, half-reclining pose, in his nudity, in the ambiguous shading of his chest, and in his long hair. More astonishingly still, the monster here – emphatically hideous in the text – is actually quite beautiful, and I can say that despite the subjective nature of such judgments because the artist clearly signifies a feminizing beauty in juxtaposing him with the *memento mori*-style skeleton, which he seems to regard in (again, effeminizing) horror.

The racial encoding of the murder of the angelic Elizabeth is even more striking in the 1831 edition, the most substantial change to which is the addition of a lengthy introduction to the character and a description emphasizing the features that German "racial science" would go on to valorize as "Aryan." Victor Frankenstein and his mother find a poor Italian family living in a cottage, wherein is one child who "appeared of a different stock." The narrator contrasts her with the Italians:

The others were *dark-eyed* hardy little vagrants; this child was thin, and very *fair*. Her hair was the *brightest living gold*, and, despite the poverty of her clothing, seemed to set a crown of distinction on her head. Her brow was *clear* and *ample*, her *blue eyes* cloudless . . . none could behold her without looking on her as of a distinct *species*, a being *heaven-sent*, and bearing a *celestial* stamp in all her features. (p. 191; emphases mine)

The passage speaks for itself, and one is not surprised to find out shortly after that the child is half German, and that her golden hair, blue eyes, pale skin, and high forehead become her ticket out of poverty; this "garden rose among dark-leaved brambles," this "child fairer than pictured cherub" who "shed radiance from her looks and whose form

T. Holst, del.   W. Chevalier, sculp.

FRANKENSTEIN.

"By the glimmer of the half-extinguished
light, I saw the dull, yellow eye of the
creature open; it breathed hard, and a
convulsive motion agitated its limbs.
... I rushed out of the room."

Page 43.

London, Published by H. Colburn and R. Bentley, 1831.

Figure 3.4. Frontispiece to Mary Shelley's *Frankenstein* (1831). Courtesy of the
New York Public Library.

and motions were lighter than the chamois of the hills" goes home
with "the guardian angel of the afflicted" (pp. 191–2), Mrs. Frankenstein.
The ethno-centrism of the inserted account is matched by (can this still
be a surprise?) its misogyny; the chapter ends in a kind of patriarchal
panic-attack:

On the evening previous to her being brought home, my mother had said
playfully, – "I have a pretty present for my Victor – tomorrow he shall have it."
And when, on the morrow, she presented Elizabeth to me as her promised gift, I,
with childish seriousness, interpreted her words literally, and looked upon
Elizabeth as mine – mine to protect, love, and cherish. All praises bestowed on
her, I received as made to a possession of my own . . . [s]ince till death she was to
be mine only. (p. 192)

It is hard to believe that Shelley, the daughter of Mary Wollstonecraft and
believer in free love, could have meant us to endorse Victor's possessive-
ness: it may well be that both the patronizing ethno-centrism of Elizabeth's
"salvation" and the fit of masculinist presumption it inspires set the
stage for the (non-white, feminized) monster's just punishment of the
Frankenstein family. In any case, the 1831 revisions are interesting in their
departure from the hazel-eyed Elizabeth with the "rich dark auburn" hair
in the 1818 version (p. 57).

Along with the emphatic blondness Shelley also intensified the "angel
in the house" rhetoric. I quote just one example: "The saintly soul of
Elizabeth shone like a shrine-dedicated lamp in our peaceful home. Her
sympathy was ours; her smile, her soft voice, the sweet glance of her
celestial eyes, were ever there to bless and animate us" (p. 194). Not that
she is the only woman so described: Victor's dead mother – herself a
victim of the monster through his stealing of her miniature portrait – is
termed "angel mother" in both editions, and even the enigmatic, exotic
Safie is granted "angelic beauty" despite her "raven black" hair (p. 87).
The first victim of the monster is not a woman but a boy (boys and
women, to paraphrase Shakespeare, being cattle of the same color [*As You
Like It*, iii.ii.371]) – yet even he is blue-eyed, dimpled, and blazoned in
angelic terms. The second victim, Justine, even betrays the Desdemonian
habit of confessing to crimes of which she is innocent. Are all the
monster's victims, in a sense, Desdemonas? The method of killing suggests so: all are strangled – or, in the case of Justine's indirect murder by
way of the incriminating miniature, hanged. The 1831 text adds an
Othellophile touch to the scene in which the monster frames her for
murder: like Othello, he soliloquizes over his sleeping victim, "Awake,

fairest, thy lover is near – he who would give his life but to obtain one look of affection from thine eyes: my beloved, awake!" (p. 216). Finally, the account of the trial encapsulates the *unheimlich* nature of her Desdemonian beauty: "[S]he . . . did not tremble, although gazed on and execrated by thousands; for all the kindness which her beauty might otherwise have excited, was obliterated in the minds of the spectators by the imagination of the enormity she was supposed to have committed" (p. 58). She later explains why she "confessed a lie" – echoing Othello on Desdemona, "like a liar gone to burning hell" (v.ii.138) – ". . . I almost began to think that I was the *monster* that he said I was" (p. 62; emphasis mine).

Indeed, monstrosity in the novel has a curious tendency to detach from the monster at the center of the story, and infect others. So much so, that it is hard to miss the powerful association between Victor and his creation, especially considering the fact that in the cultural afterlife of Shelley's novel the monster has always gone by its maker's name. Victor says, "I considered the being whom I had cast among mankind . . . nearly in the light of my own vampire, my own spirit let loose from the grave and forced to destroy all that was dear to me" (p. 55). Saving the subject of vampirism for later in the chapter, we note how the monster manifests Victor's own, so to speak, heart of darkness; we may be looking at, here, our first male "white devil."

On the other hand, this collapsing of Victor into his monster also works to transform his bride – literally "the Bride of Frankenstein" – to that other bride he tears to pieces with his bare hands, the female monster re-animated and re-named in the modern horror film.[42] As a "possession" of Victor's symbolically transferred to his monstrous alter-ego, Elizabeth becomes the monster's creature even despite her angelic countenance. Indeed, Elizabeth's pose in death – in stark contrast to the peaceful death of her predecessor, Victor's "angel mother" – bespeaks a certain monstrosity of her own: she is "thrown across the bed, her head hanging down, and her pale and distorted features half covered by her hair." The tousled hair, the bare "bloodless arms and relaxed form flung . . . on its bridal bier" constitute Elizabeth at her most erotic and earthy; indeed, for the first time we behold the hero embrace her "with ardour," until "the deathly languor and coldness of the limbs" tell him this "had ceased to be the Elizabeth whom [he] had loved and cherished" (p. 150). Simultaneously eroticized ("relaxed," languid) and made monstrous ("distorted") by death, "thrown" about like a play-thing, she is transformed; she becomes the monster's creature, his thing.

The sexualized murder that is the consummation of the *Frankenstein* marriage harks back to the plot's originary moment, itself another sexualized act: Victor's creation of the monster. Gilbert and Gubar are surely right in glossing the "filthy creation" as "filthy because obscenely sexual";[43] the loathing and fascination with which Victor describes his sexualized "secret toil" echo *Othello*'s racialist pornographic musings, its imagery of corruption and monstrosity, and its obsession with the unseen – from Iago's "monstrous birth" (i.iii.386), to Desdemona's "filthy bargain" with Othello (a bargain of which, as Emilia says, "she was too fond" [v.ii.164]). Victor's family attributes his strange behavior to indulgence in (probably sexual) "vice" – and that it is a form of vice he confirms himself by calling it "unlawful" and "unwholesome" and an interference in "the tranquility of . . . domestic affections." In animating a "filthy mass that moved and talked" (p. 110), Victor's work is not just adulterating, but also, metaphorically, adulterous.

The symbolic associations that link Victor to his monster and the monster to Elizabeth also skew – in interesting ways – the gendering of all three characters. As Gilbert and Gubar note, Victor's "labor" in his "workshop of filthy creation" is a kind of monstrous pregnancy: at the same time, his creation, though male, resembles Milton's Eve in its inferior, secondary, and derivative status, and in its threat to the order of things. Certainly, the moment in which the monster sees his reflection in a pool and despairs seems an ironic reversal of the moment in *Paradise Lost* when Eve does the same and is charmed by what she sees.[44] Creator, creature, and victim collapse into one *Über*-female, for, as Gilbert and Gubar put it, "for Mary Shelley the part of Eve is all the parts."[45]

The part of Eve in the drama of creation, however, is also Satan's part, in rebelling against divinity. Theoretically, this should mean that images of the demonic and the monstrous will inevitably be encoded as masculine–phallic–active, as the first fallen angel was Lucifer. What accounts for the masculinist reflex whereby depictions of the non-human Other hinge upon what French feminism calls "the feminine" – and not simply as victim but often as a component of the monster's monstrosity itself? The serpent in medieval and Renaissance iconography was often depicted with a female face and breasts, and the word "hell" was slang for the vagina.[46] Kristeva posits the source of these anxieties in the subject's memory of the womb and its threat to self-differentiation and identity; she writes of the "devotee of the abject" who is haunted by "the desirable and terrifying, nourishing and murderous, fascinating and abject inside of the maternal body."[47] To this we might add a simple naturalistic explanation: monsters are, after all, hard to come across, whereas (m)Others are all around. Civilized man projects his primal fears on the most proximate Other: woman. For the devil to do any work above ground, he must take on a human form. *Unheimlich.*

On the other hand, Shelley did go out of her way to make her monster and his maker, and even two of his victims, technically male. Perhaps feminist criticism does a disservice in prying wombs out of the text when a female author might be deliberately subverting stereotype and upsetting gender binaries. As one theorist of horror points out, "The monster is an ontological oddity, a being whose membership in categories of biological sex is unstable and a sham."[48] Frankenstein's monster is, in many respects, the mother of all monsters, and so it is not surprising that so many ambiguously gendered monsters followed. Indeed, *The Rocky Horror Picture Show* is a gender-bending extravaganza starring Victor Frank N. Furter, the Transvestite from Transylvania.

Let us turn to the ending of Shelley's novel to see whether she resolves any of these ambiguities. Prefiguring *Pym*, the story ends in a polar expedition – this one to the North pole. Also like *Pym*, the closing imagery turns on the black–white contrast provided by ice/snow (Poe's mysterious falling ash or, as some critics term it, warm snow) against a dark sky. The gigantic figure who looms in this wasteland is, however, not white but yellow, and by this point in the novel he is not remotely enigmatic. On the contrary, we know every detail of his past and may even, as many critics have argued, feel more compassion toward him than the hero, whose combination of arrogance and cowardice (not to mention stupidity, in assuming he and not Elizabeth would be the wedding-night victim) caused all the horror to begin with. In short, this monster is not uncanny at all. If there is a closing image of inscrutable whiteness that we might analyze along the lines suggested by Morrison, it would have to be Victor's "cold and white" corpse, which the monster – Othello-like – claims as his victim, and grieves for and reviles in turns. That the representation of Victor's death, in all editions of the story, lacks the required sublimity – that the monster, as always, steals the show – goes a long way in separating Shelley from her racist re-working by Poe.

We note one final difference between Poe's text and Shelley's: her pole seems to have no hole in it. In general, the topography of *Frankenstein* is mountainous, not cavernous; convex, not concave. The anti-hero will set himself on fire, rather than descending (as *Pym* implies) into some literal underworld: the motion is ascending. For all the earlier focus on domesticity, for all the cottages and enclosures, the final sequence leaves the reader as far outside civilization as possible. And this may be the one sense in which the monster is *unheimlich*: he does not have a home. Yet, by the end of the novel, he is the character we are most at home with. And for women readers this double valence of homeliness is significant. One sense of the word "homely" we have not yet theorized is the modern sense of homely as unattractive – a term generally reserved for women, the assumption being that a woman who is beautiful will not stay home, that she will be un-homely and hence potentially *unheimlich* in the Freudian sense. Shelley, however, has succeeded in inventing a character who is simultaneously "homely" in his appeal to readerly compassion, "homely" in his ugliness, and literally homeless, a misfit, a wanderer. For all the "angels in the house" crammed into this novel, it is the fiend who goes up in flames who steals our hearts. This is where I find Shelley's subversive message. In lieu of a dead white albatross, she gives us a yellow phoenix.

If Frankenstein's monster is ambiguously gendered, Bram Stoker's Count Dracula is an out-and-out hermaphrodite. His uncannily Petrarchan white skin and blood-red lips, combined with his penetrating, phallic teeth and his propensity to suckle as well as feed from his victims, render him beyond "effeminized." He also – like all the monsters in this chapter – has a problematic relationship with mirrors: he does not reflect, and so must shun them for fear of being exposed. At the same time, however, the description of the Count's discovery, while napping in his coffin after his latest feast, is almost comically phallic:

. . . [T]he white skin seemed ruby-red underneath; the mouth was redder than ever, for on the lips were gouts of fresh blood . . . Even the deep, burning eyes seemed set amongst swollen flesh, for the lids and pouches underneath were bloated. It seemed as if the whole awful creature were simply gorged with blood. He lay like a filthy leech, exhausted with his repletion.[49]

The hero, Jonathan Harker, shudders at the "bloated face" and is seized by "a terrible desire" to destroy him; just as he aims the blow, however, the vampire fixes him with his gaze "of basilisk horror." The description concludes, "The last glimpse I had was of the bloated face, blood-stained and fixed with a grin of malice that would have held its own in the nethermost hell" (p. 74). That the vampire is a man-sized phallus, "gorged with blood," seems almost too obvious: that, plus the hair on the backs of his hands, and his tendency to target women (saving the narrator as a special, homoerotic delicacy), renders him hyper-male at the same time that the bloody mouth suggests a vagina menstrous and/or *dentata* and the basilisk stare alludes to Medusa.

This is all fairly transparent, and has been discussed by critics prior to myself.[50] What has only begun to be theorized is the vampire's racial status. Steven Arata criticizes the feminist psychoanalytic approach for failing to recognize the fact that "the view of women encoded in the book is inextricably bound up with certain attitudes toward the cultural, racial, and social 'other.'"[51] That the Count occupies the category of "not quite/ not white" formulated by Homi Bhabha[52] is visually signaled by his strange appearance, his black clothing, and by the gypsies who accompany his travels. H. L. Malchow points out that "The savage cannibal and the gothic vampire, a species of cannibal, have much in common."[53] Malchow posits Dracula as a figure for "the nationless Jew as bloodsucker (literal and allusive), sexual threat, and corrupter of Christian morality"[54] – a reading confirmed by the silent film version, *Nosferatu* (1922), which endows the Count with a "Jewish" nose. As with Frankenstein's monster, I feel it hardly matters whether a definitive "other" can be named, nor need different readings of this racial otherness cancel one another out. But rather than take the critics' word for it, let us see what Dracula himself says about his family-tree:

[I]n our veins flows the blood of many brave races . . . Here, in the whirlpool of European races, the Ugric tribe bore down from Iceland the fighting spirit which Thor and Wodin gave them, which their Berserkers displayed to such fell intent on the seaboards of Europe, ay, and of Asia and Africa too . . . Here, too, when they came, they found the Huns, whose warlike fury had swept the earth like a living flame, till the dying peoples held that in their veins ran the blood of those old witches, who, expelled from Scythia had mated with the devils in the desert. Fools, fools! What devil or what witch was ever so great as Attila, whose blood is in these veins? (pp. 52–3)

The precise trajectory is hard to follow, but in any case the overwhelming sense of this passage is (here the nineteenth-century term seems apt) that of amalgamation. Dracula speaks of the races, plural, in his veins – a point rendered doubly meaningful considering what we know as readers and the narrator doesn't: that in speaking of the blood in his veins he alludes not only to his ancestors, but to his victims. And indeed, vampirism itself, in addition to the more obvious figuration of sexual intercourse, seems the perfect metaphor for miscegenation. There is even a hint, later in the passage, of some, shall we say, blacker blood in the mix: "Who was it but one of my own race who . . . beat the Turk on his own ground? This was a Dracula indeed! Woe was it that his own unworthy brother . . . sold his people to the Turk and brought the shame of slavery on them!" (p. 53). Altogether, the development is from light to dark, on the complexional-geographical scale: the explicit movement is from Iceland to Europe, to "Asia and Africa," then a muddled mixing in eastern Europe (whence, as Malchow usefully points out, many Jews entered the West),[55] and then finally the reference to enslavement by the Turks. The Count's pallor seems to rule out any African blood, but the aquiline nose and profuse, black, "bushy hair that seemed to curl" Aaron-like "in its own profusion" (p. 42) suggest, in addition to Malchow's Jewish thesis, some kind of Middle-Eastern mix. Notably, there is an allusion to the Amazons in the earlier reference to the "witches" from Scythia who mated in the desert – perhaps in Africa, one of their fabled domains – with the devil. In addition to signaling a concern with miscegenation (witches, as I've mentioned before, are the oldest miscegenists), the Amazonian allusion points up the vampire's association with masculinized women in the aggressive, anti-maternal, cannibalistic vampirettes (vamps?) his bite creates. This passage in the narrator's journal ends curiously: he likens his midnight conversations with the Count to "the 'Arabian Nights,' for everything to break off at cockcrow" – or to Shakespeare's depiction of "the ghost of Hamlet's father" (p. 54). Exoticism and Shakespeare, once again, go hand in hand.

The above is one of several Shakespearean citations. Some of these are significant to this study – as when Lucy, the first victim of the vampire, likens herself to Ophelia, lying in bed surrounded by garlic flowers. Or when Harker calls the three vampire women – his introduction to the vampire world – "those weird sisters" (p. 71), alluding to the witches in *Macbeth*. Most telling of all, in terms of my argument, is the one reference to Desdemona. This is Lucy again, as yet unbitten: "I sympathise with poor Desdemona when she had such a dangerous stream poured in her ear, *even by a black* man" (p. 79; emphasis mine). This sexualized "dangerous stream," alluding to Othello's "witch-craft" in wooing Desdemona (and also, perhaps, to the poison in the late Hamlet's ear), refers to, in Lucy's case, the courtship of three men among whom she does not wish to choose: "I wasn't broken to the harness" – "You will think me a horrid flirt" – "Why can't they let a girl marry three men, or as many as want her, and save all this trouble?" Not surprisingly, the *Othello* citation, like some of the other Shakespearean moments, underscores the novel's misogyny: Lucy must be rendered just sluttish enough to serve as the novel's central sacrifice, first in the arms of the vampire and then at the hand of her husband. (In Francis Ford Coppola's 1992 filmic adaptation, Lucy is an out-and-out hussy with her fluorescent red hair and aptness for remarks like "I could well stand him between my legs.") Elsewhere the letter – our introduction to the character, here a hysterical, hyper-feminine mess – deploys the classic strategy of masculinist discourse in placing misogyny in the mouth of a woman: "why are men so noble when we women are so little worthy of them?" (p. 80). I will not dwell on the other ways in which Lucy's own words – like those of her foil, the upright Mina, in the previous letter – denigrate and infantalize her (though it's tempting). The text's misogyny is far more interesting in the lady-vampire sections, to which we turn in a moment.

Christopher Craft reads the novel as a homosexual allegory – which in many ways I believe it is – but he puts this in terms useful to the focus of this chapter: "an implicitly homoerotic desire achieves representation as a monstrous heterosexuality, as a demonic inversion of normal gender relations."[56] Indeed, homosocial or homoerotic panic can often find expression in misogyny, and the events of Bram Stoker's life, as Malchow points out, shed light on the text's confused and horrified eroticism.[57] Let's look at one particularly racy passage:

The fair girl went on her knees, and bent over me, simply gloating. There was a deliberate voluptuousness that was both thrilling and repulsive, and as she arched her neck she actually licked her lips like an animal, till I could see in the moonlight the moisture shining on the scarlet lips and on the red tongue as it lapped the white sharp teeth. (pp. 61–2)

This happens to be the fair-skinned, golden-haired woman, who is offered the first taste of Harker by her dark-haired vamp cohorts. She is prevented of course – not by Harker himself, who lies "in a languorous ecstasy . . . wait[ing] with beating heart" for the bite (p. 62) – but by the Count, who wants Harker for himself.

The heart of the book's misogyny, however, lies neither in the homo-erotic subtext, nor necessarily in its animalistic blood-sucking women, like this one on all fours over an orgasmic male victim. On the contrary, I find this a deeply erotic, and even empowering image. Rather, *Dracula*'s misogyny – like its Othellophilia – is located in the rhetoric surrounding the focal wife-murder. After Lucy's seeming death by the vampire bite, she is examined in her coffin and found to be "even more radiantly beautiful than ever in death" (p. 209). This is of course because she has been preying on children. Notably, the women vampires seem limited to a diet of children, while the Count gets adults. The beauty in death is part and parcel of the vampire myth, but here it rings true to the necrophilic branch of misogynist discourse epitomized by Poe and Pre-Raphaelite paintings such as *The Lady of Shallot*. Moreover, the required method for killing her from her "undead" state and liberating her soul are all sexual metaphors: her husband, Arthur, must drive a stake through her heart (penetration); she must be beheaded (calling to mind classic puns on the removal of the "maidenhead"); and "that wicked mouth" of hers (p. 222) must be filled with garlic (again, penetration). For reasons not entirely clear, this must be done while she sleeps – thus further sexualizing the act – rather than during her midnight rambles. Indeed, more children are lost while the men wait to catch her sleeping.

In all scenes treating the vampirization of the two female characters, images of whiteness underscore the rhetoric of purity versus pollution in a way that recalls the black–white visual polarities of *Othello*. In the scene wherein Lucy is first observed indulging her vampiric appetite, she is a "white figure" (three times) holding "something dark at her breast" – a child, in this cannibalistic anti-madonna image. The white–dark contrast then inverts itself: she becomes a "dark-haired woman, dressed in the cerements of the grave," her head "bent down over . . . a fair-haired child" reminiscent of *Frankenstein*'s martyred William. The male onlookers then recognize a Lucy transformed from sweetness to cruelty, from "purity to voluptuous wantonness." That word, "voluptuous," occurs four times in the ensuing description; tropes of the demonic abound, even as she tries to seduce Arthur ("come" four times in three lines). They observe her bloody mouth: "the stream had . . . stained the purity of her lawn death-robe." That word, "stream," like "voluptuous," underscores the sexuality of the vampire; the horror of the blood-stained mouth may also register an anti-cosmetic theme – in the movies, anyway, it tends to resemble botched and over-done lipstick. Her eyes are "unclean and full of hell-fire, instead of the pure, gentle orbs [they] knew . . . her eyes [blaze] with unholy light" (pp. 218–19). The narrator then confesses, "At that moment the remnant of my love passed into hate and loathing; had she then to be killed I could have done it with *savage* delight" (p. 219; emphasis mine).

Restraint is called for here, as the novel's horror-eroticism – can one say "horroticism"? – and its Othellophilia require a bed-death. Later, asleep in her coffin, Lucy is both fair and foul: "The body lay there in all its death-beauty. But there was no love in my heart, only loathing for the foul Thing which had taken Lucy's shape . . . The blood-stained, voluptuous mouth – which it made one shudder to see – the whole carnal and unspiritual appearance seeming like a devilish mockery of Lucy's purity" (p. 221). The execution is a group effort – a kind of ghastly gang-rape – and its homosocial nature recalls the Italian novella that was Shakespeare's source for *Othello*, wherein the Iago figure aids the Moor in the murder. The Professor convinces the husband to play the main part, in impaling her, and the pseudo-sacralizing rhetoric echoes Othello's incantatory, ritualistic speech over Desdemona's sleeping form, in addition to his self-justifying eulogy over her corpse: "It was my hand that sent her to the stars; it was the hand of him that loved her best; the hand that of all she would herself have chosen, had it been to her to choose . . ." The murder is a sacrament: "Strike in God's name." Just as Othello bids Desdemona pray – "I would not kill thy soul" (*Othello*, v.ii.32) – a missal is produced and prayers are read in a kind of mock-marriage. This done, the consummation ensues: Arthur thrusts the stake into her, and produces an orgasmic result; she writhes, shakes, quivers, twists, and foams at the mouth. It gets even better: "Arthur never faltered. He looked like a figure of Thor as his trembling arm rose and fell, driving deeper and deeper the mercy-bearing stake, whilst the blood from the pierced heart welled and spurted up around it." I'm not even using italics here, as the symbolism is painfully obvious. This bit is more interesting: "His face was set, and *high duty* seemed to shine through it . . ." She dies – again – and returns to her former state of "unequalled sweetness and purity" (pp. 223–4; emphasis mine). Finally, Arthur can "Kiss her dead lips" (p. 224), fulfilling Othello's promise: "Be thus when thou art dead and I will kill thee / And love thee after" (*Othello*, v.ii.18–19). Like Desdemona, she dies twice; like Desdemona, her death redeems her; like Desdemona, her dead body is kissed by her murderer-husband.

The rhetoric of sacrament and sacrifice also surrounds the vampirizing of the next victim, Harker's wife Mina.[58] In a monstrous inversion of the Eucharist, Count Dracula chooses (for reasons unknown) not only to vampirize but vampiristically to suckle the wife of the hero. The mingling of sacred and sexual render the scene pornographic: "Kneeling on the near edge of the bed . . . was the white-clad figure of his wife." Yet she is not kneeling to pray: the Count forces "her head down on his bosom. Her white night-dress was smeared with blood" (pp. 282–3). This is clearly forced oral sex, albeit pectoral rather than penile: afterward she wails "Unclean, unclean! I must touch [Harker] or kiss him no more" (p. 285). Mina goes on to ask her husband and his friend to kneel and swear to destroy her as they did Lucy, should her vampire-self take over; the ensuing oath resembles that between Othello and Iago, when they kneel and vow to kill Desdemona. Indeed, this Mina surpasses Lucy as a Desdemonian heroine, as she, despite the bite, succeeds in suppressing her blood-thirst; she wastes away as "that sweet, sweet, good, good woman" who "with all her goodness and purity and faith" is nonetheless "outcast from God" (p. 300).

Like *Frankenstein*, the novel ends in a snowy wasteland, where the Count and his female cohorts finally meet destruction, and Mina is thus released from the spell. Count Dracula, surrounded by the usual entourage of gypsies, is dispatched in a mere ten lines of text, quite a contrast to the immediately prior full-page description of the deaths of the female vampires, and the earlier, lingering, six-page execution of Lucy at the novel's heart. Despite, however, the text's preoccupation with its women, Mina drops out of sight post-redemption; the disappearance of her scar is described indirectly, by a male observer: "The snow is not more stainless than her forehead!" (p. 368). The final "note" focuses on the son born to Mina and Harker, as the objective correlative of the mother's salvation. The last line drives home the homosocial moral: "later on he will understand how some men so loved her, that they did dare much for her sake" (p. 369).

Whether or not they loved wisely, they loved too well.

I might be accused of making too much of these echoes of *Othello*, but Stoker's biography confirms his passion for theatre in general and Shakespearean theatre in particular. Indeed, Stoker's relationship with the actor Sir Henry Irving, for whom he worked as manager for twenty-seven years, seems to have eclipsed all other relationships in his life, at least to look at the sheer bulk of correspondences and memorabilia contained in the Bram Stoker Collection at the Shakespeare Centre Library. Other evidence from the same source points to a preoccupation with *Othello*, which the author viewed four times in May, 1881, alone – he also had to be conscious of the Othellophilia of his contemporaries, as his possessions include an illustration entitled "Othello! Othello! Everywhere" (Figure 3.5), along with another of Edwin Booth as an "oriental" Othello to Irving's Iago. Indeed, based on the number of clippings and play-bills in the collection, *Othello* kept company with *Faust* and *Merchant of Venice* amongst Stoker's favorites – an observation that nicely reinforces this chapter's reading of *Dracula*'s racialist (and perhaps anti-Semitic) demonic imaginary.

However, the case for *Dracula*'s – and hence Stoker's – Othellophilia is even stronger in light of a later, and less canonical novel. Almost no one apart from specialists has heard of *The Lair of the White Worm* (1910), and it is worth asking why. This short novel features the *sine qua non* of white she-devils in the Lady Annabella March, white-clad aristocrat by day; Gargantuan, man-eating white snake by night. The descriptions of the

Figure 3.5. "Othello! Othello! Everywhere. There is no getting away from Othello." From *The Daily Critic* (1881).

Worm's lair surpass even Poe's black crannies as exemplars of not-so-sublimated misogynist nausea: the lair is incessantly termed "hole" or "well-hole" and the slime and smell associated with it are (here we go again) too gynecological to resist. Moreover, this masterwork of misogyny is also (here we go again) a masterwork of racism: the only victim of the Worm whose entrapment Stoker describes is a black man who has outraged the Lady by approaching her sexually. That her sexual repugnance toward him is expressed in searingly racist terms (she calls him "nigger" twice – as the narrator does on occasion) does not prevent Stoker from sexualizing his punishment by her. Here are some choice phrases:

> Oolanga came close behind Lady Arabella, and in a hushed voice . . . began to unfold the story of his love . . . The circumstances were too grotesque . . . The man a debased and primitive specimen and of an ugliness which was simply devilish; the woman of high degree, beautiful, accomplished.[59]

From Oolanga's name, to his mimicry of Othello's wooing (though the latter does not "unfold . . . his story" but "dilate[s]" it [1.iii.152]), to the references to the grotesque and the demonic, the passage screams Othellophilia. In a later passage, Stoker's racism gives way to misogynist nausea:

> There was certainly opportunity for the nigger's enjoyment, for the open well-hole was almost under his nose . . . In another instant she had seized him, her white arms encircling him, down with her into the gaping aperture . . . [T]he awful cry came up from that fathomless pit, whose entrance was flooded with spots of fresh blood. (p. 118)

The *pièce de resistance* is the monster's appearance on return, "calm and unruffled" despite her blood-stained hands, neck, and face. Miraculously, the white gown has escaped soiling. Lady and dress alike are "unruffled."

Stoker seems quite fond of white dresses on women. The women in *Dracula* appear to wear nothing else: reading the symbolism of their attire against the white dress of the White Worm renders this symbol of innocence, well, less than innocent. Something similar happens when we compare the overt inter-racialism of *White Worm* with the suppressed miscegeny theme in *Dracula*. The Lady's racism must be, like her white skin, skin-deep if she's that eager to pull a black man into her hole; likewise Lucy must have been "asking for it" from the cannibalistic Count. The racial encoding of *Lair of the White Worm* calls into question countless white dresses on the countless white "victims" of Gothic horror. The dress is not just white: the dress *is* the woman's whiteness, racially, morally, and sexually.

The ending of Stoker's novel *The Jewel of the Seven Stars* (1903) constitutes another white-dress fetish that looks suspicious when read racially. A group of occultists unravel an Egyptian mummy and discover within a perfectly preserved, beautiful, ivory-skinned, raven-haired woman laid out nude under a gem-encrusted, white bridal gown. Here is yet another white(washed) Egyptian queen, but one whose charms are literal and deadly, embodied in the white gown, which is left after the body goes up in smoke, taking the lives of the onlookers with it. Stoker describes the dead queen's unveiling in erotic terms: "It was not right that we should be there, gazing with irreverent eyes on such unclad beauty . . . And yet the white wonder of that beautiful form was something to dream of." If you've read *Jewel of the Seven Stars* and don't recognize this passage, you shouldn't. The passage – along with the entire, macabre ending of the novel – was expurgated in all but the first edition. Apparently, the disappearing act offended more than the impaling of Lucy or the blowing-to-pieces of the Worm.[60] It is one thing to strip and destroy a white woman, quite another to leave nothing there in her wake.

Arthur Little writes, "Woman's body as natural ritualistic object has a long history . . . it serves as a vital instrument in shaping the woman's and the community's health."[61] From the whitewashed Cleopatra's suicidal "joy of the worm" who kills her, to the white-clad Lucy who sleepwalks into the arms of the vampire, Othellophilia requires that a white woman's death be sacrificial, that it preserve the social order. That is one of the reasons why Rowley's *All's Lost by Lust* never achieved the popularity of *Othello* and why the ending of *Jewel of the Seven Stars* was censored. By the same token, though, the public prefers the narratives in which the ideological work of the text is occluded: the racism of *Lair of the White Worm* is simply too overt. I would argue, in fact, that the latter did not fall into obscurity for being unlike the famous vampire novel, but for being too much like it but too obviously racist. The same can be said of *Titus* versus *Othello*. The preference moves in both directions: overt anti-racism also works against canonicity. In horror, Anglo-American readers prefer images – but not politics – in black and white.

It is women who love horror. Shudder and cling and cry – and always willing to come back for more. (Bela Lugosi)

Frankenstein and *Dracula* both made for good theatre; both novels were adapted for the stage within the authors' lifetimes, and both plays went on to inspire "classic" film adaptations and popular parodies. Both figures make for good camp. The amiable Herman Munster of the black-and-white sitcom *The Munsters* and Bela Lugosi's heart-throb *Count Dracula* are perhaps as deeply embedded in cultural memory as Shakespeare's tragic Moor; I suspect that the first two owe their success to the last. Indeed, in the 1995 film *Interview with the Vampire*, the "bad" vampire quotes Othello's "put out the light" over one of his victims. What does this tell us about Stoker's novel; about Shakespeare; about what we take, as a culture, from both?

One thing it does tell us is that, in contrast to Poe's America, we prefer our monsters white – indeed, the vampire who quotes *Othello* is not only white, but blond and attractive, a kind of Californian "surfer-dude" vampire. And who, aside from critics of Shelley's novel, ever thinks of the Frankenstein monster as *yellow*? Blaxploitation monster fliks aside (*Blacula* and *Blackenstein* portray black monsters who prey on black victims), most contemporary movie monsters are white. This may be a sign of progress, or it may not. Judith Halberstam argues that the racial whiteness of America's current filmic monsters is a reflection of the culture's racism: because race is already "Gothicized," depicting a racially black monster would move the white, middle-class audience out of the play-world of cinema and into the psychologically "real" terror of the inner-city.[62] I think there is something to this, but it does risk a theoretical double-bind: would it be less racist to make every monster black? Clearly, there is something more complicated involved.

Let's pause for a moment on the whitewashing of Frankenstein (and I'll call him that to distinguish the film-monster from Shelley's un-named monster in the novel). This may be, in part, an accident of film technology; black and white necessarily pre-dated color, and it was the black-and-white "classics" that set the precedent in Hollywood. The original 1931 film monster in fact followed the nineteenth-century theatrical precedent, which was light blue or gray; the actor, Boris Karloff, wore a blue-green grease-paint that was supposed to photograph gray,[63] but that of course depends on the lighting and the quality of the reproduction: every Frankenstein I've ever seen has been sickly pale, particularly under the moonlight, where he tends to lurk. Many pop-culture Frankensteins have also had face-lifts: the wrinkled skin Shelley imagined is replaced by those few characteristic seams and bolts, leaving him with the marble complexion that makes Herman such a fit companion for the aptly named Lily with her ghostly pallor and matching white dress. Dracula, of course, has always been defined by his pallor; the theatrical and cinematic traditions followed suit, and the thickly applied powder and dark lipstick became his trademark. And here we reach an important juncture in the discourse. Both Frankenstein and Dracula are white-face performances: the direct inverse of the Renaissance stage Moor.

Most monsters are white – they are also mostly male. And yet. And yet. Our friendly neighborhood vampire is an arrant dandy and Bela Lugosi's first name sounds distinctly female. And as for Frankenstein: *Rocky Horror*'s Dr. Frank N. Furter, that "sweet transvestite from Transylvania," says it all. These modern monsters seem more "femme" than "butch" – no wonder we so often find them consorting with femmes fatales.

Anemia, the medical translation of the vampire's blood-thirst, is a female disease, just as the pallor associated with it is gendered female.[64] Women bleed monthly as a matter of course; it is an easy leap from this observation to the attribution of a desire to ingest blood, to make up for the deficiency. Like eating generally, cannibalism specifically is often gendered female, a kind of gross literalization and upward displacement of the *vagina dentata*. That it should be so is not logical – after all, it is women, biologically speaking, whose bodies provide nourishment – but phallocentric discourse, as we know, need not be logical or consistent. The prototypical vampire was a man, but it is women who are called "man-eaters" and "vamps."

It was Shakespeare who gave us the first man-eating woman; in the classical tradition, it was always the male parent who ate his own child. Tamora, who eats her own (if inadvertently), is the apotheosis of *Titus'* preoccupation with holes, from the pit in and around which the bloody events in the woods transpire, to Lavinia's bloody mouth, to the hole in which Aaron will be buried up to his chest and then left to starve. As Tamora eats her sons, it only makes sense that her punishment is not to starve but to be eaten, her body made piecemeal by scavenging birds, until not even Victor Frankenstein could make her whole again. Indeed, the cannibalism of *Titus* is linked to the theme of miscegenation: the Restoration adaptation foregrounds this by having Aaron offer to eat his child when he fails in preventing Tamora from killing it. Like miscegenation, cannibalism is an unholy mixing of blood. Like miscegenation, cannibalism creates a monster in the person who breaks the taboo.[65]

This chapter's titular trope foregrounds a quality common to the three central texts we have looked at, something I would call not orality but orificiality, from Poe's holes in the poles to the holes in the neck of the vampiric victim–monster. This obsession, however, has a precedent in Shakespearean inter-racialism. We have noted the orificiality of *Titus*; critics find *Othello* to be similarly haunted, in the rhetoric of dilation, of prying open of secrets, of knots, probations, and loop-holes, and even in the "O"s that resound through the text.[66] Cannibalism is there too: Othello woos Desdemona with stories of "the cannibals that each other eat" that she would "with a greedy ear / Devour" (I.iii.144); he later threatens to "chop her to messes" (IV.i.196) – that is, into servings of meat. Echoing Shakespeare, all three Gothic tales betray an obsession with a monstrous devouring or bodily immolation. *Frankenstein* may seem the exception, but the making of the monster involves a kind of reverse-cannibalism, as the "maw of death" (p. 74), the tomb, regurgitates the human remains it has consumed. Frankenstein's "filthy labor" involves dismembering corpses – that is, butchery.

Tamora, by the way, is a Goth. Shakespeare, of course, used the term to refer to a particular racial or ethnic group, but this semantic accident is worth considering. The literary genre and hence the literary usage of the term did not arise until the late eighteenth century, but there is another sense in which Tamora was "Gothic." The *OED* cites a 1695 usage of "Gothic" as "barbarous; rude; uncouth" or "savage"; this post-dates Shakespeare's play, but his portrayal of Goths is true to this tradition.[67] If we couple this sense of "Gothic" with Francesca Royster's reading of Tamora as marked by an excessive, racial whiteness, we have ourselves a female vampire who pre-dates Stoker's by some three hundred years.

Those female vampires just will not die. On the horror shelves of my local Blockbuster video store, the majority of vampire fliks feature women.

Let's take a moment to consider Lugosi's thoughts about women and horror, in the epigraph to this section. I initially found the quote rather silly: to post-modern viewers, male or female, Lugosi's Dracula is nothing at all to be scared of. Lugosi's women fans did not, clearly, "love horror": Lugosi's fans loved Bela Lugosi. Anyway, that was my first reaction; upon reflection the quote grew more sinister. It began to look, in fact, down-right creepy. They "shudder and cling and cry" – but they really want it. The sadism of this is strangely true to the character, and it somewhat mitigates my fondness for the actor whose Magyar ancestry I share. It brings to mind the fact that the vampire myth is, at basis, about rape: the bite is sexual (curiously, even more so in the 1931 film, which fades to black as the vampire leans over the bed); the bite is unwanted sex, yet the victim is hypnotized and cannot resist. *Raptus*–rapture–rape. Afterward, they come when he calls, like Katherina in *The Taming of the Shrew*; like Desdemona when Othello calls her back ("She can turn and turn . . . And turn again" [IV.i.250–1]); like Lugosi's women who "come back for more."

Women in horror must die because, deep down, they do love the monster. Deep down, in fact, they love death. Lugosi again:

Women are the ones who constantly visit cemeteries, ostensibly to grieve . . . but subconsciously to gloat over death . . . Women put forth every possible effort in their frantic desire to get to the front line trenches during the World War . . . subconsciously, they sought the savage thrill that came from being in the midst of suffering and horrible mutilation . . .[68]

These fantasies of women gloating on death and mutilation are ripe for psychoanalysis. The *OED* surmises that this usage of "gloat" associates it with "glut," to feed upon until satiation. The feminine – which, in Kristevian terms, always recalls the maternal – is the gateway of life, and thus can be imagined the gateway of death. Kristeva posits "the image of birth as a violent act of expulsion through which the nascent body tears itself away from the matter of maternal insides. Now, the skin apparently never ceases to bear traces of such matter . . . The obsession of the leprous and decaying body would thus be the fantasy of a self-rebirth on the part of a subject who has . . . incorporated a devouring mother."[69]

A leprous body is a white body – we recall Coleridge's "her skin was white as leprosy." The final chapter of Richard Dyer's book *White* is on "white death." He writes, "White people have a colour, but it is a colour that also signifies the absence of colour, itself a characteristic of life and presence."[70] Dyer posits the vampire and the zombie as epitomizing an alternative racial narrative wherein whiteness is not (as it usually is) normality, supremacy, or transcendence, but death: in George Romero's zombie trilogy, for instance, black people are the heroes.[71] Lugosi himself starred in a zombie movie, *White Zombie* (1932). The film, set in Haiti, borrows from a 1929 travel book with a chapter on "dead men working in the cane fields" – in other words, doing the work of black slaves. Lugosi's character, the zombie-maker Murder, is commissioned to help in a seduction by transforming a living woman into the walking dead: Murder himself, however, soon takes a liking to the "white zombie." The advertisements for this thinly veiled rape film were particularly lurid: "She was not dead . . . nor alive, yet she walked, breathed, and performed his every wish," and "He made her his slave." Some ads pictured Lugosi staring down at a nude female figure.[72] Here race re-enters the picture. The woman Murder desires is simultaneously corpse, slave, and (in the most literal sense) sex-object, a white surrogate for a black slave, but one with absolutely no volition: an automaton, a machine. The perfect slave, like the perfect woman, is dead, (white), and ambulatory. Poe would have loved it.[73]

Lugosi himself seems to have wanted a zombie for a wife. He boasted of one of his five marriages, "I pick out everything my wife wears. I like to see her in simple things. I don't like exotic things on women."[74] The remark is highly ironic, considering his own exoticism, evident in his aptitude for starring roles in harem films[75] and his passion for gypsy music.[76] I suspect he meant "exotic" in the sense of "exotic dancing" – that is, erotic, sexy. At least one of his ex-wives blamed his jealousy for their divorce.[77]

Dracula's "father," Bram Stoker, was himself no fan of the erotic either. Toward the end of his life – dying of syphilis – he wrote a series of scathing pro-censorship essays. Apparently, he thought his own work was not about sex. In a curious way, he was right.

CHAPTER 4

Sisters in bondage: abolition, amalgamation, and the crisis of female authorship

Reviewing Harriet Beecher Stowe's *Uncle Tom's Cabin* for the *Southern Quarterly Review* in 1853, William Gilmore Simms imagines the author in the following terms: "the petticoat lifts of itself, and we see the hoof of the beast under the table."[1] This cloven-hoofed devil in petticoats appears at a historical juncture when the discourses of inter-racialism have reached a particular pitch and intensity, pushed by the political pressure of abolitionists and fueled by the panic over "amalgamation" or racial inter-breeding, which all abolitionists were accused of favoring. The white, female, abolitionist author demonized here is the white devil at her most politically threatening; vilified for alluding – however obliquely – to the sexual use of slave women by their white masters, Stowe must be punished by way of her sexuality. Diane Roberts writes, ". . . Something else reveals itself when the petticoat of the female author rises; the 'hoof of the beast,' the 'mark' of the devil, also signifies the 'mark' of the female, that is: the genitals. The woman who speaks or writes 'in public,' who makes herself a 'display' like a prostitute, in effect flaunts her genitals."[2] It might be worth making explicit the subliminal parallel between the cleft shape of the devil's hoof and the cleft shape of the female pudendum – reinforcing the by now age-old association between hell and the female genitalia. Thus Stowe, for exposing the suppressed history of white sexual predation upon black females and the resulting "mulatto" or mixed-race offspring, must in turn be exposed to a humiliating sexualized scrutiny – a scrutiny she is understood to have invited by appearing in print in the first place.

Indeed, abolitionist writers – particularly women writers – knew they were stepping into a mine-field in making any attempt to tell this particular truth of slavery. Lydia Maria Child's introduction to Harriet Jacobs' *Incidents in the Life of a Slave Girl* (1861) makes a pre-emptive strike in addressing these concerns:

I am well aware that many will accuse me of indecorum for presenting these pages to the public; for the experiences of this intelligent and much-injured woman belong to a class which some call delicate subjects, and others indelicate. This peculiar phase of Slavery has generally been kept veiled; but the public ought to be made acquainted with its monstrous features, and I willingly take the responsibility of presenting them with the veil withdrawn. I do this for the sake of my sisters in bondage, who are suffering wrongs so foul, that our ears are too delicate to listen to them. I do it with the hope of arousing conscientious and reflecting women of the north to a sense of their duty in the exertion of moral influence on the question of slavery . . .[3]

Child's appeal to inter-racial female solidarity is the obvious corrective to the darker vision of relations between black and white women presented in the text she introduces: arguably, the most tragic element of Jacobs' story is the bitter sexual jealousy that transforms the potentially protective white mistress into the female slave's primary tormentor. Thus, despite mutual suffering at the hands of the same oppressor, white and black women become enemies, not allies.

But healing this intra-gender rift, along the lines of Child's vision in the Introduction of *Incidents*, would be no easy task. For it required, first and foremost, a critical stance toward the inter-linked ideologies of romantic love, companionate marriage, and domesticity of which even liberal abolitionists were seldom capable. Indeed, it was often by way of reference to traditional Christian values privileging the patriarchal family, the "maternal instinct," and the sanctity of the domestic sphere, that abolitionist polemic did its most effective work. Thus, for instance, William Wells Brown, in his otherwise bold novel, *Clotel; or, the President's Daughter* (1853), declares matrimony "the oldest and most sacred institution given to man by his Creator" and claims the Lucrece myth for abolitionism in his valorization of slave women who die to protect their chastity.[4] Indeed, the political purpose of the novel, which culminates in the suicide of a white woman who is "really" black (because she has an African ancestor), operates in a manner similar to the Lucrece myth: it founds a revolutionary movement on the body of a beautiful, violated, white woman.

Thus, we arrive at a paradox. For the first time in the history of inter-racialist discourse, the master narrative which I have addressed by way of the coinage "Othellophilia" is under sustained attack by authors wishing to expose the sexual hypocrisy of the slave-holding class; at the same time, however, for the counter-narrative to gain an audience at all, it must perforce borrow from the master narrative. The love-story of Desdemona and Othello is de-sexualized and becomes the love-story of Little Eva and Uncle Tom, who die in a dual – if not simultaneous – sacrifice for the sake of a similar cause: the integrity of the family unit, and (by extension) the boundaries of a social body still firmly organized around gender and racial binaries.

Not all abolitionist works are, however, equally conservative or sexually sanitized. But the relative obscurity of those works that do challenge traditional, masculinist, and even racist values attests to the aptitude of the master discourse in containing the very voices that challenge it. Thanks to the liberalizing of the American public education system in the wake of the civil rights movement and the more recent push for multiculturalism, most educated people have heard of Harriet Jacobs (though fewer than have heard of Frederick Douglas, who, being male, and married to a white woman, is of course more amenable to white mythologizing). Of those familiar with Jacobs, however, how many would recognize the name of her editor, herself a prolific and, in her time, successful author, journalist, and social activist? Not many, I would guess. Nor is this surprising, considering Child's record of advocating – to the outraged horror of abolitionists and anti-abolitionists alike, and practically to the detriment of her career – programmatic inter-marriage, which would eliminate America's racial problems by eliminating racial divisions entirely.[5] She was also a feminist, advocating women's suffrage, and critiquing, by way of her two-volume *History of the Condition of Women, in Various Ages and Nations* (1835), Victorian domestic ideology and its essentialisms about women's "natural" duties. In addition, Child proved herself something of an early feminist critic of the "classic" authors. In a letter she wrote at age fifteen, she challenges her older brother and mentor: "Don't you think that Milton asserts the superiority of his own sex in rather too lordly a manner?" (Karcher, "Introduction," p. x).

The case of Child serves as an example of the way masculinist-racist mythologies drown out other voices competing for the public ear. It is a kind of literary "white noise" – the aural equivalent of Child's metaphor of the veil. This chapter will posit the bifurcation of abolitionist literature into what I will call, in a short-hand that is as tentative as it is necessary, feminist and non-feminist, exemplified on the one hand by a white female and a black female author (Child and Jacobs) and on the other by a white female and a black male author (Stowe and Brown). My point is not to vilify the latter and extol the former: without Brown and Stowe, slavery might never have been abolished. At the same time, contemporary burlesques of *Othello* could be called (bizarrely) feminist, in putting some fight back in Desdemona, even while dealing in viciously racist caricature of Othello. My point here is to illustrate the complex and often contradictory political uses of classic inter-racialist paradigms and the potential of these paradigms for both subversion of and complicity in masculinist-racist thought. It is as though, when a racially liberal message gains air-time, it only does so by playing to its audience's sexual conservatism, and when a liberal message about gender roles makes itself heard, it does so by playing to the audience's racism. As in more recent controversies such as the Supreme Court nomination of Clarence Thomas or the O. J. Simpson murder trial, the race–gender fault line proves a political catch-22.

> A pretty piece of business it would be of a truth, to have a parcel of tawny grandchildren at your heels, squeaking *powaw*, and *sheshikwee*, and the devil knoweth what all.
>
>   Lydia Maria Child, *Hobomok*

When critics responded to the wildly successful 1824 publication of *Hobomok: A Tale of Early Times*, they assumed that the anonymous author – like the fictional author of the fictional historical source mentioned in the Preface – was male. Hence the relative lack of venom in their responses to the "revolting" inter-racialist plot. Critics praised the author for "his" skill at crafting believable characters, for historical accuracy, and for aptly rendering the "Indian character . . . and language," and they excused the distasteful plot on the basis of the author's "inexperience" – perhaps meaning "his" presumed youth (quoted in Karcher, "Introduction," p. xxxiv). What would bring outrage on a female author merely embarrasses when the author is male: no devil's hoof in sight here.

Child's novel recalls *Othello* in many ways, but one difference is crucial in explaining the critics' disapproval: the white heroine, who marries and bears the child of an Indian, does not die. In this Child departs from not only the Shakespearean ur-text, but also the more direct, contemporary inspiration: the narrative poem *Yamoyden: A Tale of the Wars of King Philip* (1820), by James Wallis Eastburn and Robert Sands. Carolyn L. Karcher notes that both *Hobomok* and *Yamoyden* "model themselves after Shakespeare's *Othello* in having their dark-skinned heroes win the love of a white woman through eloquent recitals of their exploits and adventures." But these and other similarities belie a fundamental ideological contrast between Child's version of this American *Othello,* and the male-authored tragedies it revises. As Karcher points out, even authors as progressive as Eastburn and Sands – who presented an Indian uprising from the Indians' point of view – were incapable of the critique of "white supremacy and patriarchy" legible in Child's novel (pp. xviii–xix).

To me, however, the most stunningly subversive aspect of Child's plot – and the main cause for the novel's marginalization even within the canon of abolitionist literature – is its implicit critique of the cult of female chastity, or even, arguably, of monogamy itself.[6] This is not only a novel in which a woman bears a mixed-race child and gets away with it; it is also a novel in which a woman *has sex with two men* – a white and an Indian – and gets away with it. Indeed, not even the culturally legitimate, white, second husband of the heroine chastises her for her liaison with his erstwhile rival: returning to America after being misreported as dead, he willingly adopts the son of Mary and Hobomok as his own. And if Hobomok must be sacrificed – selflessly ceding his marital rites and disappearing into the wilderness – it is still a far less violent resolution than Shakespeare's, wherein the black hero kills both himself *and* his wife, and does so in explicitly punitive terms.

Child quotes Shakespeare in some of her epigraphs, but she never quotes *Othello*. Nonetheless, there are obvious parallels between Shakespeare's "noble Moor" and Child's "tawny chieftain" who woos the white heroine with "descriptions of the Indian nations" to which "she listened with too much interest" (p. 84). Like the marriage of Desdemona and Othello, Mary's marriage to Hobomok is culturally null and void: "she knew that her own nation looked upon her as lost and degraded . . . Hobomok's connexion with her was considered the effect of witchcraft on his part" (p. 135). As in *Othello*, the bride's consent is under question: indeed, Child surpasses Shakespeare in this regard, in having Mary marry Hobomok in a moment of mental instability, deranged by grief over her beloved's rumored death. Moreover, the witch-craft charge is left unresolved in the text: in fact, the plot that propels Mary to Hobomok's wigwam begins in a moment when both characters accidentally meet in the woods while performing incantations – Hobomok's a prayer to one of his gods and Mary's an English folk charm involving a moonlit "magic circle" which would reveal her destined husband. When Hobomok unwittingly lands inside the circle, Mary's fate is sealed; as her stern Puritan father puts it, echoing Brabantio on Othello's "sooty bosom," she will "lie in the bosom of a savage" (p. 133).

Child does seem to endorse Brabantio's notion that a white woman who marries a non-white must be, by definition, deprived of her wits; moreover, the novel endorses racial hierarchies in presenting Hobomok's love for Mary as "reverence" (p. 33). However, her "savage" hero (as the text insists on calling him) more closely resembles Oroonoko than Othello in his personal charms and "natural" spirituality. The novel dwells on "the manly beauty of Hobomok." Child writes:

This Indian was indeed cast in nature's noblest mould. He was one of the finest specimens of elastic, vigorous elegance of proportion, to be found among his tribe. His long residence with the white inhabitants of Plymouth had changed his natural fierceness of manner into a haughty, dignified reserve; and even that seemed softened as his dark, expressive eye rested on Conant's daughter. (p. 36)

Like Oroonoko, this is a Europeanized savage, educated by white society. Also like Oroonoko, his religious beliefs are not dismissed as "heathen" but rather favorably contrasted to the sterile asceticism of Conant's Puritanism, which both the heroine and her mother reject in favor of their own intuitive, earth-based spirituality. Child says of Hobomok "He had never read of God, but he had heard his chariot wheels in the distant thunder, and seen his drapery in the clouds" (p. 34). Karcher is surely right in crediting Child with anticipating Transcendentalist thought through both the white female and the Indian male characters, and in aligning these views with the critique of patriarchy and religious intolerance evident both in the novel and in the author's polemical writings (pp. xxiv–xxv). From a post-modern perspective, the recurrence of the terms "nature" and "natural" in this and other descriptions of Hobomok might be seen to betray a naïve or patronizing racial essentialism. But Child's use of the "noble savage" figure appears undeniably radical when contrasted with the stereotyping of indigenous Americans by contemporaries such as James Fennimore Cooper – contemporaries who, let me emphasize, were deified by later critics for authoring *the* American classics.

Hobomok also departs from the master narrative in its systematic undoing of racial binaries. Though Child initially presents Mary's English lover, Charles Brown, as Hobomok's intellectualized and cultured foil, that binary disintegrates by the end of the novel, when the former returns from his adventures in Africa with an Indian's survival skills and the latter is proclaimed "almost like an Englishman" thanks to his contact with the settlers (pp. 137–8). Likewise, Mary's father associates both Hobomok's "heathenism" and Charles' Episcopalianism with those "who bow the knee to Baal" (p. 9); Englishman and Indian blur in perceived diabolism, while a footnote of Child's unjudgmentally translates Hobomok's term for an Indian priest as "very good devil" (p. 14). Indeed, it is worth emphasizing that *both* Charles and Hobomok are suitors unsanctioned by the Puritan patriarch's authority; in ousting Charles from his dwelling (where Hobomok, significantly, is still welcome), the "tyrannical" father growls the inescapably racialized proverb discussed in my Introduction: "A man may not touch pitch, and remain undefiled" (p. 76).

This dismantling of binaries takes place at the level of imagery as well. Though Child's text describes the Indians as "the dark children of the forest," the descriptions of Hobomok himself are markedly lacking in tropes of blackness: rather, Child singles out his "tall, athletic form" and "healthy cheek" (p. 16), or his "silent and thoughtful" demeanor (p. 88). And, in the central inter-racialist sequence – a moonlit ritual hunt on a winter's "night of . . . glittering beauty" – color binaries fail to correspond to race. Here is a key passage:

> It was indeed a strange, romantic scene. The torches sent up columns of dense, *black* smoke, which vainly endeavoured to rise in the *clear*, cold atmosphere. Hobomok stood among his brethren, gracefully leaning on his bow, and his figure might well have been mistaken for the fabled deity of the chase. The wild, fitful *light shone* upon the unmoved countenance of the savage, and streamed back unbroken upon the rigid features of the Calvinist, rendered even more *dark* in their expression by the beaver cap which deeply *shaded* his care-worn brow. The *pale* loveliness of Mary's face, amid the intense cold of the night, seemed almost as *blooming* as her *ruddy* companions; and the frozen beauty of the surrounding woods again *flashed brightly* beneath the unwonted *glow* of those artificial *rays*. (pp. 88–9; emphases mine)

Here, by a remarkable writerly sleight-of-hand, a midnight scene in the forest becomes suffused with light – a light unequivocally associated with the Indians, rather than the whites who accompany them. In fact, it is Mary's father, the Calvinist, whose face is described as "dark," while Hobomok's face shines in the torch-light; Mary's own face is simultaneously "pale" and made "ruddy" like the Indians' by the effect of the cold. In the next sentence, Child directly refers to the usual racialized binary, only to reverse it immediately: "There, in that little group . . . was the contrast of heathen and Christian, social and savage, elegance and strength, fierceness and timidity." Syntactically, Child pairs "heathen" with "social" and "elegance" as well as with "fierceness" (the "elegance" echoing the description of Hobomok as "gracefully leaning on his bow"). In a moment, two deer step – in quick succession – into the circle of light created by the Indians' torches: dazzled by "the unnatural brightness," each hesitates long enough to be struck dead by the hunters. In the "beautiful white breast displayed" by the animal, and in Mary's pain at the sight of its killing, there is a momentary, and potentially racialized identification, but the binary is lost when Child refers to the deer's "glossy brown . . . sides" (p. 89).

The complexional ruddiness that links Mary to her native cohorts here underscores the more general ways in which she is – true to the "white devil" phenomenon – metaphorically *reddened* (if not blackened) through language that emphasizes her fleshliness, her passions, and the rebellion against patriarchal rule that aligns her with the Whore of Babylon and the heathen. Thus her father accuses her of "looking back for the flesh-pots of Egypt" merely for inquiring after old friends in England (p. 9).

Child's awareness of these tropes is, however, clearly critical, as is her stance toward the patriarchalism embodied in Conant and the even more outspokenly anti-feminist John Oldham. Indeed, any express misogyny is immediately undercut in the text, and often by a male speaker. Oldham speaks of "these weaker vessels" who "are the source of every evil that ever came into the world," and is rebutted by a reference to his "care-worn and uncomplaining wife" (p. 25); he later pontificates on the vanity of "some pretty piece of Eve's flesh," and speaks of his own daughter on her wedding day as "valuable cargo" dressed in "Egyptian garments." In the latter case, it is the Governor himself who interrupts: "As for these women, it is as well to let them alone . . . It is meet they should stand by themselves . . . not to be brought under any rule whatsoever" (p. 60).

Indeed, the legitimacy of patriarchal rule comes under intense scrutiny in the novel. Unlike *Othello,* where the daughter's rebellion leads to her death at the hands of the ill-chosen spouse, in *Hobomok* the unsanctioned union directly *results* from the father's tyrannical rejection of the daughter's *prior* choice of a mate. Moreover, it is the father who is punished, in his grief and self-blame when she runs away with Hobomok, leaving her family to wonder if she has drowned herself over Charles' reported death. True, when Conant learns of her union with the Indian, he says "I could more readily have covered her sweet face with clods, than bear this" (p. 133), but the heroine's *refusal to commit suicide* at the ideologically appropriate moment – and when, indeed, the community expects it of her – strikes me as comprising the novel's boldest critique of the masculinist master narrative. Likewise, the novel's refusal to have her die at the hands of her "savage" husband – or even bear chastisement when her legitimate mate returns – proves just how far behind Child has left *Othello.*

The novel is not, of course, consistently anti-racist: Hobomok's disappearance at the end, as critics have noted, constitutes an ideologically problematic erasure. Moreover, the novel includes two "angels in the house" – Mary's mother and another exemplary Puritan wife – whose death-scenes might give a feminist critic pause. Indeed, the same reviews that expressed dismay over the inter-racialist plot praised the anonymous author for "his" skill in crafting these passages. Yet the overall radicalism of Child's novel is apparent in contrast to the "Indian tales" of her contemporaries – foremost amongst them James Fennimore Cooper who, as Karcher notes, might well have been consciously replying to *Hobomok* in his now-famous *The Last of the Mohicans* (1826), a novel that promotes "race war as the correct prototype of relations between whites and Indians" and that brutally punishes its would-be miscegenists (p. xxxv). That the latter is now enshrined on the shelves of my local Blockbuster video store – its theme song a virtual second American anthem – demonstrates once again the resilience of the master narrative. Score another one for Othellophilia.

"We are not sure that any woman in our country would outrank Mrs. Child," pronounced the *North American Review* in 1833, "Few female writers, if any, have done more or better things for our literature" (quoted in Karcher, "Introduction," p. xi). Yet who is the American woman author of her era that replaced her in cultural memory? Harriet Beecher Stowe. That American readers would prefer her sentimental, "benign," abolitionist racism to Child's amalgamationist feminism can be no surprise. And indeed, it's almost a chicken-and-egg dispute as to whether the relative conservatism of *Uncle Tom's Cabin* enabled its fame (and with it, its reputation for having "caused" the Civil War and emancipation) or whether the cause of abolition *required* a stance as conservative as Stowe's.

In the introduction to this chapter, I called *Uncle Tom's Cabin* a love-story, and I did so in all seriousness. It is the love-story not of George and Elizabeth – who are already married with a child when the book begins – but of Tom and Eva, whose love is so "star-crossed" as to be barely visible. Stowe writes, "He loved her as something frail and earthly, yet he almost worshipped her as something heavenly and divine. He gazed on her as the Italian sailor gazes on his image of the child Jesus – with a mixture of reverence and tenderness; and to humor her graceful fancies . . . was all his delight." Eva, in turn, is no "less zealous in kind offices" to him (p. 257).[7] Diane Roberts questions "the assumed sexlessness of Tom and Eva's companionship," pointing out that despite the ageing Uncle Toms of later minstrel shows, the novel depicts him as "a strong man in the prime of his life. And Eva may be prepubescent, but she is old enough to be attractive to her Byronic cousin Henrique." Building on Hortense Spillers' reading of Eva's "lush sensuality," Roberts implicates the otherwise angelic Eva in the orientalism of her surroundings – the enclosed garden within which she romps with her black playmate, ringing his neck with flowers and sitting on his knee.[8] At the height of little Eva's illness, it is Tom's job to carry her about in his arms, the image simultaneously an inter-racial, reverse-gender *pietà* and racism's worst nightmare: a blond, unresisting female body swept off her feet by a big, strong, black man.

I do not believe that the "innocent" versus "sensual" readings of Eva need contradict one another, any more than this seeming dichotomy need be resolved in regard to Shakespeare's Desdemona. Indeed, some critics have imagined Desdemona – perhaps rightly – as very young, childlike in demeanor if not literally pre-pubescent.[9] Moreover, Stowe's writing Eva as a child can be seen as calculated to make this love-story "safe" for her audiences; although her full name, Evangelina, invokes the evangelists, her nick-name recalls the epitome of the sexually "knowing" woman, Eve. As Spillers puts it: "the author invests 'Little Eva' with the desire to touch, to embrace, the forbidden, concealed like a serpent beneath a bank of flowers."[10] Underscoring the eroticism of Eva's demand of Tom's purchase, "I want him" (Stowe, p. 148), Spillers comments with dry humor, "It seems to me that Stowe dispatches the child to do a woman's job and that by doing so, she . . . spares the female for polite readers, who wanted women but not sex . . ."[11] When all's said and done, however, Eva's youth is effectively null and void, as the novel insists on Tom's own childlike quality. This is not pederasty, in the eyes of racism, but puppy-love. And what other kind of love is imaginable, between whites and blacks?

Yet even this love must be punished – perhaps to prevent its maturing into real, reproductive sex. Tom and little Eva must be sacrificed. And herein lies the best evidence that Tom and Eva constitute an Othellophile dyad. Though separated by a good chunk of text, their deaths are clearly parallel. Both go willingly and blissfully to their deaths; both die smiling. In *Uncle Tom's Cabin* the couple is sacrificed not to the cause of racism (as I've been arguing is the case in so many Othellophile legends), but to the cause of abolition – but this displacement is only possible because the eroticism is sublimated. The argument against slavery cannot go forward, can gain no support, cannot even gain an audience, unless miscegeny is ruled out a priori. Tom is already married (though, tellingly, he must be separated from his wife before meeting Eva), and "little Eva" is a child, and a dying one at that. His cradling her in his arms is their consummation.

Like Desdemona, little Eva is defined, spiritually and morally, by her complexional whiteness, linked in Tom's mind with divinity. The text harps on her "aerial grace," blonde hair, and "the spiritual gravity of her violet blue eyes." And as if the racialized language were not already over the top, Stowe clothes her perpetually in white: "Always dressed in white, she seemed to move like a shadow through all sorts of places, without contracting spot or stain; and there was not a corner or nook, above or below, where those fairy footsteps had not glided, and that visionary golden head, with its deep blue eyes, fleeted along" (pp. 143–4). Indeed, so otherworldly is this creature, that Tom equates her with "the angels that stepped out of the pages of his New Testament" (p. 144). Eva, like Desdemona, has no self-interest beyond the care of others; she is the perfect woman; she is pure charity. Eva, like Desdemona, goes to her death happily – and, more importantly, *beautifully* – and, again like Desdemona, she *returns from the dead*, haunting Tom, though lovingly and literally, the way the vengeful mulatta slave Cassy conspires to "haunt" Simon Legree by way of a white sheet. But we turn to Cassy in just a moment.

The death of Eva constitutes, indisputably, the climax of the book; as in every other Othellophile myth, the disposal of her black counterpart appears more or less an after-thought. The funerary scene is, not surprisingly, all about whiteness. The first sentence of the chapter reads "The statuettes and pictures in Eva's room were shrouded in white napkins"; the second reads "the bed was draped in white." Eva's body is, of course, "robed in one of those simple white dresses she was wont to wear when living" (p. 295), and the room is filled to bursting with white flowers (p. 296). There is the necessary touch of red, as in the roses of the soon-to-be-murdered Desdemona's breath or the strawberries on her handkerchief: "The rose-colored light through the curtains cast over the icy coldness of death a warm glow." And of course the corpse is preternaturally lovely: "there was diffused over every feature that mingling of rapture and repose" (p. 295). This is perhaps all too obvious and trite, but the white draperies do take on further significance when linked – not just to Desdemona's white bridal/death sheets ("Prithee lay on my bed my wedding sheets") and white, spotted handkerchief – but also the white sheet that enables Cassy to play ghost and drive Legree mad.

Aside from its associations with death and the spirit world, the white sheet–shroud allows Cassy – a mulatta with a "sallow" complexion – to masquerade, in effect, as little Eva – so white in life as to be described as having "transparent skin" (p. 269) and by now a *literal* ghost. Indeed, the description of Cassy's escape from the Legree house even echoes Stowe's rhapsodizing over Eva's "aerial grace" and "fairy footsteps": "some Negroes had seen two white figures *gliding* down the avenue" (p. 421; emphasis mine). But this mimicry does not mean Cassy can approximate Eva's angelic status: in fact, Legree declares Cassy the very devil (p. 401), and although Stowe goes out of her way to render her sympathetic and her aggression justified, a whiff of witch-craft (voodoo?) lingers in her power over Legree. And here the polarization of Cassy–Eva harkens to similar female juxtapositions in inter-racialist discourse: Lavinia–Tamora, Cleopatra–Ottavia, Lucy–Mina, etc. Yet the white sheet or shroud paradoxically connects the sexually "pure" child martyr to the sexually denigrated, mature slave woman. Metonymizing racial whiteness along with virginity, the sheet becomes the symbolic interface between race and sexuality: as a second skin and racial mask, Cassy's sheet is both the antithesis of Eva's "transparent" complexion and its parodic corollary, and the same is true in relation to Eva's (nominal, to follow Spillers and Roberts) sexual innocence. Like Desdemona's bridal sheets – token, in their presumably soiled state, simultaneously of virginity and its loss – the white sheet–shroud stands as objective correlative of a woman's hymen, which is to say, of her *skin*. And as fragile as this membrane is (one thinks, perversely, of Eva's "transparent skin"), it is no more fragile than a woman's cultural "whiteness" in a country where "one drop of blood" (how much does a virgin shed, when deflowered?) makes a body "black." The difference between black and white, pure and impure, proves tissue-thin. A ghostly demarcation, indeed.

According to Karen Sánchez-Eppler, "the problems of having, representing, or interpreting a body structure both feminist and abolitionist discourses," as both movements recognize "that both for women and blacks it is their physical difference from cultural norms of white masculinity that obstructs their claim to personhood."[12] White female abolitionists sexualized themselves, called attention to their embodied nature, in merely handling the theme of slavery: hence the reflex to charge them with "negrophilia." What was true of Eva's creator, Stowe, is also true of the character: her association with Tom and her fondling of him – however childish – were bound to sully her. Hence Stowe's desperate efforts to dis-flesh her; hence all the harping on her "angelic" features; hence her martyrdom. Yet the very excessiveness of Stowe's "angel in the house" rhetoric underscores the anxiety behind it. For in fact, Eva's "purity" and Cassy's carnality stand not in a binary but rather in a symbiotic relationship. As Mauri Skinfill notes, "In the South, where women were either insulated as symbols or disposed of as property, the conventions of the cult of domesticity exacerbated the conditions under which black women would by default become the locus of sexual promiscuity."[13] In light of this, white female sexual innocence begins to look less than "innocent": it begins to look almost cannibalistic.

With the "authentic ghost story" in *Uncle Tom's Cabin*, we are back to the Gothic, as explored in the last chapter. Roberts notes, "As the oriental provides *Uncle Tom's Cabin* with a means to articulate desire, the gothic provides a complementary discourse expressing the perversion of love, of order, of democracy and of the family." Roberts goes on to note, pointedly, that "as in so many gothic tales, the ghosts are women."[14] I would like to put pressure on the latter point, so resonant with the observation in Chapter 5 that in Gothic horror the monster and his victim both are female (see p. 78). What is it about women that makes them simultaneously more fleshly and more ghost-like? Clearly, we have here another literary commonplace manifesting the masculinist urge to "kill women into art" – here performed by a woman author. Spillers concludes "that the *requirements of sacrifice* . . . which Stowe enforces in the narrative's habit of pathos, seem to galvanize the murderous instincts of patriarchal, phallogocentric synthesis rather than effectively challenge them."[15] It's a harsh claim – especially considering the novel's reputation for having sparked positive social change – but then again, Lincoln himself blamed Stowe for starting a war, and what more "murderous" effect of masculinist power can one name?

On the other hand, ghosts – as opposed to angels – are victims who *will not go away.* They are oppression's nemesis and shadow. Women are ghostly, from the point of view of a "murderous" masculinist power structure – one that *still* at some level endorses the fantasy that a man has the right to kill his wife if she "cheats" on him – because *killing them does not solve the problem; you kill them, and they keep coming back.*

This is very much like white supremacy's "problem" with blacks.

The chapter on the ghost act is, perhaps gratuitously, the one place where Stowe cites Shakespeare: "The sheeted dead / Did squeak and gibber in the streets of Rome" (p. 420).[16] And Shakespeare would have loved the episode, with its *Titus*-esque black humor (pun intended) and its theatricality. Indeed the novel as a whole is highly theatrical: Stowe herself describes the book as presenting "a *living dramatic reality*" (p. 440; Stowe's italics); hence the story's popularity on stage, in minstrel shows and elsewhere. And as the grim farce of Legree's death-ravings before an imagined "stern, white, inexorable figure" (p. 421) gives way to the melo*drama* of Cassy's escape and reunion with her daughter, readers are well prepared for the theatrical metaphors in Stowe's concluding remarks. She declares, "Nothing of *tragedy* can be written, can be spoken, can be conceived, that equals the frightful reality of *scenes* daily and hourly *acting* on our shores . . ." (p. 441; emphases mine). But back to the sheets for a moment. As cartoonishly funny as we might find an adult's parading in the quintessential Hallowe'en costume, the racialized "ghost" eerily anticipates a grimmer spectacle: the theatrics of the Ku Klux Klan. Yet herein lies another irony for, like all racial drag, the KKK costume – unwittingly, for sure – parodies the racial essentialisms it holds as dogma. All cows are white at night, at a KKK rally.

We have strayed somewhat from the question of female authorship with which we began this chapter, but perhaps now, on the heels of the Child–Stowe juxtaposition, we are prepared to form some tentative conclusions (tentative in that we are not done discussing women authors). Are all female authors "black at night" from the point of view of racist-masculinist hegemony? Clearly not. The sexless and sacrificial love-story of Tom and Eva – like the mother-in-distress plot, with its sentimental-izing essentialisms about the maternal and the domestic – are a far cry from Child's brazen endorsement of female sexual agency, multiple marriage, and racial inter-breeding. Even Stowe's title betrays her invest-ment in domestic ideology: all is well in "Uncle Tom's cabin" until its patriarch is evicted (and it's worth pointing out here that the title is, legally speaking, an obfuscation: the cabin does not belong to Tom but to his master). The novel's appeal to conservative values – and its success in "selling" abolitionism – lies in its endorsement of the myth that what is "wrong" with slavery is *not* its presumption of the inferiority of the black race, and not even its treatment of human beings as chattel, but rather its failure to provide "every man his castle" – every man "his" wife, every woman her "own" child. In contrast to Stowe's sentimentalizing about hearth and home, Child gives us a heroine who runs into the forest, copulates with an Indian in his teepee, and then returns to the white settlement with a mixed-race male child to be welcomed with open arms by husband, father, and community. Of course, it is too soon to general-ize about an ideological "great divide" within the community of American women abolitionists. And in any case, as we proceed chronologically through the conversation amongst these books, it is now time to see what happened when a black man made use of Child's art.

William Wells Brown revered Shakespeare as "the world's greatest literary genius," but it was a woman and a contemporary, Child, whom he plagiarized in *Clotel*. He was also greatly indebted to Stowe. Remarking on a London performance of *Othello* starring "*Selim, an African Prince*" (in fact not a prince, but the son of an African farmer), he signals his association of Shakespeare's play with the famous abolitionist novel: "The excitement caused by the publication of 'Uncle Tom's Cabin' had prepared the public for anything in the African line."[17]

This curious notion of "Shakespearean" female abolitionist fiction (or is it "abolitionist" female Shakespearean drama?) rings true to the hybridity of Brown's *Clotel*. The central plot involving the ill-fated loves and tragic deaths of a "mulatta" slave and her daughter, derives directly from Child's short story "The quadroons," first published in 1842. Nor does Brown attempt to disguise his debt to Child: on the contrary, he lifts entire sentences, even paragraphs, verbatim from the source. Even Robert S. Levine – the editor of the most recent and authoritative edition of Brown's novel – describes Child's story as "kidnapped," though he does put the word in scare-quotes. The theoretical and cultural implications of this theft have yet, I believe, to be realized. According to the *OED*, "kidnap" came of use in the late seventeenth century, particularly in reference to the stealing of children in order to impress them into servitude in the American colonies. The editor's coolly matter-of-fact tone, plus his use of scare-quotes, suggest little sense of the irony of Brown's literary piracy. Nor is Levine alone: I am struck, reviewing the critical history of *Clotel*, by the complete lack of embarrassment on Brown's behalf in discussions of what by even nineteenth-century standards is out-and-out plagiarism.

In the case of Levine, the critical stance might even be described as enthusiastic. Brown *improves* Child's text. By cutting up the story and interspersing it with digressions both literary and polemical – bolstered by "authenticating documents" such as newspaper articles, letters, and the author's own biographical Preface – Brown reveals his source to be "overly dependent on conventional notions of race, gender, and sentiment." In other words, Brown's text is more "manly," more realistic, more interested in the socio-political context of individual suffering, while Child's remains immured in the domestic sphere and trapped by conventions of sentimentality.[18] That Brown's "authenticating machinery" is historically unreliable and inconsistent with the romance plot is not only forgivable given the nature of the genre and the worthiness of the cause; some critics find these tactics especially subversive, problematizing as they do the binary relation of natural to fictive discourse.[19] Levine goes on to contrast Brown's female characters to his literary predecessor's: "Unlike Child, Brown points to the possibilities of black rebellion, particularly among the female slaves, presenting most of the black women characters derived from 'The quadroons' as active agents who claim their rights to watch out for themselves and those they love . . ." (p. 21). Likewise Angelyn Mitchell praises Brown for crafting "female characters [who] seek freedom through heroic deeds."[20] Brown's text proves not only more rigorously masculine than Child's; it also proves more feminist.

There is some basis for the latter claim: Clotel dies attempting to escape from slavery, while Child's heroine dies passively, "of a broken heart," and seemingly in her sleep. And many readers undoubtedly appreciate Brown's breaks from sentimentality into realism and "fact." At the same time, there is something vaguely Frankensteinish about Brown's dismembering and re-stitching of Child's seamless narrative: the intactness of so much of Child's original prose produces an even more disturbing reading experience to those who know the source.

But perhaps the most striking and pregnant alteration of Child's text lies in the skin-color of its heroine: in "The quadroons," Rosaline is brown and her daughter a somewhat lighter brown, whereas Clotel is perfectly, complexionally white. Like the oxymoronic "white devil," the phrase "white slave" was designed to shock.[21] The opening scene of the novel exploits this shock-value:

The appearance of Clotel on the auction block created a deep sensation amongst the crowd. There she stood, with a complexion as white as most of those who were waiting with a wish to become her purchasers; her features as finely defined as any of her sex of pure Anglo-Saxon; her long black wavy hair done up in the neatest manner; her form tall and graceful, and her whole appearance indicating one superior to her position. (p. 87)

Brown vividly dramatizes the pandemonium that breaks out as the men scramble to out-bid one another for this beautiful female body. Saved for last in the auction "because she was the most valuable" (p. 87), Clotel's virtues are enumerated like ingredients on a soup-can, but in ascending order of value: the virtue saved for last is her chastity, which boosts her price to a presumably impressive sum of fifteen hundred dollars. As Gary Taylor has noted, the elision of slavery with prostitution here is no accident, and the titillation fostered by the spectacle of this sale of white virgin-flesh is undoubtedly Brown's point.[22] To what degree, however, is Brown cynically manipulating his white readers' prejudices – about the relative value of white women versus black, and of white virgins versus white non-virgins – and to what degree is he reinforcing them? Even Levine admits "Brown would seem to be suggesting that her tragedy is more worthy of our attention (and even more tragic) than of a dark-skinned black born into slavery" (pp. 19–20). Perhaps the assumption is that this is "okay" for a black male author, in that he could not really "believe" what he's saying, given his "natural" sympathy for women of his own race.

I want to linger on the question of chastity, which Brown's text foregrounds in a way that Child's does not, by beginning with this sensationalistic scene in which the climax is not just the sale of a virgin, but the sale *of* her virginity. Yet her chastity, though her crowning asset, is no more visible in her than the so-called "black" blood that dooms her to the auction block. That Clotel is complexionally white – if culturally "black" – makes her story more tragic (or so Brown anticipates his readers thinking). This is similar to the logic whereby the murder of an "innocent" wife is more tragic than the murder of an adulteress. Yet, as both *Othello* and *Clotel* demonstrate, these notions of purity and impurity are legal fictions; they are theoretical constructs. Iago says "Her honor is an essence that's not seen" (iv.i.16) and Othello himself admits, "I found not Cassio's kisses on her lips" (iii.iii.346). In the trial of racial and sexual purity, "ocular proof" is sometimes hard to obtain. Cut her open, and her blood will be red, regardless; we can debate ad nauseam the number of angels that danced on the pin-head of her maidenhead.

Brown's choice of a white heroine can be glossed as either conservative in playing to white prejudice – even if only strategically – or radical in deconstructing race as a biological given. But his take on sexuality is essentialist to the core, which is why, as at least one critic notes, he "can end his novel with the . . . monologic authority of high sentimentalism: a happy reunion and marriage . . ."[23] And marriage plays a key role in Brown's abolitionist rhetoric. He writes, "The marriage relation, the oldest and most sacred institution given to man by his Creator, is unknown and unrecognized in the slave laws of the United States" (p. 82). Indeed, the first four pages of the novel comprise an attack on the institution of slavery *on the sole basis* of its denial of legally valid marriages to those it subjugates. Brown complains, "Most of the slave women have no higher aspiration than that of becoming the finely-dressed mistress of some white man. And at negro balls and parties, this class of women usually cut the greatest figure" (p. 85). This begs the question of whether "this class of women" would aspire to legally binding marriages with black men, if offered the choice. Emancipation did not abolish the practice of black concubinage to rich white men. Brown, of course, could not have known this, but his logic nonetheless is open to critique.

Brown's rhetoric, however, should strike a familiar note. Placing his text in the context of the 400-year history of racial discourse, we understand that he partakes of a very old tradition – dating all the way back to Leo Africanus in 1526 – whereby female sexuality becomes the litmus-test in categorizing whole populations. The degree to which Brown blames black women – rather than the institutions that have caused their "moral degradation" (p. 84) – is of course open to debate. But the fact remains that here, as in Africanus, race somehow becomes *about* sex. Indeed, even when decrying slavery's scenes of overt brutality, sexual metaphors crop up, as when he describes the hull of a slave-ship in these terms: "men and women promiscuously, all chained two and two together, not even leaving the poor slaves the privilege of choosing their partners" (p. 51). This is followed up quickly by an anecdote about a slave who *did* escape these chains, but only to drown herself in grief over having been separated from her husband and children.

And ultimately, this is where I find Brown's text vulnerable to feminist critique. For the text is filled with black Lucreces. "I don't want, and will never have, any other man," an un-named female slave in another chapter tearfully vows (p. 104). Clotel's nieces, Ellen and Jane, choose death over "degradation" by their masters (197).[24] I do not question the emotional appeal of these moments, nor wish to "blame the victim"; I only wish to point out the way this implicates Brown in the racist-masculinist tradition that requires a female sacrifice for the building of an empire. That the empire Brown wishes to build would be first and foremost one without slavery demonstrates the more benign uses of the Lucrece paradigm. But the dead white woman remains central to his project.

One might ask, what is the alternative? How *could* Brown – or Stowe, for that matter – have imagined his slave heroine? For the answer, we turn to the work of one of his "sisters" in oppression, Harriet Jacobs, whose autobiographical narrative – interestingly enough – was edited by Child herself, after Stowe rejected it as the plot for *Uncle Tom's Cabin*. Thus Jacobs closes this "family circle" of abolitionists. In stark contrast to Brown, Jacobs presents us with a heroine who resists degradation not by suicide, but by craft, deploying as a weapon against her tyrannical and lascivious master the very thing he would degrade: her sexuality. The narrator explains that in her fifteenth year, her master, Dr. Flint, "began to whisper foul words in [her] ear."[25] From this point on, Jacobs' persona details a painfully drawn-out seduction/molestation, presenting as verbal a pattern of harassment that Anne B. Dalton suspects to have been physical.[26] Whatever the "truth," however, in the author's lived experience, the text's presentation of the *ear* as a sexualized organ recalls, not just Eve's seduction by the serpent (as Dalton points out), but also

Desdemona's seduction by Othello's "traveller's history."[27] The narrator, "Linda," continues,

Sometimes he had stormy, terrific ways, that made his victims tremble; sometimes he assumed a gentleness that he thought must surely subdue. Of the two, I preferred his stormy moods, although they left me trembling . . . He peopled my mind with unclean images, such as only a vile monster could think of. I turned from him in disgust and hatred. But he was my master. I was compelled to live under the same roof with him – where I saw a man forty years my senior daily violating the most sacred commandments of nature. (p. 470)

There is more than a touch of Prospero in this "stormy" tyrant who makes his servants "tremble," and more than a touch of Caliban too, in this "vile monster" who "people(s)" not an island but his victim's mind – when he is not literally peopling his plantation with the products of this same abuse.[28] The echoes of *The Tempest* may be accidental, but they are telling in their reversals and collapsing of binaries. Shakespeare gives us a benign if omnipotent master–father–god and a "lying slave" – member of a "vile race" – who lodges with the former until "seek[ing] to violate / The honor" of the master's "child" (1.ii.346–4). Jacobs gives us a monstrous, abusive and lascivious master and a black Miranda forced to lodge "under the same roof" and observe him "violating the most sacred commandments of nature." The Shakespearean inversions culminate in the fact that this Miranda teaches *herself* to read, only to have her master turn her literacy into another means of verbal abuse, harassing her with obscene notes, his version of Caliban's curses (after one of her many skillful evasions he hisses "Curse you!" in impotent rage [p. 504]).

Because this black Miranda has no one to protect her "honor," she does the most sensible thing: she disposes of it, and does so strategically, taking a lover who she hopes can help her in her power struggles with her master. She explains, "It seems less degrading to give one's self, than to submit to compulsion. There is something akin to freedom in having a lover who has no control over you, except that which he gains by kindness or attachment" (p. 501). She details the process that led her to this decision in painful clarity and emotional detail, appealing to her white, female audience's rational judgment and compassion rather than their prudery: "O ye happy women whose purity has been sheltered from childhood, who have been free to choose the objects of your affection, whose homes are protected by law, do not judge the poor desolate slave girl too severely!" (p. 500).

Jacobs' persona is not a passive victim but a powerfully resourceful and determined survivor. Moreover, she manifests a quality none of the women in Brown's text aspire to: she is outspoken. She actively and aggressively resists her master, Dr. Flint, and she makes no secret of her hatred of him: "How I despise you!" she declares to his face (p. 483). Even more subversively, this text gives us a heroine who not only struggles but *relishes her victories*: "I knew nothing would enrage Dr. Flint so much as the knowledge that I favored another, and it was something to triumph over my tyrant in even that small way" (p. 502). She proudly states, "My master had power and law on his side; I had a determined will. There is might in each" (p. 535). She has little patience with her grandmother's pious self-restraint: when Flint finally dies, she refuses to forgive him, simply stating, "The man was odious to me while he lived, and his memory is odious to me now" (p. 658). And her outspokenness is not limited to Flint: after her escape, she speaks out against her mistreatment by northern bigots. She concludes, "Let every colored man and woman do this, and eventually we shall cease to be trampled under foot by our oppressors" (p. 197).

Jacobs' text is also more feminist in its interest in female relationships, as opposed to "romantic" relationships between men and women. As highlighted in Child's Preface addressed to the "women of the north" (quoted earlier), the book is greatly concerned with intra-gender inter-action – particularly across racial and generational boundaries. Brown touches upon the rivalry between female slaves and their mistresses in only one sentence – "Every married woman in the far South looks upon her husband as unfaithful, and regards every quadroon servant as a rival" (Brown, *Clotel*, p. 150) – yet this arguably constitutes the main theme of Jacobs' narrative. In the second of forty-one chapters, the narrator relates a harrowing episode wherein a mistress curses the mother of her husband's "bastard" as the slave lies dying in the aftermath of childbirth. "'You suffer do you? I'm glad of it. You deserve it all, and more too,'" the jealous mistress sneers. When the slave, observing the new-born's death, says she hopes it is in heaven, the mistress retorts, "Heaven! . . . There is no such place for the likes of her and her bastard" (Jacobs, *Incidents*, p. 455). In its searchingly honest discussions of female inter-racial rivalry, the book lays bare marriage – at least in the slave-holding class – as a racist-masculinist institution that pits white women against black, ulti-mately collaborating in slavery's abuses by denying slave women potential allies against their sexually rapacious masters. The narrator notes, "The mistress, who ought to help protect the helpless victim, has no other feelings toward her but jealousy and rage" (p. 471). In an article whose title fortuitously alludes to *Othello*, Minrose C. Gwin describes this dynamic: "Powerless against a lustful husband and blind to the harsh realities of chattel slavery, the enraged wife [made a scapegoat of] the one person she *could* control, the black woman. The slave woman thus became the double victim of the two-headed monster of the slavocracy, the lecherous master and the jealous mistress."[29] Nor does Jacobs spare the latter scathing satirical commentary: "She had not the strength to superintend her household affairs, but her nerves were so strong, that she could sit in her easy chair and see a woman whipped, till the blood trickled from every stroke of the lash" (p. 453). With one deft stroke, Jacobs lays bare the hypocrisy at the heart of the cult of southern female gentility.

This is not to say the narrator shows no sympathy for the wronged southern wife. Mrs. Flint can hardly be said to deserve her sympathy, but in the following passage, "Linda" describes the plight of the white northern woman given in marriage to southern slave-owners:

The poor girls have romantic notions of a sunny clime, and of the flowering vines that all year round shade a happy home. To what disappointments are they destined! The young wife soon learns that the husband in whose hands she has placed her happiness pays no regard to his marriage vows. Children of every shade of complexion play with her own fair babies . . . Jealousy and hatred enter into the flowery home and it is ravaged of its loveliness. (p. 479)

Jacobs presents here a variation on a theme: the idyllic southern home with its flowering vines and trellises (one recalls the orientalist setting of Stowe's story of Eva and Tom), but turned dark. The theme is present also in "The quadroons" and hence in Brown's revision of the same story, but there the picturesque but unhappy home is the abode of the quadroon concubine; Jacobs, in placing the white southern mistress in the same setting, inverts expectations. Reading this passage alongside contemporary treatises on domestic architecture, Ann Gelder calls it a "critique of pastoralism as it specifically relates to domesticity."[30]

The darkened bower Jacobs makes of the southern home has great potential as a site for the *Unheimlich*: this potential comes to fruition in the story of the narrator's "escape" not out of but further *into* the domestic sphere, when she hides for seven years in a tiny crawl-space in the eaves of the house. The corollary and ideological inverse of Eliza's flight with her child gripped to her breast in *Uncle Tom's Cabin*, the self-imprisonment sequence in *Incidents* powerfully illustrates the ambivalence of domestic spaces in abolitionist texts. To the female slave – more often than not – the home is a trap, not a haven. Critics have therefore rightly described Jacobs as both "appealing to and contending with the cult of domesticity"[31] – appealing to it in her attempts to placate the moral sensibilities of her white female readers, contending with it in her negative reading of domestic space. Positing a metonymic relationship between "Jacobs' pregnant body" and the interior spaces that house it, Gelder argues,

> For Jacobs, the interiority of experience (her rape and subsequent confinement in the garret) is fact, not theory. The practice of showing spaces rather than speaking of events becomes an opportunity for Jacobs to tell her story while undermining the domestic ideology of the home as sanctified space.[32]

The Jacobs persona retreats into a coffin-like mockery of the womb metaphors surrounding the romanticized "hearth and home"; she is re-born from this space a free woman, but also disfigured from the years of confinement (and here "confinement" as euphemism for pregnancy underscores the point).[33] The domestic sphere has literally mangled her.

The novel's treatment of literal motherhood is similarly ambivalent. Speaking of her first child, the narrator admits that "its clinging fondness excited a mixture of love and pain" and that she sometimes wished for his death (p. 510). Of the birth of her second child, she says, "When they told me my new-born babe was a girl, my heart was heavier than it had been before. Slavery is terrible for men; but it is far more terrible for women" (p. 526). Interestingly, this latter quote could be plied for its ambiguity: the narrator is most likely thinking of the plight of slave women in particular, yet given what she has told us about the misery of the planta-tion wives, the absence of a racial marker seems significant. Slavery is called more than once in the narrative "the patriarchal institution": at the time "patriarchal" was a positive term, indicating a benign paternalism, and Jacobs scare-quotes the phrase for irony. But we might also read a pointed – if inadvertent – feminist comment here.

In its treatment of marriage and domesticity, *Incidents* presents a stark contrast with both Brown and his predecessor Stowe, who suggest that marriage and the patriarchal family are the antidote to slavery, rather than a comparably inegalitarian and indeed co-dependent institution. Jacobs closes her book with the following words: "Reader, my story ends with freedom; not in the usual way, with marriage" (p. 664). On the face of it, this appears a mere comment about genre, acknowledging the taste of Jacobs' female readership for melodrama and romance. But this moment in the text – like its use of the word "patriarchal" – might be pried open for feminist insight. Syntactically, the sentence suggests an antithetical relationship between "marriage" and "freedom" – an antithesis that *nothing in the book* contradicts. In retrospect, the narrator's early observation that "there is something like freedom in having a lover with no control over one" appears radically anti-marriage. This is no angel in the house talking, but rather a "madwoman" who quite literally escaped the attic.

Does marriage equal slavery? According to nineteenth-century feminists (all of whom, however, were white) the answer is "yes." Sánchez-Eppler documents the frequency with which feminist writings draw force from analogies to slavery: "marriage and property laws, the conventional adoption of a husband's name, or even the length of fashionable skirts are explained and decried by reference to woman's 'slavery' . . . At stake in the feminists' likening of women to slaves is the recognition that personhood can be annihilated and a person owned, absorbed, and un-named." Such rhetoric, however, risks perpetuating the very process it opposes, absorbing and appropriating the suffering of an entire population including men *and* women. Sánchez-Eppler concludes, "The difficulty of preventing moments of identification from becoming acts of appropriation constitutes the essential dilemma of feminist-abolitionist rhetoric."[34]

Yet Jacobs in fact *sought out* the appropriation of her autobiography by a white female author. Reluctant to tell her own story, she attempted to interest Stowe in using it as the plot for what would become *Uncle Tom's Cabin*: at the same time, she offered Stowe the services of her daughter, only to have both offers rejected.[35] That Jacobs then found and profited from Child's patronage is surely the "happy ending" to this meta-textual story of thwarted inter-racial female collaboration. Furthermore, the relationship of white female editor to black female author counters the grimmer picture of inter-racial female relations presented in the novel, and this heightens the importance of Child's appeal – in the Preface – for inter-racial female solidarity. Can we connect Child's patronage of Jacobs to her feminism? Child's phrase in her Preface "sisters in bondage" is ambiguous: we can gloss this as "sisters *who are* in bondage" or as "sisters *in their* bondage." Roberts notes that Child "insists that the white woman and the black woman make common cause instead of allowing themselves to be divided by the oppositions that delineate slave culture."[36] I would only tweak Roberts' terminology, which indicts "slave culture" as opposed to masculinist-racist power more generally. For women were pitted against women – along the lines of race, class, and sexuality – long before the advent of American slavery. Indeed, female rivalry has oiled the machine of male dominance for as long as it has existed – which is to say, forever.

What Gayle Rubin famously labeled the "traffic in women" requires that
women be divided in order to facilitate their usage in forging political
bonds between men.[37] (Interestingly, the lover of Child's "tragic mulatta"
heroine – and hence of Brown's heroine too – abandons her for a marriage
of convenience with the daughter of a white politician.) Before the particular, complexional–racial distinctions of the American slave system came to
be, those intra-gender divisions were promulgated by the cult of fairness,
and its metonymic double, the cult of chastity: hence, the Jacobs persona's
emotional appeal to her "virtuous reader[s]," strategically flattering them
for their touted modesty while also opening up a space for sympathy with
their non-virtuous (because victimized) black "sister." What Jacobs' text
could not afford to do – for fear of alienating its readers – was critique the
very notion of this "virtue," the protection of which arguably depended on
the very abuses these ladies were considered too "delicate" to behold. That
was a job for someone less vulnerable, someone who already had the public
ear, someone – in short – white. Child, in editing *Incidents* and using the
Preface to defend the author against criticism for indelicacy, had not
finished her work at what Roberts calls "redefining chastity."[38] In the final
turn in this chapter's strangely circular, if chronological, trek, we return to
Child's own vision of a truly race-less America.

A Romance of the Republic (1867) might fairly be called America's first
treatise on multiculturalism. Taking the "tragic mulatta" tradition and
rendering it tragi-comic, this novel follows the beautiful "octoroons"
Rosa and Flora, two sisters raised by their white father in ignorance of
their slave status, from another orientalist New Orleans bower, to quasi-
captivity on a tropical isle, to Italy, and finally to Boston and freedom.
The novel is checkered with Spanish and French – two other components
to the girls' ethnic mix – and chock full of references to "exotic" places
and people. Miscegeny is raised almost immediately as a theme, in the
young Flora's childish iteration of a ditty about being in love with "*un
petit blanc*" – interestingly, a "little white," gendered male. The song
signals Child's interest in the more taboo miscegenous dyad – comprising
a black woman and a white man – and references the love-story of the
dead "quadroon" mother.

In this novel, as in "The quadroons," we see an idyllic domestic space
transformed by the intrusion of slavery: the home and garden in which
the girls romped under the benevolent gaze of their father must be fled
when, after he dies, they learn that they are to be sold as slaves. Child
writes, "They went up stairs, and stood, with their arms around each

other, gazing at their once happy home"; they are afraid even to go into the garden for one last time (p. 64). When a dashing Gerald Fizgerald arrives to "rescue" the girls by buying and then "marrying" Rosa (that is, performing the ceremony despite the law's blindness to the relation), things seem to take a turn for the better, but readers distrust Fizgerald's motives from the start. Arranging the escape, he makes a telling Freudian slip – "You shall never be the property of any man but myself." She responds with outrage: "'*Property!*' she exclaimed in the proud Gonsalez tone, striving to withdraw herself from his embrace" (p. 61; Child's italics). He bumblingly apologizes, but just a few pages later we get a rather chilling glimpse of his psychology. In a passage echoing Brown's description of the sale of Clotel, Child lays bare the pornographic musings that underlie Fitzgerald's seemingly romantic impulses. Fitzgerald, awake in bed, enjoys the following fantasy:

Rosabella floated before him as he had first seen her, a radiant vision of beauty surrounded by flowers. He recalled the shy pride and maidenly modesty with which she had met his ardent glances and impassioned words. He thought of the meek and saddened expression of her face, as he had seen it in these last hurried interviews, and it seemed to him she had never appeared so lovely. He remembered with a shudder what Madame Guirlande had said about the auction-stand. He was familiar with such scenes, for he had seen women offered for sale, and had himself bid for them in competition with rude, indecent crowds. It was revolting to his soul to associate the image of Rosa with such base surroundings; but it seemed as if some fiend persisted in holding the painful picture before him. He seemed to see her graceful figure gazed at by a brutal crowd, while the auctioneer assured them that she was . . . an entirely new and perfectly sound article . . . And men, whose upturned faces were like greedy satyrs, were calling upon her to open her ruby lips and show her pearls. He turned restlessly on his pillow with a muttered oath. Then he smiled as he thought to himself that, by saving her from such degradation, he had acquired complete control of her destiny . . . (pp. 66–7)

Surpassing Brown by far in laying out the sexualized context of the sale, Child's prose underscores the complex, voyeuristic impulse that holds the fantasy in his mind's eye "as if some fiend" were forcing it on him. Roberts notes of this passage, "The implications of Rosa's 'opening' herself to other men both distresses and excites Gerald . . . If there is any degrading to be done, Gerald wants to do it himself."[39] There is more than a touch of sadism here as well: she is most "lovely" to him at her emotional worst; "her misfortunes were his triumph" (p. 67). Her object status turns him on; her hymenal intactness, the trumpeted virginity of the "article," is the icing that makes this cake irresistible. It is no wonder that, deflowered, this *rosa* loses her appeal to Gerald; sweeping her away to an isolated cottage in Nassau, he promptly begins (when he is on the island at all, that is) molesting her younger sister.

Child's text, however, does not endorse the fetishization of virginity, or the cult of female chastity of which it is a sub-set. Rosa, after losing Fitzgerald to a white wife, bears a child to him that she secretly swaps with his own legitimate child; the "changeling," left behind when she flees the island, later dies, and she is plagued with remorse. Later, a free woman in Europe with a flourishing music career, she meets a more deserving partner, and tells him his "first, fresh love . . . deserves better recompense than it could receive from a bruised and worn-out heart like mine. I can never experience the illusion of love again . . ." He replies that he is "convinced" that her "heart is noble and pure. Such natures cannot be sullied by the unworthiness of others . . ." (p. 251). Child, in celebrating a union between a "fresh" male and a "worn-out" or sexually experienced female, subverts the conventions of romance: the suitor's refusal to view Rosa as *sullied* – as, returning to the auction-block trope, un-*sound* or marred – signals the author's resistance to the cult of chastity.

Moreover, the text suggests – albeit fleetingly – that Rosa's sexuality encompasses forbidden desires beyond that of a second, more mature love. For a good fifty pages we are led to believe – and indeed her husband suspects – that she is in love with someone young enough to be her son, a dashing youth whose attentions to the seasoned but still radiant heroine make younger women jealous. The husband's suspicions (and our own) are eventually proven wrong when she confesses that the young man *is* her son (though only she knows it), thus accounting for her fevered and guilt-stricken attention to him. Though this revelation rescues – as it were – the heroine's sexual innocence, it does so retroactively and incompletely, leaving unresolved the son's unwittingly incestuous flirtation, and the jealousy of his female peers. Indeed, the revelation of young Fizgerald's status as illegitimate and racially mixed thwarts his prospect for a bride his own age – the daughter of Rosa herself, courted by him in an obvious transference of attraction – and hence sexually isolates him. The uncon-summated incest with his mother is re-cast incest with her daughter and sexual rival. The taboo is transferred from Rosa's desires to his own, just as is the stigma of her race and her sexual history. He complains, "I shall not find it easy to endure the double stain of illegitimacy and alliance with the colored race." Rosa's husband defends her thus: "Legally you are illegitimate; but morally you are not so . . . Your mother believed herself married to your father, and . . . she has proved herself a modest, pure, and noble woman" (p. 357); he goes on to praise ancestry in "the colored race" as a source of pride rather than shame and concludes, "No human being can be really stained by anything apart from his own character" (p. 358).

The idea that women – and women alone – are "stained" by sexual activity has been central to the inter-related racist-masculinist discourses epitomized by the cult of chastity and the cult of fairness. Rosa is a highly sexual protagonist, and yet Child refuses to trope her as blackened, soiled, or marked by anything other than the crimson flower that is both her namesake and the metonym for her beauty. Rosa's ardor for her first, unworthy love, the anguish with which she greets (if only forcefully to reject) his later efforts to win her back, the love she inspires in her second husband and unknowing son, and her intoxicating effect on her audiences all set her up as an erotic icon, despite her maturity and racial status.

Like Jacobs, Child gives us an outspoken heroine who triumphs in the face of oppression, a heroine who *survives*. Rejecting her first lover's excuses for his marriage to another woman, she echoes the heroine of *Incidents*: he says "You surely do not hate me?" and is answered, "No, Mr. Fitzgerald, you have fallen below hatred; I despise you" (p. 143). Rosa's sister is similarly strong-willed; rebuffing Fitzgerald's advances, she objects more strongly to his calling her "*ma petite*" than to the embrace itself: "'I am no longer a child,' she says. Eventually she escapes Nassau and Fitzgerald's harassment, leaving him to wonder whether she has "committed suicide . . . or ha[s] been drowned" (p. 111). Again, as in *Hobomok*, the old Lucrecian myths are invoked only in order to be cut down. These women, Child seems to imply, are too smart to die. In this respect the text manifests a political consciousness vastly distant from the sentimental conventions of "The quadroons." This is an author, in short, who has come of age as a feminist.

I return to the question: are all female authors "black at night"? Spillers takes issue with the claim that *Uncle Tom's Cabin* was written "'by, for, and about women' . . . [as] 'woman,' here and elsewhere . . . so elides with a *revoked* adjectival marker named 'white' that we barely notice." According to Spillers, the black women in the novel – as opposed to the "mulatta" heroine Eliza, who can pass for white – are "ciphers . . . granted *no* vocality."[40] Yet, as much as my reading of Child's amalgamation novels stresses their radical take on race and gender roles, her work is open to a similar critique. As Jean Fagan Yellin puts it, "Although proposing miscegenation as the solution to the American race problem, *A Romance of the Republic* colors the multiracial American family not from white to black, but only from white to beige."[41] Roberts concurs: ". . . In order to get her white readers to identify with her heroines . . . their blackness must be hidden, like a gothic secret, almost metaphorical." She notes that Child, despite her interest in miscegeny, shies away from it when constituted by a black man's union with a white woman.[42] Even Stowe could imagine such an embrace – albeit in the sexless figures of a dying white girl and a castrate Uncle Tom.

On the other hand, the *Othello* pattern as explored elsewhere in American literature leaves much to be desired. While Child and Jacobs were crafting their abolitionist texts, *Othello* parodies flourished on American stages. These black-face performances inevitably capitalize on stage "nigger English" and transform the murder scene into a most disturbing kind of slapstick. In one such burlesque, Desdemona and Othello sing a duet to the tune of "Dixie" that concludes "I'll love you dearly all my life, / Although you are a nigger." Entering the final scene with a black eye, Desdemona vows, "I really think Othello must be mad; / That was the hardest thump I ever had. / Just one day married, and to cut this figure – /But I'll have satisfaction on that nigger . . ."[43] When Othello threatens to kill her she defies him in a way that the original could not have conceived:

> DESDEMONA: I won't die.
> OTHELLO: Yes, you will.
> DESDEMONA: I say you won't; and you can't kill me –
> OTHELLO: Damn me, if I don't. *(Bus. with pillow, &c.)*[44]

Oddly enough, it takes a racist parody to imagine a Desdemona with a little fight in her. She does die, of course, and the ho-hum way in which the stage directions dispatch her – by way of an et cetera! – underscores the genre's connection to the casual brutality of lynch-thinking. But I wish to linger a moment on the counter-intuitive theoretical linkage between this heroine who says "I won't die" and Child's feminist inter-racialist heroines in *Hobomok* and *Romance of the Republic*: heroines who survive and triumph. The connection, I maintain, does not damn Child by association with racism any more than it marks the crude Shakespeare parody with feminist sensibilities. Rather, the parallels underscore the vexed and knotty relationship between the master narrative with its roots in Shakespeare and the feminist-abolitionist counter-narrative (if indeed such a rubric is accurate).

The minstrel Othellos themselves spawned adaptations, such as Jim "Crow" Rice's 1846 *Otello*, the only version of the story other than Child's to grant its miscegenous lovers a child. Rice's vision of this theoretical offspring is confounding in its implications: the child's face is painted half white, half black. Insofar as Rice tolerates – even, bizarrely, celebrates – the mixed-race son of Desdemona and Othello (there is no threat of harm to him, as in *Titus Andronicus*), this is a radical revision of Shakespeare; insofar as the child is visually monstrous, Rice's parody is just as racist as the rest. And there are more surprises yet. The ending grants its hero what might even be viewed as a moment of enlightenment: in lieu of Shakespeare's pre-suicide self-eulogy, Otello observes that "If his wife hab but been black, / Instead of white, all had been right / And she wouldn't hab got de sack."[45] In W. T. Lhamon's reading, this is Otello's realization "that a whole social pattern nested and determined Iago's manipulation," a moment of insight that inspires him not to suicide, but to resignation.[46] As he obediently offers to turn himself in ("So, now, if it please your will, / I'll go to de Treaden Mill"), his murdered wife miraculously *"comes to life and pops up"* and all characters join in a dance.[47] The chorus sings:

> Then dance and sing
> Till the whole house ring,
> And never more his wife he'll smother.
> And, if all right tomorrow night,
> We'll have this wedding over.[48]

What are we to make of this extraordinary mixture of racist caricature, morbid joking about domestic violence, and pro-amalgamationist comic sympathy? It might help to know a bit about the actor's preferred role: that of Jim Crow – a black-face trickster figure Lhamon sharply distinguishes from the system to which his name eventually attached. Rice, a poor white from a New York slum, might very well be called a nineteenth-century Eminem,[49] presenting to mixed-race and largely low-class audiences a kind of *anti*-Othello: "With Jim Crow facing them, Othello suddenly looked preferable, and the New York literary senators found new missions for their general. Therefore, throughout his career, there were reasons why Rice avoided playing *Othello*." And when he finally acted the role – naming it for the operatic version – he did so as much to mock the (racist), elitist literary convention as to mock black culture itself.[50]

What is the difference between mockery and mimicry? When is imitation derisive, and when is it emulative? These are knotty questions, and I don't propose a definitive answer here. That Rice's Jim Crow persona and his *Otello* faded in cultural history – that the former was absorbed into institutionalized racism and the latter into Othellophilia – seems to place

Figure 4.1. Johann Moritz Rugendas, *Voyage pittoresque dans le Brésil* (Paris, 1827–35), part 4, plate 1: "Nègres à fond de calle." Courtesy of the National Library of Jamaica.

this working-class pop hero closer to Child/Jacobs than to Browne/Stowe on the critical crux that organizes this chapter. And indeed, Rice's last great role – that of Uncle Tom – was similarly co-opted when Stowe re-vamped him as a toady to white power.

On the other hand, contrasting a minstrel show to a sentimental novel may not be entirely fair, given the rules governing genre. Parody and sentimentality work at opposite poles: the first aims to excite laughter, the latter to produce tears. Politically neutral themselves, either can be politi-cized: burlesque may ridicule the ruling class, a sentimental tale can rouse abolitionist sympathy. And here we arrive at another critical impasse, the place where gender and genre (in some languages the same word) inter-sect. It was women authors in the nineteenth century who excelled in sentiment: perhaps that is why *Clotel* is so self-conscious about genre, so determined to prove – by way of its journalistic and polemical inserts – that it is not romance, that it is not sentimental fiction. And this may be, indeed, the cause of its failure as a coherent work of art.

Another issue here is how to draw artistic materials from so *ugly* an environment as slave-holding America, and render them palatable to one's audience. And perhaps here a glance across disciplines might yield insight about the sentimental tradition in abolitionist literature. Johann Moritz Rugendas' pictorial exploration of slavery in all its Gothic fascination, *Voyage pittoresque dans le Brésil* (1827–35), is peopled with semi-naked Africans, as in this one image, purportedly depicting the hold of a slave-ship (Figure 4.1). Rugendas states in the volume, "An artist could not be allowed to depict such scenes unless he softened them as much as possible."[51] One glance at the image, and you'll say, "Indeed!" This slave-ship more closely resembles the deck of a *Royal Caribbean* cruise-liner than the sardine-can interior of the slavers grimly mapped out in abolitionist treatises. The slaves are well-fleshed, in the peak of health if not obvious contentment, lolling about like folks on a topless beach: two women even look as though they are sunbathing, their arms folded behind their heads, knees parted in either careless languor or deliberate seduction. There is ample space, some folks have blankets, and food is being distributed. The chains are barely visible, consigned to the shadowy margins of the image, and you have to look very closely before you note that the African being carried by two white sailors – only his torso and head visible – might be dead.

What does this image tell us about the making-into-art of real-life brutality? Well, that it's difficult, to say the least. That artists – whether literary or visual – are trained to deploy certain conventions predicated on pleasing the esthetic tastes of their audiences. Hence, melodrama; hence the focus on the tragic mulattas' (European) beauty; hence the eroticized slave-markets of modern films like *Roots* and *Amistad*, where people who survived the debilitating depredations of the Middle Passage miraculously emerge as oiled and muscular black beauties.[52]

At the same time, this disturbingly beautiful image might be placed on a continuum with the disturbingly *ugly* Shakespeare burlesques touched on above. Burlesque by definition subverts esthetic convention, aiming for the laughter released by observing human flaws in exaggerated form. For all their artificiality, the slave-figures in the Rugandas illustration excite sympathy – however detached and patronizing – in a way caricatures of Othello (or, for that matter, "Desdemony") do not. The intervention of the more "feminine" sentimental literary genres into the debates on slavery, hence, was one step in the right direction. Even Stowe, in the eyes of white supremacy, was a devil in petticoats.

CHAPTER 5

Handsome devils: romance, rape, racism, and the Rhet(t)oric of darkness

> Why, she's a liar to the end! Where is she? Not *there* – not in heaven
> – not perished – where? . . . Catherine Earnshaw, may you not rest
> as long as I am living! You said I killed you – haunt me then!
>
> Emily Brontë, *Wuthering Heights*

I first read Emily Brontë's *Wuthering Heights* at my mother's prompting, when I was fourteen years old. "It's so romantic!" she rhapsodized. I came back perplexed and disappointed. "Mom," I complained, "they get *one kiss!*" Margaret Mitchell's *Gone with the Wind* was more to my adolescent taste: Scarlett, at least, gets *ravished* (I did not know that the word meant rape). Unfortunately it took 929 pages to get there, and in between one had to trudge through all the tedious pages on the Reconstruction. I like to think that I only skimmed that section – hence my complete shock, when re-reading the novel as an adult, to discover Mitchell's defense of the Ku Klux Klan on p. 647.

When I ask my students to list inter-racialist stories they know of, they speak of *Othello* and *Pocahontas* and Spike Lee's *Jungle Fever*. They never name *Wuthering Heights*, the love-story of Catherine and the "gipsy brat" Heathcliff. I too missed the racialized status of Heathcliff, taking the gipsy references as metaphorical (what was a gipsy anyway? Someone in color-ful rags, who told fortunes).[1] Re-reading the novel in light of my work on Othellophilia, I was stunned at how consistently the text *blackens* him. Other scholars have picked up on this: the cover of Christopher Hey-wood's 2002 edition bears a portrait of Ira Aldridge in the role of Othello, and the introduction cites Shakespeare's play, Behn's *Oroonoko,* and anti-slavery literature as sources.[2] The young Heathcliff, woefully contrasting his looks with the blue-eyed, blond, rich Edgar Linton, is comforted with these words: "A good heart will lead you to a bonny face . . . if you were a regular black . . . Who knows but your father was Emperor of China, and your mother an Indian Queen . . . ?" (p. 151).[3] Critics do not agree on "what" Heathcliff "is" – to use one of the more tactless phrasings of the question to which my own ambiguous ethnicity so often subjects me. Yet pinpointing Heathcliff's ethnicity, as a way of dissecting a blackness that is so frequently treated as metaphorical, seems beside the point. Whether designated gipsy, simianized Irish, or Creole,[4] Heathcliff's dark-complexioned Otherness signifies in excess of itself. Dana Medoro argues, "As the fetish object of the narrators, Heathcliff both drives the plot and ruptures its surface. Although Lockwood, Nelly, and Isabella attempt to accommodate him into their frames of reference, they are never able to fill all the gaps. Heathcliff remains elusive . . ."[5] In this sense, Brontë's novel really has nothing to do with race.

Then what is it doing in this book? you might ask. Perhaps that "nothing to do with" over-states the point; I would argue that Heathcliff's blackness has less to do with race than with sex, with the sexuality of the heroine. Defending the genre of romance in 1992 against the by-then clamorous disapproval of feminist critics, Jayne Anne Krenz cited *The Taming of the Shrew* as supplying a classical prototype; Laurie E. Osborne has since substantiated romance's ongoing "romance" with Shakespeare.[6] Heywood's lineage of Shakespeare–Behn–Brontë, therefore, calls for completion in reference to more recent texts, particularly in the romance genre. And this returns me to the juxtaposition I formed when a teenager, pillaging the "classic" romance novels for the lessons in adult sexuality deprived me by my Catholic upbringing: the juxtaposition between the thwarted passion of Catherine and Heathcliff, and the smouldering if destructive sexual chemistry between Mitchell's famous Scarlett and Rhett.

As it turns out, the marked difference between the erotic content of these novels belies the many ways in which they tell the same story. And that story owes more to *Othello* than at first meets the eye. Compare, for instance, this chapter's epigraph to that which opens this book ("She's like a liar gone to burning hell: / 'Twas I that killed her"). This chapter argues that *Wuthering Heights* recalls Shakespeare's tragedy in its inter-racialist plot, its language linking blackness to the demonic, and its collapsing as one unit the inter-racial dyad – even in the seeming absence of a consummation. Mitchell re-writes *Wuthering Heights,* sublimating the inter-racialism (Rhett is only metaphorically black or gipsy) and the Gothicism (Rhett is only metaphorically a devil), while making the eroticism more overt and casting the consummation as a literal rape – even though no one calls it that.

In an infamous scene in Mitchell's novel, Scarlett gets attacked by a big black man who rips her bodice open in search of (presumably) hidden valuables. In another infamous scene in the same novel, Rhett sweeps a protesting Scarlett into his arms and carries her struggling body upstairs to the bedroom. The two scenes are related. Despite Rhett's (surprisingly) "heroic" act of riding out with the Klan to revenge the assault, the black assailant – Scarlett's bodice-ripper, if you will – is really his alter-ego, as Rhett proves when he later rapes her. That Scarlett "enjoys" the rape does not re-define the act as *not* rape but rather sets forth this heroine as the quintessential "scarlet woman" that her name so unsubtly invokes. Playing on a coinage of Catherine MacKinnon's, I will call this figure the (un)rape-able woman: a woman whose sexual status – in the eyes of masculinist discourse – renders her rape immaterial or theoretically re-dundant.[7] The direct inverse of Shakespeare's Lucrece, she is the woman who outlives her chastity, the "bad example" that must be punished because she would not punish herself.

Much feminist ink has been spilled on the romance novel – its "spirited" heroines, its "tall, dark, and handsome" heroes, and its habit of casting sex between them as rape-like if not "really" rape. By reframing these old debates in terms of the evolving discourse of inter-racialism, I hope this chapter will shed new light on both the genre of romance and the complicated issues it raises, implicating white female authors in what I have been calling Othellophilia. Finally, looking at the counter-narrative embodied in a black female author's challenge to Mitchell's classic – Alice Randall's nearly censored parody *The Wind Done Gone* – we end with a sobering acknowledgment of the ideological underpinnings of certain themes in white female fantasy. Romance as a genre is often dismissed as harmless escapism for its nearly 100 percent female readers: the feminist critique aims to expose the genre's complicity in that which women *would* escape – masculinist, or here racist-masculinist, oppression.

But romance readers (and its authors) are also predominantly white. This prompts a cynical question. If romance fans looked at every "hand-some devil" as a black man in disguise, would they be so easily "swept away"? Perhaps the brave ones. But it might also be worth asking: escape *from* what, and *into* what, and at what cost? And in a genre so defined by nostalgia, how *can* one escape history?

One thing and one thing only is clear about Heathcliff's racial status: he is not white. Readers can take the text's word for it, and call him a gipsy (by far the most consistent racial marker – used five times – and one that Heathcliff himself never rejects) or they might comb the text for instances of what Toni Morrison would call Africanism (in, for instance, the language of "acquisition" surrounding his adoption into the Earnshaw family, and his semi-slave status thereafter). For the sake of our analysis, it hardly matters "what" he "is"; as I've said before, Othellophilia, as the collective fantasy of a racist-masculinist culture, is never *about* real black people. What is more pertinent, and more obvious, is the way Brontë fetishizes his coloring: his "black eyes" appear in the very first paragraph, he is introduced in Nellie's account as "a dirty, ragged, black-haired child" (p. 129), and he scarce makes an appearance in the text without a reference to his dark skin, black hair, black eyes, and thick, black brows.[8] Indeed, six times characters call him "black" (pp. 146, 206); speak of "his own black father" (p. 268); comment on his "black tempers" (p. 133), his "black countenance" (p. 271), or the "blackness" of his "features" (p. 275); and twice he is called "blackguard" (pp. 146, 208). He may not be, in Nellie's terms, "a regular black" – that is, a sub-Saharan African – but neither, according to some critics, is his predecessor, "the Moor of Venice."

Is the pun buried in the story's setting on the *moors* an accident? Probably. But linguistic accidents yield theoretical fruit. Catherine herself likens Heathcliff to the landscape for which he is named: "Heathcliff is: an unreclaimed creature . . . without cultivation: an arid wilderness of furze and whinstone . . . he's a fierce, pitiless, wolfish man" (p. 196). His association with wilderness and wild animals like wolves and tigers points up a separate trope threaded through the novel, though one with similar racial inflections: the rhetoric of savagery. And here is the first of many ways in which Catherine partakes of Heathcliff's nature: their childhood on the moors symbolically binds them, as indicated by Nellie's comment that "they both promised to grow up rude as savages" (p. 138). I will talk about Catherine in detail below: I note this conjunction as the first reference to Heathcliff's savagery, followed up by references to his "savage ignorance" (p. 185); his "half-civilized ferocity" (p. 189); his "savage feeling" (p. 363); and, finally, his description as howling, at Catherine's death, "like a savage beast" (p. 262).

This is all fairly obvious and has been noted by others. Things get more interesting, however, when we begin to trace the rhetoric of demonism in the novel – along with its offshoots in the language of cannibalism, vampirism, and necrophilia – and note the way in which this language echoes early modern inter-racialist discourse of the "devil and his dam" variety. Hence Heathcliff's introduction to the Earnshaw family: "You must take it e'en as a gift of God; though it's as dark almost as if it came from the devil" (p. 129). This is the first and last suggestion of a duality in Heathcliff's nature; as soon as the indulgent father Earnshaw dies, Heathcliff becomes all devil. He is called "imp of Satan" (p. 132), "divil of a gipsy" (p. 180), "evil beast" (p. 201), "Satan" (p. 207), "hellish villain-fiend" (p. 232), "serpent" (p. 240), "the devil himself" (p. 362), "that devil" (p. 376), "that devil, Heathcliff" (p. 379), and "like the devil" (p. 381). He is twice called "fiend" (pp. 246, 257) and "monster" (pp. 246, 266), and he himself concedes, on his death-bed, that he is seen as a "fiend" and "worse than the devil" (p. 428); of his death, one opines that "Th' divil's harried off his soul" (p. 429). Demonic metaphors attach themselves to Heathcliff's features; his eyes are "black fiends" and "devil's spies" (p. 149). His own wife wonders, "Is he a devil?" (p. 230), and his adopted son Hareton – likened here to a "goblin" – calls him "Devil daddy" and "devil" (p. 204). People speak of "his devilish nature" (p. 266), his "fiendish prudence" (p. 267), his "fiend's existence" (p. 270), his "fiendish laugh" (p. 313), and his "evil disposition" (p. 316). Indeed, even the few people who defend him do so in reference to the demonic: Catherine, after describing him as "wolfish," adds, "he is not a fiend" (p. 196), the second Catherine echoes her with "You're not a fiend" (p. 368), and Hareton will stand by him even "if he were the devil" (p. 415). In the conclusion, the narrator muses "is he a ghoul, or a vampire?" saying she has "heard of such incarnate demons" (p. 423).

I have resisted describing this language as tropic, because it's unclear that we are not to take it as literal. Indeed, the novel never resolves Isabella's bewildered question, "What is Heathcliff? Is he a man?" (p. 230), or disproves Earnshaw's prediction that when Heathcliff dies, "hell shall have his soul!" and will thus "be ten times blacker" (p. 235). Heathcliff himself acknowledges cannibalistic or vampiric impulses: "I would have torn his heart out, and drunk his blood!" (p. 243). The vampire imagery is elsewhere reinforced by references to his "sharp cannibal teeth" (p. 271) and "sharp white teeth" (p. 429), and by the warning that "he'll tear you with his teeth" (p. 275).

The question of Heathcliff's vampiric leanings brings us to the scene I argue represents the consummation of the "love-story" – Heathcliff's digging up Catherine's grave and re-opening of her coffin. This is not, as others have treated it, *potential* necrophilia: it *is* necrophilia. It is *raptus* in the original classic sense of seizure of a woman's body, with or without sexual congress. And in fact, necrophilia might even be called the ultimate rape: there can be no consent, express or implied, where there is no will. Whether Heathcliff sexually penetrates the corpse is immaterial (though it's tempting to gloss as sexual his admission that he "gave some ease to [him]self"). The act of coitus itself has always been – in a sense – symbolic rather than constitutive of rape as the *taking* of a woman's body. In the medieval patriarchal paradigm, *raptus* was a property crime against the husband or father: hence, a woman could collaborate in her *raptus* by eloping, like Desdemona (or Brontë's Isabella).[9] But modern rape might also be considered a property crime – against the victim herself. It's about one's ownership of one's "own" body, one's "proper" (*propre*) self.

This is the second *raptus* committed by Heathcliff. The first one is both *raptus* in the classic sense and rape in the modern sense: Heathcliff cynically and coldly convinces the naïve Isabella to elope with him, only to abuse her. We know from the bridegroom himself that she cried the morning after her wedding: the abuse – emotional if not physical – probably began right away. Whether or not the wedding-night sex was rape, we cannot assume any sex following that was consensual, and Isabella's pregnancy implies that they copulated more than once. Isabella hates and, moreover, fears Heathcliff, yet she has a child by him. The evidence is conclusive: Heathcliff is a rapist.

Where there is rape, there is a rape-able woman – or, in my terms, an (un)rape-able one. And it occurs to me that this is the one component of Othellophilia so far missing in Brontë's text: the language of whoredom. Yet it is there, if not as pervasive as in *Othello*. The first instance is in Nellie's own voice. Isabella's return after her bruising nuptials presents her a changed woman: "So much had circumstances altered their positions, that he would certainly have struck a stranger as a born and bred gentleman, and his wife as a thorough little slattern!" (p. 243). The *OED* defines "slattern" as "A woman or girl untidy and slovenly in person, habits, or surroundings; a slut," and cites texts from 1639 to 1883 to support this definition. One finds an almost identical definition for the earliest occurrence of "slut," a sense still operative in the late nineteenth century: "A woman of dirty, slovenly, or untidy habits or appearance; a foul slattern." Overlapping chronologically with this seemingly asexual sense of the word "slut" one finds "A woman of low or loose character; a bold or impudent girl; a hussy, jade." By "slattern" Nellie does not seem to mean the latter; it is less clear, however, what Heathcliff means a mere three pages later when he says of his miserable bride "She degenerates into a mere slut!" (p. 245). Heathcliff is the only character who uses this word, and he uses it twice more, in reference to Isabella (again) and Catherine the younger, who are, respectively "wicked slut" (p. 302) and "insolent slut" (p. 414).

Curiously, the original Catherine herself is never subject to this stigmatizing language – Brontë does not even let us know she is pregnant (by her racially and socially legitimate mate) until after she dies giving birth, and even then the birth is reserved for a separate chapter, leaving her death-bed drama strangely virginal. Indeed, there's more than a touch of Ophelia in her mad ravings over her pillow, her plucking of feathers from it as Ophelia plucked wild-flowers: "this is a wild duck's . . . this is a pigeon's . . . And here is a moor-cock's . . ." (p. 216). Perhaps Brontë spares this symbolic virginity because Catherine's passion for Heathcliff is not consummated during her life. Catherine the second, as her daughter *and* her re-incarnation, of necessity bears the mark of her mother's sexuality, having entered the world through the latter; it thus makes sense that Heathcliff calls her names like "slut" and (another one) "witch" (p. 381), and that even the phlegmatic Lockwood remarks, "She's a beauty . . . but not an angel" (p. 392). The same may be said of the ghost of Catherine, whom Lockwood calls "little fiend" and "wicked little soul" (p. 119) and whom Heathcliff himself calls a "devil" (p. 383).

And this moment is significant, replicating as it does the mutual demonism that defines the inter-racial dyad. In both veins of rhetoric – the demonic and the savage – Catherine is racialized alongside Heathcliff, just as physically she is linked to him through her black eyes. Nellie calls Catherine a "wild, wicked slip" (p. 134) and "a wicked, unprincipled girl" (pp. 175–6); Isabella calls her "a vixen" and "a tigress" (p. 200); she will later call Heathcliff a tiger too (p. 240). We've already glanced at the way in which Catherine's childhood on the moors alongside Heathcliff rendered her "rude as" a savage – a rearing in "absolute heathenism" (p. 142), producing a "wild, hatless little savage" who cannot help but "grow wild" (p. 145). On her death-bed, Catherine rues her taming as Linton's ladylike wife: "I wish I were a girl again, half savage and hardy, and free" (pp. 219–20). In her ravings she threatens "I shall get wild" (p. 210), and she follows through with her threat: at one point Nellie observes, with horror, a vampiric trickle of blood on her lips (p. 212). True, at one point Catherine declares "I'm an angel!" (p. 193), but this is clearly self-ironizing; the only other whiff of an "angel in the house" is Nellie's description of Catherine's smiling corpse: "no angel in heaven could be more beautiful" (p. 259). This is followed immediately, however, by Heathcliff's "May she wake in torment!" and his insistence that she is "not in heaven" (p. 262). And, indeed, Lockwood's dream has prepared us – from the first pages of the novel – to believe him.

"I am Heathcliff!" (p. 175) – what reader can forget the line? And herein lies the crucial peg to our reading of the text as Othellophile. Heathcliff and Catherine are one: "He is more myself than I am" (p. 173), she says, and then asks, rhetorically, "Who is to separate us?" (p. 174).

Here she echoes Heathcliff in an earlier scene, as he scoffs at the Lintons for quarreling "divided by a whole room" (p. 140). Her death underscores the collapse of their identities: "You have killed me" (p. 253), she says; "You have killed yourself" (p. 255), he says. Compare the sequence to *Othello*: "Who has done this deed?" – "Nobody. I myself. Farewell" – "'Twas I that killed her." Years later, in digging up her corpse, Heathcliff imagines "dissolving with her" in the earth (p. 382); he even makes preparations to do so, removing one side of her coffin so that he can – as it were – crawl in, from his own coffin. The grave's a fine and quiet place and these two, I think, do there embrace.

But Heathcliff has work to do before he can enjoy this union in death. He first must revenge his wrongs on the Linton family, largely through its women. Anyway, that's what Heathcliff *thinks* he is doing, in tormenting Isabella and the second Catherine: in my reading, however, there's a disjunction between Heathcliff's express purpose – revenge on his dead rival Edgar through his sister and daughter – and the *novel's* purpose for him, which is to revenge, or rather punish, the heroine for her illicit desire for *him*. Because Catherine dies midway through the novel, Heathcliff must seek an alternative Desdemona in Isabella. This proxy figure allows the racially marked member of the inter-racial dyad to fulfill his role as executor of the cultural punishment for breaking the miscegeny taboo. (Heathcliff, remember, is what father Earnshaw brought Catherine home from London *instead of a whip* – a whip, I would argue, that can as easily be turned on herself.)[10] And indeed, Isabella's initial suicidal impulses reflect the model. Fortunately, though, Brontë lets her break free: "I've recovered from my first desire to be killed by him. I'd rather he killed himself!" (p. 266). When she escapes, he then turns his violence on Catherine the younger, linked to Isabella not just by family likeness, but in his calling her, like his estranged wife, "slut."

The topic of family likenesses turns us to the one crux in this analysis: Heathcliff's biological son. The logic of an inter-racialist reading would call for racialized offspring for the gipsy Heathcliff. But Linton is, as his name indicates, one hundred percent Linton, composed of all the (racial) family weaknesses magnified: effeminacy, pallor, sickliness, petulance. Heathcliff even suggests – echoing Shakespeare's Aaron – that this "whey-faced whining wretch" might have *literally* "white blood" (p. 302). It's as if Isabella gave birth to her own brother's son. What happened to the inter-racialism? One explanation is simple: Brontë lost heart. She simply could not allow Heathcliff – "a nameless man" himself (p. 194), outside the system of patrolineage – to sire a "gipsy brat" of his own.

Another explanation is offered in Heywood's introduction to the novel, where he places Heathcliff at the far end of the Spanish racial circuit: "The stages were termed mulatto, quadroon, octoroon, mustee, mustefino, and white. In that circuit of seven generations, all partners except the first must be white" so that the end result, the child of the mustefino, was classified as racially white. "As the father of a blonde girl's white child, Heathcliff occupies the rank of *mustefino,* the last black position in that Creole circuit."[11] Viewed in this light, Heathcliff's role in the novel is purgative of Catherine's miscegenous desire for him. It lets the novel have its ideological cake and eat it too.

In any case, all is well at Wuthering Heights once Heathcliff is dead. And his death, typically, mirrors Catherine's. Both Catherine and Heathcliff kill themselves through self-starvation, sleep deprivation, and exposure to the elements through an open window. Both die smiling, though Heathcliff's smile provokes no pious meditations in Nellie: noting that ". . . he seemed to smile," she tries to close his eyes "to extinguish . . . that frightful, life-like gaze of exultation" (p. 429). Her horror at failing to do so recalls the abjection of Othello and Desdemona's corpses, indistinguishably hideous in death: "This object poisons sight, / Let it be hid." That Heathcliff and Catherine are rumored to haunt the moors hereafter may be their final triumph over the forces that separated them in life. Or it may be, merely, the author's attempt to punish them further.

"How black was Rhett Butler?" the title of an essay by Joel Williamson memorably asks. The author makes a compelling case for a lost predecessor for *Gone with the Wind* (1936) in a manuscript that Mitchell – after criticism from her husband – burned. This manuscript told the story of Europa Carmagin: a white woman in love with a mulatto.[12] The precursor to Rhett Butler *was,* Williamson suggests, a black man, and the template for *Gone with the Wind* was a story about miscegenation. Williamson notes, "One of the most striking paradoxes in American literature is that Margaret Mitchell was born into a social universe that was obsessed with blackness, and yet she wrote a novel that seemed so totally white." Yet this might not have been the case were it not for her husband's influence; his objection to Mitchell's previous project was specifically the miscegenous story-line.[13] Mitchell whitewashed Rhett, it seemed, to get him past the censors.

Perhaps whitewashing is the wrong idiom: the only thing white about Rhett is his teeth. Even more so than with Heathcliff, however, his complexional darkness is less a racial marker than a signifier of animal sexuality. Indeed, it would not be an exaggeration to say that Rhett, for Scarlett, *is* sex, embodied. The first thing we are told about him is that his stare arouses the heroine. Let's look at his first appearance in the novel:

. . . Her eyes fell on a stranger . . . staring at her in a cool impertinent way that brought her up sharply with a mingled feeling of feminine pleasure . . . and an embarrassed sensation that her dress was too low in the bosom. He looked quite old, at least thirty-five. He was a tall man, and powerfully built. Scarlett thought she had never seen a man with such wide shoulders, so heavy with muscles, almost too heavy for gentility. When her eye caught his, he smiled, showing animal-white teeth below a close-clipped black mustache. He was dark of face, swarthy as a pirate, and his eyes were as bold and black as any pirate's appraising a galleon to be scuttled or a maiden to be ravished . . . There was undeniably a look of good blood in his dark face. It showed in the hawk nose over the full red lips, the high forehead and the wide-set eyes.[14]

The progression of this description is telling: from his stare, to her bosom, to his mouth – with its *animal*-white teeth (an odd compound, surely: one thinks of dental care as distinctly human) – to the *black* mustache, to the *dark, swarthy* face, back to the now explicitly *black* eyes, and then to the notion of rape. Rhett's dark coloring is, immediately and henceforth, inextricably bound up with his sexuality – or, more accurately, with *Scarlett's* – and with the possibility of sexual violence.

Indeed, the fetishizing of Rhett's coloring even precedes his entry into the narrative. The black hair and mustache make a solo appearance – curiously disembodied, like the Cheshire cat's grin – as early as p. 11 of this 1000-plus-page novel. Scarlett says, "I don't like Mammy Jincy's fortunes . . . She said I was going to marry a gentleman with jet-black hair and a long black mustache, and I don't like black-haired gentlemen." The presumably black, though perhaps Creole, fortune-teller exoticizes Rhett by association in a way that recalls *Wuthering Heights*, wherein Heathcliff is likened to the "son of a fortune-teller" (Brontë, *Wuthering Heights*, p. 44). Body-hair is, of course, an ever-ready sexual symbol: it might not even be too much of a stretch to theorize the mustache as alluding not so much to the male but the *female* genitals, by its proximity to the mouth. And Mitchell does make a point of telling us Rhett has a lot of body-hair: "His shirt, open to the waist, showed a brown chest covered with thick black hair" (p. 846).

Close-reading for complexional references, I used a whole pack of Post-its: the adjective "black" or "dark" occurs no fewer than forty-five times in reference to Rhett's hair, eyes, mustache, profile, head, face, or brow(s). His face is called "swarthy" or "brown" fourteen times, and his white or flashing teeth or smile appear more than half a dozen times in the text. In addition to harping on Rhett's complexional darkness, Mitchell repeatedly tropes him as black: he is thrice called the "black sheep of the Butler family" and thrice called "blackguard" (once, "the blackest of blackguards"); he is "a clever black hearted wretch" (p. 243) and bears more than one moral "black mark"; in the dark his body is a "black bulk" (p. 922); he rides a "wild black stallion" (p. 224); and when Mitchell mentions his clothing at all, it is black. Beyond this, one cannot miss the tropes of savagery, foreign-ness, and exoticism: he has a "peculiarly lithe, Indian-like gait" (p. 179) that is elsewhere described as the "springy stride of a savage" (p. 371) and a "light Indian-like tread" (p. 612); he is likened to "a pagan prince" (p. 371) enjoying "pagan freedom"; he is a "savage stranger" (p. 930) who acts with "sinister savagery" (p. 625) and has a "face dark as an Indian's" (p. 952).

Rhett is also exoticized in his interest in self-adornment. Mitchell writes,

His severe black suit, with fine ruffled shirt and trousers smartly strapped . . . was oddly at variance with his physique and face, for he was foppishly groomed, the clothes of a dandy on a body that was powerful and latently dangerous in its lazy grace. His hair was jet black, and his black mustache was small and closely-clipped, almost foreign-looking compared with the dashing, swooping mustaches of the cavalry men nearby. He looked, and was, a man of lusty and unashamed appetites. (p. 179)

Later we learn that his interest in clothes extends to women's fashions: "Had he been less obviously masculine, his ability to recall details of dresses, bonnets and coiffures would have been put down as the rankest effeminacy" (p. 225). This gender ambiguity appears in later blazons of the hero: a reference to "his mouth, red-lipped, clear cut as a woman's [and] frankly sensual" is quickly followed up by a description of his hyper-masculine physique. Mitchell writes, "His body seemed so tough and *hard*, as tough and *hard* as his keen mind. His was such an *easy, graceful strength, lazy as a panther* stretching in the sun, alert as a *panther* to spring and strike" (p. 298; emphases mine). The whiff of effeminacy in the interest in clothes, in the shape of the mouth, is true to the inter-racialist paradigm: the racial Other, feminized by definition in his subordination to white power, is doubly effeminized in his sensuality, despite the paradoxically hyper-male appearance of the package. Further, the panther metaphor links Rhett to the jungles of Africa. The way in which the above passage racializes him becomes clear just a few pages later, in the parallels with a description of a "real" black man: ". . . her eyes lighted on a singing black *buck* . . . He stood nearly six and a half feet tall . . . ebony black, stepping along with the *lithe grace of a powerful animal,* his *white teeth flashing*" (p. 300; emphases mine). How black is Rhett Butler? Black enough.

Rhett's "savage" sexuality often threatens to find expression in violence – or, seen in a different light, his sexuality gets written in the text *as* violence, either latent or symbolic. Indeed, it is hard to distinguish between real brutality in Rhett's actions and the language of brutality, of physical force, with which his most innocent actions are described: "There was something exciting about him that she could not analyze . . . There was something breath-taking in the grace of his big body which made his very entrance into a room like an abrupt physical impact." Scarlett admits to herself in astonishment: "It's almost like I was in love with him! But I'm not and I just can't understand it" (p. 219). We may have to surpress a smirk at her naïveté here – obviously, the poor girl is experiencing her first hormonal rush – but it is not altogether clear that the author understands Rhett's effect on Scarlett either. When she comes to him for the money to save Tara, his actions toward her are repeatedly described in the language of propulsion and force: "He had her hands in both of his and . . . there was something hot and vital and exciting about his grip . . . he bent and kissed her cheek . . . As he felt the startled movement of her body away from him, he hugged her about the shoulders . . . as if he relished her helplessness in resisting his caresses" (p. 561). He maintains this grip another page or so, where Mitchell has him push her about some more, pulling her to her feet and propelling her into another room. Scarlett anticipates an aggressive kiss: "his hands closed over hers in so hard a grip that it hurt . . . Now, in an instant his lips would be upon hers, the hard insistent lips which she suddenly remembered with a vividness that left her weak. But he did not kiss her." Momentarily disappointed, she is then startled when he gently kisses her hand, for she had been "expecting violence" (p. 568).

These tropes are tired enough and explicable in terms of the attitude – fortunately fading now – that women shouldn't want *any* sex, so that all sex (at least the good sex) is at some level coerced. Clearly, the "violence" in the kiss Scarlett expects – indeed, desires – is purely metaphorical. But elsewhere in the novel Rhett threatens or commits real violence: twice he tells her she deserves "beating with a buggy whip" (p. 821); once he chokes her unconscious; once he threatens, Othello-like, to "tear [her] to pieces" or crush her skull (p. 926); and once he out-and-out rapes her. Maybe it's time we looked at the infamous passage, which I will do my best to edit to a reasonable length:

He swung her off her feet into his arms and started up the stairs. Her head was crushed against his chest . . . He hurt her and she cried out, muffled, frightened . . . He went in the utter *darkness*, up, up, and she was *wild* with fear. He was a mad *stranger* and this was a *black darkness* she did not know, *darker than death*, carrying her away in arms that hurt. She screamed, stifled against him and he . . . bent over her and kissed her with a *savagery* and a completeness that wiped out everything from her mind but the *dark* into which she was sinking . . . She was *darkness* and he was *darkness* and there had never been anything before this time, only *darkness* . . . She tried to speak and his mouth was over hers again. Suddenly, she had a *wild* thrill such as she had never known: joy, fear, madness, excitement, surrender to arms that were too strong, lips too bruising . . . For the first time in her life she had met someone, something stronger than she, someone she could neither bully nor break, someone who was bullying and breaking her. Somehow, her arms were around his neck her lips trembling beneath his and they were going up, up into the *darkness* again, a *darkness* that was soft and swirling and all enveloping. (p. 929; emphases mine)

This is not consensual sex: the victim struggles and screams. What makes it "not rape" in the eyes of some readers is what follows the break in the text, when we witness Scarlett waking up the next morning. To the chagrin of a legion of feminists, Mitchell writes,

He had humbled her, used her brutally through a wild mad night and she had gloried in it.

Oh, she should be ashamed, should shrink from the memory of that hot swirling darkness! A lady, a real lady, could never hold up her head after such a night. But stronger than shame, was the memory of rapture, of the ecstasy of surrender. (p. 930)

We've known now for quite some time that Scarlett is no Lucrece – Rhett himself comments with dry humor on her offer to "part with that jewel which is dearer than life" (p. 821). But this reaction is far from what we expect from a woman subjected to bullying, breaking, and bruising treatment. Scarlett has been raped, and has not been raped: she certainly doesn't seem to *feel* raped. And that's because she is not a "real lady," not rape-able as a "real lady" is. The obsessive tropes of darkness surrounding the sexual act darken her in complicity with Rhett's "savagery." She goes on to rhapsodize, "Rhett loved her! . . . he loved her, this savage stranger . . ." and then to fantasize about "hold[ing] the whip over his insolent black head" (p. 930).

We have seen that whip before: Catherine had it in Heathcliff and passed it on to Rhett and Scarlett. Scarlett's whip-fantasy in fact only reverses Rhett's characterization of their relationship: "I'm riding you with a slack rein, my pet, but don't forget that I'm riding you with curb and spurs just the same" (p. 850). Arguably, though, Shakespeare had the whip first: in eighteenth- and nineteenth-century productions of *The Taming of the Shrew* – that predecessor of the romance novel, in the words of an author of romance – Petruccio inevitably carried a whip. I don't believe we need choose a single Shakespearean ur-text here: Mitchell's novel invokes Shakespeare (as well as other authors) in any number of ways. Indeed, Rhett twice compares Scarlett to Lady Macbeth, quoting her about the blood on her hands and describing Scarlett as "unsexed" (p. 937) – the latter also echoes an earlier Shakespeareanism, when Scarlett inadvertently cites Beatrice (yet another "spirited heroine") in *Much Ado about Nothing*: "I wish I was a man" (p. 221).

Scarlett's – if you will – whip-envy is only one of numerous ways in which Mitchell conflates her and Rhett. The most obvious of these is their names, both metonyms for the social stigma they carry and the question-mark haunting their seeming racial whiteness. Scarlett's name also links her to the prostitute Belle Watling with her signature, dyed red hair, while the latter's own name – in a wonderful hermeneutic boomerang – doubles back as a pun on Scarlett's reputation as "the belle of five counties." The symbolism of red also operates in Scarlett's linkage to the red earth of Tara, itself linked to her Irish father's "florid" complexion and unrefined (read: not-white-enough) ways. She may resemble the perfect southern lady in her "magnolia-white skin," but her "thick black brows" and "turbulent, willful, lusty" eyes associate her with Rhett (p. 3).

Interestingly, it is Rhett who harps on Scarlett's Irish heritage, and he does so in explicitly racial terms: "The Irish . . . are the damnedest race," he says (p. 574). Eliza Russi Lowen McGraw notes, "Scarlett's Irishness holds the possibility of positioning her alongside the Southern 'other' – African Americans . . . Irish people fought that linkage . . . But Mitchell's treatment of Scarlett's ethnicity borrows from depictions of the tragic mulatta figures who populate nineteenth-century novels."[15] As is often the case in this book, I feel we need not argue over the "correct" reading of the character's ethnicity: Scarlett is both Irish and not Irish, white and not white, and in the latter she is like Rhett, because the red name that links her red blood to the red earth is not so much about a country of origin but about that "something coarse and earthy in her" that enables her to laugh at Rhett's bawdy stories (p. 844). In a word, it is her sexuality that constitutes her marginal racial status.

For Scarlett's sexuality is the one thing that can blacken her. Once caught in Ashley's arms, she has, in Desdemonian fashion, "blackened Ashley's name" and enabled people "to blackguard her" (p. 916). Rhett –

black-hearted himself – is fond of exposing her inner darkness: "Certainly I'm a rascal and why not? . . . It's only hypocrites like you . . . just as black at heart but trying to hide it, who become enraged when called by their right names" (p. 221). And the right name for Scarlett, in at least one point in the novel, would be "hussy." Driven to offer herself sexually to Rhett in exchange for the money to save Tara, she visits him in jail and is taken for the likes of Belle Watling: "'She thinks I'm a hussy,' thought Scarlett. 'And perhaps she's right at that!'" (p. 558). Rhett too chastises her for "frisking like a prostitute with a prospective client" (p. 570) and then delivers the final blow to her pretensions: "What makes you think you are worth three hundred dollars? Most women don't come that high" (p. 573).

In fact, Rhett sells her short: he seems to forget that he paid $150 for a mere dance with her, in a mock "auction" to raise money for the Confederate troops that even the naïve, asexual Melanie sees as associating white ladies with slaves. Indeed, throughout the novel the rhetoric of prostitution and sexual compromise links white and black women, as when Rhett says that "Belle and her girls will lie themselves black in the face" (p. 801). With Scarlett, however, what we might call the "belle–Belle continuum" is only one element in a larger discussion of female sexuality wherein adultery, prostitution, and rape are inter-linked and racialized. Rhett's reaction to the suspicions about Scarlett and Ashley foreground the complexional/racial language in which adultery is so easily troped. When Scarlett tries to back out of attending the party, he calls her a "white livered, cowardly little bitch." He goes on to say, "while I may endure a trollop for a wife, I won't endure a coward" (p. 918), and he forces her not only to attend but to wear a trampy jade-green dress (in the film it is red). He fumes, "No modest, matronly dove grays and lilacs tonight . . . And plenty of rouge. I'm sure the woman the Pharisees took in adultery didn't look half so pale." He ties her stays himself, pulling them painfully tight: "'Hurts, does it?'. . . Pity it isn't around your neck" (p. 919).

The whiff of *Othello* in the latter threat is worth at least a passing glance, as is the way in which it participates – however subtly – in the lynch-logic rampant elsewhere in the text. But let's save the more serious implications of this passage until we have finished contextualizing it. The above is not the first episode in which Scarlett rouges up. Mammy – being the "good nigger" and hence enforcer of white, upper-class values – disapproves: "Face paint! Well, you ain' so big dat Ah kain whup you! [That whip again!] Miss Ellen be tuhnin' in her grabe dis minute! Paintin' yo face like a –" (p. 591). Mammy doesn't fill in that blank, but we know what she's thinking: "Paintin' yo face like a *ho*." And this earlier episode calls our attention to the more subtle way in which Scarlett is stigmatized throughout the text: the charge that she is – as in Rhett's first conversation with her – "no lady" (p. 122). From her early wish to be "compromised" by Ashley, to her self-accusation of behaving in a way that is "common . . . like white trash" (p. 126), to her "downright common" ease in giving birth (p. 135), to her fascination with "bad women" (p. 149), to her toying with the idea of abortion (p. 872), Scarlett falls far short of the standard set by her "angel in the house" mother, Ellen. Furious with Rhett, she thinks, "'If I just wasn't a lady, what I wouldn't tell that varmint!'" (p. 248). And while female readers are bound to sympathize with her resistance to the stifling norms of southern female gentility, we must also bear in mind that, according to the logic of the text, the final proof that she is *not* a "real lady" is her enjoyment of her rape. It seems our heroine is caught between a rock (a Rhett?) and a hard place.

And herein lies the crux of the text's problematic feminist appeal. Scarlett's freedom-loving spirit is what sets her up as a target for violence, and that violence cannot be imagined in the text in anything but racist terms. Learning of her pregnancy, Rhett delivers the following lecture:

> . . . It's dangerous for you to drive alone . . . If you don't care personally whether or not you are raped, you might consider the consequences. Because of your obstinacy, you may get yourself into a situation where your gallant fellow townsmen will be forced to avenge you by stringing up a few darkies. And that will bring the Yankees down on them and someone will probably get hanged. Has it ever occurred to you that perhaps one of the reasons the ladies do not like you is that your conduct may cause the neck stretching of their sons and husbands? And furthermore, if the Ku Klux handles many more negroes, the Yankees are going to tighten up on Atlanta in a way that will make Sherman's conduct look angelic . . . They mean to stamp out the Ku Klux even if it means burning the whole town again and hanging every male over ten. (p. 676)

From the casual misogyny of "you might not care personally if you are raped" to the even more shockingly casual treatment of lynching (the Klan *handles* its victims), the passage exemplifies the perplexing way in which Mitchell implicates white female sexuality in racist violence. And while we may not be surprised to see racism justify itself as "protection" of white women, Rhett goes one step farther than the usual propaganda in implying that the white women the Klan "protects" are not even worthy of its protection. In this instance of naked ideology, the white female body is revealed not merely as an *excuse* for lynching, and not even as a *prop* for lynching (her object status apparent in the fact that she wouldn't *mind* being raped), but as another *target* for denigration, if not the actual target of mob violence. Carried to its logical conclusion, lynch-thinking would "string up" the woman too. "Hurts, does it?" Rhett sneers, "Pity it isn't around your neck."

Racist propaganda such as that mouthed by Rhett presents lynching as a preventative of violence against women, while in fact encouraging misogynist violence by asserting male propriety of the (un)rape-able female body. Indeed, one wonders whether the black male victim isn't at some level a surrogate – a, as it were, "whipping boy" – for the white female he allegedly raped, who, as the anti-Lucrece, the woman who defiantly outlives her rape, really should be dead also. Mitchell delivers some proof for the latter hypothesis in another chilling discussion of lynching:

A negro who had boasted of rape had actually been arrested, but before he could be brought to trial the jail had been raided by the Ku Klux Klan and he had been quietly hanged. The Klan had acted to save the as yet unnamed victim from having to testify in open court. Rather than have her appear and advertise her shame, her father and brother would have shot her, so lynching the negro seemed a sensible solution . . .

This *quiet* hanging (something the Klan is famous for, surely) serves as an alternative to the murder of the rape victim (for her own good, of course: how could she bear to "advertise her shame" in court?). That lynching is a threat to black men – "Don't touch our women" – has always been clear; here, we see that it's a threat to white women as well: "You're next." In order to get raped, a woman would have to be gadding about in the wrong parts of town – like Scarlett in her buggy alone – and consorting with black men (since white men don't rape unless they're Yankees). So any white woman raped by a black man would in fact at some level have "asked for it." Scarlett, reflecting on the lynching de-scribed in the above quote, thinks, "Probably the girl hadn't been raped after all" (p. 738). Of course, because such a "girl" cannot be properly raped: such a "girl" would be, by virtue of her having been raped, (un)rape-able.

Scarlett should recognize this, because it's what *she* is. And so she ignores Rhett's warning and goes riding through Shantytown. And though she shudders at the sight of the "drunken negro slatterns sitting along the road" she is, the text suggests, only a buggy's wheel above them in the southern hierarchy. They know this, too: "The negro sluts seemed to try themselves whenever she drove by" (p. 770). Finally attacked by a "black ape" who rips open her dress and a white-trash accomplice who shouts encouragement, she is told, "What happened to you . . . was just what you deserved and if there was any justice you'd have gotten worse" (p. 786).

When it is not so blatantly perpetuating blame-the-victim misogyny, lynch-thinking of the variety laid out by Mitchell operates more subtly to keep women – at least the "good women" of the southern aristocracy – in their place, locked up at home. Indeed, those ghastly pages justifying the Klan on the basis of the "terrors of the Reconstruction" for white women bring home powerfully the double-reflex of lynch thinking. If lynching causes white female terror *and* black terror, racist-masculinist oppression has killed two birds with one stone. Mitchell harps on this white female terror in a way that suggests no consciousness of the way it has been manufactured. The effect of the above-mentioned lynching, for instance, is to threaten not only black men like the one accused (perhaps falsely, as Scarlett suspects) of rape and killed by mob justice, but to terrify the white women allegedly vindicated by the lynching. Mitchell writes, "since the Ku Klux lynching, the ladies had been practically immured" (p. 743). The same thing happens when, in reprisal over Scarlett's attack in Shantytown, the men of her social circle ride out (unbeknownst to her) with the Klan. That Scarlett's own husband – the pathetically doting Frank, whom Scarlett married for money – is killed as a "result" of her unseemly behavior skews the usual kill-the-bitch adultery plot so that Scarlett can blame herself for murdering a man who, as Rhett jocularly underscores, wouldn't even think to run around on her.

"Thar ain't but one reason for killin' a woman" (p. 746). The words are not Rhett's but those of the white trash racist avenger Archie. But Rhett partakes of this philosophy, as we see when he tells Scarlett that had Ashley really loved her he would have killed her rather than let her come to Atlanta alone, where she made her indecent proposal. Why, then, does Rhett not kill Scarlett, in the end, over her adulterous leanings? From the whip he threatens to wield over her, to his wish to "string [her] up" by her stays, Rhett continually sets her up as *deserving* of a violence she somehow sweet-talks her way out of. The fact that he desists in violence (not counting the rape, of course, which does her good) sets him up not as her oppressor, but as her savior. Indeed, he even moves in to "protect" the pregnant Scarlett from those "free issue niggers" who might rape her, when he rides out with the Klan. At the same time that he is her rescuer (even the rape, as the text presents it, liberates her), his complexional darkness makes him the objective correlative of her sexual guilt, the very thing she should be punished for. This paradox rings true to the discourse of inter-racialism, where the hero plays two roles: that of "black" villain and that of castigator, executor of white justice on black people and the women who love them.

By whitewashing Rhett Butler, Mitchell retains the exoticism and danger associated with black male sexuality, while purging her text of the taint of miscegeny that drove her to burn her earlier manuscript. At the same time, emphasizing Scarlett's Irishness, problematic sexuality, and failure to fit codes of southern female gentility allows the author to superimpose the "scarlet woman" on the figure of the tragic mulatta, thus doubly saving the text for racist ideology. Hence, *Gone with the Wind* celebrates white supremacy and sentimentalizes the antebellum, slave-holding south while yet, in its ideological contradictions and its covertly racialized hero and heroine, bearing buried within it its own deconstructive "shadow text." That a black female author eventually unearthed that text and re-shaped it as a creative parody seems the perfect, as it were, poetic justice.[16] But before plunging forward to the year 2001 and leaving romance behind, let us look back on the Shakespeare–Brontë–Mitchell triad and see what we've learned from the conversation between these authors.

My titular "handsome devil" is, of course, not really one: coinage of a secular culture, the expression seems roughly coincident with the rise of the quaint, red-leotard-clad, pitch-fork-toting figure with the black goatee. I wonder about that goatee: in my memory it was ubiquitous in the cartoons produced by the same company that produced a jillion copies of that singular image of a mustachioed Clark Gable – framed by fire – bent over Vivian Leigh's barely covered bosom. Mitchell's description of the scene may be the one place where the diabolism so pervasive in Brontë's archetypal romance bubbles to the surface: "In the unholy glow that bathed them, his dark profile stood out as clearly as the head on an ancient coin, beautiful, cruel and decadent" (p. 377). Elsewhere in the novel, however, Mitchell paints this "arrogant devil" (p. 115) in somewhat less grandiose a fashion: the "diabolic gleam" in his eye tends to appear when he's thinking of seducing Scarlett (p. 574), and the only time Scarlett calls him "devil" is during a less-than-heated and rather banal disagreement over her budding saw-mill business (p. 620).

This may be the one significant alteration of the Shakespearean–Brontëan inter-racialist paradigm taken up by Mitchell. The rhetoric of darkness is there, as is the potential for rape, but Mitchell transforms the language of demonism into what it arguably sublimates in Brontë: the language of primitive and potentially violent sexuality. This transformation should not surprise us, given the ideological shifts set in motion by the Reformation and the "Age of Discovery" and solidified by the Scientific Revolution and the establishment of a secular American state. As I have argued elsewhere at length, the secularization of Anglo culture that began in Shakespeare's day resulted in the sacralization of sexuality in popular forms of entertainment like that of the theatre; one main offshoot of this discursive trajectory was the cult of romantic love.[17] Hence the modern romance novel. Hence those handsome devils.

There is one other notable difference between Brontë's and Mitchell's novels: the ending. In Mitchell the central couple does not implode, like Catherine and Heathcliff or Desdemona and Othello. Violence does happen in the novel, but the hero and heroine survive, and even hope for a better life: "Tomorrow is another day" (p. 1024), Scarlett famously declares at the end. Scarlett's ultimate punishment for her transgressive desires is separation from Rhett, not death at his hands. In feminist terms, this is *some* good news, and certainly more realistic than the "happy endings" that later became a staple of romance. On the other hand, one wonders whether Mitchell's departure from the tragic conclusion would have been possible had she retained the aborted inter-racialist plot. Did she have to whitewash the hero in order to save the heroine? Are we trapped in another gender/race impasse?

The traditional inter-racialist heroine does have a certain feminist appeal – as is evident in the plethora of articles celebrating Tamora as an "empowered" heroine, or arguing that Desdemona, despite her whimpering end, is no passive victim.[18] The inter-racialist heroine is, after all, defined by her willful transgression of taboo. But our feminist enthusiasm can only go so far, because the Desdemonian heroine is also defined by her *masochism* – hence Desdemona's forgiving her murder, hence Catherine's self-starvation, hence Scarlett's "enjoyment" of her rape. Whether or not this masochism is psychologically convincing (as some of my students have tried to argue), we cannot afford to separate it from its ideological utility: for me, the masochism of the inter-racialist heroine is first and foremost a racist projection. According to racist ideology, any woman who would wish, even subconsciously, to be sexual with a black man (or a gipsy) must want to demean herself, because such relationships are intrinsically demeaning for the racially superior party. She also, by definition, deserves to be punished for her transgression. And what better punishment than self-punishment, and/or punishment at the hands of the beloved? This is why figures like Catherine and Scarlett will inspire both condemnation *and* applause in feminist criticism. In pursuing their desires, they are gutsy, strong, active, even heroic – but ultimately their desire is unmasked as a desire for rape ("She gloried in it") and annihilation of self ("I *am* Heathcliff!" – "Nobody. I myself."). Heathcliff's express sadism in the face of Isabella's masochism – "Are you sure you hate me? If I let you alone for a half a day, won't you come sighing and wheedling to me again?" (Brontë, *Wuthering Heights*, p. 141) – enacts on the narrative level the meta-narrative of the sado-masochistic relation between the romance reader and the romance heroine. Doesn't everyone want to see Scarlett "get what she deserves"?

Romance in general is a problematic genre for women. Indeed, browse through criticism of romance and you find a good deal of apologizing and explaining. One need look no farther than the title of Krentz's anthology, *Dangerous Men and Adventurous Women: Romance Writers on the Appeal of the Romance*. In defending a literary genre that routinely peddles the notion that "dangerous men" are sexy, its authors like to emphasize the courage of its heroines. One essay in the volume explains, "What critics don't realize is that it is the hero's task in the book to present a suitable challenge to the heroine. His strength is a measure of her power. For it is she who must conquer him."[19] And how does she "conquer" him? By marrying him, of course. Or, before that "happy" ending – by "taming" him so that when he rapes her, he does it *nicely*. That is, in this romance author's terms, "power." That is empowerment.

Maybe for white girls. I suspect that for romance's potential black readership, empowerment would mean something else. A master's degree, a six-figure income – or even the leisure time to read romance novels. I suspect empowerment, to the great-grand-daughters of slaves, would mean something other than the "power" to be raped nicely, or be raped by somebody who happens to be "tall, dark, and handsome." Or the "power" to marry him, so one can be raped every day. In the introduction to this chapter, I asked – rhetorically – whether mainstream romance would lose its white female readership, were its heroes actually, racially "dark." The difficulty then would be that, thanks to racist mythology, those scenes of "ravishment" might be taken at face-value; they might be taken as representing real rape, rather than rape fantasies come to life. Titillation would turn to the real thrill of fear, mere fascination to its always latent extreme in fascinated horror. I'm not saying that there aren't many white women who would enjoy a love-story wherein the hero is "tall, *black*, and handsome." But that wouldn't be romance. That would be *To Sir, with Love*.

United States Court of Appeals, Eleventh Circuit.

SUNTRUST BANK, as Trustee of the Stephens Mitchell trusts f. b. o. Eugene Muse Mitchell and Joseph Reynolds Mitchell, Plaintiff-Appellee,
v.
HOUGHTON MIFFLIN COMPANY, Defendant-Appellant.
No. 01-012200.
May 25, 2001.

Owners of copyright in novel "Gone With the Wind" brought action under Copyright Act, seeking temporary restraining order (TRO) and preliminary injunction to prevent publication and distribution of allegedly infringing book "The Wind Done Gone." The United States District Court for the Northern District of Georgia, No. 01-00701-CV-CAP-1, Charles A. Pannell, Jr., J., granted preliminary injunction, and appeal was taken. The Court of Appeals held that unwarranted grant of preliminary injunction amounted to unlawful prior restraint in violation of First Amendment.

Vacated.

What if it wasn't Mitchell's fault? What if her husband (if not the devil) "made" her "do it," made her re-write her original, now lost, inter-racial love-story as *Gone with the Wind*? For the sake of this analysis, it doesn't, in fact, matter. Individuals are sometimes willing to tell their own story; it is the culture that determines which stories deserve an audience. And so it is perfectly fitting – both deeply ironic, and absolutely unsurprising – that the Mitchell estate attempted to bar publication of *The Wind Done Gone*, a novel that takes the form of a diary written by Scarlett's mulatta half-sister, the child of her father and Mammy. Othellophilia's hegemonic status could hardly be more obvious than a law-suit aiming to censor the counter-narrative. Randall's narrator, Cynara, signals her interest in exploding America's racial mythologies: she says simply, "I read *Uncle Tom's Cabin*. I didn't see me in it" (p. 7). She could have said, "I read *Gone with the Wind*. I didn't see me in it." But then again, the entire book says that.

Cynara has something to say about Shakespeare's *Othello* also. "If I had been Othello's friend, Desdemona would still be alive, and they'd have plenty of pretty babies" (p. 114). Here, at last, is Othello's sister. And here, at last, is the topic of miscegeny – not merely unmasked but also celebrated. References to the complexional spectrum produced by inter-breeding abound in the text: "He didn't want any bastards, beige or white" (p. 17); "Men don't love the brown babies as they love the pale white ones" (p. 132); "You still wanted to marry him, and bear his little may-be-brown babies" (p. 132). This is not the only way Randall blurs the color binary so pronounced in Mitchell's novel: she also does so at the level of plot. The half-black narrator – nick-named Cinnamon for her complexion, in direct contrast to Mammy's "coffee" – tells of the strange emotional dynamic whereby she and her half-sister effectively trade mothers. Mammy openly prefers her white charge to her own daughter, and continues to breast-feed Scarlett – who Cynara calls (appropriately) Other – well into childhood. Meanwhile, Ellen – called Lady in the text – is drawn to the effectively motherless Cynara and proffers her frustrated mother-love, and her own milk, to her. Lactation and nursing enact on the literal level a different kind of mingling of the races, while also eroding racial binaries on the symbolic level: milk is white, whether from a black mother or a white. Right away, we begin to sense that inter-racialism, in this particular novel, plays out not just between men and women, but between women and women: Randall literalizes the inter-racial sisterhood invoked by Lydia Maria Child's introduction to *Incidents in the Life of a Slave Girl*, making this sisterhood – however emotionally fraught – her focus.

Cynara and Scarlett/Other do not just share mothers: they also share a lover, Rhett, whom Cynara cheekily refers to as Debt. Cynara even has him first, and takes pride in the fact that he loves her better: "She was your daylight version of me" (p. 196). The heroine also recognizes her rival's hidden blackness: "She has the vitality, the vigor, and the pragmatism of a slave, and into this water you stir as much refinement as you can pour without leaving any grains of sugar at the bottom of the glass. She was a slave in a white woman's body, and that's a sweet drink of cold water" (p. 47). (As she notes of her rival's Irish heritage: "All white skins are not created equal" [p. 135].) Finally, the ultimate boundary between Cynara and Scarlett/Other collapses when the former learns – after the latter's death – that Ellen/Lady too had African ancestry, thus rendering Scarlett/Other not just metaphorically, but socially "black," according to the one-drop-of-blood rule. "She was just a nigger. Their [Rhett's and Scarlett's] baby was just a high-yellow gal in a blue velvet riding habit" (p. 133). The symbolic merging of the inter-racial couple in mainstream myths of the *Othello* variety is replaced, here, by a female inter-racialist dyad, in which racial divisions break down and the identity of self and "Other" melt together.

Randall's interest in an inter-racial sisterhood is not limited to the heroine and Scarlett/Other: the narrator works for Belle (here translated as Beauty) and the two share a kind of mentoring relationship. Once again confronting head-on the issues Mitchell tends to skirt, Randall points up the parallel between prostitution and slavery: Cynara notes, "The girls who sell themselves at Beauty's are saved the pain of words on paper; their prices disappear, spoken and forgotten in the air" (p. 77). Yet Cynara, herself a slave, is set up in moral contrast to the prostitutes whose sheets – significantly – it is her job to bleach: at Beauty's she is "the only *female* virgin in the house" (p. 21; emphasis in original). In stark contrast to the "negro sluts" abjected in Mitchell's novel, here is a sexually inexperienced, black heroine – although one who goes on to experience a satisfying adult sexual life. Indeed, there is a curious innocence about Cynara – an innocence that is all the more real and compelling for not being sentimentalized. Until she falls in love with – and seduces – the black Congressman, she prides herself "on being the only colored girl" she knows with "only one man and no children" (p. 184). She also sees Beauty for who she is – neither a monster nor a hero – commenting drily that "This whore had no 'heart of gold,' but then again, she didn't pretend to" (p. 24).

There is no sexual violence in *The Wind Done Gone*. The sex between Rhett/Debt and the heroine is, in fact, mutually pleasurable, even loving. This hero is not violent: one time and one time only he strikes her, and she snaps: "The only thing you can beat out of me is my love for you." She then explains, "Beauty taught us to say that, and say it quick . . . It stopped her from having to shoot a man or two" (p. 19). Clearly this is not a heroine who needs to be "bullied" and "broken" in order to experience sexual "rapture"; she tells us, "I seen children play . . . I had no place to play then. My body became my place to play. I became my own playing ground" (p. 29). When she meets the Congressman, she realizes that her life with Rhett/Debt was more about ownership than mutuality: "Redeemed as I was, I was sold and he bought me . . . I have let him be my God." She then alludes to the story of the woman caught in adultery – that favorite of Rhett and Scarlett's – asking rhetorically, "Where do I go, to go and sin no more?" (p. 145). The citation is clearly ironic, though: Cynara shows no sign of feeling "sinful," only of wishing to escape the God-like control of her owner/husband. So she leaves him, telling him tartly, "You have been a father to me, and now that you look the part, I don't want you" (p. 197). She winds up bearing a child to a man who "has never in his life touched a white woman" (p. 188).

The child born at the end of the novel – the Congressman's love-child, which she offers as a gift of love to his barren wife – represents the non-miscegenous resolution of the miscegenation plot. Cynara says, "I bore a little black baby and I knew – what every mother should know and has been killed out of too many of my people, including my mother – I bore a little black baby and knew it was the best baby in the world." This conclusion also resolves the second inter-racialist plot-line, the conflict between the two half-sisters: ". . . A lifetime of hating Other has made me fit for an eternity of loving her" (p. 206). Considering the vehement racism of the text Randall critiques, it is hard not to be moved by so forgiving a final gesture. In one of the most stunning insights of the book, the heroine observes, "One way of looking at it, all women are niggers. For sure, every woman I ever knew was a nigger – whether she knew it or not" (p. 177).

Hélène Cixous and Catherine Clément re-phrase the "Song of songs," having it speak for all women: "We are 'black' *and* we are beautiful."[20] Randall – herself a musician – sings the same song in a different key.

Romance is a nostalgic genre. Indeed, the very title of Mitchell's Pulitzer-Prize-winning "classic" bemoans a world that is gone. This is another way in which romance as a genre seems fundamentally Shakespearean. Shakespeare never set a play in his own time and he spent a good deal of ink commemorating – like Mitchell – a heroic age that preceded his birth. The histories and tragedies in particular are full of elegiac and nostalgic moments: "This blessed plot, this earth, this realm, this England / This nurse, this teaming womb of royal kings . . . is now leased out – I die pronouncing it" – "The oldest hath borne most. We that are young / Shall never see so much, nor live so long" – "O withered is the garland of the war. / The soldier's pole is fall'n . . . /Young boys and girls / Are level now with men. The odds is gone, /And there is nothing left remarkable / Beneath the visiting moon."[21] It is much easier to sentimentalize a world one has not known – or a world that preceded a war that one's ancestors lost. Randall's title alone signals the author's resistance to these conventions, deflating her source's over-blown, nostalgic pronouncements. The wind done gone, but we still here, stupid; let's make the best of it.

Randall's narrator comments, "Othello's just a creation. Maybe just like me" (p. 114). Maybe. But all lies are not created equal: all fictions are not equally false. And I am probably not the only female reader who finds Randall's heroine more "like me" than Mitchell's. I read *Gone with the Wind.* I didn't find me in it. I read *Othello.* I didn't find me in that either. Cynara says, "Someone else has written the play. I wish I could think it was God. I merely take my place on the stage" (p. 164). And indeed, the author learned personally, after penning these lines, just how powerful cultural scripts can be, just how hard it is to be heard when one is not parroting the same clichés, reciting the same old myths.

And times do, like it or not, change. *Gone with the Wind* was the last romance novel I read, as a young person. Once I'd discovered Judy Blume's *Forever*, I realized I didn't have to settle for fade-to-black and the ambiguous language of "ravishment." When I first watched the film of Mitchell's "classic" novel, I found its treatment of sex ridiculous, its heroine's coquettish games tiresome and infantile. And later, reading up on the feminist debate about the infamous scene, I had no patience with the Mitchell apologists. Suggesting that women like non-consensual sex is just flat out dumb and wrong.

Rape fantasies in women have been theorized as products of sexual repression and the double standard: the idea of getting "raped" by the likes of Clark Gable allowed his fans an erotic thrill free from guilt and sexual accountability.[22] By the same token, though, where sexual repression is minimal, coercion should, theoretically, have no place in a woman's erotic inner life, and should therefore appear infrequently in the collective fantasies of a sexually liberated culture. My sense is that this is already happening. Paula Kamen argues that the sexual revolution has produced a generation of women who are sexually assertive and relatively guilt-free about it: the generation of Monica Lewinsky and the hit TV series *Sex and the City*.[23] These women came of age exposed to a media wherein the "dominatrix" has replaced the dominator as the symbol of coercive sex. Whether this is a good thing for women is open to debate, but it certainly leaves the whip-snapping Rhett Butlers in the historical dust-bin.

On the other hand, though, cultural myths – as we've seen again and again in this exploration – do tend to reproduce themselves, with relatively slight alterations. Also, the relationship between individual and collective fantasy is not a one-way street. To what degree were the rape fantasies of the post-Mitchell generation *created* by the infamous stairway scene? Who can say?

I use the word "scene" ambiguously above, but perhaps I should be more precise. Most readers come to Mitchell's novel these days having seen the movie first, and the movie is not the novel. Indeed, in that infamous stairway scene, Scarlett does not scream and only struggles – very weakly – at first. Likewise, most readers of *Taming of the Shrew* come to the text having seen the film – featuring another "tall, dark, and handsome" star – first. This is the film of *Shrew* wherein Elizabeth Taylor's Kate winks after delivering that nauseating final lecture on wifely duty.[24] Students read the text through the film and do not believe what the author says.

Fans of *Gone with the Wind* – of which there are many in the American Deep South where I teach – inevitably fail to grasp, or perhaps turn a blind eye to, Mitchell's defense of the Klan. I don't believe they're pretending for the sake of their liberal, "ethnic"-looking, New York-born professor: few if any closet racists enroll in the kinds of courses I teach. And in any case, I "missed" it too, apparently, when I read the book the first time. It's not, after all, in the movie. Nor should it be: the movie is better that way. But I find that, once these students get the "unedited" version, they view the whole story differently. Once they connect the novel's treatment of race to its treatment of rape, they view the stairway scene differently. Once they learn that the actress who played Mammy – Hattie McDaniel – was both the first black performer to win an Oscar, and the *last for thirty years*, they wonder whether the censoring of the pro-lynching material was sincere, or simply strategic. Once they connect Scarlett's seventeen-inch waist to the corset that maintains it, to the psychological corset that keeps the women of Atlanta "practically im-mured" in fear of black rapists, and then connect these *stays* to the terrorist tools of the lynch-rope and the burning cross, they are less likely to lapse into wistful smiles at those well-worn strains of the movie's theme song.

History too is a form of fantasy. That's why it must be continually re-examined and re-written. And a genre like romance – which purports to offer the past in the form of pure fantasy, "pure escapism" – is thus doubly likely to bury ideological pills in a deep sugar coating. I say this as an avid Tolkien fan and someone who went ga-ga over the opening of *The Fellowship of the Ring*. Don't think I don't sometimes ruin my *own* fun. But it's important to bear in mind that what a culture does in the name of "fun" is often in dead earnest. Whether or not a woman can "enjoy" being raped, a rapist must, at some level, find gratification in the crime. And people made postcards from photos taken at lynchings. Wish you were here. Or: wish you were dead. Depending upon the audience.

And therein lies the crux of the problem. In these pictures from an execution, with whom do you identify? I read *Othello*, and I did not see me in it. I did not, in particular, see me in Desdemona. If I had, it would have been even worse. "This object poisons sight: let it be hid." That's why it will take some courage for me to write – and perhaps for you to read – the next chapter, where we look at modern female victims of black literary violence, a product of those "black nights of the soul" endured by the racially conscious.

CHAPTER 6

Invisible men, unspeakable acts: the spectacle of black male violence in modern American fiction

Not all inter-racialist narratives of the early twentieth century fixate on the black male–white female dyad; not all occlude women of color as erotic objects; not all punish female sexuality with violence or confuse seduction with rape. I have found one exception, and its author is male and of African descent. Jean Toomer's *Cane* (1923) opens with lyrics praising an explicitly black female beauty: "Her skin is like dusk on the eastern horizon . . . When the sun goes down . . . Men had always wanted her, this Karintha, even as a child, Karintha carrying beauty, perfect as dusk when the sun goes down."[1] The short stories in the book include many love-stories that cross racial boundaries in either direction, such as "Fern," which celebrates a woman of mixed African and Jewish ancestry, whose particular fascination attracts both whites and blacks: "Men were everlastingly bringing her their bodies" (p. 25). There is also "Becky," which begins, "Becky was the white woman who bore two Negro sons," and "Esther," about a fair-skinned girl who falls in love with a dark-skinned black man, only to be laughed at: "What brought you here, lil milk-white girl?" (p. 47). In "Blood-burning moon," we are told the story of a black woman whose white lover is killed in a tussle with his black rival, who of course then gets lynched. For its celebration of women of color, its appreciation of the human complexional rainbow, and its haunting eroticism, the book is unique.

But *Cane* is also virtually unknown when compared to contemporary works dealing with racial issues, and not entirely because Toomer resisted marketing his work as African-American literature.[2] Course syllabi are far more likely to feature works by William Faulkner – or, when looking to "diversify" the reading-list, one turns to the major figures of the "Harlem Renaissance": Richard Wright and Ralph Ellison. And this is how Othellophilia wins the day again. True, this is Othellophilia in a different guise. The black authors in particular approach the myth – arguably, of necessity – with a critical eye or ironic detachment of which Faulkner, with his privileged position and classical education, seems incapable. And even Faulkner, for all his Shakespearean leanings, twists the myth in *Light in August* (1932) – re-imagining, for example, the inter-racialist hero as a man who can "pass" and whose true racial status remains, right through the end of the novel, a mystery.

This chapter's title comments on Ellison's notion in *Invisible Man* that black men are culturally invisible. I wish to problematize this invisibility in two ways: firstly, it is not so much black men but black *women* who are told to disappear – indeed, they are barely visible in Ellison's own novel – and, secondly, as often as racist culture turns a blind eye to black men, it also, perversely and almost despite itself, turns the spotlight on them. This dynamic of peek-a-boo is of course not new, and can be traced back to *Othello*, where the hero's brutal exposure to white voyeurism concludes with the imperative: "This object poisons sight. Let it be hid." Racist culture, in other words, when it directs its gaze at all at black men, only does so to make a spectacle of them (just look at the prominence of black men in spectator sports and the entertainment industry).[3]

This hyper-visibility, however, is a visibility on racist culture's own terms: there is always a script, and the black male must learn it by heart. Ellison knows this: hence the sequence of events wherein the hero is made to perform a (usually disagreeable) role for the titillation or amusement of his (usually white) audience. Hence the hero's flight from a white woman who wants him to "play rapist" with her; hence his ultimate retreat into a private, underground world. Wright's *Native Son*, similarly, likens the criminal actions of his protagonist, the doomed Bigger Thomas, to the performance of a socially scripted meta-narrative, one including the smothering in bed of a white woman followed by the dismemberment and burning of her remains. And indeed, these two episodes – the "rape fantasy" of the white woman in Ellison, and the Othello-like smothering of the white woman in Wright – represent, in my reading, parallel comments on Othellophilia, however much the two scenes contrast in tone and effect. These authors' comprehension of the social conditioning behind such unspeakable acts sets them apart from previous white authors of inter-racialist texts. Even Faulkner – by far the least racist of the canonical authors this book examines – leaves unresolved the nature–nurture riddle, in accounting for the violent actions of his racially marked protagonist: whereas Faulkner clearly critiques religious fanaticism when it serves racist ends, his metaphorical language suggests higher forces at work.

This chapter reads Faulkner's, Wright's, and Ellison's novels as inter-linked inter-racialist narratives whose central tropes of blindness or

darkness-versus-light signal their common interest in questions of spec-
ularity, knowledge, and human motivation, particularly as these themes
play out in the theatre of American race relations. However, at the same
time that these texts interrogate certain forms of willed or collective
blindness, they share one common blind-spot themselves: blindness
toward women of color – itself a sub-category of each text's broader lack
of sympathy for women. Both Faulkner and Wright feature a black
protagonist whose defining actions constitute violence against women –
both white and black – and whereas sympathy for the victim might be
evoked, the adventure-narrative involving the murderer's flight, and the
sacrificial nature of his death, set him up as, in all senses, the hero. The
murderer is redeemed and the victim is, merely, dead. Ellison improves
on this paradigm by *not* having the protagonist commit the misogynist
violence that racism expects of him – yet the book is, as we'll see, suffused
with hostility toward women, a hostility that at times erupts in the form
of symbolic violence. All three novels valorize black manhood at the
expense of women, and above all women of color.

This is an observation, not a condemnation. Indeed, we have seen again
and again the way ideology works to occlude the inter-dependency of
racism and misogyny in order to insure that total equality across gender
and racial divisions can never be achieved. It simply does not serve
masculinist-racist power to discourage misogyny in black males or racism
in white women – culture, after all, chooses its rebels as well as its heroes,
and the safest rebels are the ones with only *one* cause, their own. And so
it is that Eldridge Cleaver, in his memoir *Soul on Ice* (1968), can be
applauded for calling white women "the Ogre" and calling homosexuality
"a disease."

Cleaver presents an unusual case, and one with which I aim to conclude
this chapter. A reformed black rapist who claimed that his career in crime
was politically motivated – an enraged attempt to correct his socially
programmed preference for white women – Cleaver represents the real-
life embodiment of Wright's tragic "outlaw" hero, as well as an example
of what I'd like to call internalized Othellophilia.[4] To the young Cleaver,
white female bodies were appropriate targets for violence, as their mythic
desirability and unattainability was cynically manipulated by racist power
in making enemies of black men and black women. As property and tool
of the oppressor, therefore, white women were the best means of revenge.
This, needless to say, is no easy book for a woman (of any race) to read.
And yet – astonishingly – even this convicted criminal recognizes what so
many authors of inter-racialist myths did not: that his actions against

white women – though conceived initially as rebellion – ultimately only furthered racist ideology, fulfilling its most pernicious predictions. And he ends his book with a stunningly moving prose-poem in praise of black women.

And this is where I hope to end our exploration – with insight, reconciliation, and maybe even hope. It's an ending, also, which steps outside fiction – outside fantasy – and onto (insofar as we can get there in a book) the "stage" of all the world. It might, of course, be said that Cleaver's memoir is as much a construct as a literary text – his persona is as much a persona, his justifications of his life as consciously crafted as the characters and motives in a novel. I've said this before: it's not a question of who's telling the "truth" but a question of which lies hurt the most. And when all's said and done it might prove – paradoxically – that the one who has done the most harm tells the least hurtful lies. That is, if we are willing to listen.

There is one good woman in *Light in August.* This in itself is not surprising: Shakespeare himself made a point of including one Cordelia for every pair of bad women. What is surprising about Faulkner's novel is that the good woman is pregnant, visibly pregnant, and pregnant out of wedlock: she is, in short, a "bad woman" from the point of view of her culture. And yet Faulkner redeems her, and sets her up as the frame and moral reference point for his novel.

The good news for feminists ends there, as this character differs from the conventional good woman only in her physical state, and insofar as that state evidences the fact that she has had sexual intercourse. The novel begins and ends with the heavily pregnant Lena Grove, a poor white young woman on the road in search of the no-good scoundrel who knocked her up and then fled. Faulkner also makes it clear immediately that the no-good scoundrel who knocked her up will keep fleeing, while she keeps pursuing him, on foot if folks don't offer her a ride (which they tend to do, merely because she's the kind of girl that inspires spontaneous kindness in people – especially men). Indeed, in her futile search for the father of her child, and in her repeated rejection of the overtures of a man who loves her enough to raise another man's child with her, she may even be said to represent chastity itself; even the Church fathers analogized chastity and virginity, praising female fecundity when contained by the monogamous unit. Lucrece, we recall, was not a virgin either.

Having said that, I want to argue that there is, in fact, a kind of virginal quality to Lena. Her comportment and her face are repeatedly described as youthful, serene, and vacant of thought: in a word, childlike. Faulkner describes her as she confronts the bitter and judgmental wife of one of her benefactors: "Her face is calm as stone, but not hard. Its doggedness has a soft quality, an inwardlighted quality of tranquil and calm unreason and detachment."[5] Despite her obvious pregnancy and absence of either a husband or a ring, she acts unashamed – "like she never had nothing particular to either hide or tell" (p. 21). When she tells her story to folks on the road she does so "with that patient and transparent recapitulation of a lying child" (p. 22). Fecundity divorced from sensuality, experience divorced from knowledge, Lena embodies all that is unthreatening in the archetypal female principle. Indeed, Faulkner even invokes Keats' Grecian urn (an allusion we'll look at more closely below) in describing Lena's pilgrimage, suggesting – as Diane Roberts has noted – that she too is an "unravished bride."[6] Like the Virgin Mary, Lena is simultaneously pregnant and virginal, an unbreached vessel. Her unborn child's conception seems curiously non-sexual, standing outside the narrative and referred to only elliptically in the mention of her climbing out of her bedroom window. She shows, moreover, no signs of erotic desire for the father of her child even as she tirelessly pursues him, repeating simply to the folks who help her along the way, "I reckon a family out to be together when a chap comes . . . I reckon the Lord will see to that" (p. 18). This strangely virginal quality of Lena is so complete that the man who falls in love with her heavily pregnant self is stunned and dismayed finally to see the newborn baby in her arms, realizing for the first time, "*She is not a virgin*" (p. 380; emphasis in text). When the child's father eludes her again after a sole glance at his baby, she picks it up and toils doggedly on. Here, more than half a century before the American Republican party popularized the term, is the modern answer to Lucrece: the "family values" woman.

That Lena is no reason for feminist enthusiasm becomes clear when we look at the terms in which most critics celebrate her. Sally R. Page, for instance, writes:

Lena Grove is Faulkner's most fascinating portrayal of a woman fulfilling her natural destiny. It is with the understanding of Faulkner's view of women offered by his early works – the initial despair in the face of the failure of the virginal ideal and the subsequent devotion to woman the nourisher and sustainer of life – that his portrait of Lena Grove can best be comprehended as a wholly favorable one.[7]

Roberts is rightly suspicious of this reading, paraphrasing Page's essentializing with wry humor: Lena, Roberts writes, is "born to get pregnant."[8]

Such skepticism is not limited to recent feminist critics like Roberts and myself. Leslie A. Fiedler, writing in the mid sixties, categorizes Lena as the first of two Faulknerian stereotypes: "great, sluggish, mindless daughters of peasants, whose fertility and allure are scarcely distinguishable from those of a beast in heat; and the febrile, almost fleshless but sexually insatiable daughters of the aristocracy." Like Eula Varner in *The Hamlet* and Dewey Dell in *As I Lay Dying*, Lena is "the peasant wench turned earth goddess," pure, inarticulate, reproductive "'womanflesh.'"9

Roberts, to be fair, views Fiedler's dualistic reading of Faulkner's female characters as reductive, and indeed her book's table of contents – naming six different "types" of Faulknerian womanhood – evidences a more complex picture. It is not my goal, here, to settle the broader question of Faulkner's feminist sympathies or lack thereof. My point about Lena is that Faulkner sets her up – and immediately, in this novel – as the Good Woman. And that means a bad one is bound to come along soon.

Let us return to the Keats allusion on which feminist readings of Lena place such importance. The urn arises in Faulkner's early description of her travel: "a long monotonous succession of undeviating changes from day to dark to day again, through which she advanced in identical and anonymous . . . wagons . . . like something moving forever and without progress across an urn" (p. 5). Keats calls the urn "Thou still unravished bride of quietness" and meditates on the way the figures upon it are trapped in time: "Bold lover, never, never canst thou kiss, / Though winning near the goal – yet do not grieve . . . / Forever wilt thou love, and she be fair."10 In Faulkner, hence, the unkissed nymph is conflated with the urn itself, an association not obviously conscious in Keats. Lena, moreover, is an "unravished bride" in at least two senses: in her self-image as perpetual bride and in her "unravished" or sexually "pure," if not literally virginal, status. I want to pause to point out the double sense of "ravished" as raped – by token of which Lena is literally and not just figuratively "unravished" – only to come back to it later, when we are ready to talk about Lena's foil, the (un)rape-able Joanna Burden. Suffice it to say here that the urn–bride linkage works well for Lena as both a bride in waiting and the fecundated womb by which she is metonymized.

This reading works, but at the risk of sounding persnickety I want to return to the fact that Faulkner only *implicitly* likens Lena to the urn itself: the *explicit* analogy is to the figure *on* the urn. And which figure would that be? Oddly enough, the details of Lena's case invite her comparison not so much to the nymph as to the swain: she is the one in erotic pursuit. At the same time, though – and this, I believe, is more to Faulkner's point – it is a pursuit that is *trapped in time*. I therefore quarrel with Roberts' phrasing when she says that "in her wandering, [Lena] represents the unfettered feminine . . ."[11] She might represent that to the men off whom she bums rides – one of whom surmises that her search for the father of her child is merely an excuse to travel ("You can't beat a woman," he misogynistically declares [pp. 479–80]) – but in my mind this woman is as "fettered" as one can be. Because the fact is, in Faulkner's text, Lena cannot properly be said to move at all: she is "something moving forever without progress" – like the earth itself. Faulkner's ability to describe motion in the paradoxical terms of stasis – where Lena is concerned – seems one of the novel's most brilliant rhetorical achievements. Lena herself is perpetually astonished at the fact that she gets anywhere at all: "'My, my,' she says; 'here I aint been on the road but four weeks, and now I am in Jefferson already. My, my, a body does get around'" (p. 26). This becomes the refrain of the Lena frame-narrative, and Faulkner returns to it in the very last sentence of the novel: "My, my. A body does get around. Here we aint been coming from Alabama but two months, and now it's already Tennessee" (p. 480). I hope it is only my paranoia that makes me want to see this as an authorial joke at the dumb woman's expense. As an earth–goddess figure, Lena's motion is both theoretically constant and definitionally imperceptible: only in earthquakes and blues songs do we "feel the earth move" under our feet. As Michael Millgate notes, Lena is "a kind of impersonalised catalytic force, effecting change but itself unchanging."[12] The positive inverse of Joe Christmas – who eventually realizes that the long road of his life is *circular* (p. 321) – Lena moves without progressing. Having taken two months to get from Alabama to Tennessee, she can hardly be said even to move in an orbit. Lena does not move: she rotates.

To say this is not to diminish the positive energy with which Faulkner fills this female receptacle. Roberts notes that the vessel image for the female body also represents, in Faulkner, art. She writes, "Faulkner's metaphor for creation is the female body . . . The urn is the womb, to which he strives to return, as well as the vagina, the desired space to be penetrated by male agency. In all his work, the body of the woman and the body of the fiction are conflated; in his words, he tries to control and regulate the woman/art into a perfect, seamless vessel, yet the woman/art sometimes erupts, resists, proves to be cracked, flawed, or a space that becomes engulfing instead of chaste, 'polluted' instead of pure."[13] And that brings us to Joanna Burden.

Joanna is introduced in the text as "a woman of middleage" who "lives in the big house alone . . . a stranger, a foreigner . . . A Yankee, a lover of Negroes, about whom there is still talk of queer relations with Negroes . . ." The barren "spinster" polarized in relation to Lena's youthful maternity, Joanna's body and its metonymy in the big, dark house inspire distrust and fear: ". . . it still lingers about the place: something dark and outlandish and threatful, even though she is but a woman" (p. 42). Readers learn the gruesome details of her murder before we learn much else about her:

Her head had been cut pretty near off . . . he was afraid to pick her up and carry her out because her head might come clean off . . . So he . . . jerked a cover off the bed and rolled her onto it, and caught up the corners and swung it onto his back like a sack of meal and carried it out of the house and laid it down under a tree. And he said that what he was scared of happened. Because the cover fell open and she was laying on her side, facing one way, and her head was turned clean around like she was looking behind her. (p. 85)

The repetition of "clean off" and "clean around" ironically underscores the way in which Joanna's body is treated – by other characters and by the text – as anything but clean. This is abjection in the classic Kristevian sense: a mature female body – already threatening in its non-reproductive and non-maternal status – not even fully but *partially* decapitated, and carried "like a sack of meal" – that is, animal food – to be dropped in this distorted posture. The body, monstrous to begin with in the mind of a culture that can only conceive of women as virgins or mothers, is triply monstrous in its mutilation and the freakish Janus-like position it winds up taking.[14] The speaker goes on to make a comment the chilling flippancy of which signals the degree to which this woman – treated as so much baggage (a *Burden*) in death – was denigrated in life: ". . . if she could have done that [i.e., turned her head backward] when she was alive, she might not have been doing it now." Later in the novel, Faulkner returns to the spectacle of Joanna's corpse:

The people began to gather . . . the sheriff . . . thrust away those who crowded to look down at the body on the sheet . . . the casual Yankees and the poor whites and even the southerners . . . believed aloud that it was an anonymous negro crime committed not by a negro but by Negro and [they] knew, believed, and hoped that she had been ravished too: at least once before her throat was cut and at least once afterward. The sheriff came up and looked himself once and then sent the body away, hiding the poor thing from the eyes. (pp. 271–2)

The naked voyeurism of the crowd is skillfully and believably drawn, as is the correlating counter-reflex that leads the sheriff to veil the body: "This object poisons sight, let it be hid" (*Othello* v.ii.374–5). Faulkner powerfully conveys the double-impulse of abjection, as well as hinting at its connection to lynch-thinking. And the murderer *will*, of course, be lynched; however much the town despised his victim, she was still a "white lady."

Or rather, in her rape/murder she *becomes* a "white lady" – as Roberts points out – because the town can make use of her death.[15] Or, in the darkly ironic phrasing of Deborah Clarke, "being murdered is the best thing she ever did for them."[16] By the same token, her murderer, Joe Christmas, is publicized a "nigger" – as opposed to the dark-complexioned "foreigner" that the town initially takes him for – when evidence arises for his guilt. Joe and Joanna, with their interlocked names and their shared outsider status, become joint victims of a sacrificial ritual set in motion long before the violence that allegedly justifies Joe's lynching. It's as though the town was merely waiting for – indeed, in Faulkner's terms, it *hoped* for – the rape/murder to happen. Now, the fun begins for them.

This does not, however, make the townspeople at fault for what happened to Joanna. The one at fault – certainly in Joe's mind, but quite possibly in Faulkner's as well – is Joanna herself.[17] The story of her relationship to Joe – in typical Faulknerian fashion – emerges piecemeal and out of chronological order, but by the end of the novel the reader feels little sympathy for the woman he butchered. As Laura L. Bush notes, "Faulkner's novel requires readers to view, like voyeurs, Joe's brutality from a one-sided, abuser's prospective."[18] Joe, adrift and hungry as he so often is, steals into her kitchen for food and finds her coolly willing to provide it; he then moves into the "negro cabin" behind her house and partakes of her charity for three years. It is unclear when he starts having sex with her, but it is perfectly clear that the first episode – and others as well – constitutes rape.

Even after a year it was as though he entered by stealth to despoil her virginity each time anew. It was as though each turn of dark saw him faced again with the necessity to despoil again that which he had already despoiled – or never had and never would.

Sometimes he thought of it in that way, remembering the hard, untearful and unselfpitying and almost manlike yielding of that surrender. A spiritual privacy so long intact that even its own instinct for preservation had immolated it . . . There was no feminine vacillation, no coyness of obvious desire and intention to succumb at last. (pp. 221–2)

Joe repeats the latter misogynist reflection the next day, when he sees her in daylight and is stunned and enraged to see her act as though nothing has happened. "'My God,' he thought, 'it was like I was the woman and she was the man' . . . Because she had resisted to the very last. But it was not woman resistance, that resistance which, if really meant, cannot be overcome by any man for the reason that the woman observes no rules of physical combat" (p. 222). These passages are confusing, and it is not clear whether the confusion is Joe's or the author's. If typical "woman resistance . . . cannot be overcome," clearly women can never *really* be raped: a "real" victim would successfully resist her attacker. This is misogynistic sophistry, but we can put it aside for the moment as Joe seems to be excluding Joanna – with her "hard . . . manlike . . . surrender" – from this category of "feminine" behavior. But wait a minute. Just one page later he is raping her again, and it is unclear whether this second rape happens on the ensuing night, after he was enraged to find her spiritually unvanquished, or whether Joe is simply replaying the first rape in his memory, as he does obsessively – the text has already told us – for at least a year. And during this second rape – or second account of the same rape – he says, "She did not resist at all. It was almost as though she were helping him, with small changes of position of limbs . . ." At the same time, however, that he fantasizes her assistance in the rape, he says, "But beneath his hands the body might have been the body of a dead woman not yet stiffened" (p. 223). So, does she resist, or doesn't she? Even within what is clearly an account of the same attack, Joe contradicts himself: how can a corpse "assist" its attacker by moving its limbs?

At this point, it becomes necessary to re-examine Joe's initial musings about the rape, which he sees as re-enacted each time he goes to her "to despoil again that which he had already despoiled – *or never had and never would*" (emphasis mine). Has Joanna "really" been raped? Is she even *capable* of being raped? Joe posits that "*Under her clothes she cant even be made so that it could have happened*" (p. 222; italics in original). Joanna is simultaneously sexually impregnable – thanks to that "spiritual privacy so long intact" – and unrape-able because totally available, totally "open," like the back door she refuses to lock against him, even after the attack. Again, it becomes necessary to re-quote and re-analyze Faulkner's prose to untangle the dizzying indeterminacy of his depiction of the rape: Joanna's "spiritual privacy" has been "so long intact that its instinct for preservation had immolated it." Her virginity – as she heads toward menopause – simply, and of itself, implodes, leaving nothing in its wake for Joe to violate. Roberts notes, "Joanna Burden acts as both a body that cannot be raped and a body that is raped."[19] She is, in a word, (un)rape-able.

That she falls into this paradoxical category of woman becomes all too clear when we learn how she ultimately reacts to the rape(s). She becomes her rapist's willing lover, and from there descends into a maniacal sexuality that Faulkner describes as "nymphomania." Faulkner writes, "It was as though he had fallen into a sewer . . ." The sewer is Joanna's sexuality and moral perversion – the negative flip-side of Lena's fecundated womb and "inwardlighted" spiritual state. "The sewer ran only by night," Faulkner writes. "The days were the same as they had ever been . . . But he knew that she was in the house and that the coming of the dark within the old walls was breaking down something and leaving it corrupt with waiting" (p. 243). The "something" that is "corrupt with waiting" is Joanna's middle-aged, unfructified womb, transformed into something sewer-like from years of stagnant sexual desire.

> At first it shocked him: the abject fury of the New England glacier exposed suddenly to the fire of the New England biblical hell. Perhaps he was aware of the abnegation in it: the imperious and fierce urgency that concealed an actual despair at frustrate and irrevocable years, which she appeared to attempt to compensate each night as if she believed that it would be the last night on earth by damning herself forever to the hell of her forefathers, by living not alone in sin but in filth. (p. 244)

The language of damnation so central to earlier discourses of inter-racialism returns here with a vengeance, and as in Brontë it is unclear whether this damnation is literal, psychological, or symbolic. Joanna turns her affair with Joe into a series of bizarre sex-games: she talks dirty to him; enacts scenes of jealousy despite the absence of a rival, "playing it out like a play"; she forces him to re-enact the role of rapist, climbing in through a window while she hides in a closet or empty room, "her eyes in the dark glowing like the eyes of cats." The description builds in intensity, and Joanna – already an animal with her glowing eyes – becomes increasingly monstrous:

> Now and then she appointed trysts beneath certain shrubs about the grounds, where he would find her naked, or with her clothing half torn to ribbons upon her, in the *wild* throes of nymphomania . . . She would be *wild* then, in the close, breathing halfdark without walls, with her *wild* hair, each strand of which would seem to come alive *like octopus tentacles*, and her *wild* hands and her breathing: 'Negro! Negro! Negro!'" (p. 245; emphases mine)

The suggestion that a white female advocate of "the negro cause" could find a certain erotic thrill in calling her black lover "negro" is not what I object to in this passage; indeed, I find it one of the more psychologically plausible aspects of this portrait of a "nymphomaniac." It is the imagery that troubles me – the medusa-like hair, for instance – and that imagery derives from the author, not the character, in this passage that distinguishes between Joe's thoughts and the narrative "truth" ("*Perhaps* he was aware . . ."). Faulkner writes, "Within six months she was completely corrupted. It could not be said that he corrupted her. His own life, for all its anonymous promiscuity, had been conventional enough, as a life of healthy and normal sin usually is . . . In fact, it was as though . . . *she began to corrupt him*" (p. 246; emphasis mine).

Now wait a minute. Didn't *he* rape *her*? And as to that "life of healthy and normal sin" Joe led until this point, I have to wonder what Faulkner was smoking when he penned the line. Had he forgotten what he'd written about Joe in the previous 245 pages? This is a man who, when offered his first sexual experience, chooses to *beat* the girl rather than lose his virginity with her. His second experience is not much better: the prostitute/waitress tells him she has her period and he reacts by hitting her, running off, and vomiting in misogynist horror at the images menstruation brings to mind. When he finally has sex with her, it's after dragging her into the woods and ripping her dress; he hits her again when he realizes she is a prostitute, and he begins routinely calling her his "whore." After Bobbie there is the series of anonymous white women Joe copulates with and then tells he is a "nigger," sado-masochistically relishing their racist horror and sense of having been corrupted: when one woman fails to react this way, he beats her within inches of her life. Can it be anything but authorial amnesia that presents this as "a life of healthy and normal sin"? I think even the stoutest moralist would prefer Joanna's kinky version of hide-and-seek.

Doreen Fowler concedes that "*Light in August* is . . . a feminist's nightmare" – she then goes on to argue, however, that the novel "is not a facile affirmation" of misogynist ideology, but rather "an indictment and a warning."[20] Apologists like Fowler will argue that the misogyny of the above reflections must not be ascribed to the author, but to the character. And Joe does hate women. As a boy he is routinely beaten by his fanatically religious adopted father, but he prefers the beatings to his adopted mother's pathetic attempts at intimacy. Faulkner writes, "It was not the hard work which he hated, nor the punishment and injustice . . .

It was the woman: that soft kindness which he believed himself doomed to be forever victim of" (p. 158). And maybe there is a bizarre, if neurotic logic here; it is not inconceivable that, to a psychology hardened by violence, it is kindness – which makes one emotionally vulnerable – that victimizes. Hence, in Joe's psychology, the mother's slipping him petty cash or food behind the father's back, or attempting to intervene in his punishments, manifests not kindness or the desire to bond through a sense of co-conspiracy, but rather "a woman's affinity and instinct for secrecy, for casting a faint taint of evil about even the most trivial and innocent actions" (p. 157).

But not every eruption of misogyny in the novel can be traced to Joe's psychology. Some appear in passages that call attention to the limits of the character's knowledge, as in this description of Joe's first lover, the prostitute Bobbie: "Even a casual adult glance could tell that she would never see thirty again. But to Joe she probably did not look more than seventeen too, because of her smallness . . . But the adult look saw that the smallness was not due to any natural slenderness but to some inner corruption of the spirit itself . . ." (p. 161). This spiritual corruption – invisible to Joe – corresponds to the horrified vision he has when she lets him in on the secret of a woman's "periodical filth" (p. 173): "he seemed to see a diminishing row of suavely shaped urns in moonlight, blanched. And not one of them was perfect. Each one was cracked and from each crack there issued something liquid, deathcolored, and foul" (p. 178). Viewing this as the negative counterpart to the early Keats allusion, we note that the urns here are *multiplied* – as, indeed, "bad women" highly outnumber the "good" in this novel. Also, the substance the urns leak is not clearly blood: it is ambiguously "deathcolored," which the reader is likely to imagine as black, particularly in contrast to the "blanched" exterior of the vase. An allusion to the "whited sepulchres" of the gospel according to Matthew,[21] these urns are white without and black within – like Joe himself, who passes for white but who thinks of himself as a "nigger."

The notion of Bobbie's internal corruption – whether imagined in spiritual or in physical terms – is quickly confirmed by her behavior, and in this the author is ultimately implicated in Joe's misogyny. Called "harlot" by Joe's adopted father she flies into a violent rage that doesn't cease even as he lies unconscious on the floor, knocked over the head with a chair by Joe: "He looked and saw two men holding her and she writhing and struggling . . . her white face wrung and ugly beneath the splotches of savage paint, her mouth a small jagged hole filled with shrieking. 'Calling me harlot!' she screamed" (p. 192). With her "white face" and "savage paint," Bobbie enacts the (racialized) part of the Whore of Babylon, even as she violently rejects the label. She continues to struggle with the men who detain her, trying to bite them, and finally turns her rage on Joe as well, hurling abuse at him. The hypocritical over-reaction to being called "harlot" (she is, after all, a prostitute) and the futile (only because she's female and small) attempts at violence squelch any inkling of sympathy we have for the poor, stunted creature, especially when she throws yet another temper tantrum hours later, attacking Joe in the most racist and obscene of terms: "'He told me himself he was a nigger! The son of a bitch! Me f – ing for nothing a nigger son of a bitch . . .'" (p. 204). Significantly, this is the only place Faulkner indicates the "F-word"; Bobbie is not only a hysterical and deludedly vain prostitute, but she also has a "filthy mouth" – that "jagged hole" from which racism and obscenity stream. Here she mirrors Joanna, who enjoys "the forbidden wordsymbols" (p. 244) – the word "fuck" probably foremost among them.

We have strayed somewhat from Joanna in contextualizing Joe's reaction to her: it's hard, if not impossible, to be linear when reading Faulkner. Let us return to the "sewer" passage, to see what conclusions, if any, Joe or Faulkner draw from Joanna's descent into "nymphomania." Joe wishes to leave her, feeling himself "sucked down into a bottomless morass," but he stays nonetheless, partially out of curiosity, "watching the two creatures that struggled in the one body like two moongleamed shapes struggling drowning in alternate throes upon the surface of a black thick pool . . ." These two selves are the cool and collected daylight Joanna, who "even though lost and damned, remained somehow . . . impregnable," and "the other . . . who in furious denial of that impregnability strove to drown in the black abyss of its own creating that physical purity which had been preserved too long now even to be lost." The racial inflection of this rhetoric is telling: "Now and then they would come to the black surface, locked like sisters; the black waters would drain away . . ." (p. 246). The second self begins to win out: she begins "to get fat," sensuality and earthiness displacing the "manlike" spinster-self that had preceded the loss of her virginity. When Joe sees her in the daytime he senses "beneath the clean, austere garments which she wore that rich rottenness ready to flow into putrifaction at a touch, like something growing in a swamp"; he then wonders whether "what he now saw during daylight was a phantom of someone whom the night sister had murdered" (p. 248).

The misogyny of these passages is merciless, and I've quoted more than enough to make my point (though there's more). It is more important to bear in mind the overall effect of the narration: the chapter that tells the story of the descent into the "sewer" is inserted between the chapter that tells of the rape, and the chapter which returns, again, to the spectacle of Joanna's mutilated body. The chapter, hence, develops sympathy for the murderer, describing the ways in which the victim "drove" him to violence. Faulkner surpasses prior inter-racialist narratives by making the white female not only a partner-in-crime or moral "twin" – meta-phorically, inwardly blackened – but by making *her* the victimizer and *him* the victim. And in fact we learn, at the very end of the chapter, that Joe literally killed her in self-defense: she pulls a gun on him in which he later finds two bullets – "'For her and for me'" (p. 270). Joanna becomes the Othello figure, planning a murder–suicide. At this point – scarcely more than halfway through this very long novel – sympathy is turned entirely to Joe, whom we must follow through an agonizing hunt that we know will conclude in his lynching.

Roberts frames her reading of *Light in August* in reference to the real history of lynchings in Faulkner's Mississippi, especially the case of Claud Neal, who – two years before the publication of the novel – was "tortured, mutilated, forced to eat his own penis, and hanged" for allegedly raping and murdering a young white woman. Roberts observes, "Faulkner's fiction in the thirties reflects the climate of racial and sexual terrorism. His work tries to understand and, in a way, contain the terror through a shift in the blame from black man to white woman." Claud Neal's alleged victim was later rumored to have had a long-standing consensual affair with him, and medical examiners even suggested that she had not been raped.[22] Faulkner, in diagnosing a social illness that confronted him practically every day, had seen enough atrocities practiced upon black men in the name of a white female "purity" he had to know was often a sham. Published in 1932 – four years before Mitchell's *Gone with the Wind* made monolithic the mythologies of the old south – his revision of the Claud Neal story was a bold critique of white supremacy and white sexual hypocrisy.

And ultimately, neither Joe nor Joanna is the villain. The villain is Joe's grandfather and chief enemy, Doc Hines – the walking embodiment and grim parody of everything sick about Faulkner's culture. Doc is insane, but Faulkner crafts his insanity to reflect – or telescope – the collective insanity that is lynch-thinking. And here Faulkner does right from a feminist point of view, as he throws just enough misogyny into Doc's racist hellfire-and-brimstone ravings to signal the interdependence of these two forms of intolerance, and their amenability to the discourse of religious fanaticism. Doc's refrain of "bitchery and abomination!" and "God's abomination of womanflesh!," his railing against "niggers" and "sluts" – in particular the "slut" who is his daughter, and the "nigger" she gave birth to – and, finally, his willingness to lynch his own grandson, set him up as the key source and touchstone of all the malevolence of Joe's world. He – not Joe, rapist and beheader of white women – is the novel's heart of darkness.

Doc might also be viewed as the main cause of everything wrong with Joe, starting from before the latter's birth. Joe's obsession with the idea that he is a "nigger" has its roots in Doc's insistence that Joe's father lied in calling himself Mexican. His orphanhood is directly a result of Doc, who shot his father (perhaps moments after Joe's conception), denied his mother medical care during the birth, and then took the baby away to an orphanage, where he quietly took up a job as guard in order to torment the child and poison his mind as he grew up. Of course, we learn none of this until the very end of the novel: the pathological grandfather appeared only briefly – as an anonymous, crazy old man stalking the playground – in the account of Joe's childhood at the orphanage. From the child Joe's point of view, everything wrong in his life began with the white nurse whom he accidentally witnessed in an illicit tryst, and who made him a scapegoat for her sexual guilt, shipping him off to the orphanage for "niggers."

In Doc's mad ravings, we see the apotheosis of the obsession with the demonic recurrent in inter-racialism. Doc believes that Joe, as the product of miscegeny, *is* "the devil's spawn" (p. 423). Yet, clearly, it is Doc who is the demon of the novel. Moreover, in his death, Joe becomes a Christ figure, as his initials and Christmas birthday have signaled all along. Toward the end of the novel, the metaphor of the ongoing road that Joe imagines as his life becomes the circle that he now realizes this road has been tracing; this metaphor is replaced, in the episode describing his death, by the metaphor of the chess-board and the omniscient Player. The bloody scene takes place in the house of the aptly named minister Hightower, where Joe has turned for sanctuary. Faulkner's metaphors enact the collapsing of racial and moral binaries as the fanatical white supremacist Percy Grimm – his expression akin to "that serene, unearthly luminousness of angels in church windows" – hunts Joe with the recklessness of one "under the protection of a magic or of providence" (p. 437). As the pursuers enter the minister's house, the "stale and cloistral dimness" of the place is penetrated by "savage summer sunlight," which seems to linger on them "in its shameless savageness." The rest of the passage is full of Christological imagery:

Out of it their faces seemed to *glare* with *bodiless suspension* as though from *haloes* as they stooped and *raised* Hightower, his face *bleeding*, from the floor where Christmas, his *raised* and armed manacled hands full of *glare* and *glitter* like *lightning bolts*, so that he resembled a vengeful and furious *god* pronouncing a doom, had struck him down. (p. 438; emphases mine)

Religious references clash and jangle in Faulkner's prose: Hightower "swears to God" and Grimm cries, "'Jesus Christ!,' his young voice clear and outraged like that of a young *priest*" (emphasis mine). When he finds, shoots, and dismembers Joe he does so in these terms: "Now you'll let white women alone, even in hell" (p. 439). But the victim's manner in death belies Grimm's prediction about the destination of Joe's soul:

For a long moment he looked up at them with peaceful and unfathomable and unbearable eyes. Then his face, body, all, seemed to collapse, to fall in upon itself, and from the slashed garments about his hips and loins the pent black blood seemed to rush like a released breath. It seemed to rush out of his pale body like the rush of sparks from a rising rocket; upon that blast the man seemed to rise soaring into their memories forever and ever. They are not to lose it, in whatever peaceful valleys, beside whatever placid and reassuring streams of old age . . . It will be there, musing, quiet, steadfast, not fading and not particularly threatful, but of itself alone, serene, of itself alone triumphant. Again from the town . . . the scream of the siren mounted toward an unbelievable crescendo, passing out of the realm of hearing. (pp. 439–40)

The imagery here is of ascent, not descent; of light, not darkness of ablution, not pollution. At the same time, the imagery is profoundly – if ambiguously – sexual. I concur with Roberts' reading of the "black blood" as less a racial marker than a symbol of the feminine in him, recalling the "deathcolored" substance leaking from the white urns of his misogynist vision of menstruation. Roberts writes: "The ejaculatory nature of Joe's death is suggested by the 'rising rocket.' In the end Joe incorporates both white and black, both male and female," and in so doing is "erased."[23] Perhaps not entirely, though, as the spectacle of this font of blood will forever haunt its audience, troubling the psalm-like metaphors they hope will populate their descent toward old age and the Valley of Death.

One question remains to be asked of *Light in August*: where are the black women? For a novel so preoccupied with race and gender relations

– a novel in which almost every page contains a racial reference, and many pages are positively checkered with terms like "black," "white," "negro" or "nigger" – the absence of black women is striking. There is the anonymous "negro girl" waiting passively in a shed to service Joe and his teen-aged friends, whom Joe decides to beat instead; there is another woman "who resembled an ebony carving," whom the text mentions his living with; and there is finally the black woman with whom he swaps shoes while in flight, in order to throw the dogs off his scent. None of these women is given a name or dialogue: the first two, indeed, seem almost mute. And in fact, they might as well be the same woman: the universal, archetypal Black Woman, who is pure flesh, pure sexuality. In the scene in the shed, Joe does not even see the girl with whom he is supposed to lose his virginity; he stumbles into the darkness and *smells* her, "smelling the woman, smelling the negro all at once; enclosed by womanshenegro . . ." Are "woman" and "negro" merely different names for the same entity? Faulkner implies, here, that they are. M. J. Burgess notes, "In [Joe's] world, gender *is* race and blackness and femaleness – structural homologies in their shared position of subordination – become identical terms."[24] Moreover, this is femaleness at its most debased. When the girl speaks, it is not speech but "a guiding sound that was no particular word and completely unaware" (p. 147). As Beth Widmaier notes, "She cannot communicate in symbolic discourse, cannot vocalize a personal will, and speaks from her position in the abject semiotic before identity is individu-ated."[25] The description continues to elide not just the black girl's subjectivity, but her humanity: Joe discerns her in the darkness as "some-thing, prone, abject; her eyes perhaps. Leaning, he seemed to look down into a black well and at the bottom saw two glints like reflections of dead stars." He starts to kick her, maniacally, until "There was no She at all" (p. 147). The second interaction with a black woman is not violent, but similar in its conflation of negritude with the flesh and the femi-nine: "At night he would lie in bed beside her . . . trying to breathe into himself the dark odor, the dark and inscrutable thinking and being of negroes" (p. 212).

Where are the black women in *Light in August*? Everywhere and nowhere. When Joe's late-night wanderings bring him near the "negro section" of town, he likewise associates and abjects blackness and the feminine: "On all sides, even within him, the bodiless fecundmellow voices of negro women murmured. It was as though he and all other manshaped life about him had been returned to the lightless hot wet primogenitive Female. He began to run" (p. 107). Escaping into the white

section, he looks back in terror at "the black pit from which he had fled
. . . No light came from it . . . It just lay there, black, impenetrable . . . It
might have been the original quarry, abyss itself" (p. 108). Interestingly,
foremost in Joe's reaction to the sound of black female voices is his sense
that he hears them *within him*. It's as though he assumes his racially
"black" blood is the blood of a black *woman* – yet we learn by the end of
the book his mother was white – or as though his body, his sexuality itself,
is where his blackness resides. Faulkner writes, "In the halflight he
appeared to be watching his body, seeming to watch it turning slow and
lascivious in a whispering of gutter filth like a drowned corpse in a thick
still black pool of more than water" (p. 99). Clearly, the "sewer" Joe sees
in Joanna's sexuality is also inside himself. And that's why, fleeing it down
the long, lonely road of his life, he winds up tracing a circle. He winds up
exactly where he started: a figure trapped in time, like an image painted
on an urn. Like the hero of a tragedy. Each time we see it, he makes the
same mistake.

Bigger Thomas, the protagonist of Richard Wright's *Native Son*, kills *two*
women – a rich, white virgin and a poor, black maid – but he is only
punished for killing the former. Indeed, the murderer himself nearly
forgets the second victim until her bloody remains are unveiled at the
inquest. Bigger's amnesia is his culture's. In flight after the murder of
Mary Dalton, he kills his girlfriend in order to prevent her from turning
him in or otherwise bungling his escape: the second murder is a result of
the first and utterly eclipsed by it in the outraged eyes of the white masses
on his trail. Yet, the second murder – in narratological and moral terms –
is also far more terrible: Mary dies suddenly and painlessly, in a drunken
stupor, while Bessie's death is premeditated, painful, and horrifically
drawn out. Mary dies accidentally and at the hands of a stranger: Bessie
has a relationship with her murderer and has foreknowledge of the
murder. Before murdering Bessie, Bigger bullies her, terrorizes her, and
rapes her; he then beats her over the head with a brick and throws her
down a garbage shaft. We later learn her suffering doesn't even end there:
the poor creature regains consciousness, tries to climb her way out, and
finally freezes to death.

This disparity is no doubt part of Wright's point, in underscoring the
hypocrisy of white justice in making the brutalized, black female body a
literal prop in the court-room drama surrounding a *white* girl's murder.
Still, this doubling of female bodies carries a theoretical significance that
seems to me outside the scope of authorial consciousness. Bigger murders

two women, but he only rapes one: it is in the novel's treatment of the issue of rape that the race–gender fault-line seems to have tripped up the author as well.

Let us start with the first, precipitous murder, and its racial encoding by Wright. It is Bigger's first day on the job at the Dalton household, where he will be chauffeur. Eerie images of whiteness Gothicize the setting, reversing the usual binaries in order to underscore the protagonist's anxiety and sense of alienation in the world of rich whites: particularly prominent is the ghostly "white figure" of the aged, blind Mrs. Dalton, who is usually accompanied by a big, white cat (a negative allusion to Poe's "The black cat"). Bigger, enlisted to drive Mary to an evening lecture, gets embroiled in her tryst with her communist boyfriend and ultimately winds up – to his supreme agitation – having to carry her limp, drunken body to bed. Wright's figurative language underscores this as a kind of pre-ordained script, a kind of theatre wherein racism stages its own nightmares: "He felt strange, possessed, or as if he were acting upon a stage in front of a crowd of people."[26] Leaning over her on the bed, he hesitates, transfixed by the allure of this attractive, forbidden, and unconscious body; seemingly despite himself, he steals a furtive caress only to turn in "hysterical terror" when the door opens and the "white blur" of Mrs. Dalton appears. Panicking as Mary begins to mumble and stir, he puts a pillow over her head and smothers her, unwittingly, to death, before this paradoxically blind audience. The color binaries comprised by the bed, the pillow, the white young woman, and the repeatedly described "white blur" underscore the allusion to *Othello* legible in the (aborted) inter-racial eroticism, in the tropes of demonic possession and theatre, and of course in the smothering of this "nouvelle Desdemona."[27]

What follows, however, surpasses any Othellophile precedent for Gothic horror. In disposing of the body, Bigger realizes he must sever its head. He has carried it down to the basement and shoved it into the furnace, but the head does not fit. (This is witnessed by the white cat, whose accusative stare almost paralyzes Bigger.) Wright's language hammers home the racial point as Bigger steels himself to cut Mary's "white throat," places the knife against "the white flesh," and then pauses, staring at the fire-lit "edge of the blade resting on the white skin." His knife fails to do the job; he must resort to an ax – I will spare you the horrific realism of Wright's description – and when it's finally done, Bigger is haunted by "the sight of this bloody throat" and the blood-soaked black curls around it (p. 79).

Wright is merciless in keeping that image in our minds, and in the protagonist's. When it reappears, there is again the reference to the blood-soaked black curls – black curls that were never noted in descriptions of the living Mary. Roberts notes of the decapitation in *Light in August* that "in cutting Joanna's throat Joe gives her another orifice."[28] I would point out a similar – if hideous – sexual metaphor operant here, in the allusion to defloration and the resulting blood-soaked pubic hair. Bigger will be accused not just of murder, but of rape. Indeed, the fear of being caught in a seeming rape-attempt is precisely the *reason* Bigger kills Mary. That he didn't rape her will become the central irony of the trial sequence. And indeed, decapitation has a long history as a sexual euphemism, dating back to those Shakespearean puns on the loss of a maidenhead.[29] Decapitation imagery literalizes the mind–body split that governs sexual repression and misogynist constructions of woman as pure flesh.

Later in the novel, Bigger's reflections about Bessie evidence a subtler decapitation urge:

As he walked beside her he felt that there were two Bessies: one a body he had just had and wanted badly again; the other was in Bessie's face; it asked questions; it bargained and sold the other Bessie to advantage. He wished he could clench his fist and swing his arm and blot out, kill, sweep away the Bessie on Bessie's face and leave the other helpless and yielding before him. He would then gather her up and put her in his chest, his stomach . . . keeping her there just to feel and know that she was his to have and hold whenever he wanted to. (p. 119)

From *Titus Andronicus* on, we have seen these tropes: dismemberment, rape, even cannibalism (the latter a variation on Bigger's earlier comment that "the white folks live . . . in [his] stomach" [p. 18]). The urge to blot someone or something out is also habitual to Bigger. An outgrowth of the book's preoccupation with blindness/vision and black/white, the idea of blotting – as one does with ink – underscores the latent violence in representation, and implicates the collective, willed blindness Bigger sees all around him in the violence he is driven to. Unable to blind himself willingly to what is in front of him – as so many others do – Bigger wants to blot it out, erase it, remove it. That he can only do this in the most brutal and literal way, rather than by authoring his own fate and hence ordering his reality – like the Daltons in their big white house, removed from the ugly realities of Southside – underscores, from Wright's point of view, not his potency but his impotence.

This is, I believe, an accurate and compelling analysis of the way social impotence leads to violence. But there are blind spots in Wright's critique, evident in the verbal treatment of Bigger's violence. For instance, the three words "he had killed" become a refrain in the novel; after he kills Bessie, the refrain is "he had killed twice." At a certain point I became uncomfortable with the past participle standing there alone, "killed," as though there had been no victims, and as though both victims had not been female.[30] It should read, "He had killed *women.*" But, as a refrain, this would not have had the effect Wright seems to have intended by the incantatory repetition of "he had killed": to insert "women" would have diminished the act. After all, killing – as rebellion against oppression – can be heroic. But killing someone weaker than oneself – killing a slender, young woman when she is passed out drunk; killing a presumably stronger, but exhausted, working woman when she is asleep – is cowardice and villainy. Such violence merely repeats – at the next level – the oppression that arguably led to it.

Bigger doesn't just kill: he also rapes. In the freezing, dark, abandoned building to which they flee when Mary's bones are discovered in the Daltons' furnace, he rapes Bessie even after deciding that he has to kill her. "Imperiously driven, he rode roughshod over her whimpering protests feeling acutely sorry for her as he galloped a frenzied horse down a steep hill in a resisting wind" (p. 198). As she finally drifts off to sleep, he listens to her breathing, imagining it "as a white thread stretching out over a vast black gulf." This image recurs when the wind outside shrieks "like an idiot in an icy black pit" – that black pit prefiguring the air-shaft in which Bessie will eventually freeze to death. Arguing with himself all the while, Bigger turns the flashlight on her tear-stained and sleeping "black face," then shuts it off so as not to witness his own crime (p. 200). Pausing with the raised brick only once in anguished and horrified reluctance, he brings it down on her head mercilessly and repeatedly, not stopping until it is a "sodden mass." Afterward, Bigger does not want to look at Bessie, but feels he has to. "There! Blood and lips and hair and face turned to one side and blood running slowly." This is almost the same nightmare-image of Mary's head, but the racial photo-negative; he later calls it "the face of death and blood" (p. 202) – as though it did not even belong to Bessie at all, and never had. When he throws the body into the air-shaft it goes "down into blackness" – hitting the bottom with a thud – never to resurface in his thoughts until the law drags it up again.

Bigger's first reaction to this second crime – and first willful murder – is not regret (although he curses himself for forgetting to remove the money from Bessie's pocket before throwing her down the airshaft) but exhilaration: "And yet, out of it, over and above all that had happened, impalpable but real, there remained to him a queer sense of power. *He had done this* . . . In all his life those two murders were the most meaningful things that had ever happened to him" (p. 203). Yet the meaning he attributes to Bessie's death is paltry compared to that of Mary, as he realizes fifty-five pages later when a detective stuns him with the question "where's Bessie?" Wright outlines Bigger's bewilderment in shocking detail: "Bigger's eyes widened. He had not thought of Bessie but once since his capture. Her death was unimportant beside that of Mary; he knew that when they killed him it would be for Mary's death, not Bessie's" (p. 258).

Why does Wright have Bigger kill Bessie? Couldn't the same story – about race relations, about black male despair, disempowerment, and violence – have been told without the second murder? Wouldn't readers feel more sympathy for Bigger if he had not killed a second time, and deliberately? They certainly would, and perhaps that was part of Wright's point – to present as morally perplexing, as conflicted a picture as possible. But Bessie's murder also serves an important narratological purpose in the book: her body will later be used as "evidence" against Bigger, "proving" not that he murdered Mary, but that he also raped her.

Interestingly enough, it was Bessie who first pointed this out to Bigger – "They'll . . . they'll say you raped her" – and Bigger realized that "there would be no way to prove that he had not" (p. 193). Indeed, the prosecuting attorney even claims that he burned Mary's body in order to destroy the evidence of rape: "He killed her because he *raped* her! Mind you, Your Honor, the central crime here is *rape!*" (p. 345). In Wright's scathing social critique, the murder, butchering, and burning of a young woman are of less interest to white justice than the question of her sexual and racial purity, and the former, gruesome details of the case become a mere excuse for prurient speculations as to whether a black penis penetrated a then intact, virginal, white, female body. (That Mary was a virgin is evident in the fact that, even while drunk, she only "makes out" with her boyfriend – and then there is her name, of course.) Even worse, the bones of the victim are trotted out and exhibited to the horrified and fascinated audience as proof, not of murder, but of rape – and, if this is not enough to prove the latter, there is the *pièce de résistance* of Bessie's "raped and mutilated body" (p. 280).

I want to pause over this juxtaposition of two forms of "ocular proof." A better metaphor for the racial binary of black versus white femininity seems scarcely possible: the white bones of the virgin sacrifice versus the "bloody and black" spectacle of Bessie's remains, the sight of which causes Bigger – for the first time in the novel – to shrink and cover his eyes. Here we have, vividly literalized, the notion of black woman as all-body, as mute, mindless flesh, that Faulkner cites without critique – and, counterpoised against it, the clean, white bones that manifest and metonymize white woman's alleged "angelic," anti-material, anti-sexual nature. At the same time, however, that exhibits A and B materialize this binary, the narrative context undercuts it, by making the black body a *surrogate* for the obliterated white flesh that encased those white bones. Using Bessie's body as "evidence" that Mary was not just killed but raped, on the one hand subordinates the former to the latter, but it also in effect *superimposes* Bessie on Mary. In an odd sort of way, Bessie (to use Bigger's favorite term) *blots out* or erases Mary.

To Bigger, however, the cynical use of Bessie's body here is primarily a lesson in white hypocrisy, and it incites in him a rare moment of cross-gender empathy:

. . . he felt a deeper sympathy for Bessie than at any time when she was alive. He knew that Bessie, too, though dead, though killed by him, would resent her dead body being used in this way. Anger quickened in him: an old feeling that Bessie had often described to him when she had come from long hours of hot toil in white folks' kitchens . . . He was their property, heart and soul, body and blood; what they did claimed every atom of him, sleeping and waking; it colored life and dictated the terms of death. (pp. 281–2)

Viewing the prop made of his girlfriend's body, he realizes that he too is "property." He is also made to appreciate retrospectively an experience he, because generally unemployed, has been spared, an experience particular to working black women: he realizes the way in which a life of service to others denies one a sense of personhood, a sense of owning one's own life. This is not the only time in the novel Bigger identifies with one of his victims: at one point during his flight from the law he has a nightmare in which he finds himself carrying his *own* bloody head wrapped in newspapers. In both cases, however, the collapse of the murderer into his victim is brief – yet another way in which Wright *subverts* Othellophilia, which, in abjecting a "Nigger lover" like Joanna Burden, must make her a black man's double or soul-mate. Wright is far too invested in his hero's subjectivity to have him annihilate himself in identification with any woman, white or black.

And herein lies both the emancipatory vision of *Native Son* – for black men – and its greatest blind spot. On being reminded, by Bessie, that he will be accused of rape, though innocent of it, Bigger reflects, "Had he raped her? Yes, he had raped her. Every time he felt as he had felt that night, he raped. But rape was not what one did to women. Rape was what one felt when one's back was against a wall . . . He committed rape every time he looked into a white face . . . But it was rape when he cried out in hate deep in his heart. That, too, was rape" (p. 193). Rape, here, becomes curiously abstract – a feeling, and a frequent one, almost a habit of thought – and divorced from its victim. Rape becomes an intransitive verb, just like "killed" in the passages I've already highlighted. Above all, though, "rape" is an act divorced from the gender of its victim: it becomes something one "does" to, or in the presence of, a genderless "white face." If this is the novel's definition of rape, then, does Bigger or does Bigger not "rape" Mary Dalton?

According to the newspapers, it's a foregone conclusion. The first account Bigger sees reads "REPORTERS FIND DALTON GIRL'S BONES IN FURNACE. NEGRO CHAUFFEUR DISAPPEARS. FIVE THOUSAND POLICE SURROUND BLACK BELT. AUTHORITIES HINT SEX CRIME . . ." Bigger re-reads the line: "AUTHORITIES HINT SEX CRIME. Those words excluded him utterly from the world. To hint that he had committed a sex crime was to pronounce the death sentence . . ." (p. 206). At this point, I want to ask Bigger – or ask his world – or ask his author – or ask his author's world – "why?" Why is the phrase "sex crime" more shocking to the white male reader than the phrase "girl's bones in furnace"? How is cutting someone's head off and burning her body somehow less wrong than putting a penis in her, even if it *is* a black penis? It makes no sense, and I'm not sure that Wright's hero – or even his novel – really wants to make sense of it. Subsequent newspaper snippets harp on the charge of rape. "24-HOUR SEARCH FAILS TO UNEARTH RAPIST" (p. 216); "Bigger Thomas, 20-year-old Negro rapist and killer" (p. 217); "NEGRO RAPIST FAINTS AT INQUEST . . . Bigger Thomas, Negro sex-slayer . . . This man, in the grip of a mind-numbing sex passion, overpowered little Mary Dalton, raped her, murdered her . . ." The same story boasts, "Down here in Dixie we keep Negroes firmly in their places and we make them know that if they so much as touch a white woman, good or bad, they cannot live" (p. 239). For the sake of argument, I'll resist theorizing the qualifier "good or bad," as at issue here is a more basic problem of logic. Is Bigger on trial for *touching* a white woman, or for decapitating and burning her?

This iteration of rapist, rapist, rapist continues in the trial scene: it is always "rape and kill," and the bodies are "ravished," and the final words of the prosecutor's closing statement are "Bigger Thomas, this despoiler of women!" (p. 323).

These iterations read as ironic, but that irony works to occlude Wright's own plot. *Because Bigger* is *a rapist. Bigger raped Bessie.*

Why does the novel "forget" that Bigger raped Bessie? For it must have forgotten: otherwise the hysterical repetition of "Negro rapist" would *not* be ironic, and what then would be Wright's point in such repetition? Is it perhaps Wright's point that what happened between Bigger and Bessie – when she repeatedly said "Don't Bigger, don't" and he overpowered her – only "became" rape when superimposed over the same act with a white woman? Or is it the case, rather, that Bessie wasn't raped – from the point of view of the omniscient narrator – because she was (un)rape-able? If rape is a political crime – as Wright seems to conceive it – then its target is political, not personal: its target is not a person, but a *group* of people. As this is not the "reason" Bigger rapes Bessie, she has not been raped at all.

Trudier Harris is therefore not without justification in the claim that "Ultimately, Bessie is victimized by everyone, including Wright . . . and the reader."[31] It is all too easy to "forget" – as Bigger does – the rape of Bessie, to forget even her horrible death, so caught up are readers in the excitement of the flight, capture, and trial of the protagonist. And as we are dragged through the excruciating wait for his death, it is hard, it is very hard, not to forgive him. The last time I read the book, I burst into tears to hear his sentence pronounced – even though I knew what was coming – and I cried non-stop through the final pages. I hated Bigger, but I did not want him to die: he was a victim too. Wright does such an exquisite job laying bare the way social conditioning scripts human behavior, making us all actors in the great, white spotlight of American racism. As Bigger explains, "I knew what I was doing, all right. But I couldn't help it . . . It was like another man stepped inside my skin and started acting for me . . ." (p. 298). His lawyer then uses this metaphor in his defense, calling Bigger "the hapless actor in this fateful drama" (p. 327). That he refuses, when driven back to the Dalton home by a bunch of leering reporters, to re-enact, for their titillation, the presumed rape and murder of Mary, only underscores the way in which the "real" crime was play-acted, pre-ordained – indeed, a command performance for racism. "'Come on. Show us what you did,'" they taunt, cameras poised, "'. . . Get over there by that bed and show us how you raped and murdered that girl'" (p. 285). The lurid voyeurism here resonates perfectly with

Faulkner's description of the crowd's eye-balling Joanna's corpse and speculating – or fantasizing, rather – about her presumed rape.

I want to return to "if they so much as touch a white woman, good or bad . . ." One way that Wright does right by women is in not blaming the victim of black male violence – Bigger does ("hell, she *made* me do it!" [p. 97]), but Wright clearly does not endorse this blame. Neither does he polarize his female characters, pitting saintly virginal Lenas against nympho-bitches like Joanna. Bessie and Mary are foils only in social and racial terms, not on the symbolic or moral level: both are sympathetic characters, both mean well, and they even share the same weakness for liquor. Their manner of deaths is similar: both are prone, unconscious, or asleep, and are attacked on the head with household objects. Both women arouse the protagonist sexually, and though Bigger claims he "hates" Mary Dalton, he also cannot confirm that he loves Bessie. Bessie and Mary are metaphorical twins, even if no one in the novel can see it.

And therein lies the potential feminist message that we can only wish Wright had articulated. Because Bessie did not have to disappear after the inquest scene. Arguably, she had to die – for the sake of the plot-line – but she did not have to disappear. In a book so fascinated with notions of blindness, of blotting out, of vision and insight, darkness and light, the black woman is the beam in the author's eye.

In the introduction to *Invisible Man*, Ellison scoffs at the "pseudoscientific sociological" discourse that blames America's racial problems on the "high visibility" of black people. In reply, he puts forth his own thesis on the *invisibility* of black men. And while the novel does offer a radical critique of the notion of "high visibility," it often does so by underscoring the paradoxical double-gesture of racism, which wishes simultaneously to make a *spectacle* of black men, and to keep them out of sight.

For of course it is only the blindness of racism that renders the un-named protagonist invisible.[32] Speaking to us from inside his "hole," the disembodied voice of the narrator explains, "A beautiful girl once told me of a recurring nightmare in which she lay in the center of a large dark room and felt her face expand until it filled the whole room, becoming a formless mass while her eyes ran in bilious jelly up the chimney. And so it is with me." This is the first of many theoretically complex and not always positive cross-identifications with the feminine. He goes on, explaining why he fills his underground lair with light-bulbs powered by stolen electricity: "Without light I am not only invisible, but formless as well, and to be unaware of one's form is to live a death."[33] By the same token, though, isn't being *trapped* in one's form – being all-form, all-flesh – also a living death? The woman's fascinatingly Kristevian nightmare – that "bilious jelly" so suggestive of the abject interior of the body, of the entrails, of the womb, ejected through the birth-canal/chimney – could translate as simple female body dysmorphia or dread of becoming "fat." In any case, the fact that the "girl" is "beautiful" seems important in interpreting the dream: is she white or black, one wonders? It is unusual for Ellison to leave this ambiguous, particularly for women. A couple of pages later – in the narrator's marijuana-induced vision, another "beautiful girl" appears, this one white: "*I saw a beautiful girl the color of ivory pleading in a voice like my mother's as she stood before a group of slaveowners who bid for her naked body*" (p. 9; italics in original). Ellison may have Clotel in mind: he does later reference Thomas Jefferson's non-white children. In any case, inter-racialism arises in Chapter 1 as a concern of Ellison's: the same vision contains an exchange with a black woman who confesses loving her master ("You should have hated him," the narrator says), because "he gave [her] several sons" (p. 10).

The next time a white woman – or any woman at all – appears in the novel, she is once again naked. The young narrator and a group of boys from his all-black school have been chosen to attend an alleged "charity" event at a club for the white male elite: as it turns out, they're to be used as entertainment of the crudest sort, a "Battle Royal." But before the main event, there is the opening act, at which the drunken, cigar-smoking throng pushes them to the front of the ballroom to view the show. Ellison describes the spectacle thus:

A sea of faces, some hostile, some amused, ringed around us, and in the center, facing us, stood a magnificent blonde – stark naked . . . I felt a wave of irrational guilt and fear. My teeth chattered, my skin turned to goose flesh, my knees knocked. Yet I was strongly attracted and looked despite myself. *Had the price of looking been blindness, I would have looked.* The hair was yellow like that of a circus kewpie doll, the face heavily powdered and rouged, as though to form an abstract mask, the eyes hollow and smeared a cool blue, the color of a baboon's butt. I felt a desire to spit upon her as my eyes brushed slowly over her body. Her breasts were firm and round as the domes of East Indian temples, and I stood so close as to see the fine skin texture and beads of pearly perspiration glistening like dew around the pink and erected buds of her nipples. I wanted at one and the same time to run from the room . . . or go to her and cover her from my eyes and the eyes of the others with my body . . . to caress and destroy her, *to love her and murder her* . . . and yet to stroke where below the small American flag tattooed on her belly her thighs formed a capital V. (p. 19; emphases mine)

The paralysis brought on by looking subtly evokes Medusa, and the theme of blindness is linked to the problem of white women – for white women *are* a problem, to the narrator. The combination of fear, fascination, and loathing the dancer inspires in him is excruciating; in this context, the whiff of Othellophilia in "love her and murder her" makes psychological sense, however troubling. The boys tremble at the sight of this woman; some lower their heads. But the crowd forces them to look. "And then she began to dance, a slow sensuous movement; the smoke of a hundred cigars clinging to her like the thinnest of veils . . ." He describes the "big shots yelling" at them: "Some threatened us if we looked and others if we did not. On my right I saw one boy faint . . . Another boy began to plead to go home. He was . . . wearing dark red fighting trunks much too small to conceal [his] erection. He tried to hide himself with his boxing gloves" (pp. 19–20). The abject humiliation and terror of this situation for the reluctant, yet mesmerized black boys, and the white crowd's sadistic and prurient enjoyment of their guilty and terrified fascination, impress powerfully on the reader the complex cultural dynamic involved when white female and black male sexuality collide.

The description of the dancer is also interesting in its tropic language – an odd combination of exoticism (the mask, the baboon, the Indian temples, the veil) and Americana (the flag and the red, white, and blue of her make-up). As the dance quickens in tempo, the crowd takes greater liberties with the poor trapped creature, and they finally wind up catching her and tossing her up in the air. Ellison writes, "above her red, fixed-smiling lips I saw the terror and disgust in her eyes, almost like my own terror and that which I saw in the other boys" (p. 20). Indeed, the boys are terrified: some are reduced to hysterical tears. The black boys and the white dancer occupy identical positions in this sadistic pornographic spectacle in which they are forced to perform. Ellison gives the lie to Othellophilia, exposing the derisive, white male gaze it serves – a gaze at once punitive, jealous, and fascinated.

The detail of the boy's erection, and his shame and horror over it, brings to mind the stereotype of black male phallic endowment that has been so richly theorized by black cultural critics. Marlon B. Ross comments on the treatment of the myth by Richard Wright in his autobiography *Black Boy*: "The charge of a larger penis ironically marks the young black boy's *lack* of masculine power within Jim Crow society. Even when white men's fantasy gaze is turned onto a black man's admirable endowment, it is the black man who is being emasculated."[34] Wright's autobiography recounts a joke made at his expense by an older white co-worker: "'I heard that a nigger can stick his prick in the ground and spin around on it like a top . . . I'd like to see you do that. I'd give you a dime, if you did it.'"[35] Ross comments, "Just as [the co-worker] has every right to expose the young Wright's penis to humorous contempt covered by admiration (or is it admiration covered by contempt?), so, if the boy responds with any signal of self-affirmative manliness, [the co-worker] would have every right to expose that penis to the white mob's castrating rage."[36] A similar dynamic is at work in the Ellison passage, wherein a degrading white male voyeurism makes a spectacle of black male arousal before a white female, while yet holding forth (those contradictory threats) the likelihood of violent retribution should that arousal be acted on.

That the black male body is the focus of the spectacle – not the blonde erotic dancer – is confirmed when the boys take center stage. In keeping with the blindness/invisibility theme, they are forced to fight one another blindfolded: "I felt a sudden fit of blind terror. I was unused to darkness," the narrator says (p. 21). This scene foreshadows another crucial performance for the hero, when he gives his speech for his Brotherhood while blinded by the spotlight. This early scene also involves a speech, which the hero is allowed to deliver only after bloodying himself in the Battle Royal and participating in the equally degrading and painful game of gathering coins off an electrified carpet. The two performances – separated by the years of the hero's adolescence – at first seem polar opposites, but are not so. The teen-aged narrator is a kind of clown-figure – target of the author's own dark satire – in his blindness to the cruelty of the games and his pathetic pride in the fawning Uncle Tom speech he doggedly delivers through bloody lips. In contrast, the adult narrator seems to triumph in his inspired and radical speech before the Brotherhood: the crowds go wild and he is catapulted into fame. As it turns out, though, this fame is short-lived and it soon becomes clear that the Brotherhood will only tolerate this visibility if it serves their cynical ends: in other words, he has no control over the script. In both episodes, the hero is made a puppet of racism. He is an actor in someone else's play.

Ellison explicitly draws this analogy at key points in the novel: "I walked out of the building with a queer feeling that I was playing a part in some scheme which I did not understand" (p. 170); "Everyone seemed to have some plan for me, and beneath that some more secret plan" (p. 194); "I had a feeling that somehow he was acting a part" (p. 288); "I must have looked silly . . . like a black-face comedian shrinking from a ghost" (p. 294); "Everyone smiled . . . as though they all knew the role I was to play" (p. 311); "'I realize how you feel,' he said, becoming an actor who'd just finished a part in a play and was speaking again in his natural voice" (p. 476). These theatrical tropes strongly suggest a critique of Othellophilia – especially when they arise in reference to Paul Robeson himself (p. 409), the first black actor to play Othello and the first who rose to fame that way.

To me the most interesting of these metaphors involve the protagonist's encounters with white women. The first time a white woman elicits erotic contact, he has the strange sense that he "had been through it all before." Ellison writes, "I couldn't decide if it were from watching some similar scene in the movies, from books I'd read, or from some recurrent but deeply buried dream. Whatsoever, it was like entering a scene which . . . I had hitherto watched only from a distance" (p. 300). In this instance, the physical contact itself – though aggressively initiated by her – is not unpleasant, but on other occasions, there is an element of coercion, coupled with the same socially programmed fear he felt facing the white erotic dancer, as a teenager. New to the north's more permeable racial boundaries, he is horrified to find himself crushed against an overweight white woman on the subway: ". . . I was trapped, so close that simply by nodding my head, I might have brushed her lips with mine. I wanted desperately to raise my hands to show that *it was against my will.* I kept expecting her to scream . . ." It takes him a while to recover from this: "I was *limp*, my clothing *wet* . . . suppose she had screamed. . . . The next time I used the subway I'd be sure to enter with my hands grasping my lapels" (p. 158; emphasis mine). In this perfect demonstration of the emasculated black male, the protagonist here uses the language of rape to describe his physical contact with a white woman. There is a near repeat of the experience after he delivers his blind lecture to the Brotherhood: "I couldn't see and there was much confusion and suddenly someone spun me around, pulling me off balance, and I felt myself pressed against warm feminine softness, holding on" (p. 347).

It is no accident that the narrator's interactions with white women peak once he enters the Brotherhood; as it turns out, he becomes for them a kind of mascot, a decorative, exotic figure employed more for image than for any real interest in the social advancement of his fellow blacks. So it is no surprise that, in its first effort to curtail his visibility and influence, the Brotherhood transfers his assignment from Harlem to "the Woman Question." For the time being, I will leave aside the question of whether the hero's reaction reflects his author's views as well (though the evidence, as we'll see, is damning) and focus instead on the Brotherhood's cynical exploitation of Othellophilia in its female audience. The hero fumes: "I stood there . . . thinking the *woman question* and searching their faces for signs of amusement . . . I had just been made the butt of an outrageous joke . . ." (p. 407; emphasis in original). Nonetheless, he recovers from the shock and the disappointment of losing his Harlem assignment (temporarily, he tries to convince himself), and bolsters himself up for his first feminist lecture. Interestingly enough, he has Othellophilia in mind: "If only I were a foot taller and a hundred pounds heavier," he muses. ". . . I'd no more have to speak than Paul Robeson had to act; they'd simply thrill at the sight of me" (p. 409).

And they do. The same evening he winds up alone in the apartment of a woman who speaks of his "great throbbing vitality": she coos, "You give me such a feeling of security – although. . . . I must confess that you also make me afraid." The exchange is as disturbing as it is humorous:

> "Really . . . It's so powerful, so – so *primitive!*"
> I felt some of the air escape from the room, leaving it unnaturally quiet.
> "You don't mean primitive?" I said.
> "Yes, *primitive*; no one has told you, Brother, that at times you have tom-toms beating in your voice?"
> "My God," I laughed, "I thought that was the beat of profound ideas."
>
> (p. 413; italics in original).

As this tête-à-tête grows increasingly intense, the hero begins to panic. Echoing the mingled hostility and attraction of the erotic dancer episode, he says, "I wanted both to smash her and to stay with her and knew I should do neither" (p. 415). He does stay and go to bed with her, only to be awakened by the return of her husband, who, utterly non-plussed, tells her good-night and goes into his separate bedroom. Bewildered, the hero slips out, fearing that she had not really been awake when she'd seen her husband, and that if she did awake now, "she'd scream, shriek" (p. 417). He wonders in anguish, "Why did they have to mix their women into everything? Between us and everything we wanted to change in the world they placed a woman: socially, politically, economically. Why, goddamit, why did they insist upon confusing the class struggle with the ass struggle, debasing both us and them – all human motives?" (p. 418). Well, any feminist – and, particularly, any black feminist – knows that the "ass struggle" *is* a "class struggle." The protagonist of *Invisible Man* does not – and I wonder whether the same can be said of its author. The hero may have been offended by the suggestion that there are "tom-toms" and not ideas in his speech, but Ellison does not grant this white woman many ideas in this exchange either: on the contrary, she utters nothing but inanities and stereotypes. But, again, Ellison's position is a different matter.

If the Brotherhood exploits Othellophilia in drawing female followers and making a puppet of the hero, the hero himself – once he realizes this – does the same. Recognizing his disempowerment in the Brotherhood – recognizing his invisibility – he deliberately pursues the girlfriend of one of the movement's leaders, in order to get information. His language as he comes to this decision recalls the Battle Royal scene: "They seemed to have me blocked at every turn, forcing me to fight them in the dark" (p. 511). The metaphor of fighting in the dark then materializes as he goes on to "fight" them in the bedroom. It goes badly from the beginning:

> She was more interested in the drinks, in which I had to join her glass for glass, and in little dramas which she had dreamed up around the figures of Joe Louis and Paul Robeson . . . I was confounded and amused and it became quite a contest, with me trying to keep the two of us in touch with reality and with her casting me in fantasies in which I was Brother Taboo-with-whom-all-things-are-possible. (p. 517)

She finally works up the courage to ask him to play rapist with her. He is shocked: "There was a pristine incorruptibility about her face now that upset me all the more, for she was neither kidding nor trying to insult me" (p. 517). He is fascinated by her blushing and wonders, "Was this meant to excite me, or was it an unconscious expression of revulsion?" (p. 518). Yet he himself can't seem to choose between attraction and disgust; at one point he tells himself – in the first of a number of derogatory comments on her body – "She would soon be a biddy, stout, with a little double-chin and a three-ply girdle" (p. 519). His date continues to horrify him, telling him of her fascination with the story of a friend's rape by a black man. The hero opines, "Maybe a great number secretly want [rape]; maybe that's why they scream when it's farthest from possibility" (p. 520). Nothing in the scene – or in the book, for that matter – counters the thought.

Indeed, this bitch has it bad. She rhapsodizes over the hero's black skin against her white sheets: "You're beautiful . . . Like warm ebony against pure snow." She even steals (with slight alterations) one of Othello's lines: "Look at me like you want to tear me apart" (p. 520), she says, paraphrasing "I will chop her to messes" (*Othello* IV.i.195). It gets worse: "Come on, beat me, daddy – you – you big black bruiser . . ." He feels both "confused pity" and anger: "I was annoyed enough to slap her. She lay aggressively receptive, flushed, her navel no goblet but a pit in an earth-quaking land, flexing taut and expansive." Fortunately, she passes out before he can "rape" her, and he merely scrawls in lipstick on her stomach, "SYBIL YOU WERE RAPED BY SANTA CLAUS SURPRISE" (p. 522).

The stereotype of the black rapist is also invoked in a key speech of Ras the Exhorter, the black nationalist who stands as the alternative to the Brotherhood for the hero's political action. In stark contrast to the narrator's befuddlement over the "ass"/ "class" dilemma, Ras has thought it all through and has come to his own conclusions about the political uses of Othellophilia. Railing against the hero for his disloyalty to blacks, he asks, "What they give you to betray – their women? You fall for that?" He goes on, "In Africa this mahn be a chief, a black king! Here they say he rape them godamn women with no blood in their veins. I bet this mahn can't beat them off with baseball bat – shit!" His reflections are peppered with misogyny, but also often perceptive: "He take one of them strumpets and tell the black mahn his freedom lie between her skinny legs . . . The good white women he tell the black mahn is a rapist and keep them locked up and ignorant while he makes the black mahn a race of bahstards" (p. 373). Whereas I cringe at the binary he sets up between the "strumpets" black men are offered, and the "good women" who are kept in fear of black rapists, he nonetheless manifests awareness of white women's entrapment by the same system. Indeed, we saw in the previous chapter the way lynch-logic kept white women "immured" (to use Mitchell's own term); here Ellison – through Ras – allows, at least briefly, for cross-identification with the *other* pawn to racist-masculinist power.

Would that this cross-gendered sympathy had extended to the white women the narrator becomes involved with. Or toward *any* woman – white or black – in the novel. As Mary Rohrberger notes, "Nowhere in *Invisible Man* is there a woman not characterized as automaton."[37] Indeed, Ellison may slight white women, but he almost completely ignores black women. The only black female character, the hero's land-lady, is a Mammy figure, plain and simple: she exists to serve the narrator tea. And as for the fate of Sybil, the hero's rape-fantasizer, her final appearance in the novel says it all. Left wandering drunk in the dark, snowy, city streets, she disappears from the plot, but only after making one ghostly re-appearance. Ellison writes,

Ahead of me the body hung, white, naked, and horribly feminine from a lamp-post. I felt myself spin around with horror and it was as though I had turned some nightmarish somersault. I whirled . . . and now there was another and another, seven – all hanging before a gutted store-front. I stumbled, hearing the cracking of bones underfoot and saw a physician's skeleton shattered on the street, the skull rolling away from the backbone, as I steadied long enough to notice the unnatural stiffness of those hanging above me. They were mannequins – "Dummies!" I said aloud. Hairless, bald, and sterilely feminine . . . But are they unreal, I thought; *are* they? What if one – even *one* is real – is . . . Sybil?

(p. 556)

In lynching, white female sexuality justifies racist violence: in Othellophilia, the woman is lynched too. True to Ellison's dark ironizing – his gift for taking the horror of *Native Son* and making it bearable, making it "black" humor – this mock-rape leads to a mock-lynching, albeit of the "victim." Indeed, it is a scary moment if you don't know the book – almost, for a few seconds, as scary as *Native Son*, to which Ellison seems to allude in the reference to the bones (the skeleton, too, has been decapitated, and the bones' whiteness links them, as imagery, to the dummies).

I called this a lynching, but it is a reverse lynching in every respect – it is Ras and his followers who have "lynched" these white mannequins, as is clear when he threatens to hang the protagonist too. As an "Uncle Tom" and a betrayer of his people, the protagonist deserves no lesser treatment by Ras. (This is not the first time the novel has implicated black people in lynching: problematically enough, to some critics, the worst racist in the novel is arguably one of the black characters, the hypocritical president of the hero's black college, who at one point declares he will "have every Negro in the county hanging on tree limbs . . . if it means staying" in power [p. 143].) Yet, as extreme as we find Ras' threats, he is not altogether "wrong" in calling the narrator an Uncle Tom, considering his play-acting with Sybil. And if, as a radical black nationalist who "goes wild when he sees black people and white people together" (p. 365), Ras' loathing of inter-racialism is as intense as any white supremacist's, there is a certain consistency to his racially inverted lynch-logic: Sybil did, in fact, try to *force* the narrator into "rape" (we remember his phrasing in his earliest contact with a white woman: "*It was against my will*"), which makes her, in essence, a white "rapist" of a black man. So, in a reverse-racism scenario, lynch-logic would wish to string her up first, and use her body to threaten her black "victim" into racial solidarity.

Oddly enough, this may be the moment where Ellison is at his best, with regard to the political implications *for white women* of Othellophilia: at least there is recognition, in this scene, that they can be victims too. And there is – as in the Battle Royal episode – that momentary cross-identification, as he too is threatened with hanging. From that moment until the end of the penultimate chapter, he is on the run, in darkness, and he finally winds up diving into a manhole, where his underground life begins. There he has a dream: they castrate him, and throw his testicles in the river. The culmination of his symbolic "lynching," this reference to the punitive dismemberment of black men is theoretically pregnant, particularly in the context of the novel's discussion of rape. Harris argues that the sexual violence – most often genital mutilation – enacted upon black males during lynching is a kind of "communal rape."[38] Marlon B. Ross problematizes this theorization, pointing out that it constructs "violence against women as deriving ultimately and/or solely from sexual oppression and violence against black men as deriving necessarily from racial oppression." In other words, the operation of racial politics in the rape scenario and the operation of a sexual politics in the symbolic rape (i.e., genital mutilation) of black men, are occluded by the analogy. These phenomena are never about "just" race, or "just" sex.[39]

Ironically, the dream of castration is the means whereby Ellison's hero gains insight. Poignantly, he says in the final pages, "I'm invisible, not blind" (p. 576). Even after descending into his (another feminine image) "hole," he can see the world more clearly than most – for his "hole is warm and full of light" (p. 6). And one of these insights will, he promises, eventually drive him up into the world again: the book's final theatre metaphor is a positive one: "Even an invisible man has a socially responsible role to play" (p. 581). And maybe being invisible makes that easier – acting not in the spotlight, but behind the scenes.

> "Who knows when some slight shock, disturbing the delicate balance between social order and thirsty aspiration, shall send the skyscrapers in our cities toppling?" Richard Wright, *Native Son*

Richard Wright might not have been the only prophet of the event whose horror so stupefied America that, several years later, we can still only call it by a number: "9/11." In my post-9/11 re-reading of the novel, this rhetorical question, posed by Bigger's lawyer, Max, during his impassioned speech on American race relations, stunned me for its clairvoyance. Yet I did not at first think I could use the quote in this book. For what, I asked myself, did the attack on the World Trade Center on September 11, 2001 have to do with the individual, fictional episodes of violence in these three American novels? But that was before I finished the book, and surprised myself by feeling compassion as Bigger faced his execution. For I realized then what I did not realize the first time I read the book, when I was too young and (I suppose) innocent to see beyond the horror of Bigger's crimes: I realized that this is a book everyone should read (and at least twice) in order to *understand* hatred, rather than merely react to it.

Max is doing what too few Americans did in the year following the catastrophe in New York: he is contextualizing it, pointing out its situation in time and history, its relationship to a vast and ongoing series of actions on the part of American political power. He is answering the question in the minds of the horrified white audience of the trial: why do they (blacks) hate us so? To understand violence is, of course, not to condone or even forgive it: it is merely to understand it, and hence, hopefully, prevent it. What Max says of the execution of Bigger, American liberals (along with much of the rest of the world) said of the invasion of Afghanistan: "The surest way to make certain that there will be more such murders is to kill this boy" (p. 330). They kill him nonetheless, answering blind hate with blind hate. An eye for an eye.

To Eldridge Cleaver's persona in *Soul on Ice*, white women *are* the Twin Towers. They are the Statue of Liberty, the White House, the Washington Monument, and Mount Rushmore too. In a bitterly satiric dialogue between young black radicals and an older "Infidel" or Uncle Tom, the latter expounds on his contempt for women of his own race, and his worship of white women: "The white man made the black woman the symbol of slavery and the white woman the symbol of freedom."[40] From the perspective of the authorial persona, however, white women are the symbol of a freedom he, as a black man, is *denied*, and hence they are ultimately a symbol of oppression.

Of course to view women as symbols is to blind oneself to their humanity. And so the Cleaver persona explains his career as a rapist in terms of a lashing out at "the Ogre" in revenge over his internalized Othellophilia, his programming by white supremacy to worship at the altar of white female beauty. In prison for possession of marijuana, he is furious to find one day that a white guard has torn down and torn up his white pin-up, throwing the pieces in the toilet: "Get yourself a colored girl for a pin-up . . . and I'll let it stay up," the guard says (pp. 26–7). This catapults the speaker into self-examination, at the end of which he realizes he *does* prefer white women; subsequent interviews with his jail-mates prove that they share this "sickness." The final blow to his psyche comes when he looks at – and finds beauty in – a photograph of the woman Emmet Till was lynched for whistling at. When he gets out of prison, he becomes a rapist, first "practicing on black girls in the ghetto" then systematically turning to "white prey." Cleaver writes, "Rape was an insurrectionary act. It delighted me that I was defying and trampling upon the white man's law, upon his system of values, and that I was defiling his women – and this point, I believe, was most satisfying to me because I was very resentful over the historical fact of how the white man has used the black woman" (p. 33). It is not enough to call this offensive to white women: its sincerity toward black women can also be questioned. Would the black women on whom Cleaver "practiced" his "technique" appreciate his pseudo-feminist reflections on their historical mistreatment by white men? Ishmael Reed comments in his introduction to the book, "In this war, women are regarded as bargaining chips and loot for both sides . . . [The guard who ripped up Cleaver's pin-up,] like many white men regarded all white women as his property, while black men feel that black women belong to them. Both groups were upset when the women declared they owned their own bodies, their souls, and their minds" (p. 3).

It takes courage to *look at* rather than just to react to hatred, but the insight gained is always worth it. And it's worth reading *Soul on Ice* for the final chapter, where Cleaver strives to make peace with the black women he doubly victimized, first passively and then actively, in his love–hate mania over white women. In "To all black women, from all black men," Cleaver sings a love song to his "Queen," his "Black Bride of My Passion," his "Sable Sister," and "Eternal Love." The last sentence of the book reads, "Put on your crown, my Queen, and we will build a New City on these ruins" (p. 242). It is a visionary ending, a note of hope against the dire prophecy of this conclusion's epigram. After all, the Towers *have* fallen: our monuments have been desecrated, our twin cities of glass brought to the ground. I don't need to belabor the 9/11 connection: much has already been said about the dangers of the new racism parading as American patriotism. I might also point out that, in this new race war, western (read: white) women are once again symbols of freedom, the contrast with their veiled eastern sisters a justification for "liberating" the latters' country through war. Will we build a New City – as Cleaver envisions – or simply resurrect the old? What will the new Towers look like? "Rebuild 'em bigger," said President Bush in undisguised phallic nostalgia.

I say we ask the Queen, once she is elected.

Conclusion. *"White women are snaky":*
Jungle Fever and its discontents

From *Guess Who's Coming to Dinner* (1967) to *Jungle Fever* (1991) to *Save the Last Dance* (2001), inter-racialism in mainstream cinema has historically highlighted the *Othello* configuration, effacing the real history of white male–black female relations, from slavery on. Not until Halle Barry and *Bullworth* (1999) could Hollywood imagine a love-story across racial boundaries featuring an African-American woman – in other words, it took a "black" woman who was almost white. Even the unprecedented *Bringing Down the House* (2003) raises and thwarts the inter-racialist drive of its plot by keeping the emphatically white-haired, WASPy Steve Martin at a safe distance (with some humorously misinterpreted exceptions) from Queen Latifah's zaftig heroine; she does – surprisingly enough – wind up with a white boyfriend at the end of the movie, but this is Martin's exaggeratedly semitic, black-haired side-kick. Likewise, the heroine of Spike Lee's *Jungle Fever* is emphatically ethnic: the heavy-browed, raven-haired, "Italyun" Angela Tucci with her colorful "New Yawk" accent (Annabella Sciorra). Deconstructing racial binaries is, of course, part of the director's point: Lee excels in his analysis of the dark side of the so-called melting pot, wherein the contest for social privilege pits minority groups against one another.[1] But there is also a curious way in which Lee's Italianism echoes Shakespeare, who can only imagine inter-racial love as a possibility on the Italian peninsula. By way of balancing, if only somewhat, the latent Othellophilia of the central love-story, Lee includes some brief flirtation between the heroine's jilted Italian-American boyfriend and a black female patron at his diner. One of the Italian-American men observes crudely, "Colored women, they like to fuck." "How do you know?" one of his buddies answers. "He asked his mother," another rejoins. The first speaker flies into a rage: "My mother's not black! She's *dark*! There are dark Italians!"[2]

There are, indeed. More on that below.

Jungle Fever is also curiously Shakespearean in its discussions of the heroine's sexuality – though here the parallels more likely arise from Lee's satire against Italian-American Catholic conservatism, rather than any conscious allusion to the classical paradigms. Early in the film Angela's brothers threaten her boyfriend in protecting what they hope is their sister's virginity. "Angela's not some slut you find on the street," they say. Nonetheless, she is also pitted against the memory of not one but *two* angel-in-the-house dead mothers – her own and her boyfriend's (the boyfriend's father makes him pray daily at a shrine to her on the mantelpiece). And once the secret of her affair with Flipper comes out, this woman named for an angel is demonized in both her own and her lover's communities: her father beats her black and blue, and her lover's father invites her to dinner only to insult them both at the table, declaring, "I don't eat with whoremongers."

In *Othello* the inter-racial sex is metaphorically adulterous – in the sense that it is adulterating, impure, and thereby adulteress-making of Desdemona, whether she's faithful to Othello or not – while *Jungle Fever* presents us with inter-racial sex that is *literally* adulterous. To emphasize the double-illegitimacy of the affair, the director sets up Flipper's family life as idyllic: the film opens with a homey shot of a newspaper-boy en route through a charming neighborhood of brownstones, then cuts to the window toward which he casts the morning paper. Inside we witness the exuberant morning love-making of husband and wife along with the irresistibly cute daughter's gleeful listening-in. This is followed by a breakfast exchange between mother and daughter about "the birds and the bees" (actually, "the pigeons and the squirrels") wherein the child feigns a disturbed naïveté about the sounds she heard through the bedroom wall, only to reveal finally – to charming effect – her simultaneously precocious and innocent delight in her parents' sex-life ("I would really like a baby brother"). The sequence functions quite effectively to associate Flipper's marital sex with the positive values of childhood and nature, thus framing the inter-racial sex-on-the-drawing-board that takes place in Flipper's office as debased and anti-family. The contrast is especially clear when the frame is complete at the end of the film: Lee returns to the morning sex sequence (newspaper and all) after Flipper has had his affair, has been kicked out, has repented, and been tentatively forgiven. This time, however, as the daughter eavesdrops, grinning, on her parent's lovemaking, she misinterprets as pleasure the sound of her mother's weeping. The message is clear: Flipper's affair with a white woman has indelibly damaged a pristine family life.

Lee presents an interesting reversal of the hegemonic narrative in casting inter-racial sex as corruptive of an essentially natural and positive African-American sexuality (I hesitate to call it "black" as Flipper's wife, Drew, is very light-skinned, and the film makes a point of exploring the way this problematizes her racial outrage). Despite the radical nature of the reversal, though, it leaves essentially unchanged the position of the white female in the inter-racial dyad: Angela is the white devil – or "that white bitch," as Drew calls her repeatedly. Similarly, the film plays with, and again radically twists, the trope of the black rapist and his morally dubious white target. After her humiliation by Flipper's father, Angela takes it out on her lover, hitting him hard on the chest and inciting a tussle that is only half playful; they try to vent their hurt and frustration by mock-boxing and bantering about Italian versus black prize-fighters, and Angela gets the upper hand by stealing Flipper's glasses. She winds up splay-legged under him on the hood of his car, teasingly waving his glasses around. The police arrive, predictably enough, seeing only a black man on top of a white woman: "That's my boyfriend!" she screams as they throw him against the wall. Still, it is only when she violently defends Flipper that they take the gun from his temple. "Waste of time" the one cop sneers, clearly at Angela's expense. This is not a Faulknerian (un)rape from the point of view of the film, but it may well be in the eyes of the racist cops. And Flipper, not Angela, is clearly the victim. He ends the relationship shortly after, and tries to make peace with his wife. As he walks the irresistibly cute daughter to school again, she says, "I wish you and Mommy were back together making those funny noises in the morning."

From my description so far it might appear that Lee offers a race-reversed Othellophilia – essentially conservative in its approach to race relations – in its idealization of the racially "pure" marriage between Flipper and Drew. But in fact the film's message is far more complex. For *Jungle Fever* also criticizes black bigotry, and exposes the fault-lines within the black community introduced by questions of racial pedigree, authenticity, and class. At one point, despairing of their relationship, Flipper tells Angela, "No children. No babies . . . No half-black, half-white babies for me, no." Angela calls him on his hypocrisy, pointing out the mixed blood of his own child and his own wife, and concluding, "You know, you're not much different than my family." He adds, "Except that *your* family is *racist.*" "And what's this stuff coming out of your mouth?" she rejoins. The film gives her the last word. Along the same lines, Lee resists idealizing black family life generally: the scenes of cozy

African-American domesticity, of Flipper walking his too-cute daughter to school, are counter-poised against scenes involving his crack-addict brother, addled mother, and fanatical ex-preacher father.

The ex-preacher father – the "Good Reverend Doctor," as his own wife still calls him – is worth a word or two, in that he functions in the film as a mouthpiece for ideology. He constantly quotes the Bible, and frequently its most misogynistic, flesh-phobic passages. His stentorian pronouncements and biblical language render him almost Shakespearean, even Othellophilic ("I know the devil's handiwork when I see it," he says, staring straight at Angela). Curiously, though, in one crucial point, he summarizes the history of American inter-racialism – telling this time the *other* side of the story. The monologue takes place at the dinner-table, where Angela and Flipper still think they are welcome. He addresses her exclusively.

"You think I don't understand the white woman's committing black adultery, but I do. You see, there was a lot of lynchings . . .where I come from as a boy . . . White man say to his woman, baby you are the flower of white southern womanhood, too holy and pure to be touched by any man, including me; I'm gonna put you up on a pedestal for the world to fall down and worship you, and if any nigger so much as look at you I'll lynch his ass. She believed him, thought she really was holy and pure, like the Virgin Mary . . . Meanwhile, the husband, no sooner night fell, [went] down to the slave quarters, grabbin' up every piece of black poontang he could lay his hands on . . . And that's how our blood got diluted . . . Now I'm sure that most of those high and mighty white ladies felt abandoned, but they were so proud to be white and therefore superior, they kept their mouths shut and their legs locked tight. But in the midnight hour, laying there alone on the hot bed of lust, I'm sure they must have thought what it would be like to have one of them big black bucks their husbands were so desperately afraid of. I feel sorry for you. Here it is the nineties – still trying to make up for what you missed out on. Well, I don't blame you. As for the black man, like my own son Flipper, who ought to know better . . . still got to fish in the white man's cess-pool – I have nothing but contempt."

As drama the passage is painful – Angela listens with polite dignity. The misogyny – and even a whiff of the racism – of the master discourse is there: black woman as "poontang," white woman as a "cess-pool" (we recall Faulkner's description of the "sewer" of Joanna Burden's sexuality). But as critique of Othellophilia the passage is, I think, without peer in contemporary film. The Good Reverend Doctor is not, of course, the moral spokesman of the film: Lee generally reserves that role for himself, and he does so here, as Cyrus, Flipper's best buddy. In fact, Flipper's father may even be the villain, like Faulkner's fanatical, infanticidal Doc

Hines: in a harrowing later scene, the Good Reverend Doctor shoots his own son, Flipper's drug-addict brother. The patriarchal violence Angela endured at the hands of her racist Italian-American father is finally eclipsed. Neither black nor white has a monopoly on intolerance, hatred, and violence.

The same even-handedness applies to Lee's approach to black versus white sexuality. I have emphasized the contrast between the adulterous inter-racial sex which is the film's theme and the marital *intra*-racial sex that frames it – but Lee complicates this binary by way of the black "crack whore" who haunts the route Flipper takes as he walks his daughter to school. The film ends in a moment of profound anguish and ideological ambivalence: walking off after the tearful sex with his not very forgiving wife, Flipper is accosted by the same drug-addict, who offers him oral sex for five dollars. This time, instead of pushing her off, the hero seizes her in a paternal embrace and howls a resounding "No!" Lee freeze-frames this ambiguous denial, rendering an African-American version of the famous painting by Edvard Munch, *The Scream*. It is no less wrenching – and far more complex – an ending than the abjection of Shakespeare's black tragic hero. *Jungle Fever* might justifiably be called an American tragedy, even if its protagonist lives.

What we learn from Spike Lee's film are all the ways in which *Othello* both is and is not still relevant. Illuminating the cultural forces that continue to punish inter-racial love – and the way in which these forces operate on *both sides* of the racial binary – Lee presents us with a *plus ça change, plus c'est la même chose* parable. But Lee also more clearly critiques the social policing of inter-racialism; though the hero gives up on the relationship, he does not punish his lover – or himself – for her transgressive desire. At the same time, though, I wonder to what degree the film's treatment of inter-racialism merely reinforces the taboo: Diana R. Paulin notes the way the title – which is "never deconstructed" – reinforces "the notion that inter-racial love is the result of irrational, racialized, heated passion."[3] With a colloquial levity belying the mood of the movie itself, the title diagnoses Flipper and Angela with a sickness out of the "jungle" – with all the attendant connotations of African "primitivism." Indeed, by definition a "fever" is temporary – or at least one hopes it is. A fever can also cause hallucinations: it is the secular diagnosis of Othello's suspected witch-craft.

That Lee too harshly judges inter-racialism – and that he slights the central love-story even despite good performances from the principals – are central themes in the reviews. One critic calls Lee "despairing and separatist" because he renders "the sexual affair a localized social disaster and not a personal event."[4] Another complains "Snipes and Sciorra are left flailing in a limbo, trying to give depth to characters whose *raison d'être* is simply to provide an excuse for this chorus of disapproval."[5] This becomes the critical refrain: "We never get any idea of the feeling between the two lovers . . ."[6] – ". . . Their romance seems . . . an excuse for the other events of the movie . . ."[7] – "Spike Lee is less interested in their affair than the environment in which it takes place"[8] – "Lee is so interested in the ripple effect they cause, he almost forgets the affair itself."[9] One critic even quotes Flipper as though he speaks for the director when he tells Angela, "I give up. It's not worth it. I don't love you and I doubt seriously you ever loved me."[10] Indeed, Lee himself has confirmed the claim, explaining that the central characters "are meant to represent two people who come together because of sexual mythology instead of love."[11]

One can find *some* filmic treatments of inter-racialism that are more or less celebratory, if in their own way bitter-sweet. A sub-genre of Othello-philia in film is the *To Sir, with Love* (1967) story, itself a somewhat less patronizing revision of the sexless love-story of Tom and little Eva. Here, Uncle Tom grows up and is endowed with a mind of his own and a good dose of classic black dignity, and he becomes the object of an innocent infatuation that he is too morally upright to take advantage of. Arguably, *Driving Miss Daisy* (1989) falls into this category, with old age replacing youth and innocence as the element that sexually sanitizes the white heroine (and, to some degree, her black male counterpart). *Far from Heaven* (2002) brings us another dignified black hero, in another uncon-summated love-story between the long-suffering, sexless wife of a closet gay man, and her compassionate gardener. These dramas need not punish the inter-racial couple, as miscegeny remains only a distant prospect.

What by now is impossible to ignore, however, is the overwhelming *negativity* of depictions of inter-racial couples since Shakespeare. And yet the population that produced *Jungle Fever* and *O.* includes, in fact, numerous happy inter-racial couples.[12] Indeed, we are all familiar with the way black-on-white handshakes and embraces function automatically as pictorial slogans advocating inter-racial reconciliation and multicul-turalism: these seem essentially *positive* images. I do find it curious that just such an image – the clasped black and white hands – became the promotional image for Lee's film, and then found its way into Oliver Parker's 1995 *Othello*, flashed on-screen to represent the (literal) climax of the inter-racial nuptials. And perhaps it is partially a hunger for these images that keeps audiences coming to see *Othello*: many do, like Alice

Randall's heroine in *The Wind Done Gone*, want Othello and Desdemona to live "happily ever after." This is the flip-side of Othellophilia and the more optimistic reading of the media fascination with that image of O. J. and Nicole – the "happy in love" one. *Othello* is a love-story – even if it masks, or serves, or ultimately constitutes, a hate-story. And this is one reason why *it will not go away.*

It will not go away. Not as long as Shakespeare remains the crown jewel of the western canon and *Othello* remains *the* classic drama of inter-racial love. For as long as there are black actors wanting to prove their talent – and as long as Shakespeare remains the bar against which this talent is measured – they will continue to succumb to the siren-song that Hugh Quarshie cautions against. I cite the actor himself:

> . . . If a black actor plays Othello does he not risk making racial stereotypes seem legitimate and even true? When a black actor plays a role written for a white actor in black make-up for a predominantly white audience, does he not encourage the white way, or rather the wrong way, of looking at black men, namely that black men . . . are over-emotional, excitable and unstable . . .? Of all the parts in the canon, perhaps Othello is the one which should most definitely not be played by a black actor.[13]

Let's take Lawrence Fishburne's Othello, in the Parker film mentioned above. Pascale Aebischer is surely right in calling Parker's version one of the most racist ever, in the way Fishburne's body comes to naturalize stereotype. Aebischer notes Parker's adornment of the actor's body with "jewelry and tattoos" that render him "an eroticized, exoticized, violently inscribed 'Other' . . ."[14] Aebischer is concurring with Francesca T. Royster, who writes that "The audience . . . is encouraged to enjoy" the actor's frequently semi-nude, athletic body, "to take pleasure . . . in his rages and even in his murder of the play's heroine."[15] I too find the film's eroticizing of Fishburne troubling in a way that the campy racial drag of Olivier's "classic" performance cannot approach; I feel coerced into voyeuristic complicity. This becomes especially uncomfortable in the murder scene. On the one hand Fishburne's approach is counter-stereotype in its resistance to hyper-emotionality: he carries out the violence with slow, studied motions and a sad, stoic countenance; on the other hand, though, his very coolness in this scene – and those lingering shots of the tear trickling down his perfectly sculpted, dark jaw – allows the viewer to relish the choreography of this beautiful, black-on-white murder. Indeed, the aestheticization of the murder allows what I find the film's most offensive detail to look almost plausible:

when her body *should* be spasming uncontrollably in the final throes of asphyxiation, Desdemona languidly caresses her strangler's head.

It will not go away. At least not as long as producers "modernize" it, plumbing this four-centuries-old artifact for parallels to contemporary affairs. Hence our final stop in this trek through the afterlife of Shakespeare's tragedy: Tim Nelson's film adaptation, *O.*, released in 2001 after a delay due to the film's perceived resemblance to a shocking mass-murder at an elite American high school.[16] The first point I wish to make about this film is that its female lead, Julia Stiles, had not only starred in two previous pseudo-Shakespeare fliks for the American teen screen (*Ten Things I Hate about You* and *Hamlet*): after playing Desdemona, she went on to star in another inter-racial love-story, *Save the Last Dance* (2001). This type-casting of Stiles as both a "Shakespeare flik chick" and a lover of black men deserves note, especially in light of a parallel episode on the Shakespearean stage: Zoë Waites' casting both as Juliet to Ray Fearon's black Romeo in 1996, and as Desdemona to his Othello in 1999. I wonder what this means. Could there be something on her résumé about black men? Or, a more disconcerting and more likely possibility, does starring in an inter-racial love-story somehow subtly "mark" an actress? In any case, it seems at the very least unfair to all the under-employed actresses of color out there: where a racial "cross-over" movie gets done, the role inevitably goes to a white girl, and sometimes the same one twice.

Even more so than *Jungle Fever*, *O.* encapsulates a lesson in just how much use we can still make of *Othello*. Critics almost unanimously complain of the problem of motivation in *O.* – they don't "believe" the hero, Odin's, violence. Some have the insight and knowledge of the Shakespeare to trace this problem back to the original, rather than blaming the adaptation. Some even call the movie's premise – and hence, implicitly, the source – out-dated. But most simply dispraise the film in terms that reveal their ignorance of the source. "The movie dabbles unpleasantly with the black-man-as-untamed-beast iconography of yesteryear," one online critic complains.[17] But so does the play, of course. ". . . Completely dated . . .," declares another.[18] "We don't see a violent tendency or any psychological motivation in Odin," observes yet another.[19] ". . . Devoid of motivation, incredulously acted [*sic*]," states a fourth.[20] And again: "When the inevitable carnage ensues, there's not enough dramatic weight to justify it, let alone make it remotely plausible."[21] At least one critic has a theory as to why we accept the same plot in Shakespeare, but not in the modernized teen film: "Shorn of [Shakespeare's] language, the plot, the characters and their motivations seem fairly uncompelling – even foolish."[22] Other comments directly impugn Shakespeare's politics: "While 'O.' carries a sense of its cleverness about how it parallels the original text, some things should have changed. A so-easily duped black man might be one of them. A barbaric attitude toward homicide [I would say, femicide] could well be another."[23]

We have seen this before: a contemporary director trying to "sell" early modern ideology to liberal-minded, multicultural, anti-sexist, post-modern audiences. And in these cases, the film can only succeed insofar as it does *not* resemble the Renaissance original. Stiles' previous pseudo-Shakespeare role in Gil Junger's *10 Things I Hate About You* required her to insert a back-bone into Shakespeare's most problematic of heroines, Katherina from *The Taming of the Shrew.* Junger's Kat, moreover, is not just *not* a door-mat; she is a Germaine-Greer-quoting feminist. Her love-object is no Petruccio, either: on the contrary, he's a perfectly sensitive nineties male whose only mis-step is entering into a tacky bet about her. Instead of an obedience speech, Kat recites a love-poem in her English class, from which we get the title of the movie. This is the extent of "taming" that contemporary American teen-aged girls will stomach.[24]

O. is more daring insofar as it tries to stick to Shakespeare's plot. Still, changes had to be made. Shakespeare's tragic hero is not a teenager: on the contrary, the play emphasizes his advanced age relative to Desdemona. Nelson, in representing Othello as a teenager, makes his rashness more credible, as he does his susceptibility to gulling and manipulation. In other words, stereotype needn't work as hard, in *O.*, to explain violence, as Hugh Quarshie compellingly argues it does in *Othello.*[25] Nelson also expands the time-frame (Parker does this as well), rendering the hero's psychological transformation more gradual and hence (with another nod to Quarshie's critique) more plausible.

Despite all this, the murder scene is *still* incredible to me – incredible in that I can't believe the story, and incredible in that *I can't believe* the director tried to make me. The image of a black male straddling and kissing his white lover, and then putting his very dark hands on her very pale throat and strangling her, would be hard enough to bear on grounds of its explosive implications for gender and racial politics – but as the climax to this particular story it feels utterly, utterly wrong. If a white teenager strangled his girlfriend on the mere *suspicion* that she was "two-timing" him, he would be dismissed as a psychopath: here we are supposed to take him for a tragic hero. In both Shakespeare's play and the film it inspired, skin-color explains violence. And that is a racist premise.

The aftermath of the murder also poses problems to modern viewers, particularly female viewers. How plausible is it that an American female teenager in the twenty-first century, within seconds of discovering her room-mate's freshly strangled corpse, would stand around defending the victim's chastity to her killer, rather than screaming her head off and running to the police?

There are also some problematic additions, most the result of clumsy translations of the play's language of whoredom. Desi gives up her virginity in these ambiguous terms: "I want you to be able to do anything. I want you to do what you want to me." Odin then overpowers her during sex, hurting her and ignoring her pleas to stop. The rape sub-text to *Othello* is thus graphically literalized, and it's not clear why. Later Odin throws the phrasing of her erotic invitation back at her, "How come when we were doin' it you were actin' all freaky and stuff? Tellin' me I could do whatever I wanted wit you, hmm?" The film's Iago figure exploits this suspicion, rendering in modern idiomatic American English the old Renaissance tropes of demonized female sexuality: "White women are snaky. White women are horny snakes," he says. Commenting on this statement, a blonde, female student of mine wondered whether the moral of the film inverted what many have taken to have been Shakespeare's original (racist) moral. Does the film constitute a warning against inter-racial sex on behalf of *black men*, against white women – similar to *Jungle Fever*? In this context, Stiles' character's requisite sass (Desi is another pseudo-Shakespearean heroine with an inserted post-modern back-bone) might redound against her, casting her as just another uppity white bitch.

I wonder about the title of the film, which resembles the title of what may very well be the most dangerous book a young woman might pick up, Pauline Réage's sado-masochistic porno-Bible, *The Story of O.*, in which the heroine revels in her violent, sexualized debasement by her pimp-lover.[26] What *are* we supposed to think when Desi tells Odin to "Do anything" he wants to her? Indeed, in both the novel and the play, the letter or the phoneme "O" signifies the voiding or annihilation of the hero and heroine's identities and subjectivities. In Shakespeare's play the hollow vowel resounds through the text, above all in the murder scene. Othello's name disintegrates into his repeated howlings of "O, O, O!" – as does Desdemona's name, in his stammering "O Desdemon! Dead Desdemon! Dead! O! O!" (v.ii.288) – and we have already talked about the couple's verbally paralleled renunciations of self ("Nobody. I myself" and "He that was Othello, here I am").[27] Similarly, the abbreviated name of Réage's modern, pornographic heroine is symbolized by the ring she is forced to wear in her anus, to facilitate sodomitical rape by her lover-master's patrons.

"White women are snaky." This is a new version of a very old statement: women are snaky. Woman-Eve has kept notoriously close company, in the masculinist imaginary, with the devil, from the beginning. Many depictions of the serpent in medieval and Renaissance iconography endow him with female breasts and a female face. Throughout this book, we've traced the language of demonized (white) female sexuality and its connection with a demonized black male sexuality from *Titus Andronicus* on. That racism and misogyny reinforce one another has become a critical commonplace. Works like Kim Hall's *Things of Darkness*, however, make it increasingly difficult to speak of these discourses as ontologically separate (if compatible) entities, rather than different inflections of the same hegemonic discourse. When it was no longer safe to tell nigger jokes, the blonde joke was invented. Racism will turn to misogyny on a dime; misogyny often obscures racism. Is the man who beats his daughter for sleeping with a black man (as in *Jungle Fever*) a sexist or a racist? When a rap song inveighs against "bitches" it is not only sexist but racist: unless the modifier "white" is used, "bitch" is synonymous with "black female." Along the same lines, pornographic websites lure white men with the sadistic racist-misogynistic thrill of watching "Huge black cocks pound[ing] squealing white bitches."

Only one critic of *O.* – in my research – comes close to addressing what is, to me, the most troubling aspect of *Othello*'s politics. This critic writes:

'O' is a tragedy, all right – a tragedy of failed metaphors . . . Taking all the heavy stuff that goes on in 'Othello' and applying it to the adolescent just doesn't pan out. Othello and his posse were soldiers, fighting a war in which lives were lost; Odin is leading his high school basketball team to the state championship. Sorry, it's not the same thing. Othello and Desdemona were married; Odin and Desi are youthful sweethearts. Why doesn't it ever occur to Odin to just break up with her?

This critic goes on to take issue with "the implied message that Desi's tragic end is only tragic because Odin was duped. Had she actually been seeing someone on the side, would that have made it OK for him to kill her?" Then, this critic lets me down: "In Shakespeare, stakes are high." In other words, it's *more* "OK" for Othello to kill Desdemona because they are married, and he thinks she is unfaithful.

"If my wife cheated on me," a student of mine said, "I'd kill her."

The fact that the film *O.* was delayed in distribution because of the shootings at Columbine High School simply demonstrates how blind American culture is when it comes to race, gender, and violence. As Tim Wise points out in his bold essay, "School shootings and white denial," mass-murder in American high schools, along with a host of other "delinquent" behaviors, is statistically *white*.[28] Connecting the Columbine massacre to Shakespeare's fantasy of black-on-white uxoricide is yet another way of blaming minorities for America's (white) social ills and obscuring the ideological underpinnings of what is, first and foremost, the story of the murder of a *woman* for the sake of a man's claim on her body. If the film had to be censored, it should have been censored for its problematic racial and gender politics, not its insensitivity to the white families of the white victims of white, adolescent, male violence.

After all, Shakespeare was writing in 1603. He had an excuse.

LEPIDUS: What manner o' thing is your crocodile?
ENOBARBUS: It is shaped, sir, like itself, and it is as broad as it hath breadth. It is just so high as it is, and moves with it own organs. It lives by that which nourisheth it, and the elements once out of it, it transmigrates.
LEPIDUS: What colour is it of?
ENOBARBUS: Of it own colour, too.
LEPIDUS: 'Tis a strange serpent. (William Shakespeare, *Antony and Cleopatra* II.vii.32–6)

In a graduate seminar I taught on the subject of this book, a bright young poet once objected to the critical lens I brought to inter-racialist texts like *Othello*, on the basis of his understanding of the creative process. "The black–white binary has got to be *the* central trope in literature," he said, inadvertently paraphrasing Jacques Derrida. "How can an author compose without it? If I worry that every time I use 'black' with a negative inflection, I'm being racist, I'll get nothing written." He had a point. And this point was driven home to me when I tried to write my own "traveler's history" on sabbatical in Sicily, confronted daily with what to my middle-class American gaze was a dark-skinned "exotic" population – much more exotic than America's own population of color, so familiar to me, and so often (let's face it) not very dark-skinned at all. Interestingly, Spike Lee himself, commenting on the antagonism between blacks and Italians dramatized in his film, observes that "Sicily is not that far from Africa."[29] Indeed, Italians of the north insult those of the south by calling them either *Albanesi* or *Africani*.

I must admit, however, I was particularly intrigued by the Sicilian men. As an American feminist, I was alarmed by their overt patriarchalism: I felt distinctly uncomfortable crossing the *piazze*, all-male domains according to unwritten cultural codes. As an American woman and a heterosexual, though, I found the *Siciliani* beautiful to look at, and they kept cropping up in my poetry. It wasn't "jungle fever" in that reductive, complexional sense: it was the whole strange, gorgeous, and disturbing picture that was Sicily. The sheer, heart-breaking lines of the mountains; the winding, cliff-side roads lacking guard-rails. The volcano – which was active during my stay there, and spewing ash across one side of the isle. The *scirocco*, a hot wind out of Africa that carries in it the desert sand. The seemingly lawless streets of Palermo – a city of over a million with hardly any traffic-lights. The men: when "white," never lighter than brown, and when black – meaning African – *really* black. This ambivalent fascination became even more pronounced when visa problems necessitated a brief trip to Tunis: the city streets were virtually devoid of women, which meant that in my eyes the rush-hour crowds seethed as one black-haired, brown-skinned, hyper-male human mass. Fascination turned to anxiety: I glued myself to my partner when in public, and couldn't wait to get "home" to Sicily. Later, when polishing my writings on these travels, I noticed a persistent vein of Orientalist tropes. Complexional tropes; tropes of exotic spices, sphinxes and sultans marched across the page. Yet I liked the poems. Disconcerted, I went into my closet and dug up the journal I kept during freshman year in college, when I dated a Jamaican. Appalled at what I found, I burned the evidence.

When writing on the topic of race, there comes a point where it's almost impossible to avoid the confessional mode. All of the major characters in *Jungle Fever* enter it at some point – Flipper listing his childhood nick-names as a dark-skinned black; his wife rattling off hers as a light-skinned black; even Angela, with her talk of Catholic school and her overbearing brothers. So I might as well tell you that I think I can see Othellophilia from both sides, as I have lived all my life in the "Other" slot of the ethnic questionnaire. It was a black man who asked me "What are you?" when I was in line at Blockbuster. Maybe I was renting a "black" film – or maybe not. Put off by his bluntness I answered, "*Homo sapiens sapiens.*" Normally, I make people guess, if they haven't initially posed the question by way of a guess. "Are you Cuban?" – "Are you Thai?" – "Are you mixed?" – "*Sei Siciliana?*" – "Are you Svengali?" – "Are you Jewish?" – "Are you Polynesian?" – "Are you from my country [Saudi Arabia]?" – "Are you Cherokee?" – "Are you East Indian?" – "Are y'all [myself and an Indian friend] sisters? No? But y'all're from India." – "Do you know that Iranian professor in the Business School? No? Do you know those Mexicans who just moved in down the block?" – "What kind of name is 'Daileader'?" – "Where are you from? . . . No, I mean originally." – "You're not from around here, are you?" – "Hey. She black or *not*?"

Not all Othellophiles are racist. Most, in fact, are emphatically anti-racist – or try to be. Which is why I encounter so much resistance when I read *Othello* politically. People get defensive – or get ugly. Occasionally, they tell me more than I want to know ("If my wife cheated on me . . ."). And I have to admit that in writing this book I came a long way from my original hostility toward Shakespeare's paradigm, if only because *so few* white authors in the intervening four centuries succeeded in imagining something better for members of different races who happened to fall in love, or for men who suspected or found out that their wives were having affairs. In fact, it increasingly seemed that the more obviously, clinically racist and/or misogynist versions of the same story were produced within my own century, despite all our alleged "progress" and moral relativism. There is no poetry, no beauty, in the love-story – or is it hate-story? – of Joanna Burden and Joe Christmas. There is no "If it were now to die / 'Twere now to be most happy," no "Perdition catch my soul / But I do love thee" (*Othello* II.i.190–1; III.iii.91–2). There is only a decapitated woman, and a metaphorical sewer, and a horrific lynching.

The tragedy of Othellophilia is this: it tends to take the most negative elements of Shakespeare's tragedy, and exaggerate them. It tends to lose the wonder – a wonder that, as Paul Yachnin has shown, is central to both the play and our experience of it.[30] A wonder that surely characterized the first encounters between Europeans and non-Europeans.[31] A wonder that is integral to travel and discovery, integral to art. "'Twas strange, 'twas passing strange" (I.iii.159). There is nothing inherently wrong with the wonder that people feel encountering Otherness. It is nobody's particular fault if his or her background did not prepare him or her to see such dark or fair skin, or hear this foreign tongue – and it is nobody's particular fault to be fascinated. Where it all goes wrong is when fascination becomes polluted with fear, with hostility, with condescension. It all goes wrong, in short, when ideology harnesses that wonder, and forces it to serve its own purposes. And though I am speaking just now about racial or ethnic difference, this is true also of men and women, confronting the difference of the Other's body. "'Twas strange, 'twas passing strange."

Shakespeare most likely never saw Italy, and he certainly never saw Africa. His explorations of the Mediterranean, of the Other, of the Orient, were entirely imaginary. Yet there is a way in which *all* explorations of the foreign are imaginary: confronting Otherness, we attempt to frame it, describe it in terms familiar to us. It is the only way we know how. "What manner o' thing is your crocodile?" – "It is shaped, sir, like itself." Caesar worries that "this description" of the crocodile will not "satisfy" (Shakespeare, *Antony and Cleopatra* ii. vii.40–9) and he is right. And so I, in describing Sicily – the mountains, the winding roads, the men milling about in the *piazza* – resorted to Shakespearean tropes; I wrote of jet, of ebony, of spices, of desert sands. And it seems fitting, now, that this intellectual journey that began with a book, with a play, with a cultural fantasy, should have reached its conclusion on an island in the Mediterranean, more than midway between Italy and north Africa. Like Prospero's island or Cyprus, neither Europe nor Africa, neither "here" nor quite "there." Where the essence of that "dark continent" is as formless and as wayward as sand blown in the wind.

Notes

INTRODUCTION. OTHELLOPHILIA

1 David M. Friedman, *A Mind of Its Own: A Cultural History of the Penis* (New York: Free Press, 2001), p. 2. Friedman draws upon many sources, including Henry Charles Lea, *Materials toward a History of Witchcraft* (Philadelphia: University of Pennsylvania Press, 1939); Rossell Hope Robbins, *The Encyclopedia of Witchcraft and Demonology* (New York: Crown, 1959); Robert E. L. Masters, *Eros and Evil* (New York: Julian Press, 1962); Ann Llewellyn Barstow, *Witchcraze* (San Francisco: HarperCollins, 1994); Joseph Klaits, *Servants of Satan* (Bloomington, Ind.: Indiana University Press, 1985); and Brian P. Levack, *The Witch-Hunt in Early Modern Europe* (New York: Longman, 1987).

2 Quoted in Friedman, *A Mind of Its Own*, p. 114. In a later chapter, Friedman dates the myth of the "macrophallic" black male back to 1623 (p. 103).

3 All quotations of Shakespeare in this book will be from *The Complete Works of William Shakespeare*, ed. Gary Taylor and Stanley Wells (Oxford: Oxford University Press, 1986).

4 Michael Neill, " 'Mulattos,' 'Blacks,' and 'Indian Moors': Othello and early modern constructions of human difference," *Shakespeare Quarterly* 49.4 (Winter, 1998), 361–74; p. 361. Similarly but more exhaustively, Mary Floyd-Wilson situates the play "on the cusp – between old ethnological values and emergent racial ones" (Mary Floyd-Wilson, *English Ethnicity and Race in Early Modern Drama* [Cambridge: Cambridge University Press, 2003], p.18).

5 On the genre of "domestic tragedy" see Henry Hitch Adams, *English Domestic; or, Homiletic Tragedy: 1575–1642* (New York: Benjamin Bloom, 1965). On *Othello* in particular see G. W. Knight, *The Wheel of Fire* (London: Methuen, 1949), p. 108; M. R. Ridley's introduction to his edition of the play (London: Methuen, 1958), p. xlv; Peter L. Rudnytsky, "*A Woman Killed with Kindness* as subtext for *Othello*," *Renaissance Drama* 14 (1983), 103–24; and Brian W. Shaffer, " 'To manage private and domestic quarrels': Shakespeare's *Othello* and the genre of Elizabethan domestic tragedy," *Iowa State Journal of Research* 62.3 (1988), 443–57.

6 Linda Charnes, "What's love got to do with it? Reading the liberal humanist romance in Shakespeare's *Antony and Cleopatra*," *Textual Practice* 6.1 (Spring,

1992), 1–2. For a less "academic" critique of our most sacred institution, see Laura Kapnis, *Against Love: A Polemic* (New York: Pantheon, 2003).

7 Ronald Huebert's reading of Thomas Heywood's *A Woman Killed with Kindness* persuasively debunks the widely held assumption that a woman caught in adultery could be murdered by her husband with no legal repercussions. In seventeenth-century England "adultery was not a crime but an offence under canon law. The church courts tended to subject offenders to a variety of shame punishments . . . such as . . . 'carting, ducking, and doing of open penance in sheets'" (*The Performance of Pleasure: A Reading of English Renaissance Drama* [New York: Palgrave, 2003], p. 92). Huebert is quoting William Harrison's *Description of England*, ed. Georges Edelen (Ithaca, N.Y.: Cornell University Press, 1968), p. 189. Oddly enough, critics who endorse Heywood's message in the play, citing an "unwritten law" exonerating wife-murder on the basis of adultery, have tended to cite – when citing any historical source at all – a case in which a man was hanged for the murder of his adulterous wife. See F. G. Emmison, *Elizabethan Life: Disorder* (Chelmsford: Essex Historical Society, 1970), p. 154.

8 See Katherine Eisaman Maus, *Inwardness and the Theatre of the English Renaissance* (Chicago: University of Chicago Press, 1995), pp. 104–27.

9 Shaffer goes so far as to credit Shakespeare for *improving upon* the genre with respect to its treatment of women, by way of the innovation of Desdemona's "innocence." This critic opines, "if Elizabethan domestic tragedy is a drama of crime and punishment, *Othello* is one in which 'punishment' (Othello's murder of Desdemona) becomes the crime itself (because gratuitous violence)" ("*Othello* and domestic tragedy," p. 451). In other words, in this play the bitch *didn't* have it coming to her; this proves how much Shakespeare loved women.

10 Cassio's wife disappears after this one puzzling reference: later on he presents himself as a bachelor ("I marry!" [IV.i.120]).

11 In fact, Iago is not white in the racial sense, nor is any other character in the play, as Gary Taylor points out (see *Buying Whiteness: Race, Culture, and Identity from Columbus to Hip-Hop* [New York: Palgrave, 2005], pp. 39–45). Iago may be either Spanish or Italian – both objects of vicious stereotyping by the English.

12 See S. T. Coleridge, *Lectures 1808–1819 on Literature*, ed. R. A. Foakes, 2 vols. (1987), II, p. 315.

13 Only in recent years have Shakespeareans begun to consider the plays' representations of conjugal violence as having anything to do with the dangers women faced in the home in early-modern England – as well as today, when more than half of female homicides are at the hands of a partner. So far, however, the discussion has been limited to *The Taming of the Shrew* with its more overt and pervasive treatment of male power and spousal violence. See, for example, Emily Detmer, "Civilizing subordination: domestic violence and *The Taming of the Shrew*," *Shakespeare Quarterly* 48.3 (Fall, 1997), 273–94.

14 M. P. Tilley, *A Dictionary of Proverbs in England in the Sixteenth and Seventeenth Centuries* (Ann Arbor: University of Michigan Press, 1950), E186 and P358. See also Jean Michael Massing, "From Greek proverb to soap advert: washing the Ethiope," *Journal of the Warburg and Courtauld Institutions* 58 (1995), 180–201, and Carolyn Prager, "'If I be devil': English Renaissance response to the proverbial and ecumenical Ethiopian," *Journal of Medieval and Renaissance Studies* 17 (1987), 257–79.

15 Toni Morrison, *Playing in the Dark: Whiteness and the Literary Imagination* (New York: Vintage Books, 1992), p. 17.

16 Such reactions to the plot have been documented from fairly early in the play's performance history. There is, for example, Thomas Rymer's famous exclamation of incredulity over the inter-racial marrage: "With us a *Moor* might marry some little drab, or Small-coal Wench: *Shake-spear*, would provide him the Daughter and kin of some great Lord, or Privy-Councillor." Charles Gildon concurred, stating that "every one almost starts at the Choice" of Desdemona for Othello. Quoted in Virginia Mason Vaughan, *Othello: A Contextual History* (Cambridge: Cambridge University Press, 1994), p. 94.

17 Thomas Adams, *The White devil; or, the Hypocrite Uncased: in Sermon Preached at Pauls Cross, March 7. 1612* (London, 1613), pp. 1–2. The date in the title refers to the old calendar, in which the year began on March 21.

18 Mary Floyd-Wilson, *English Ethnicity and Race in Early Modern English Drama* (Cambridge: Cambridge University Press, 2001), pp. 140, 142.

19 See Hugh Quarshie, *Second Thoughts about "Othello,"* International Shakespeare Association Occasional Papers, no. 7 (Chipping Camden, 1999).

20 Celia R. Daileader, "Casting black actors: beyond Othellophilia," in *Shakespeare and Race*, ed. Catherine M. S. Alexander and Stanley Wells (Cambridge: Cambridge University Press, 2000), pp. 177–202.

21 My attention was brought to this pattern by the coincidence of three inter-racial productions of *Romeo and Juliet* within the space of a couple of years: in 1996 the theatre department in my own University of Alabama presented a consciously racial interpretation, casting the entire house of Montague as black; one year later the RSC cast black actor Ray Fearon in the role of Romeo; during this same period ACTER featured a black Romeo–white Juliet performance. My research on the Stratford, Ontario, Festival and the Alabama Shakespeare Festival uncovered no inter-racial productions at all. To my knowledge only two major festivals have cast black Juliets opposite a white Romeo: the Washington DC Summer Shakespeare Festival (1968) and the Shakespeare Society of America at the Globe Playhouse in Los Angeles (1977), both described in Errol Hill, *Shakespeare in Sable: A History of Black Shakespearean Actors* (Amherst, Mass.: University of Massachusetts Press, 1984), pp. 156, 158. The pattern may hold in adaptations as well: the Toronto Fringe Festival recently put on a "rave" *Romeo/Juliet Remixed* with a black Romeo and white Juliet. Finally, personal conversations with black

performers have confirmed this working thesis: Hugh Quarshie has a distinguished Shakespearean career but, as of my last conversation with him, he has never been cast romantically opposite a black actress in English classical drama. Such anecdotal evidence, of course, can never be considered conclusive: there are always likely to be exceptions. But one can safely say that the most recent and most visible inter-racial Romeos have been black, as in the RSC's critically acclaimed production. My thanks to Jill Levenson and Peter Holland for help with this question.

22 Francis Fletcher, *The World Encompassed by Sir Francis Drake, Being His Next Voyage to That to Nombre de Dios, XVI* (London: Hakluyt Society, 1854), p. 183.

23 David Eltis, *The Rise of African Slavery in the Americas* (Cambridge: Cambridge University Press, 2000), pp. 95–6.

24 A. Leon Higginbotham, *Shades of Freedom: Racial Politics and Presumptions of the American Legal Process* (Oxford: Oxford University Press, 1996), pp. 34–5.

25 Hilary McD. Beckles, "Property rights in pleasure: the marketing of enslaved women's sexuality," in *Caribbean Slavery in the Atlantic World,* ed. Verene Shepherd and Hilary McD. Beckles (Kingston, Jamaica: Ian Randle Publishers, 2000), pp. 692–701; David W. Cohen and Jack P. Greene, eds., *Neither Slave nor Free: The Freedman of African Descent in the Slave Societies of the New World* (Baltimore: Johns Hopkins University Press, 1972), pp. 1–18; and Winthrop D. Jordan, *White over Black: American Attitudes toward the Negro 1550–1812* (Chapel Hill: University of North Carolina Press, 1968), pp. 78–80.

26 Beckles, "Property rights in pleasure," p. 698. Another interesting observation is that "The money paid to owners of slave women for sexual services frequently exceeded the slaves' market value" (p. 695).

27 Kim F. Hall, *Things of Darkness: Economies of Race and Gender in Early Modern England* (New York: Cornell University Press, 1995), p. 9.

28 William Wells Brown, *Clotel; or, The President's Daughter,* ed. Robert S. Levine (Boston: St. Martin's, 2000), p. 81.

29 See Celia R. Daileader, "The uses of ambivalence: pornography and female heterosexual identity," *Women's Studies* 26.1 (January 1997), 73–88. For a theorization of the erotic, see Daileader, *Eroticism on the Renaissance Stage: Transcendence, Desire, and the Limits of the Visible* (Cambridge: Cambridge University Press, 1998). My definition of "eroticism" is on p. 5.

30 See, for instance, Michel Foucault, *The Archaeology of Knowledge* (New York: Pantheon, 1972), pp. 3–17.

31 This wave of resistance might even be strong enough to be called a movement now: scholars such as Hugh Grady and Terence Hawkes advocate "Presentism" as an alternative to New Historicism. Presentism holds that our responsibility to understand the present is at least as important as our responsibility to understand the past. See Hugh Grady, *The Modernist Shakespeare: Critical Texts in a Material World* (Oxford: Clarendon Press, 1991), and Terence Hawkes, *Shakespeare in the Present* (London: Routledge, 2002).

32 Arthur J. Little Jr., *Shakespeare Jungle Fever: National-Imperial Re-Visions of Race, Rape, and Sacrifice* (Stanford: Stanford University Press, 2000), p. 6.

33 Neil L. Whitehead, Introduction to Sir Walther Ralegh, *Empire of Guiana*, ed. Whitehead (Norman: University of Oklahoma Press, 1997), p. 53.

34 I use the term "black/feminist" in recognition of the growing scholarly consensus on the inseparability of social constructions of race and gender, and their mutual complicity in economic exploitation and social injustice generally. In early-modern studies in particular, post Kim Hall's analysis of "the cult of fairness" in the literature of the period, white feminists can no longer afford to take as a given a female discursive subject whose cultural production is somehow "innocent" of the rise of colonialism and the slave trade.

35 Bell hooks, *Salvation: Black People and Love* (New York: HarperCollins, 2001), pp. 55–70.

36 Ania Loomba, *Shakespeare, Race, and Colonialism* (Oxford: Oxford University Press, 2002), p. 5.

37 Jyotsna Singh, "Othello's identity, postcolonial theory, and contemporary African rewritings of *Othello*," in *Women, "Race," and Writing in the Early Modern Period*, ed. Margo Hendricks and Patricia Parker (London: Routledge, 1994), p. 291.

38 Joseph Roach builds on Paul Gilroy's concept of "the black Atlantic" in formulating the notion of a "circum-Atlantic world (as opposed to a transatlantic one)" – a concept that "insists on the centrality of the diasporic and genocidal histories of Africa and the Americas, North and South, in the creation of the culture of modernity" (Joseph Roach, *Cities of the Dead* [New York: Columbia University Press, 1996], p. 4).

39 See Joel Williamson, "How black was Rhett Butler?" in *The Evolution of Southern Culture*, ed. Numan V. Bartley (Athens, Ga.: University of Georgia Press, 1988), pp. 87–107.

40 Gary Taylor, "The greatest lie ever told," *The Observer* (October 9, 1994).

I WHITE DEVILS, BLACK LUST: INTER-RACIALISM
IN EARLY MODERN DRAMA

1 Horatio F. Brown, ed., *Calendar of State Papers and Manuscripts, Relating to English Affairs, Existing in the Archives and Collections of Venice, and in Other Libraries of Northern Italy, Vol. XI, 1607–1610* (London: Mackie and Co., 1904), p. 322. See also Brown's description of the controversy in his Preface, pp. xxviii–xxx. The original pamphlet is by John Wilson writing as Horatius Dolabella, *Purit-anus* (Lambeth, 1609); the English ambassador is paraphrasing p. 9.

2 Hall, *Things of Darkness*, p. 9. Additionally, Gary Taylor argues that the English did not use the noun "white" or "whites" in the collective racial sense until later in the seventeenth century; rather, "white" skin in the early

modern period was an attribute of (aristocratic) English women, and not at all desirable in men, for whom a healthy complexion was "ruddy" or even "brown" (*Buying Whiteness: Race, Culture, and Identity from Columbus to Hip-Hop* [New York: Palgrave, 2005], pp. 6–58).

3 Francis Fletcher, *The World Encompassed by Sir Francis Drake, Being His Next Voyage to That to Nombre de Dios, XVI* (London: Hakluyt Society, 1854), p. 183.

4 A seminal essay on the subject is Lynda E. Boose, "The getting of a lawful race: racial discourse in early modern England and the 'unrepresentable' black woman," in *Women, "Race," and Writing in the Early Modern Period*, ed. Margo Hendricks and Patricia Parker (London: Routledge, 1994), pp. 35–54. Since the publication of the former, critics such as Hall in *Things of Darkness* and Joyce Green MacDonald (*Women and Race in Early Modern Texts* [Cambridge: Cambridge University Press, 2002]) have fruitfully complicated Boose's theoretical paradigm. MacDonald, for instance, studies the whitewashing of African women in early modern drama, arguing that "The racial 'sameness' that these women's white skin apparently proclaims does not, in fact, repudiate the idea of racialized norms of femininity, since other kinds of difference – sexual, political, behavioral – will be fully identified as racial matters within the newly whitened social body" (pp. 13–14). For discussions of race in the literature of the period generally, see, in addition to Hall and MacDonald, Anthony Barthelemy, *Black Face, Maligned Race: The Representation of Blacks in Renaissance Drama from Shakespeare to Southerne* (Baton Rouge: Louisiana State University Press, 1987); Emily C. Bartels, "Making more of the Moor: Aaron, Othello, and Renaissance refashionings of race," *Shakespeare Quarterly* 41 (1990), 433–54; Jack D'Amico, *The Moor in English Renaissance Drama* (Tampa, Fla.: University of South Florida Press, 1991); Eldred Jones, *Othello's Countrymen: The African in Renaissance Drama* (Oxford: Oxford University Press, 1965); Ania Loomba, *Gender, Race, Renaissance Drama* (Oxford: Oxford University Press, 1992); Michael Neill, "Unproper beds: race, adultery, and the hideous in *Othello*," *Shakespeare Quarterly* 40 (1989), 383–412; Jyotsna Singh, "Caliban versus Miranda: race and gender conflicts in postcolonial rewritings of *The Tempest*," in *Feminist Readings of Early Modern Culture*, ed. Valerie Traub, M. Lindsay Kaplan, and Dympna Callaghan (Cambridge: Cambridge University Press, 1996), pp. 191–209; Virginia Mason Vaughn, *Othello: A Contextual History* (Cambridge: Cambridge University Press, 1994); and Mary Floyd-Wilson, *English Ethnicity and Race*. See also the essays in Hendricks and Parker, eds., *Women, "Race," and Writing* and *Shakespeare and Race*, ed. Catherine M. S. Alexander and Stanley Wells (Cambridge: Cambridge University Press, 2000).

5 On Peele's collaboration on *Titus Andronicus*, see Brian Vickers, *Shakespeare, Co-author: A Historical Study of Five Collaborative Plays* (Oxford: Oxford University Press, 2002), pp. 148–243. The play is identified as co-authored in

the revised edition of the *Complete Works of William Shakespeare*, ed. Stanley Wells and Gary Taylor (Oxford: Oxford University Press, 2005).

6 D'Amico, *The Moor in English Renaissance Drama*, pp. 98–132.

7 Hall, *Things of Darkness*, pp. 134–5.

8 A note on terminology might be called for here. The slippery and confused nature of early modern racial taxonomies has been well noted by scholars (see, for example, Neill, "'Mulattos,' 'Blacks,' and 'Indian Moors'" and Bartels, "Making more of the Moor"). I will use each of the above-mentioned early modern terms in accordance with each text to be discussed. When speaking generally of the early modern period, I will use the term "racialist" to denote discursive treatments of race that seem to prefigure modern racist discourse (racism being recognized as a nineteenth-century invention), and "anti-black" or "color-phobic" to denote the sentiment expressed in denigrations of a racialized blackness or dark skin; following Taylor's caveat in *Buying Whiteness*, I will use "white" only as a modifier of (usually female) skin-color and not in its generic racial sense.

9 I am alluding here to Gary Taylor's *Reinventing Shakespeare: A Cultural History from the Restoration to the Present* (Oxford: Oxford University Press, 1989).

10 Ravenscroft's adaptation ratchets up the racialist rhetoric and makes the relationship between Tamora and Aaron central to the play; Aaron is given dialogue in the first act (unlike in Shakespeare's play, where he is silent throughout it), and Ravenscroft makes his spectacular punishment (burning alive) the climax of the show, in sharp contrast to Shakespeare, who has him punished offstage. See Joyce Green MacDonald, "'The force of imagination': the subject of blackness in Shakespeare, Jonson, and Ravenscroft," *Renaissance Papers* 1991, pp. 53–74.

11 See especially Hall, *Things of Darkness*, pp. 11–24, 211–53. Most of Hall's examples post-date the composition of *Titus Andronicus*; in particular, the portraits featuring decorative black servants in pearl necklaces date from the middle to the late 1600s, when the fashion for such human accessories began to peak. In *Titus Andronicus*, as in *Othello*, Shakespeare appears one step ahead of the trends in racial discourse.

12 Mary Floyd-Wilson emphasizes the asexual nature of Aaron's self-portrait here in a way that strengthens her case for a lingering classical, geo-humoral understanding of Africans as wise and chaste in earlier Renaissance texts. By the time Shakespeare wrote *Othello*, however, that discourse was already being tempered by the new, proto-racist stereotype of the "lascivious Moor," as Floyd-Wilson's own analysis makes clear. I take seriously her caveat against projecting backward from *Othello* the discourse of African hyper-sexuality and irrationality that the play itself helped foster, but I do find that the sexualized imagery in Aaron's speech here – along with his complicity in the rape of Lavinia – strongly qualifies his disassociation from Venus in this speech.

13 Little, *Shakespeare Jungle Fever*, pp. 59–60.

14 John Marston, *The Wonder of Women; or, the Tragedy of Sophonisba*: *The Selected Plays of John Marston*, ed. Macdonald P. Jackson (Cambridge: Cambridge University Press, 1986), iii.i.10–11.

15 Little, *Shakespeare Jungle Fever*, pp. 58–9.

16 See Francesca Royster, "White-limed walls: whiteness and Gothic extremism in Shakespeare's *Titus Andronicus*," *Shakespeare Quarterly* 51.4 (Winter, 2000), 432–55. The classical paradigm that grounds racial difference in the physiological effects of climate, and the endurance into the early modern period of this "geo-humoral" model, is exhaustively laid out in Mary Floyd-Wilson's *English Ethnicity and Race*.

17 For a more detailed reading of this language, see Daileader, *Eroticism on the Renaissance Stage: Transcendence, Desire, and the Limits of the Visible* (Cambridge: Cambridge University Press, 1998), pp. 34–40, 120–5.

18 This was pointed out by Stanley Cavell in "Epistemology and tragedy: a reading of *Othello* (together with a cover letter)," *Daedalus* 108.3 (1979), p. 42. In addition, the word "devil" occurs twenty times in the play in association with Desdemona and Othello almost equally.

19 *Le Nord*, November 23, 1858. Quoted in Herbert Marshall and Mildred Stock, *Ira Aldridge: The Negro Tragedian* (London: Camelot Press, 1958), p. 227.

20 *Tallis's Dramatic Magazine*, April, 1851, p. 168. Quoted in Carol Jones Carlisle, *Shakespeare from the Greenroom: Actors' Criticisms of Four Major Tragedies* (Chapel Hill: University of North Carolina Press, 1969), p. 244.

21 Most of these moralistic critiques are also racist. Samuel Taylor Coleridge opines, "[I]t would be something monstrous to conceive this beautiful Venetian girl falling in love with a veritable Negro. It would argue a disproportionateness, a want of balance, in Desdemona, which Shakespeare does not appear to have in the least contemplated" (Samuel Taylor Coleridge, *Coleridge's Shakespearean Criticism*, 2 vols., ed. Thomas Middleton Raysor [Cambridge, Mass.: Harvard University Press, 1930], i, p. 47). John Quincy Adams raises even stronger objections: "Upon the stage, her fondling with Othello is disgusting. Who, in real life, would have her for a sister, daughter, or wife? She is not guilty of infidelity to her husband, but she forfeits all the affection of her father and all her own filial affection for him." He goes on to say that her character "is always deficient in delicacy. Her conversations with Emilia indicate unsettled principles, even with regard to the obligations of the nuptial tie, and she allows Iago, almost unrebuked, to banter with her very coarsely upon women. This character takes from us so much of the sympathetic interest in her sufferings, that when Othello smothers her in bed, the terror and pity subside immediately into the sentiment that she has her deserts" (quoted in James Henry Hackett, *Notes, Criticisms and Correspondence upon Shakespeare's Plays and Actors* [London: Benjamin Blom, 1968], pp. 225–6).

22 I agree here with Joyce Green MacDonald, who says that *Othello* "suggests a broadly racialized connection between prostituted Bianca and virtuous

Desdemona, because of their mutual association with a bestialized female sexuality" ("Black ram, white ewe: Shakespeare, race, and women," in *A Feminist Companion to Shakespeare*, ed. Dympna Callaghan [Oxford: Blackwell, 2000], p. 196).

23 Dympna Callaghan, *Woman and Gender in Renaissance Tragedy* (Atlantic Highlands, N.J.: Humanities Press International, 1989), p. 141.

24 Thomas Dekker, *Lust's Dominion; or, the Lascivious Queen*, in *The Dramatic Works of Thomas Dekker*, ed. Fredson Bowers (Cambridge: Cambridge University Press, 1968).

25 See the introduction to Aphra Behn, *Abdelazer: or, The Moor's Revenge*, in *The Works of Aphra Behn*, 7 vols., ed. Janet Todd (Columbus: Ohio State University Press, 1996), v, p. 241.

26 See Celia R. Daileader, "Back-door Sex: Renaissance gynosodomy, Aretino, and the Exotic," *ELH* 69.2 (Summer, 2002), 303–34; p. 322.

27 Joyce Green MacDonald calls attention to the critical silence surrounding Cleopatra's racial identity and offers an insightful corrective in her essay, "Sex, race, and empire in Shakespeare's *Antony and Cleopatra*," *Literature and History* 5.1 (Spring, 1996), 60–77.

28 Samuel Daniel's *Tragedy of Cleopatra* (1594) does not specify the heroine's skin-color, Mary Sidney's *Antonie* (1595) depicts her as white, Elizabeth Cary's *Tragedy of Mariam, Fair Queen of Jewry* (1613) calls her "the brown Egyptian" (1.ii.190), and Thomas Dekker's *The Wonder of a Kingdom* (1636) calls her black. On the racial whiteness of Sidney's and Daniel's Cleopatras, see MacDonald, *Women and Race in Early Modern Texts*, pp. 41–85.

29 Marvin Hunt, "Be dark but not too dark: Shakespeare's Dark Lady as a sign of color," in *Shakespeare's Sonnets: Critical Essays*, ed. James Schiffer (New York: Routledge, 1999), pp. 369–89.

30 The acclaimed 1982 RSC production is just one example.

31 John Webster, *The White Devil*, ed. John Russell Brown (Manchester: Manchester University Press, 1977). All quotations are from this edition.

32 See Daileader, "Casting black actors," pp. 184–92 and *passim*.

33 Ania Loomba, "The colour of patriarchy: critical difference, cultural difference, and Renaissance drama," in *Women, "Race" and Writing in the Early Modern Period*, ed. Hendricks and Parker, pp. 27–8.

34 On the play's canine imagery and its linkage to racial difference see Francesca Royster, "Working like a dog: (e)racing the animal–human divide," in *Writing Race across the Atlantic World*, ed. Philip Beidler and Gary Taylor (New York: Palgrave, 2005).

35 Dympna Callaghan, *Woman and Gender in Renaissance Tragedy*, p. 142.

36 On skin-color tropes in the Petrarchan tradition, see Hall, *Things of Darkness*, pp. 62–122.

37 In calling her Zanthia I am departing from the Cambridge edition, which uses the speech-prefix Abdella. With this one qualification, all quotations are from John Fletcher, Philip Massinger, and Nathan Field, *The Knight of*

Malta, in *The Dramatic Works in the Beaumont and Fletcher Canon*, 8 vols., ed. Fredson Bowers (Cambridge: Cambridge University Press, 1966), VIII.

38 For a fascinating discussion of the prosthetic woman on the early modern stage, see Ann Rosalind Jones and Peter Stallybrass, *Renaissance Clothing and the Materials of Culture* (Cambridge: Cambridge University Press, 2000), pp. 207–19. Stallybrass and Jones do not, unfortunately, have an answer to the technical question of whether the boys wore prosthetic breasts, a practice for which there seems to be no historical record (p. 210).

39 For a more complete theorization of the absence of female performers on the early modern stage, see Daileader, *Eroticism on the Renaissance Stage*.

40 William Rowley, *A Tragedy Called All's Lost by Lust* (London: 1633).

41 Floyd-Wilson, *English Ethnicity and Race*.

42 D'Amico, *The Moor in English Renaissance Drama*, p. 104.

43 Barthelemy, *Black Face, Maligned Race*, p. 135.

44 An underlying question here and throughout this study is whether misogyny is older than these other forms of cultural and social "othering." This is probably an unanswerable question, bound up in the theoretical problem of whether subjects are gendered before they are constituted as "white" or "black," "us" or "them." Kaja Silverman argues that "race and class identities are best understood as ideological interpolations" but that these differences are articulated with the help "of an even more inaugural difference . . . sexual difference." Jean Walton disputes this position, building on Lévi-Strauss in stating that "Kinship, through the exogamous exchange of women, is the means by which subjects are 'masculinized' or 'feminized' . . . But through the racially defined endogamous exchange of women, kinship is also the means by which subjects are 'raced' . . ." (*Fair Sex, Savage Dreams: Race, Psychoanalysis, Sexual Difference* [Durham, N.C.: Duke University Press, 2001], p. 10). I lean toward Silverman in this debate, but confess to doing so entirely on intuitive and personal grounds, as a female subject of ambiguous ethnicity who has always been baffled by the choice of "white/black/other."

45 Even Coleridge finds *Antony and Cleopatra* the "most wonderful" play of Shakespeare's (*Coleridge's Shakespearean Criticism*, I, p. 86).

46 Taylor, *Cultural Selection. Why Some Achievements Survive the Test of Time – and Others Don't* (New York: Basic Books, 1996).

47 Taylor, *Reinventing Shakespeare*, pp. 100–61.

48 See Thomas Middleton's (1613) city pageant, *The Triumphs of Truth*, in *The Collected Works of Thomas Middleton*, ed. Gary Taylor (Oxford: Oxford University Press, forthcoming).

49 See especially Taylor, *Reinventing Shakespeare*, pp. 100–11, 157–61.

50 Nabil Matar, *Turks, Moors and Englishmen in the Age of Discovery* (New York: Columbia University Press, 1999), p. 13.

51 *Ibid.*, pp. 40–1.

52 Quoted in *ibid.*, p. 41.

53 Joyce Green MacDonald, "Black Ram, White Ewe," p. 197.

54 Henry Neville, *The Isle of Pines; or, a Late Discovery of a Fourth Island in Terra Australis, Incognita* (London, 1668).

2 THE HEATHEN WITH THE HEART OF GOLD: OTHELLOPHILIA COMES TO AMERICA

1 MacDonald, *Women and Race in Early Modern Texts* (Cambridge: Cambridge University Press, 2002), pp. 252–3.
2 The only other favorable portrayal of an African couple that I know of is in Thomas Middleton's city pageant, *The Triumphs of Truth* (1613). See Taylor's discussion in *Buying Whiteness: Race, Culture, and Identity from Columbus to Hip-Hop* (New York: Palgrave, 2005), pp. 145–9.
3 Laura Brown, *Ends of Empire: Women and Ideology in Early Eighteenth-Century English Literature* (Ithaca: Cornell University Press, 1993), pp. 49, 23–63.
4 All quotations are from Aphra Behn, *Oroonoko*, ed. Joanna Lipking (New York: Norton, 1997).
5 Adaptations of Behn's novella include Thomas Southerne's as well as John Hawkesworth's (1759), Francis Gentleman's (1760), John Ferriar's (1788), and the anonymous *Royal Captive* (1787). See MacDonald's discussion in *Women and Race in Early Modern Texts*, pp. 122–56. Biyi Bandele's 1999 adaptation for the RSC restores the black Imoinda; this production brought a record number of black performers to the company.
6 See Elizabeth D. Gruber, "Dead girls do it better: gazing rights and the production of knowledge in *Othello* and *Oroonoko*," *Literature, Interpretation, and Theory* 14.2 (2003), 99–117.
7 Jane Spencer, *The Rise of the Woman Novelist: From Aphra Behn to Jane Austen* (Oxford: Blackwell, 1986), p. 52. Margaret W. Ferguson, similarly, sees the relationship between author and heroine as problematic, arguing for "an implicit competition between the white English female author and the black African female slave-wife-mother-to-be . . . for Oroonoko's body and its power to engender something in the future, something that will outlive it." The author, according to Ferguson, wins the competition by destroying Imoinda and her unborn child, replacing the latter with her own narrative (Margaret W. Ferguson, "Juggling race, class, and gender," in *Women, "Race," and Writing*, ed. Margo Hendricks and Patricia Parker (London: Routledge, 1994), pp. 209–24; 220). It's a powerful point and worth considering. I would ask, however, whether the textual violence enacted on Imoinda is worse than Southerne's violence in removing her entirely.
8 Brown, *Ends of Empire*, p. 40.
9 Quarshie, "Second thoughts about Othello," *International Shakespeare Association Occasional Papers*, no. 7 (Chipping Camden, 1999), p. 12.
10 Margaret Mitchell, *Gone with the Wind* (New York: Warner, 1993 [1936]), p. 371.

11 Gretchen Holbrook Gerzina, *Black London: Life before Emancipation* (New Brunswick: Rutledge Press, 1995), pp. 4–6.

12 *Ibid.*, pp. 53–4.

13 Quoted in *ibid.*, p. 17.

14 George Winchester Stone's *The London Stage* (Carbondale, Ill.: Southern Illinois University Press, 1962) cites hundreds of performances between the years 1695 and 1800.

15 The original account appears in *The Gentleman's Magazine* 19 (February 16, 1749), 89–90, and in *The London Magazine* 18 (February 1749), 94. On the story of Prince William, see Wylie Sypher, "The African Prince in London," *Journal of the History of Ideas* 2.2 (April, 1941), 237–47 (p. 242); David Brion Davis, *The Problem of Slavery in Western Culture* (Ithaca, N.Y.: Cornell University Press, 1966), p. 477; and Gerzina, *Black London*, pp. 11–12.

16 Gronniosaw's story was published in James Gronniosaw, *A Narrative of the Most Remarkable Particulars in the Life of James Albert Ukasaw Gronniosaw, an African Prince, as Related by Himself* (Leeds: Davies and Booth, 1814).

17 Some fifteen ships by the name *Othello* sailed slaving missions between 1755 and 1774 (David Eltis, Stephen D. Behrendt, David Richardson, and Herbert S. Klein, *The Trans-Atlantic Slave Trade: A Database on CD-ROM* [Cambridge: Cambridge University Press, 1999]).

18 Gerzina, *Black London*, pp. 54–5; 48–50.

19 See Vincent Carretta, "Olaudah Equiano or Gustavus Vassa? New light on an eighteenth-century question of identity," *Slavery and Abolition: A Journal of Slave and Post-Slave Societies* 20.3 (December, 1999), 96–105.

20 All quotations are from Olaudah Equiano, *The Interesting Narrative of the Life of Olaudah Equiano, Written by Himself*, ed. Robert J. Allison (Boston: Bedford Books, 1995).

21 I find it interesting that this places the narrator in a position parallel to that of Behn's female narrator in *Oroonoko*. Spencer observes that the gender of Behn's persona "saves her from sharing the guilt of her countrymen's treatment of the noble black prince, and by implication, from sharing in the general corruption of the society she criticizes." Like the female relatives who witness Oroonoko's execution she is, throughout, "a spectator, but because of her femininity, a helpless one" (p. 50).

22 In responding to a published attack on a fellow abolitionist, Equiano offers – or perhaps threatens – a solution to the problem of racial prejudice in the elimination of race altogether through "open, free, and generous loves upon Nature's own wide and extensive plain, subservient only to moral rectitude, without distinction of the color of a skin" (quoted in Allison's introduction, *Interesting Narrative*, pp. 12–13).

23 Kim F. Hall, *Things of Darkness: Economies of Race and Gender in Early Modern England* (New York: Cornell University Press, 1995), pp. 28–40.

24 Malcolm X used the phrase in various speeches. Here is one quote in context: "We declare our right on this earth . . . to be a human being, to be respected as a human being, to be given the rights of a human being in this society, on

this earth, in this day, which we intend to bring into existence by any means necessary" (OAAU Founding Rally, June 28, 1964).

25 For a comprehensive theorization of the seraglio, see Alan Grosrichard, *The Sultan's Court: European Fantasies of the East*, trans. Liz Heron (London: Verso, 1988).

26 Loomba, *Shakespeare, Race, and Colonialism* (Oxford: Oxford University Press, 2002), p. 100.

27 In using the term "Orientalist" I draw upon Edward Said's paradigm in his influential book, *Orientalism* (New York: Random House, 1978). Although Said's landmark study posits Orientalism as an Anglo-French cultural enterprise, the discourse was bound to influence Anglo-American authors as well, particularly when these authors wished to take a peep inside the seraglio. For a compelling feminist re-working of Said's theories, see Meyda Yegenoglu, *Colonial Fantasies: Toward a Feminist Reading of Orientalism* (Cambridge: Cambridge University Press, 1998).

28 All quotations are from Susannah Haswell Rowson, *Slaves in Algiers; or, A Struggle for Freedom*, in *Plays by Early American Women, 1775–1850*, ed. Amelia Howe Kritzer (Ann Arbor: University of Michigan Press, 1995).

29 In one estimate, 76,000 African slaves were transported to America between the years 1791 and 1800 (Allison, ed., *Interesting Narrative*, p. 199).

30 This will not be the last time jingoism masquerades as concern for women. Witness the United States' apathy toward the plight of women in Afghanistan before September 11, 2001 versus afterward.

31 Elizabeth Schafer, ed., "Introduction," to William Shakespeare, *The Taming of the Shrew*, Shakespeare in Production Series (Cambridge: Cambridge University Press, 2002), pp. 49–51.

32 Philip Beidler observes the way in which Islamic seamen "were legendarily feared as notorious enslavers of Europeans – the fact notwithstanding, of course, that the same Europeans had been taking them captive in substantial numbers since the crusades" ("Mustapha Rub-a-Dub Keli Khan and other famous early American literary Mahometans," in *Writing Race across the Atlantic, World*, ed. Philip Beidler and Gary Taylor [New York: Palgrave, 2005] p. 6). And whereas earlier in the century there may indeed have been more English slaves in Muslim north Africa than African slaves under English control, in part the former fueled the explosion of the latter. David Brion Davis notes that "the continuing enslavement of Christians by Muslims and of Muslims by Christians actually conditioned both groups to accept the institutionalization of slavery on a wider scale and thus prepared the way for the vast Atlantic slave system" (*The Problem of Slavery in Western Culture*, p. 51). Rowson's play, written at the time that the enslavement of Christians was coming to a halt and the enslavement of Africans reaching its peak, passively perpetuates the latter institution.

33 Washington Irving, *Washington Irving: History, Takes and Sketches*, ed. James W. Tuttleton (New York: Library of America, 1983), p. 79. All quotations are from this edition.

34 See Taylor, *Buying Whiteness*, pp. 6–24, on the idea of white female sexual enslavement.

35 On the history of the "tawny" Othello, see, for instance, Ruth Cowhig, "Blacks in English drama and the role of Shakespeare's *Othello*," in *The Black Presence in English Literature*, ed. David Dabydeen (Manchester: Manchester University Press, 1985), pp. 1–25; Virginia Mason Vaughn, *Othello: A Contextual History* (Cambridge: Cambridge University Press, 1994); Marvin Rosenberg, *The Masks of Othello: The Search for the Identity of Othello, Iago, and Desdemona by Three Centuries of Actors and Critics* (Berkeley: University of California Press, 1961). On *Othello* in the American south, see Charles B. Lower, "Othello as black on southern stages: then and now," in *Shakespeare in the South*, ed. Philip C. Kolin (Jackson: University Press of Mississippi, 1983), pp. 199–228, and Woodrow L. Holbein, "Shakespeare in Charleston, 1800–1860," in the same volume, pp. 88–111.

36 John Lambert, *Travels through Lower Canada, and the United States of North America, in the Years 1806, 1807, and 1808*, quoted in Holbein, "Shakespeare in Charleston," pp. 98–99.

37 On the relationship between Thomas Jefferson and Sally Hemings, see Robert S. Levine's introduction to *Clotel; or, The President's Daughter*, ed. Robert S. Levine (Boston: St. Martin's, 2000), pp. 8–17. See also Elise Lemire's discussion of the satiric verses produced by the affair in *Miscegenation: Making Race in America* (Philadelphia: University of Pennsylvania Press, 2002), pp. 11–34.

38 George C. D. Odell, *Annals of the New York Stage*, 15 vols. (New York: Columbia University Press, 1927), II, p. 229.

3 HOLES AT THE POLES: GOTHIC HORROR AND THE RACIAL ABJECT

1 Toni Morrison, *Playing in the Dark: Whiteness and the Literary Imagination* (New York: Vintage Books, 1992), pp. 12–13.

2 *Ibid.*, p. 17.

3 S. T. Coleridge, *Table Talk* (London: 1822).

4 S. T. Coleridge, *The Rime of the Ancient Mariner*, in *Poetical Works*, ed. Ernest Hartley Coleridge (Oxford: Oxford University Press, 1974), lines 181–90; italics in original.

5 Deirdre Coleman, "Conspicuous consumption: white abolitionism and English women's protest writing in the 1790s," *ELH* 61 (1994), 341–62; p. 345.

6 *Ibid.*, p. 356.

7 Quoted in *ibid.*, p. 357.

8 Julia Kristeva, *Powers of Horror: An Essay on Abjection*, trans. Leon S. Roudiez (New York: Columbia University Press, 1982).

9 Edgar Allen Poe, *Selected Writings of Edgar Allen Poe*, ed. Edward H. Davidson (Boston: Houghton Mifflin, 1956), p. 458. All future quotations will be from this edition and will be referenced in the text.

10 On Poe's racial politics, see, for instance, Ernest Marchand, "Poe as social critic," *American Literature* 6 (1934), 28–43; F. O. Matthiesen, "Edgar Allen Poe," in *The Literary History of the United States*, 3 vols., ed. Robert Spiller *et al.* (New York: Macmillan, 1948), I, pp. 321–42; Bernard Rosenthal, "Poe, slavery, and the *Southern Literary Messenger*: a reexamination," *Poe Studies* 7 (1974), 29–38; and any of the essays in J. Gerald Kennedy and Liliane Weissberg, eds., *Romancing the Shadow: Poe and Race* (Oxford: Oxford University Press, 2001).

11 Buttressing this claim on Egypt was the theory of polygenesis, which held that the human population originated simultaneously in separate and incommensurable races, of which the Negro was the most inferior. See Dana D. Nelson, "The haunting of white manhood: Poe, fraternal ritual, and polygenesis," *American Literature* 69.3 (September, 1997), 515–46.

12 Poe, *Philosophy of Composition*, p. 82.

13 See Sandra M. Gilbert and Susan Gubar, *The Madwoman in the Attic: The Woman Writer and the Nineteenth-Century Literary Imagination* (New Haven: Yale University Press, 1979), pp. 16–20 and *passim.*

14 John Carlos Rowe, "Poe, slavery, and modern criticism," in *Poe's "Pym": Critical Explorations*, ed. Richard Kopley (Durham: Duke University Press, 1992), pp. 117–38; p. 118.

15 On the approach to *Pym* as an allegory of antebellum southern racism, see Sidney Kaplan's introduction to Edgar Allen Poe, *The Narrative of Arthur Gordon Pym of Nantucket* (New York: Hill and Wang, 1960); Harold Beaver's introduction to *Pym* (Harmondsworth: Penguin, 1975); Kenneth Alan Hovey, "Critical provincialism: Poe's poetic principle in antebellum context," *American Quarterly* 4 (1987), 341–54; and Rowe, "Poe, slavery, and modern criticism," *passim.* On Coleridge's *Mariner* as a source see Burton R. Pollin, *The Imaginary Voyages: Collected Writings of Edgar Allen Poe*, I (Boston: G. K. Hall, 1981), pp. 268, 270–1, 283–4.

16 Edgar Allen Poe, *Edgar Allen Poe: Essays and Reviews*, ed. G. R. Thompson (New York: Library of America, 1991), p. 762.

17 Elise Lamire, "'The murders in the Rue Morgue': amalgamation discourses and the race riots of 1838 in Poe's Philadelphia," in *Romancing the Shadow*, ed. Kennedy and Weissberg, pp. 177–204.

18 Marie Buonaparte's exhaustive and seminal Freudian reading posits the entire journey as Poe's imaginary search for the body of the mother who died when he was two, evident in the profusion of womb-images and the horrified fascination with decomposing corpses and biological processes in general (Buonaparte, *The Life and Works of Edgar Allen Poe*, trans. John Rodker [London: Imago, 1949], pp. 290–352). My own reading attaches these tropic patterns to a different unconscious more particular to Poe's culture than to his peculiar family history and less dependent on Freud's theories of the Oedipal complex and castration anxiety, which as a feminist I find problematic. Sexual symbolism, after all, is older than Freud.

19 Rowe, "Poe, slavery, and modern criticism," p. 127.

20 J. Gerald Kennedy is one critic who reads the "hybrid" as an indication of Poe's ideological inconsistencies. Kennedy challenges the reading of *Pym* as straightforwardly racist by pointing out the way Poe "ironizes the position of his own picaresque narrator" and thereby "both affirms and questions Anglo-Saxon racial hegemony" ("'Trust no man': Poe, Douglass, and the culture of slavery," in *Romancing the Shadow*, ed. Kennedy and Weissberg, pp. 225–7, 243–4). Rowe, on the other hand, reads "Peters' status as a 'half-breed'" as something that "allows Poe's Pym to liberate a savage without succumbing to the southern heresy of liberating a perfectly good piece of property, that is, a black slave" (Rowe, "Poe, slavery, and modern criticism," p. 132).

21 Dennis Alan Pahl, *Architects of the Abyss: The Indeterminate Fictions of Poe, Hawthorne, and Melville* (Columbia: University of Missouri Press, 1989), p. 56.

22 Kristeva, *Powers of Horror*, p. 101.

23 When the Tsalan chief sees his reflection in one of the white men's mirrors, he throws himself down and covers his head; on one level, this might be Poe's own racist joke at the Tsalalans' expense, but on another this superstitious dread of the image is consistent with Tsalalan literal-mindedness. Either way, the power of the mirror over the Tsalalans feminizes them. We will return to the topic of mirrors later in the chapter.

24 Marie Buonaparte makes the point that the word "indenture," repeatedly used to refer to the chasms, is related to dentures or teeth, and is therefore "an allusion to the fantasy of the vagina dentata" (Buonaparte, *Life and Works of Edgar Allen Poe*, p. 342).

25 The amenability of the work of Poe to deconstructionist criticism is best exemplified by the influential volume *The Purloined Letter: Lacan, Derrida, and Psychoanalytic Reading*, ed. John P. Muller and William J. Richardson (Baltimore: Johns Hopkins University Press, 1988).

26 Morrison, *Playing in the Dark*, p. 33.

27 *Ibid.*, p. 37.

28 Alexis de Tocqueville, *Democracy in America*, trans. Henry Reeves, ed. Rev. Francis Bowen, 2 vols. (1863), II, 66 (Book I, Chapter xiii).

29 The originator of the concept of language as a differential system is Ferdinand de Saussure; see his *Course in General Linguistics*, trans. R. Harris (London: Duckworth, 1983).

30 See, for instance, Jean Ricardou, "Le caractère singulaire de cette eau," *Critique*, n.s. 14 (1967), 718–33, trans. Frank Towne, as "The singular character of the water," *Poe Studies* 9 (1976), 1–6; John Carlos Rowe, *Through the Custom House: Nineteenth-Century American Fiction and Modern Theory* (Baltimore: Johns Hopkins University Press, 1982), pp. 91–110, 205–7; Pahl, *Architects of the Abyss*, pp. 41–56; John Irwin, *American Hieroglyphics: The Symbol of the Egyptian Hieroglyphics in the American Renaissance* (New Haven: Yale University Press, 1980); J. Gerald Kennedy, *Poe, Death, and the Life of Writing* (New Haven: Yale University Press, 1987), pp. 145–76, 221–2.

31 Rowe, "Poe, slavery, and modern criticism," pp. 136–7.

32 For Kristeva's theorization of the death-bearing woman see *Black Sun: Melancholia and Depression* (New York: Columbia University Press, 1987), pp. 28–30.

33 See George C. D. Odell, *Annals of the New York Stage* 15 vols. (New York: Columbia University Press, 1927), particularly vol. iii, and David Grimsted, *Melodrama Unveiled: American Theatre and Culture 1800–1850* (Chicago: University of Chicago Press, 1968), pp. 249–56; on *Othello's* popularity on American stages generally, see Tilden G. Edelstein, "*Othello* in America: the drama of racial intermarriage," *Interracialism: Black–White Intermarriage in American History, Literature, and Law*, ed. Werner Sollors (Oxford: Oxford University Press, 2000), pp. 356–69.

34 Gary Taylor, "Gender, hunger, horror: the history and significance of *The Bloody Banquet*," *Journal for Early Modern Cultural Studies* 1.1 (Summer, 2001), 1–45; p. 24.

35 Linda Williams, "When the woman looks," in *Re-Vision: Essays in Feminist Criticism*, ed. Mary Ann Doane, Patricia Mellencamp, and Linda Williams (Los Angeles: University Publications of America, 1984), p. 90.

36 The dichotomy is explored throughout Gilbert and Gubar, *The Madwoman in the Attic*; see especially pp. 3–44.

37 See, for instance, Rhona J. Berenstein, *Attack of the Leading Ladies: Gender, Sexuality, and Spectatorship in Classic Horror Cinema* (New York: Columbia University Press, 1996); Carol J. Clover, *Men, Women, and Chainsaws: Gender in the Modern Horror Film* (Princeton: Princeton University Press, 1992); Barbara Creed, *The Monstrous-Feminine: Film, Feminism, Psychoanalysis* (New York: Routledge, 1993); and Barry Keith Grant, ed., *Dread of Difference: Gender and the Horror Film* (Austin: University of Texas Press, 1996). For an approach that reconsiders the prevailing reading of the genre as anti-feminist, see Isabel Cristina Pinedo, *Recreational Terror: Women and the Pleasure of Horror Film Viewing* (Albany: State University of New York Press, 1997).

38 All quotations are from Mary Shelley, *Frankenstein: or, the Modern Prometheus*, in *The Novels and Selected Works of Mary Shelley*, 8 vols., ed. Nora Crook (London: William Pickering, 1996), 1. This edition very usefully includes the substance of the 1818, 1823, and 1831 editions.

39 Anne K. Mellor, "*Frankenstein*, racial science, and the yellow peril," *Nineteenth-Century Contexts* 23 (2001), 1–28; p. 10.

40 See Joseph W. Lew, "The deceptive other: Mary Shelley's critique of Orientalism in *Frankenstein*," *Studies in Romanticism* 30 (1991), 255–83; Harold L. Malchow, "Frankenstein's monster and images of race in nineteenth-century Britain," *Past and Present* 139 (1993), 90–130, and *Gothic Images of Race in Nineteenth-Century Britain* (Stanford: Stanford University Press, 1996), pp. 9–40; Guyatri Chakravorty Spivak, "Three women's texts and a critique of imperialism," *Criticial Inquiry* 12 (1985), 243–61; and Zohreh T. Sullivan, "Race, gender, and imperial ideology in the nineteenth century," *Nineteenth-Century Contexts* 13 (1989), 19–32.

41 Mellor, "*Frankenstein*, racial science, and the yellow peril," p. 11.

42 Regrettably, I don't have the space here to embark on a reading of the 1935 film spin-off, *The Bride of Frankenstein*, which strikes me as relevant to our discussion. One aspect of the film worth theorizing is the fact that they made the monster's female counterpart so un-monstrous, so good-looking. It is as if, like Victor in his laboratory, audiences were expected to find it unbearable to look at a real female monster, a male one being scary enough.

43 Gilbert and Gubar, *The Madwoman in the Attic*, p. 232.

44 *Ibid.*, pp. 213–47.

45 *Ibid.*, p. 230.

46 Two medieval wood-cuts of the Temptation of Eve that feature half-female serpents can be found at New York's Metropolitan Museum of Art (Elisha Whittelsey Fund, 1951; Harris Brisbane Dick Fund, 1931). On "hell" as vagina see Stephen Booth in William Shakespeare, *Shakespeare's Sonnets*, ed. Booth (New Haven: Yale University Press, 1977), pp. 499–500.

47 Kristeva, *Powers of Horror*, p. 54

48 Berenstein, *Attack of the Leading Ladies*, p. 4.

49 Bram Stoker, *Dracula*, ed. John Paul Riquelme (New York: Palgrave, 2002), p. 47. All subsequent quotations are from this edition.

50 Naturally, much discussion of the sexuality of the vampire comes from psychoanalytic criticism. See, for instance, Ernest Jones, *On the Nightmare* (New York: Liveright Publishing, 1951) pp. 98–130; C. F. Bentley, "Monster in the bedroom: sexual symbolism in Bram Stoker's *Dracula*," in *Dracula: The Vampire and the Critics*, ed. Margaret L. Carter (Ann Arbor: UMI Research Press, 1988), pp. 25–34; Joseph S. Bierman, "*Dracula*: prolonged childhood illness and the oral triad," in *Dracula: The Vampire and the Critics*, ed. Carter, pp. 51–5; Thomas B. Byers, "Good men and monsters: the defenses of Dracula," in *Dracula: The Vampire and the Critics*, ed. Carter, pp. 149–57; Maurice Richardson, "The psychoanalysis of ghost stories," *Twentieth Century* 166 (December, 1959), 419–31. For an argument against the Freudian reading, see J. A. Stevenson, "A vampire in the mirror: the sexuality of Dracula," *PMLA* 103 (March, 1988), 139–49.

51 Burton Hatlen, "The return of the repressed/oppressed in Bram Stoker's *Dracula*," in *Dracula: The Vampire and the Critics*, ed. Margaret L. Carter (Ann Arbor: UMI Research Press, 1988), pp. 117–35, 133. Building on this reading, Steven Arata reads the vampire as manifesting the fear of "reverse colonization." See Steven Arata, "The occidental tourist: *Dracula* and the anxiety of reverse colonization," *Victorian Studies* 33.4 (Summer, 1990), 621–46.

52 The concept is laid out in Homi Bhabha, "Of mimicry and man: the ambivalence of colonial discourse," in *The Location of Culture* (New York: Routledge, 1994), pp. 85–92.

53 Malchow, *Gothic Images of Race*, p. 124.

54 *Ibid.*, pp. 124–66, 130.

55 *Ibid.*, p. 162.

56 Christopher Craft, "Kiss me with those red lips: gender and inversion in Bram Stoker's *Dracula*," in *Dracula: The Vampire and the Critics*, ed. Carter, pp. 170–1. Here I wish to point out that the homoerotic reading does not preclude the connections to *Othello* that are my focus here: Shakespeare's play also lends itself to such a reading in regard to Iago's interactions with Othello.

57 Malchow, *Gothic Images of Race*, pp. 138–41.

58 For a nuanced theorization of the links between rape, race, and sacrifice evident in the classical and Shakespearean traditions, see Arthur J. Little, *Shakespeare Jungle Fever: National-Imperial Re-Visions of Race, Rape, and Sacrifice* (Stanford: Stanford University Press, 2000), esp. pp. 1–67.

59 Bram Stoker, *The Lair of the White Worm* (London: Jarrolds Publishers, 1966), p. 91. All subsequent quotations are from this edition.

60 The expurgated ending is reprinted as "The bridal of death" in Bram Stoker, *Midnight Tales*, ed. Peter Haining, pp. 151–82; p. 174. See the introduction (pp. 151–2) for an account of the original complaints.

61 Little, *Shakespeare Jungle Fever*, p. 3.

62 Judith Halberstam, *Skin Shows: Gothic Horror and the Technology of Monsters* (Durham, N.C.: Duke University Press, 1995), p. 4.

63 The monster of the nineteenth-century theatrical adaptations wore a light blue or gray body-suit or else one of very pale yellow highlighted with blue to show the shape of the musculature (apparently some monsters were quite buff): his hair was always black (Steven Earl Forry, *Hideous Progenies: Dramatizations of Frankenstein from Mary Shelley to the Present* [Philadelphia: University of Pennsylvania Press, 1990]). On Boris Karloff's make-up, see Albert Manguel, *Bride of Frankenstein* (London: British Film Institute, 1997), p. 22.

64 Gary Taylor points out that one effect of pre-pubertal castration is soft, pale skin; the characteristic pallor of the eunuch led men in the classical world to despise pale skin, associated with a defective manhood (*Castration: An Abbreviated History of Western Manhood* [New York: Routledge, 2000], pp. 140–4).

65 Taylor, "Gender, hunger, horror," pp. 27–8.

66 See Patricia Parker, "*Othello* and *Hamlet*: dilation, spying, and the 'secret place' of woman," *Representations* 44 (Fall, 1993), 60–95. On the sound of "O" see Joel Fineman, *The Subjectivity Effect in Western Literary Tradition: Essays Toward the Release of Shakespeare's Will* (Cambridge, Mass.: MIT Press, 1991), p. 151; Daileader, *Eroticism on the Renaissance Stage*, p. 125; and Bruce R. Smith, *The Acoustic World of Early Modern England: Attending to the O Factor* (Chicago: University of Chicago Press, 1999).

67 The first *OED* example of "Gothic" is 1611: "of or pertaining to the Goths"; the word was used to describe architecture as early as 1641; the now obsolete sense of "Gothic" as "barbarous" came into usage in 1695; the *OED* does not cite the literary usage, but it seems co-terminous with the rise of the genre in the late eighteenth century. I have been coupling the term with "horror" to

emphasize Gothicism's ancestral relation to the modern, now primarily filmic genre, as well as, more generally, the artistic elements designed to arouse a sense of horror.

68 Gary Don Rhodes, *Lugosi: His Life in Films, on Stage, and in the Hearts of Horror Lovers* (London: Macfarland, 1994), p. 292; the epigraph is on p. 14.

69 Kristeva, *Powers of Horror*, pp. 101–2.

70 Richard Dyer, *White* (Routledge: New York, 1997), p. 207.

71 *Ibid.*, p. 211.

72 Rhodes, *Lugosi*, pp. 93–4.

73 It is worth noting that Lugosi starred in *Murders in the Rue Morgue* a year after his debut as Dracula. Interestingly, *Dracula*, *Frankenstein*, *Murders*, and *White Zombie* were produced by Universal Studios within the space of about a year (Rhodes, *Lugosi*, pp. 17–18).

74 *Ibid.*, p. 19.

75 To name just a few, *Caravan of Death* (1920), *Arabesque* (1925), and *Women of All Nations* (1931). Lugosi also played a Native American in *Leatherstocking* (1920) and a gypsy in *The Wolf Man* (1941). See Rhodes, *Lugosi*, pp. 152–87.

76 Bela Lugosi, Jr., "A personal note," in Robert Cremer, *Lugosi: The Man behind the Cape* (Chicago: Henry Regnery Company, 1976), pp. x, xii.

77 Rhodes, *Lugosi*, p. 19.

4 SISTERS IN BONDAGE: ABOLITION, AMALGAMATION, AND THE CRISIS OF FEMALE AUTHORSHIP

1 William Gilmore Simms, "Stowe's key to *Uncle Tom's Cabin*," *Southern Quarterly Review* 8 (July, 1853), 226.

2 Diane Roberts, *The Myth of Aunt Jemima: Representations of Race and Region* (London: Routledge, 1994), p. 62.

3 Lydia Maria Child, "Introduction by the editor," in Harriet Jacobs, *Incidents in the Life of a Slave Girl*, in *The Classic Slave Narratives*, ed. Henry Louis Gates, Jr. (New York: Signet Classics, 2002), pp. 441–2. Future citations of Harriet Jacobs' narrative will be drawn from this edition and will be cited in the text.

4 William Wells Brown, *Clotel; or, the President's Daughter*, ed. Robert S. Levine (Boston: St. Martin's, 2000), p. 82.

5 Child denounced the anti-miscegenation laws in her 1833 treatise, *An Appeal on Behalf of That Class of Americans Called Africans*; as a result, she faced complete ostracism from the literary elites who had praised *Hobomok*, and the children's magazine she had founded and edited for eight years folded (Carolyn L. Karcher, "Introduction," in Lydia Maria Child, *Hobomok and Other Writings on Indians* [New Brunswick, N.J.: Rutgers University Press, 1986], p. xiii). Further citations from this introduction will appear in the text.

6 In underscoring Child's radical view of sexual relations I would only point out how rare it is even today to hear someone critique that aspect of "heteronormativity" that enforces, if not marriage, then certainly monogamy.

Monogamy is the final "m" in the Shakespearean trinity (monarchy, monotheism, monogamy) that cultural relativism has largely left unmolested. Indeed, even Queer/gender/feminist thought has left the monogamy ideal – which, practically speaking, no one is really living – an unmolested article of dogma. For a brave vision of the alternative, which contemporary sexologists call "polyamory" or "responsible non-monogamy," see Deborah M. Anapol, *Polyamory: The New Love without Limits* (San Rafael, Calif.: ItiNet Resource Center, 1997). See also David P. Barash and Judith Eve Lipton, *The Myth of Monogamy: Fidelity and Infidelity in Animals and People* (New York: W. H. Freeman, 2001).

7 Harriet Beecher Stowe, *Uncle Tom's Cabin* (New York: Bantam Books, 1981), p. 257. All further quotations will be from this edition, and will be cited in the text.

8 Roberts, *The Myth of Aunt Jemima*, p. 37; see also Hortense J. Spillers, "Changing the letter: the yokes, the jokes of discourse, or, Mrs. Stowe, and Mr. Reed," in *Slavery and the Literary Imagination*, ed. Deborah E. McDowell and Arnold Rampersad (Baltimore: Johns Hopkins University Press, 1989), pp. 25–61; p. 42.

9 See, for instance, E. A. J. Honigmann's Introduction to the Arden edition (Walton-on-Thames: Nelson, 1997), pp. 41–3.

10 Spillers, "Changing the letter," p. 43.

11 *Ibid.*, p. 44.

12 Karen Sánchez-Eppler, "Bodily bonds: the intersecting rhetorics of feminism and abolition," in *Interracialism: Black–White Intermarriage in American History, Literature and Law*, ed. Werner Sollors (Oxford: Oxford University Press, 2000), pp. 408–37; p. 409.

13 Mauri Skinfill, "Nation and miscegenation: *Incidents in the Life of a Slave Girl*," *Arizona Quarterly* 52.2 (Summer, 1995), 63–79; p. 71.

14 Roberts, *The Myth of Aunt Jemima*, p. 39

15 Spillers, "Changing the letter," p. 40.

16 She is quoting, from memory, *Hamlet* 1.i.8–9.

17 William Wells Brown, *The American Fugitive in Europe*, in *The Travels of William Wells Brown*, ed. Paul Jefferson (New York: Markus Wiener, 1991), pp. 203–4. For his reflections on Shakespeare see pp. 183–6.

18 William Wells Brown, *Clotel; or, The President's Daughter*, ed. Robert S. Levine (New York: St. Martin's, 2000), p. 21.

19 On Brown's inaccuracies, see Lee Schweniger, "Clotel and the historicity of the anecdote," *MELUS* 24.1 (Spring, 1999), 21–36. On Brown's tactics for self-authorization, see William Andrews, "The novelization of voice in early African American narrative," *PMLA* 105 (1990), 23–34; Richard O. Lewis, "Literary conventions in the novels of William Wells Brown," *CLA Journal* (December, 1985), 129–56; and Robert B. Stepto, *Behind the Veil: A Study of Afro-American Narrative* (Urbana: University of Illinois Press, 1979). For an insightful commentary on the scientific verification of Brown's "source" in American oral history, see Ann duCill, "Where in the world is William Wells

Brown? Thomas Jefferson, Sally Hemings, and the DNA of African-American literary history," *American Literary History* 12.3 (Fall, 2000), 443–62.

20 Angelyn Mitchell, "Her side of his story: a feminist analysis of two nineteenth-century antebellum novels – William Wells Brown's *Clotel* and Harriet E. Wilson's *Our Nig,*" *American Literary Realism* 24.3 (Spring, 1992), 7–21; p. 8.

21 For a fascinating discussion of the process by which the word "black" became implicit in "slave," see Gary Taylor, *Buying Whiteness: Race, Culture, and Identity from Columbus to Hip-Hop* (New York: Palgrave, 2005).

22 *Ibid.*, pp. 10–15.

23 R. J. Ellis, "Body politics and the body politic in William Wells Brown's *Clotel* and Harriet Wilson's *Our Nig,*" in *Soft Canons: American Women Writers and Masculine Traditions*, ed. Karen L. Kilcup (Iowa City: University of Iowa Press, 1999), pp. 99–122; p. 115.

24 Brown's narrative of his escape – included in Levine's edition of *Clotel* – makes his endorsement of the Lucrece myth even clearer; he writes, "How infinitely better is it for a sister to 'go into the silent land' with her honour untarnished . . . than for her to be sold to the sensual slave-holders" (p. 56).

25 Harriet Jacobs, *Incidents in the Life of a Slave Girl*, in *The Classic Slave Narratives*, ed. Henry Louis Gates, Jr. (New York: Penguin, 2002), p. 470. Further quotes from Jacobs' narrative will be from this edition, and will be cited in the text.

26 Anne B. Dalton, "The devil and the virgin: writing sexual abuse in *Incidents in the Life of a Slave Girl,*" in *Violence, Silence, and Anger: Women's Writing as Transgression*, ed. Deirdre Lashgari (Charlottesville: University of Virginia Press, 1995), pp. 38–61.

27 In a note Dalton also draws a parallel with Claudius' poisoning of Hamlet senior (p. 60, n. 23). To me the link with *Othello* is more pertinent for its racial reversal: Othello's stories include his "being sold into slavery" and his "redemption thence" (I.iii.137).

28 In glossing the verb "people" as "populate" I am following Dalton, who views this as further evidence of the text's sublimation of the physical abuse in the author's life (p. 44).

29 Minrose C. Gwin, "Green-eyed monsters of the slavocracy: jealous mistresses in two slave narratives," in *Conjuring: Black Women, Fiction, and Literary Tradition*, ed. Marjorie Pryse and Hortense J. Spillers (Bloomington: Indiana University Press, 1985), p. 40.

30 Ann Gelder, "Reforming the body: 'experience' and the architecture of imagination in Harriet Jacobs' *Incidents in the Life of a Slave Girl,*" in *Inventing Maternity: Politics, Science, and Literature, 1650–1865*, ed. Susan C. Greenfield and Carol Barash (Lexington: University of Kentucky Press, 1999), pp. 437–668; p. 255.

31 Skinfill, "Nation and miscegenation," p. 68. Hazel Carby seems to have been the first critic to note Jacobs' subversion of domesticity, describing her text as "an exposition of womanhood and motherhood contradicting and transforming an ideology that could not take account of her experience"

(Hazel Carby, *Reconstructing Womanhood: The Emergence of the Afro-American Woman Novelist* [New York: Oxford University Press, 1987], p. 49). See also Harryette Mullen, "Runaway tongue: resistant orality in *Uncle Tom's Cabin, Our Nig, Incidents in the Life of a Slave Girl*, and *Beloved*," in *The Culture of Sentiment: Race, Gender, and Sentimentality in Nineteenth-Century America*, ed. Shirley Samuels (Oxford: Oxford University Press, 1992), pp. 244–64; Gelder, "Reforming the body"; and Caroline Levander, "'Following the condition of the mother': subversions of domesticity in Harriet Jacobs's *Incidents in the Life of a Slave Girl*," in *Southern Mothers: Fact and Fictions in Southern Women's Writing*, ed. Naguelalti Warren and Sally Wolff (Baton Rouge: Louisiana State University, 1999), pp. 28–38.

32 Gelder, "Reforming the body," pp. 252–4. Earlier criticism notes the text's equation of "Linda" with domestic space. Sánchez-Eppler, for instance, says that "She never comes to inhabit the domestic; rather, as a slave and particularly as a female slave she *is* the domestic" (Karen Sánchez-Eppler, *Touching Liberty: Abolition, Feminism, and the Politics of the Body* [University of California Press, 1993], p. 87.

33 Gelder reads the attic sequence as empowering for the narrator, who thus "becomes her own mother, giving birth to herself as she reconstructs the ideological norms imposed on her body" (p. 261). I would add that no such "reconstruction" by way of a subversive text can counter the way in which slavery has damaged this particular female body: rather, the hope is that Jacobs' putting her damaged body into discourse will prevent future damage to other bodies.

34 Sánchez-Eppler, "Rhetorics of feminism and abolition," p. 412.

35 Sánchez-Eppler, *Touching Liberty*, p. 85. On the Stowe–Jacobs connection, see also Phyllis Cole, "Stowe, Jacobs, Wilson: white plots and black counterplots," in *New Perspectives on Gender, Race, and Class in Society*, ed. Audrey T. McCluskey (Indiana University Press, 1990), pp. 23–46.

36 Roberts, *The Myth of Aunt Jemima*, p. 137.

37 Gayle Rubin, "The traffic in women: notes on the political economy of sex," in *Toward an Anthropology of Women*, ed. Rayna Reiter (New York: Monthly Review, 1975), pp. 157–210.

38 Roberts, *The Myth of Aunt Jemima*, pp. 136–41.

39 *Ibid.*, p. 144.

40 Spillers, "Changing the letter," p. 35.

41 Jean Fagan Yellin, *Women and Sisters* (New Haven: Yale University Press, 1989), p. 75.

42 Roberts, *The Myth of Aunt Jemima*, p. 149.

43 Stanley Wells, ed., *Nineteenth-Century Shakespeare Burlesques* (Wilmington, Del.: Michael Glazier, 1978), p. 131.

44 *Ibid.*

45 W. T. Lhamon, Jr., ed., *Jump Jim Crow: Lost Plays, Lyrics, and Street Prose of the First Atlantic Popular Culture* (Cambridge, Mass.: Harvard University Press, 2003), p. 383.

46 *Ibid.*, p. 88.
47 *Ibid.*, p. 383.
48 *Ibid.*
49 On the Eminem analogy, see Taylor, *Buying Whiteness*, pp. 341–62.
50 Lhamon, *Jump Jim Crow*, pp. 24–5.
51 Quoted in Hugh Honor, *The Image of the Black in Western Art, vol.* IV: *From the American Revolution to World War I* (Cambridge, Mass.: Harvard University Press, 1976).
52 Paul Gilroy makes this point about *Amistad* in *Against Race: Imagining Political Culture beyond the Color Line* (Cambridge, Mass.: Harvard University Press, 2000), pp. 25–6.

5 HANDSOME DEVILS: ROMANCE, RAPE, RACISM, AND THE RHET(T)ORIC OF DARKNESS

1 Gilbert and Gubar's seminal reading of the novel brings home the race-blindness of early feminist criticism: they place the word "gipsy" in scare-quotes, assuming it is a metaphor and not a literal ethnic/racial marker. Correspondingly, they share Nellie's mis-characterization of the child Heathcliff's native speech as "a kind of animal-like gibberish" (Sandra M. Gilbert and Susan Gubar, *The Madwoman in the Attic: The Woman Writer and the Nineteenth Century Literary Imagination* [New Haven: Yale University Press, 1979], pp. 264, 294).
2 Christopher Heywood, "Introduction," to Emily Brontë, *Wuthering Heights*, ed. Heywood (Ontario: Broadview, 2002), pp. 63–8. There is evidence that Brontë attended at least one performance of the play, as she refers to Macready's *Othello* in two separate letters. See Marianne Novy, ed., *Women's Re-Visions of Shakespeare: On Responses of Dickinson, Woolf, Rich, H. D., and Others* (Chicago: University of Illinois Press, 1990), p. 87 n. 1.
3 I cite Heywood's edition throughout this chapter.
4 In addition to Heywood's Introduction, cited above, see Elsie Michie, "From simianized Irish to Oriental despots: Heathcliff, Rochester and racial difference," *Novel* 25 (1992), 125–140.
5 Dana Medoro, "'This thing of darkness I / acknowledge mine': Heathcliff as fetish in *Wuthering Heights*," *English Studies in Canada* 22.3 (September, 1996), 267–81; p. 290
6 See Jayne Anne Krenz, ed., *Dangerous Men and Adventurous Women: Romance Writers on the Appeal of the Romance* (Philadelphia: University of Pennsylvania Press, 1992), p. 139. See also Laurie E. Osborne, "Romancing the bard," in *Shakespeare and Appropriation*, ed. Christy Desmet and Robert Sawyer (New York: Routledge, 1999), pp. 47–82; and "Sweet, savage Shakespeare," in *Shakespeare without Class: Misappropriations of Cultural Capital*, ed. Donald Hedrick and Bryan Reynolds (New York: Palgrave, 2000) pp. 135–51.

7 MacKinnon coins the term "rap*able*" to theorize rape as a cultural construct: "To be rap*able,* a position which is social, not biological, defines what a woman *is*" ("Feminism, Marxism, method and state: toward a feminist jurisprudence," *Signs* 8 [1983], p. 651 [italics in original]).

8 My own close-reading for color yielded these results: "black eyes" (p. 1), "dark-skinned gipsy" (p. 3), "dark face and hair" (p. 84), "eyes full of black fire" (p. 87), "his reflections revealed their blackness through his features" (p. 165), "black hair and eyes" (p. 189), "dark face" (p. 262), "black hair" (p. 296), "black brows" (p. 299), "little dark thing" (p. 301), "black long hair" (p. 306). This is only counting references to his literal, complexional darkness, not the language of demonism or moral darkness, which I deal with in the chapter.

9 See, for instance, J. B. Post, "Ravishment of women and the statutes of Westminster," in *Legal Records and the Historian,* ed. J. H. Baker (London: Royal Historical Society), pp. 150–64; and James A. Brundage, *Law, Sex, and Christian Society in Medieval Europe* (Chicago: University of Chicago Press, 1987), p. 209.

10 It is Gilbert and Gubar who first treat Heathcliff as Catherine's metaphorical whip (*Madwoman in the Attic,* p. 264).

11 Heywood, "Introduction," p. 66.

12 Joel Williamson, "How black was Rhett Butler?" in *The Evolution of Southern Culture,* ed. Numan V. Bartley (Athens, Ga.: University of Georgia Press, 1988), pp. 87–107.

13 *Ibid.,* pp. 87, 103.

14 Margaret Mitchell, *Gone with the Wind* (New York: Warner, 1936), pp. 98–9. Further quotations will be from this edition and will be cited in the text.

15 Eliza Russi Lowen McGraw, "A 'Southern belle with her Irish up': Scarlett O'Hara and ethnic identity," *South Atlantic Review* 65 (2000), 123–31; p. 127. The most thorough treatment of the question of Irish ethnicity, and in particular of the Irish struggle to disassociate themselves from American people of color, is Noel Ignatiev's *How the Irish Became White* (New York: Routledge, 1995).

16 I had hoped to have something interesting to say in this chapter about the "sequel" to *Gone with the Wind,* Alexandra Ripley's *Scarlett* (New York: Warner, 1991), which was also a best-seller. But the novel disappoints in a way that makes Mitchell's text – for all its offensive ideas – look almost radical. First of all, Ripley has nothing at all to say about race: there are almost no black characters at all, and the few there say almost nothing. One almost prefers the honest racism of Mitchell: at least you know where she stands. There is also almost no sex. Scarlett – chastened by the double loss of Melanie and Rhett – recognizes the error of her ways and spends the entire 884 pages fighting to "win" him back. Which of course she does: first by becoming a "lady," then by getting pregnant by him (conveniently, in the sole instance of sex in the novel). It amazes me that the Mitchell estate let this one get by: surely, it is much more an insult to the original than Alice Randall's parody,

which at least constitutes art (Alice Randall, *The Wind Done Gone* [New York: Houghton Mifflin, 2001]). All quotes will be from this edition, and will be cited in the text.

17 See Celia R. Daileader, *Eroticism on the Renaissance Stage: Transcendence, Desire, and the Limits of the Visible* (Cambridge: Cambridge University Press, 1998).

18 See, for instance, Emily C. Bartels, "Strategies of submission: Desdemona, the Duchess, and the assertion of desire," *Studies in English Literature* 36.2 (Spring, 1996), 417–33; Carol Thomas Neeley, *Broken Nuptials in Shakespeare's Plays* (New Haven: Yale University Press, 1985), pp. 105–35; and Margaret Loftus Ranald, "The indescretions of Desdemona," in *Shakespeare and His Social Context: Essays in Osmotic Knowledge and Literary Interpretation* (New York: AMS Press, 1987), pp. 135–52.

19 Robyn Donald, "Mean, moody, and magnificent: the hero in romance literature," in *Dangerous Men*, ed. Krenz, pp. 81–4; p. 81.

20 Hélène Cixous and Catherine Clément, *The Newly Born Woman*, trans. Betsy Wing (Minneapolis: University of Minnesota Press, 1986), p. 69. The biblical "Song" reads "I am black but beautiful"; changing the "but" to "and" is surely part of Cixous and Clément's feminist-anti-racist point.

21 The quotes are from, respectively: *Richard II* (II.i.49–59); *The History of King Lear* (II.iv.320-1); and *Antony and Cleopatra* (v.ii.66–70).

22 It was Helen Deutsch who famously (or infamously) argued for the universality of female rape fantasies as evidence of inherent female masochism (*The Psychology of Women* [New York: Grune & Stratton, 1944], pp. 219–78). For a critique of Deutsch and other psychoanalytic theorizations of rape fantasy, see Susan Brownmiller, *Against Our Will* (New York: Simon and Schuster, 1975), pp. 322–46; and Molly Haskell, "Rape fantasy: The 2,000-year-old misunderstanding," *Ms.* (November, 1976), pp. 85–98.

23 Paula Kamen, *Her Way: Young Women Remake the Sexual Revolution* (New York: New York University Press, 2000).

24 This is only one of any number of "revisionist" takes on the play. A popular production amongst my students was one by the Alabama Shakespeare Festival in 1998, wherein Kate concludes her speech by stripping down to a black leather body-suit and mounting a motor-cycle: summoning Petruccio to ride piggy-back behind her, she then roars offstage to a life of, we presume, Gen-X sexual freedom.

6 INVISIBLE MEN, UNSPEAKABLE ACTS: THE SPECTACLE OF BLACK MALE VIOLENCE IN MODERN AMERICAN FICTION

1 Jean Toomer, *Cane* (New York: Harper and Rowe, 1969 [1923]), p. 1. Future quotations will be from this edition and will be inserted into the text.

2 On the debate surrounding Toomer and racial categorization, see Charles Harmon, "*Cane*, race, and 'neither/norism,'" *Southern Literary Journal* 32.2 (Spring, 2000), 90–101.

3 Lisa Maria Hogeland notes that "the visibility/invisibility trope is, of course, ironic in that it turns *hyper*visibility into *in*visibility (italics in original). That is, the Other named as invisible is unseen as an individual, while simultaneously hypervisible as a stereotype" ("*Invisible Man* and invisible women: the sex/race analogy of the 1970s," *Women's History Review* 5.1 [Spring, 1996], 31–53; p. 36). That the trope has feminist theoretical potential is obvious, and Ellison's influence on women authors has been duly noted by Hogeland and others. My reading, however, seeks to underscore the irony of Ellison's relationship to feminism in his rendering women of color "invisible."

4 For an explication of the Wright–Cleaver connection, see Robert Felgar, "*Soul on Ice* and *Native Son*," *Negro American Literature Forum* 8.3 (Autumn, 1974), 235.

5 William Faulkner, *Light in August* (New York: Modern Library/McGraw-Hill, 1932), p. 15. Future quotations will be from this edition and will be inserted into the text.

6 Diane Roberts, *Faulkner and Southern Womanhood* (New York: Routledge, 1994), p. xv.

7 Sally R. Page, *Faulkner's Women: Characterization and Meaning* (Deland, Fla.: Everett/Edwards, 1972), p. 140.

8 Roberts, *Faulkner and Southern Womanhood*, p. 203.

9 Leslie A. Fiedler, *Love and Death in the American Novel* (New York: Stein and Day, 1966), pp. 300, 321. Numerous critics have described Lena as an "earth goddess" figure. See, for instance, Judith Bryant Wittenberg, "The women of *Light in August*," in *New Essays on "Light in August,"* ed. Michael Milgate (Cambridge: Cambridge University Press, 1987), pp. 103–22; and Deborah Clarke, "Gender, race, and language in *Light in August*," *American Literature* 6.3 (October, 1989), 398–413. For an alternative reading, see Mary Joanne Dondlinger, "Getting around the body: the matter of race and gender in Faulkner's *Light in August*," in *Faulkner and the Natural World: Faulkner and Yawknapatawpha*, ed. Donald Kartiganer and Ann J. Abadie (Jackson: University of Mississippi Press, 1999), pp. 98–125.

10 John Keats, "Ode on a Grecian urn," *The Norton Anthology of English Literature*, ed. M. H. Abrams, 6th edn. (New York: W. W. Norton, 1996), pp. 1793–5.

11 Roberts, *Faulkner and Southern Womanhood*, p. 185.

12 Micheal Millgate, *The Achievement of William Faulkner* (New York: Random House, 1966), pp. 125–6.

13 Roberts, *Faulkner and Southern Womanhood*, p. xv.

14 Wittenberg views the position of the corpse as reflecting the irreconcilability of Joanna's masculine (i.e., head, rationality) and feminine (i.e., body, sensuality) aspects (p. 118).

15 Roberts, *Faulkner and Southern Womanhood*, p. 183.

16 Clarke, "Gender, race, and language in *Light in August*," p. 99.

17 John N. Duvall goes so far as to argue that were Joe's case heard in a modern, unbiased court, he would not be charged with murder, having acted in self-defense. See *Faulkner's Marginal Couple: Invisible, Outlaw, and Unspeakable Communities* (University of Texas Press: Austin, 1990), pp. 19–24.

18 Laura L. Bush, "A very American power struggle: the color of rape in *Light in August*," *Mississippi Quarterly* 51.3 (Summer, 1998), 483–501; p. 483.

19 Roberts, *Faulkner and Southern Womanhood*, p. 176.

20 Doreen Fowler, "Joe Christmas and 'Womanshenegro,'" in *Faulkner and Women*, ed. Doreen Fowler and Ann J. Abide (University of Mississippi Press, 1986), pp. 158–9.

21 The King James version reads: "Woe unto you, scribes and Pharisees, hypocrites! For ye are like unto whited sepulchres, which indeed appear beautiful outward, but are within full of dead *men's* bones, and of all uncleanness" (Matthew 23.27; italics in original). The relevance to this book's central trope – the white devil as hypocrite – should be obvious.

22 Roberts, *Faulkner and Southern Womanhood*, p. 151.

23 *Ibid.*, p. 184. On this racialized "crucifixion," see also James A. Snead, "*Light in August* and the rhetorics of racial division," in *Faulkner and Race*, ed. Doreen Fowler and Ann J. Abadie (Jackson: University of Mississippi Press, 1987), pp. 152–69.

24 M. J. Burgess, "Watching (Jefferson) watching: *Light in August* and the aestheticization of gender," *Faulkner Journal* 7.1 (Fall, 1991), 95–114; p. 108. Joseph R. Urgo presents an interesting – because counter-intuitive – reading of Joe's abjection of femaleness, blackness, and his own corporality, pointing out that his horror of menstruation has a positive flip-side: "The 'victims' of menstruation are also the beneficiaries of . . . a *purifying* ordeal" (italics in original) to which he, as a male – and one polluted by "nigger blood" – has no access. Likewise, Joanna's menopausal status "reminds him of his own secret, pent-up filth," hence, the sacrificial imagery surrounding his death. See "Menstrual blood and 'nigger' blood: Joe Christmas and the ideology of sex and race," *Mississippi Quarterly* 41.3 (Summer, 1988); 394–401; p. 400.

25 Beth Widmaier, "Black female absence and the construction of white womanhood in Faulkner's *Light in August*," *Faulkner Journal* 16.3 (Fall, 2000–Spring, 2001), 23–39; p. 28.

26 Richard Wright, *Native Son* (New York: Harper and Brothers, 1949), p. 72. Future citations will be from this edition and will be given in the text.

27 Maria K. Mootry calls Mary a "nouvelle Desdemona," but does not explicate the comparison. See Maria K. Mootry, "Bitches, whores, and woman haters: archetypes and typologies in the art of Richard Wright," in *Richard Wright: A Collection of Critical Essays*, ed. Mootry (Englewood Cliffs, N.J.: Prentice-Hall, 1984), 117–27; p. 123.

28 Roberts, *Faulkner and Southern Womanhood*, p. 183.

29 See *Romeo and Juliet* 1.i.20–30.

30 A number of critics have taken issue with Wright's erasure of Bigger's victims. Trudier Harris, for instance, notes that "Wright directs our

sympathies so that [Bessie's] death does not evoke the outrage that might be anticipated in reaction to such graphic brutality" ("Native sons and foreign daughters," in *New Essays on "Native Son,"* ed. Kenneth Kinnamon [Cambridge: Cambridge University Press, 1990], p. 79). See also Kimberly Drake, "Rape and resignation: silencing the victim in the novels of Morrison and Wright," *Literature, Interpretation, Theory* 6.1 (April, 1995), 63–72; Jane Davis, "More force than human: Richard Wright's female characters," *Obsidian II* 1.3 (Winter, 1986), 68–83; and Mootry, "Bitches, whores, and woman haters" pp. 123–7. For a defense of Wright's art against charges of misogyny, see Sondra Guttman, "What Bigger killed for: rereading violence against women in *Native Son*," *Texas Studies in Literature and Language* 43.2 (Summer, 2001), 169–93.

31 Harris, "Native sons and foreign daughters," p. 80.

32 For a Foucauldian reading of the anonymity/invisibility of Ellison's persona, see Frederick T. Griffiths, "Copy Wright: what is an (invisible) author?" *New Literary History* 33.2 (Spring, 2002), 315–41.

33 Ralph Ellison, *Invisible Man* (New York: Vintage, 1981), pp. 6–7. All future citations will be from this edition, and will be inserted into the text.

34 Marlon B. Ross, "Race, rape, castration: feminist theories of sexual violence and masuline strategies of black protest," in *Masculinity Studies and Feminist Theory*, ed. Judith Kegan Gardiner (New York: Columbia University Press, 2002), pp. 305–43; p. 320.

35 Richard Wright, *Black Boy* (New York: HarperCollins, 1989 [1945]), pp. 222–3. Quoted in Ross, "Race, Rape, Castration," p. 320.

36 Ross, "Race, Rape, Castration," p. 320.

37 Mary Rohrberger, "'Ball the jack': surreality, sexuality, and the role of women in *Invisible Man*," in *Approaches to Teaching Ellison's 'Invisible Man,'*" ed. Susan Resneck Parr and Pancho Savery (New York: Modern Language Association, 1989), pp. 124–32; p. 130. For another discussion of Ellison's trafficking in stereotype, see Catherine Saunders, "Makers or bearers of meaning: sex and the struggle for self-definition in Ralph Ellison's *Invisible Man*," *Critical Matrix* 5 (1989), 1–28.

38 Trudier Harris, *Exorcising Blackness: Historical and Literary Lynching and Burning Rituals* (Bloomington: Indiana University Press, 1984), p. 109.

39 Ross, "Race, Rape, Castration," pp. 306–7.

40 Eldridge Cleaver, *Soul on Ice* (New York: Random House, 1992 [1968]), p. 189. Future citations will be from this edition, and will be inserted into the text.

CONCLUSION. "WHITE WOMEN ARE SNAKY":
JUNGLE FEVER AND ITS DISCONTENTS

1 Arguably, Wesley Snipes' Flipper and his family are "whiter" socially than any of the Italian-Americans in the film. They are certainly more high-class: their speech far more closely approximates radio English, their lifestyle is far more

"civilized." Also, Flipper's wife is only a shade darker than Angela: she is, like Halle Barry, complexionally not "black" at all.

2 *Jungle Fever,* film, directed by Spike Lee (USA: Universal Pictures, 1991).

3 Diana R. Paulin, "De-essentializing interracial representations: black and white border-crossing in Spike Lee's *Jungle Fever* and Octavia Butler's *Kindred,*" *Cultural Critique* 36 (Spring, 1997), 165–93; p. 168. Paulin also faults Lee – not without reason, I feel – for denying Angela "voice and agency. Her interpretation of the relationship is never vocalized or revealed . . . Flipper interprets, names and defines the terms of the relationship" (p. 172).

4 Benjamin Saltman, "Jungle Fever," *Film Quarterly* 45.2 (Winter, 1991), 37–40; p. 38.

5 Anne Billson, "Mixed message. Spike Lee deserves a slap on the wrist," *New Statesman of Society* 4.167 (September 6, 1991), 31–2.

6 Stephen Farber, *"Jungle Fever,"* http://movieline.standard8media.com/reviews/junglefever.shtml.

7 Roger Ebert, *Jungle Fever* review, *Chicago Sun-Times* (June 7, 1991), http://rogerebert.suntimes.com/apps/pbcs.dll/article?AID=/19910607/REVIEWS/106070305/.

8 Peter Travers, *Rolling Stone,* http://www.rollingstone.com/reviews.

9 Dessen Howe, *Washington Post* (June 7, 1991).

10 Samuel G. Freedman, "Love and hate in black and white," *New York Times* (June 2, 1991), http://query.nytimes.com/gst/fullpage.html?res=9D0CE7D81438F931A35755C0A967958260.

11 Quoted in *ibid.,* p. 10.

12 The 2002 US Census counted 1,674,000 African-American–Caucasian couples.

13 Hugh Quarshie, *Second Thoughts about "Othello,"* International Shakespeare Association Occasional Papers, no. 7 (Chipping Camden, 1999), p. 5.

14 Pascale Aebischer, *Shakespeare's Violated Bodies: Stage and Screen Performance* (Cambridge: Cambridge University Press, 2004), p. 148.

15 Francesca T. Royster, "The 'end of race' and the future of early modern cultural studies," *Shakespeare Studies* 26 (1998), 59–70; p. 66.

16 *O.,* film, directed by Tim Blake Nelson (USA: Chickie the Cop, Daniel Fried Productions, FilmEngine, Rhulen Entertainment, 2001).

17 Matthew Wilder, "Miramax was right. Keep it in the vault" (September 3, 2001), http://www.imdb.com/title/tt0184791/usercomments-31.

18 Curatorfilm, Chicago (September 2, 2001).

19 Victoria Alexander, *O,* http://www.filmsinreview.com/Film%20Reviews/O.htm.

20 John Anderson, "'O' brother, what is this?" *Newsday* (August 31, 2001).

21 Adele Marley, *O* review, *Orlando Weekly* (August 29, 2001), http://www.citypaper.com/film/review.asp?id=2160.

22 Robert W. Butler, "'O,' where's the bard?" *Kansas City Star* (August 30, 2001).

23 Anderson, "'O' brother, what is this?"
24 *10 Things I Hate About You*, film, directed by Gil Junger (USA: Jaret Entertainment, Mad Chame, Touchstone Pictures, 1999).
25 Quarshie, *Second Thoughts about "Othello."*
26 Pauline Réage, *The Story of O* (New York: Ballantine Books, 1981).
27 On the "O" in the final scene, see also Celia R. Daileader, *Eroticism on the Renaissance Stage: Transcendence, Desire, and the Limits of the Visible* (Cambridge: Cambridge University Press, 1998), p. 125.
28 Tim Wise, "School shootings and white denial: a white person's perspective" (March 6, 2001), http:www.alternet.org/story/10560.
29 Quoted in Freedman, "Love and hate in black and white," p. 12.
30 Paul Yachnin, "Wonder effects: Othello's handkerchief," in *Staged Properties in Early Modern England*, ed. Jonathan Gil Harris and Natasha Korda (Cambridge: Cambridge University Press, 2002), pp. 316–34.
31 See Mary Baine Campbell, *The Witness and the Other World: Exotic European Travel Writing, 400–1600* (New York: Cornell University Press, 1988), and *Wonder and Science: Imagining Worlds in Early Modern Europe* (New York: Cornell University Press, 1999); Stephen Greenblatt, *Marvellous Possessions: The Wonder of the New World* (Chicago: University of Chicago Press, 1991). See also J. V. Cunningham, *Woe or Wonder: The Emotional Effect of Shakespearean Tragedy* (Denver: Denver University Press, 1951).

Index

abolitionism 111–13, 120, 122, 124–8
Adams, John Quincy 230
Aebischer, Pascale 221
amalgamation *see* miscegenation
Arata, Steven 97

Barber, Francis 60
Barthelemy, Gerard 43
Behn, Aphra 10–11
  Abdelazar; or, the Moor's Revenge 27, 50–2
  Oroonoko; or, the Royal Slave 50, 53–4, 64, 233, 234; and Olaudah Equiano 62–3; and Lydia Maria Child 116
Beidler, Philip 235
Bhabha, Homi 97
Boose, Lynda E. 228
Bride of Frankenstein, The 240
Brome, Richard
  English Moore; or, the Mock Marriage, The 15–16
Brontë, Emily
  Wuthering Heights 143–4, 145–51; and Margaret Mitchell's *Gone with the Wind* 163
Brown, Laura 53
Brown, William Wells 244
  Clotel; or, The President's Daughter 9, 44, 112, 113, 130, 141
Buonaparte, Marie 105, 238
Burgess, M. J. 187
Bush, Laura L. 178

Callaghan, Dympna 25, 33
Carby, Hazel 244
Charnes, Linda 3
Child, Lydia Maria 111–12, 113, 124–7, 130, 165, 242
  Hobomok 114–19, 137
  'The quadroons' 125
  Romance of the Republic, A 134–8
Cixous, Hélène and Catherine Clément 167

Clarke, Deborah 178
Clay, E. W.
  Fruits of Amalgamation, The 87–8
Cleaver, Eldridge
  Soul on Ice 172–3, 206–7
Congreve, William 54–6, 73
Coleman, Deirdre 77
Coleridge, Samuel Taylor 76–8, 230
  Rime of the Ancient Mariner 76–8, 79, 85, 87
Cooper, James Fennimore
  Last of the Mohicans, The 119
Craft, Christopher 99

D'Amico, Jack 15–16
Dalton, Anne B. 113
Davis, David Brion 235
Dekker, Thomas
  Lust's Dominion 16, 26–8, 39, 50
Deutsch, Helen 248
Drake, Sir Francis 8, 15, 47
Dryden, John
  All for Love 29
Duvall, John N. 250
Dyer, Richard 109

Elizabeth I, Queen of England 14, 46
Ellison, Ralph 170–2
  Invisible Man 11, 196–205
Equiano, Olaudah 52, 61–3

Faulkner, William 170–2
  Light in August 173–88
Fearon, Ray 6–7, 31
Ferguson, Margaret W. 233
Fiedler, Leslie 175
Field, Nathan, John Fletcher, and Philip Massinger
  Knight of Malta, The 16, 35–40
Fletcher, John
  Knight of Malta, The see under Field, Nathan, John Fletcher, and Philip Massinger

Floyd-Wilson, Mary 6, 42, 223, 229, 230
Foucault, Michel 9, 10
Fowler, Doreen 181
Freud, Sigmund 88, 89, 105
Friedman, David M. 223

Gelder, Ann 131, 132, 245
Gilbert, Sandra M. and Susan Gubar 89,
    94, 168
Gilroy, Paul 227
Gothicism and Gothic horror 78, 89, 108,
    241–2
Greenaway, Peter
    Prospero's Books 22
Gronniosaw, James 60
Guttman, Sondra 251
Gwin, Minrose C. 131

Halberstam, Judith 97
Hall, Kim 9, 14–15, 16, 30, 34, 46, 53, 62, 229
Harris, Trudier 250
Heywood, Christopher 143, 151
Heywood, Thomas
    Fair Maid of the West, Part 2, The 17
Hogeland, Lisa Maria 249
hooks, Bell 10
Huebert, Ronald 224
Hunt, Marvin 30

Irving, Washington
    Salmagundi 52, 64, 67–74

Jacobs, Harriet 12, 113
    Incidents in the Life of a Slave Girl 11, 111–12,
        113, 128–34
Jefferson, Thomas 70
Jones, Ann Rosalind 232

Kamen, Paula 168
Karcher, Carolyn L. 114, 119
Keats, John 175
Kennedy, J. Gerald 238
Krenz, Jayne Anne 144, 163
Kristeva, Julia 78, 94, 109
Ku Klux Klan 124, 158–9
Kyd, Thomas
    Spanish Tragedy, The 44

Lamire, Elise 79–80
Lee, Spike 219
    Jungle Fever 208–13, 220, 252; reviews of
        212–13
Levine, Robert S. 125–6
Lhamon, W. T. 139
Little, Arthur 10, 21–2, 105

Loomba, Ania 10, 31, 64
Lugosi, Bela 105, 106, 108–10, 242
lynching 158–60

MacDonald, Joyce Green 46, 50, 228, 230, 231
McGraw, Eliza Russi Lowen 156
MacKinnon, Catharine A. 145, 247
Malchow, H. L. 97
Malcolm X 63, 234
Marston, John
    Sophonisba 21
Massinger, Philip
    Knight of Malta, The see under Field, Nathan,
        John Fletcher, and Philip Massinger
    Parliament of Love, The 15–16
    Renegado, The 14
Matar, Nabil 45–6
Maus, Katherine Eisaman 3
Mellor, Anne K. 90
Middleton, Thomas 45, 233
    The Lady's Tragedy (*The Second Maiden's
        Tragedy*) 35
Millgate, Michael 176
miscegenation 8–9, 48, 77, 78, 79, 107, 111, 120, 161
Mitchell, Angelyn 126
Mitchell, Margaret
    Gone with the Wind 12–13, 143, 151–63,
        164, 184
Morrison, Toni 4, 75, 84

Neill, Michael 2
Nelson, Tim
    O. 13, 215–19; reviews of 215–16, 218
Neville, Henry
    Isle of Pines, The 47–9
New Historicism 9–10
"Noble Savage" 52–3, 116

Osborne, Laurie E. 144
Othellophilia 6–13, 15, 31, 46, 54–5, 58–9, 64, 67,
    73, 102–4, 105, 112, 143, 145, 146, 148, 164,
    170, 171, 172, 193, 198, 200, 202, 203, 204,
    211, 221

Page, Sally R. 174
Parker, Oliver
    Othello 25, 214–15
Paulin, Diana R. 212, 252
Peele, George
    Old Wives Tale, The 15
Poe, Edgar Allen 78–80
    *Narrative of Arthur Gordon Pym of Nantucket,
        The* 78, 79, 80–7; prefigured in Mary
        Shelley's *Frankenstein* 95
presentism 226

Quarshie, Hugh 6, 214, 216

Randall, Alice
   Wind Done Gone, The 11, 12, 145
rape 18, 20–2, 40–1, 61, 108, 145, 147–8, 154–5,
   158–9, 163, 168, 175, 178–81, 192–3, 194–6,
   202–3, 205, 217, 248
Ravenscroft, Edward 17–24, 229
Réage, Pauline
   Story of O., The 217
Reed, Ishmael 207
Rice, T. D. ("Jim Crow") 138–41
Ripley, Alexandra
   Scarlett 247–8
Roach, Joseph 12, 52, 227
Roberts, Diane 111, 119, 123, 133, 135, 137, 174,
   176, 184, 186, 190
Rohrberger, Mary 203
romance 144, 145, 162–3, 167–9
Ross, Marlon B. 205
Rowe, John Carlos 87, 89, 105
Rowley, William
   All's Lost by Lust 16, 40–3
Rowson, Susannah Haswell
   Slaves in Algiers 52, 64–7, 73, 235
Royal Shakespeare Company 6, 7, 13, 31, 34, 233
Royster, Francesca T. 22, 214
Rubin, Gayle 134
Rugendas, Johann Moritz
   Voyages pittoresques dans le Brésil 141–2
Rymer, Thomas 46

Said, Edward 235
Sánchez-Eppler, Karen 122, 133, 245
Shaffer, Brian W. 224
Shakespeare, William 16
   Antony and Cleopatra 7, 28–31, 43, 57, 219
   King Lear 45
   Merchant of Venice, The 14, 15, 23, 26
   Much Ado about Nothing 33
   Othello 1, 2–7, 12, 16, 22–6, 27, 35, 37, 40, 49,
      107, 124, 127, 208; and Behn's *Abdelazar*
      52; and Behn's *Oroonoko* 54; and
      Brontë's *Wuthering Heights* 144; and
      Child's *Hobomok* 114, 115; Desdemona as
      literary prototype 90, 120–2, 129, 162;
      and Ellison's *Invisible Man* 202; and
      inter-racialism in film 208, 209, 210, 212,
      215; and Irving's *Salmagundi* 68–70, 73;
      parodies of 138–41; popularity of 9, 42,
      44–6, 88; and Randall's *The Wind Done
      Gone* 164; and Southerne's *Oroonoko*

56–7; and Stoker's *Dracula* 98, 101, 102;
   and Wright's *Native Son* 189
   Rape of Lucrece, The 21–2
   Romeo and Juliet 57; inter-racial productions
      of 7, 225–6
   Sonnets 30
   Taming of the Shrew, The 66–7, 108, 156, 168,
      216, 224
   Tempest, The 22, 46–7; and Harriet Jacobs 129
   Titus Andronicus 17, 26, 27, 42, 44, 107
   Winter's Tale, The 35
Shelley, Mary
   Frankenstein 89–96, 102, 105
Silverman, Kaja 232
Singh, Jyotsna 11
Skinfill, Mauri 122
slavery 53, 56, 59, 67, 77–8, 124, 126, 128, 130–3,
   141–2, 235
Southerne, Thomas 44, 54–7
Spencer, Jane 58, 234
Spillers, Hortense J. 120, 123, 137
Stallybrass, Peter 232
Stoker, Bram 96–105, 110
   Dracula 78, 102, 105
   Jewel of the Seven Stars, The 104–5
   Lair of the White Worm, The 102–4, 105
Stowe, Harriet Beecher 119
   Uncle Tom's Cabin 12, 44, 111, 113, 119–24, 131

Taylor, Gary 13, 44–5, 50, 88, 126, 227,
   229, 241
Toomer, Jean
   Cane 170

Urgo, Joseph R. 250

Walton, Jean 232
Webster, John
   White Devil, The 5, 16, 31–5, 44
Whitehead, Neil L. 10
Widmaier, Beth 187
Williams, Linda 89
Williamson, Joel 151
Wise, Tim 219
witch-trials 1–2, 4
Woolf, Virginia 13
Wright, Richard 170–2
   Black Boy 198–9
   Native Son 188–96, 204, 205–6

Yachnin, Paul 221
Yellin, Jean Fagan 137